Virgil and the Myth of Venice

Virgil and the Myth of Venice

Books and Readers in the Italian Renaissance

CRAIG KALLENDORF

CLARENDON PRESS · OXFORD

1999

Oxford University Press, Great Clarendon Street, Oxford OX2 6DP

Oxford   New York

Athens   Auckland   Bangkok   Bogotá   Buenos Aires   Calcutta
Cape Town   Chennai   Dar es Salaam   Delhi   Florence   Hong Kong   Istanbul
Karachi   Kuala Lumpur   Madrid   Melbourne   Mexico City   Mumbai
Nairobi   Paris   São Paulo   Singapore   Taipei   Tokyo   Toronto   Warsaw
and associated companies in   Berlin   Ibadan
Oxford is a registered trade mark of Oxford University Press

Published in the United States
by Oxford University Press Inc., New York

© Craig Kallendorf 1999

The moral rights of the author have been asserted

British Library Cataloguing in Publication Data

Data available

Library of Congress Cataloguing in Publication Data

Virgil and the myth of Venice: books and readers in the Italian
Renaissance/Craig Kallendorf.

Includes bibliographical references

1. Virgil—Appreciation—Italy—Venice. 2. Authors and readers—
Italy—Venice—History—16th century. 3. Books and reading—Italy—
Venice—History—16th century. 4. Authors and readers—Italy—
Venice—History—To 1500. 5. Books and reading—Italy—Venice—
History—To 1500. 6. Latin poetry—Appreciation—Italy—Venice.
7. Italy—Civilization—Roman Influences. 8. Venice (Italy)—
Civilization. 9. Reader–response criticism. 10. Renaissance—
Italy—Venice. I. Title.
PA6825.K36   1998   873'.01—dc21   98–40795
ISBN 0–19–815254–X

1 3 5 * 7 9 10 8 6 4 2

Typeset by Cambrian Typesetters, Frimley, Surrey
Printed in Great Britain on acid-free paper by
Biddles Ltd., Guildford and King's Lynn

PREFACE

I am grateful to a number of institutions and individuals for supporting this project in various ways. This kind of work cannot be done without travel to the sources and time to write, and I am grateful to the Delmas Foundation, the National Endowment for the Humanities, and the American Council of Learned Societies for funds. Additional support came from the Departments of English and of Modern and Classical Languages, and from the College of Liberal Arts, at Texas A&M University, and support of another but equally valuable nature came from the Interlibrary Loan Service at the University's Sterling B. Evans Library. Among the individuals who have answered my requests for information, read sections of the book, and written letters on my behalf, I would like to single out Lilian Armstrong, Daniel Bornstein, Douglas Brooks, A. C. de la Mare, Rona Goffen, Paul Grendler, Daniel Javitch, Margaret King, Alexander McKay, Ray Petrillo, Patricia Phillippy, Wayne Rebhorn, Margaret Rosenthal, and Warren Tresidder. I am also grateful to Charles Martindale and to three other anonymous readers engaged by Oxford University Press for a number of very helpful suggestions. The merits of the following study are due in part to these people, while the short-comings, of course, are entirely my own. Finally, the friendship of Marino and Rosella Zorzi deserves special mention; not only have they provided invaluable scholarly guidance and support, but they have made Venice a place of warm and lasting memories for me.

In this study, names of scholars and printers generally appear in the form most commonly used today. I have preferred a Latin form in discussions of those who wrote in Latin and an Italian form for those who wrote in the *volgare*, but I have ultimately favoured intelligibility over consistency here. Usage of i/j and u/v has been adjusted to modern standards; otherwise my quotations from early texts preserve the original orthography but not the vagaries of Renaissance punctuation and capitalization. Translations are my own unless otherwise indicated.

Preliminary versions of some material have been published in the *Journal of the History of Ideas*, *Miscellanea Marciana*, and the *Acta* of the Ninth International Congress of the International Association for Neo-Latin Studies, and I am grateful to the editors of these publications for permission to draw on previous work in the present study.

Finally, I would like to dedicate this book to my wife Hilaire. This project came to completion under her watchful eyes, and I am grateful for her love and support.

C.K.

CONTENTS

LIST OF ILLUSTRATIONS

1

Introduction

The value of a book lies in its being read. ... Without an eye that reads it, a book does not effect the production of ideas, and therefore it is mute.[1]

This is a book about books—viewed as both carriers of ideas and as material objects, as both records of intellectual and social relationships and as forces that are themselves able to do work in history. The books under consideration are editions of the Roman poet Virgil—132 in Latin, sixty-four in Italian—published in Venice and the surrounding area between 1470 and 1600. I am less interested in production and distribution than in consumption—specifically, consumption by readers in the area around Venice during the late Renaissance. My argument, stripped of all its accompanying nuance and qualification, is that the poetry of Virgil became a best-seller in Renaissance Venice because it sometimes challenged, but more often confirmed, the specific moral, religious, and social values that these readers brought with them to their books.

Part of this argument can be made using the methods of traditional intellectual and literary history. Much of it, however, cannot, for such standard surveys as Rudolf Pfeiffer's *History of Classical Scholarship 1300–1850*[2] rest on a concept of reading that

[1] Umberto Eco, *Il nome della rosa* (Milan, 1980), 399, qtd. in Christian Bec, *Les Livres des Florentins (1413–1608)*, Biblioteca di 'Lettere Italiane', Studi e testi, 29 (Florence, 1984), 145.

[2] (Oxford, 1976). In a review of my *In Praise of Aeneas: Virgil and Epideictic Rhetoric in the Early Italian Renaissance* (Hanover, NH, 1989), Ronald MacDonald observed that in studying the ms culture of Florentine humanism, I did not pay much attention to the social and political concerns of the readers (*Speculum*, 67 (1992), 168–9). The point is well taken, and the present study takes up questions that remained largely unasked in the previous one. For a more general treatment of this same problem, see my 'Philology, the Reader, and the *Nachleben* of Classical Texts', *Modern Philology*, 92 (1994), 137–56.

separates Greek and Latin texts from the social and political
values of those who studied them—a concept that many scholars
of our day find increasingly outmoded. What is more, traditional
methods pay far less attention than I feel they should to the physical attributes of the books that readers of the past used, for typeface and page layout have ideological ramifications, and
ownership notes and marginalia provide valuable, concrete
records of what kinds of people bought specific books and how
they understood the books they read. Since the methods
employed in this study are both indebted to and different from
such recent approaches as the history of the book, the sociology
of literature, and reader-response criticism, I would like to begin
by explaining in fairly general terms how I have tried to
contribute toward the writing of a new literary history. I shall
then turn to the basic ideological framework of Renaissance
Venice, the so-called 'myth of Venice', to suggest what readers
of this period would have been prepared to see in the books they
read. Finally, I would like to sketch out the general parameters
of Venetian humanism and Virgil's role in it, as preparation for
the study that follows.

Until the 1960s, studying books as physical objects usually
meant doing descriptive or analytical bibliography: patiently
identifying editions, describing them in terms of collation, typeface, and so forth, and analysing how an understanding of the
process of printing could aid in understanding a particular
book.[3] Traditional bibliography remains essential, of course;
indeed, the analysis that follows rests on two such studies of my
own.[4] Yet beginning in the 1960s, books have been approached
in different ways by practitioners of the *histoire du livre*, the

---

[3] The classic example of this approach in the Anglo-American tradition remains
Fredson Bowers, *Principles of Bibliographical Description* (Winchester, 1987; repr. of Princeton,
1949 edn.); see also Philip Gaskell, *A New Introduction to Bibliography* (New York, 1972). A
number of issues raised in the following pages are also covered by Deborah Parker,
Commentary and Ideology: Dante in the Renaissance (Durham, NC, 1993), 124–30; and
William H. Sherman, *John Dee: The Politics of Reading and Writing in the English Renaissance*,
Massachusetts Studies in Early Modern Culture (Amherst, Mass., 1995), 54–9, although
these scholars have organized their material somewhat differently to reflect their own
approaches.

[4] Craig Kallendorf, *A Bibliography of Venetian Editions of Virgil, 1470–1599*, Biblioteca
di bibliografia italiana, 123 (Florence, 1991); and id., *A Bibliography of Renaissance Italian
Translations of Virgil*, Biblioteca di bibliografia italiana, 136 (Florence, 1994).

history of the book.[5] This method took root in such institutions as the École Pratique des Hautes Études and has spread through the works of such scholars as Lucien Febvre and Henri-Jean Martin, whose *L'Apparition du livre* has been very influential.[6] These studies have brought the book into the range of objects studied by the Annales School of social and economic history, so that requests for permission to print books, inventories of the contents of private libraries, and neglected genres like the *bibliothèque bleue* have come under systematic analysis. Americans like Robert Darnton have been pursuing similar studies,[7] so that a significant body of information is now available about the relationship between books and the societies in which they were created.

By this point, however, the field has reached sufficient maturity that it seems reasonable to follow such distinguished practitioners as Roger Chartier in questioning some of its basic operating principles.[8] For one thing, like the Annales School in general, historians of the book tend to favour quantitative analysis: one thinks immediately of Christian Bec's *Les Livres des Florentins (1413–1600)*, a statistically based study of small- and medium-sized library inventories preserved among the documents relevant to the

[5] A basic orientation to this approach and its history may be found in Robert Darnton, 'What is the History of Books?', *Daedalus*, 111/3 (1982), 65–83, repr. in Cathy N. Davidson (ed.), *Reading in America: Literary and Social History* (Baltimore, 1989), 27–52; John P. Feather, 'The Book in History and the History of the Book', in John P. Feather and David McKitterick, *The History of Books and Libraries: Two Views* (Washington, 1986), 1–16; Cathy N. Davidson, 'Toward a History of Books and Readers', *American Quarterly*, 40/1 (Mar. 1988), 7–17, repr. in ead. (ed.), *Reading in America*, 1–26; and I. R. Willison, 'Remarks on the History of the Book in Britain as a Field of Study within the Humanities, with a Synopsis and Select List of Current Literature', *Library Chronicle*, 21/3–4 (1991), 95–145.

[6] Darnton, 'What is the History', 28–29. Febvre and Martin's book has been translated into English as *The Coming of the Book: The Impact of Printing 1450–1800*, trans. David Gerard (London, 1990). A good orientation to this approach, its development, and its place in modern French historiography in general may be found by examining Roger Chartier and Daniel Roche, 'Le Livre: Un changement de perspective', in Jacques Le Goff and Pierre Noya (eds.), *Faire de l'histoire: Nouveaux objets*, 2 vols. (Paris, 1974), ii: 115–36; and Wallace Kirsop, 'Literary History and Book Trade History: The Lessons of *L'Apparition du livre*', *Australian Journal of French Studies*, 16 (1979), 488.

[7] Darnton, 'What is the History', 28–9.

[8] Chartier, 'L'Ancien Régime typographique: Réflexions sur quelques travaux récents', *Annales: Économies, sociétés, civilisations*, 36 (1981), 191–209. A survey of early work with suggestions for future research can also be found in R. Birm, '*Livre et société* after Ten Years', *Studies in Voltaire and the Eighteenth Century*, 151 (1976), 287–312.

Magistrato de' Pupilli in the Florentine state archives.[9] Such studies as these can be enormously useful in establishing which books people owned and in tracing shifts in taste. However, they tell us next to nothing about what the owners of these books thought about them—or whether they even read their books at all, as Bec himself admits.[10]

And again, like the Annales School in general, historians of the book tend to favour popular writing at the expense of high culture. As a result, the *bibliothèque bleue* is studied much more intensely than editions of the classics, the ordinary reader much more than the noble one.[11] What is more, as several others have noted, this procedure has been slow to catch on among Italian scholars, for many of whom bibliography remained until recently a field isolated from larger social and historical movements.[12] As a

[9] A similar example of this approach as applied to mss is Carla Bozzolo, Dominique Coq, and Ezio Ornato, 'La Production du livre en quelques pays d'Europe occidentale aux XIVᵉ et XVᵉ siècles', *Scrittura e civiltà*, 8 (1984), 129–60. As Robert Darnton has pointed out more generally, 'The French have been quantifying culture for a generation' ('History and the Sociology of Knowledge', in *The Kiss of Lamourette: Reflections in Cultural History* (New York, 1990), 303–4).

[10] Bec, *Livres*, 15–16. As Deborah Parker has reminded me, however, Bec does provide some information in another study, *Les Marchands écrivains, affaires et humanisme à Florence (1375–1434)* (Paris, 1967), about how early owners read their books (personal communication).

[11] Darnton, 'What is the History', 28–9. This same point is also made by Sandra Hindman in a response to Darnton's essay, 'Introduction', in S. Hindman (ed.), *Printing the Written Word: The Social History of Books, circa 1450–1520* (Ithaca, NY, 1991), 1–2, 6.

[12] Furio Diaz, 'Metodo quantitivo e storia delle idee', *Rivista storica italiana*, 78 (1966), 932–47; the absence of a section on Italian scholarship in Willison, 'Remarks', 95–110, makes the same point by default. I know of three notable exceptions to this generalization. The first is Amedeo Quondam, ' "Mercanzia d'onore" / "Mercanzia d'utile": Produzione libraria e lavoro intellettuale a Venezia nel Cinquecento', in Armando Petrucci (ed.), *Libri, editori e pubblico nell'Europa moderna: Guida storica e critica*, Biblioteca Universale Laterza, 291 (Bari, 1989), 51–104, which specifically addresses such key questions as 'which books, for whom, made by whom, edited by whom, carried where, in exchange for what, paid for by whom' (57); this is the exception that proves the rule, however, for Quondam's essay is one of only two in the vol. not originally written in French or English. A second exception is Claudia Di Filippo Bareggi, *Il mestiere di scrivere: Lavoro intellettuale e mercato librario a Venezia nel Cinquecento*, 'Europa delle Corti', Centro Studi sulle Società di Antico Regime, Biblioteca del Cinquecento, 43 (Rome, 1988), in which the work of a group of active editors is placed within the development of the press in Cinquecento Venice. The third exception is Lodovica Braida, *Il commercio delle idee: Editoria e circolazione del libro nella Torino del Settecento*, Fondazione Luigi Firpo, Centro di Studi sul Pensiero Politico, Studi e testi, 2 (Florence, 1995), although this study covers post-Renaissance material. A good example of a book originally written in Italian that approaches bibliography as an essentially self-contained, closed field is Luigi Balsamo, *Bibliography: History of a Tradition*, trans. William Pettas (Berkeley, Calif., 1990).

result, much material has been left unexplored and emphases have been somewhat skewed.

The study that follows is intended to correct some of these imbalances. To begin with, my material is Italian. Secondly, the text from which my study begins was originally written in Latin, so that the surviving evidence forces us to begin with the judgements of the upper-class males who most often read such books, although I should note that since translations into the *volgare* were also common, we can in fact recover some of the responses of other readers as well. Finally, although I shall cite occasional statistics in the chapters that follow, my principal interest is interpretive rather than quantitative, for my focus is on how books were read. That is, I am responding to Chartier's conclusions about what is currently needed in this field, for 'it is clear, in effect, that after twenty years and more of research into the circulation of books, the problem to be posed now is that of the different modalities in their *consumption*'.[13]

This problem is addressed in part by the sociology of literature, a field that traces its origins back to around 1800 but has actually come into its own only since World War II, under the stimulus in particular of Robert Escarpit and his colleagues at the Centre de Sociologie des Faits Littéraires in Bordeaux.[14] This approach distinguishes itself with particular vigour from the formalist interests of the New Criticism dominating Anglo-American scholarship during the years immediately following World War II:

Since sociology has as its object of research the social, that is, intersubjective transactions, it does not interest itself in the literary work as aesthetic object, but literature is only meaningful for sociology insofar as it is brought to completion within the world of special human interactions. The sociology of literature therefore has to do with the transactions of people who have a stake in literature; its object is the interaction of people having a stake in literature.[15]

---

[13] Chartier, 'Ancien Régime typographique', 206. On the application of this approach to literary texts in particular, see Michael Warner, 'Literary Studies and the History of the Book', *Book*, 12 (July, 1987), 3–9.

[14] Escarpit traces the origins of the systematic study of literature and society to Mme de Staël's *De la littérature considérée dans ses rapports avec les institutions sociales* (1800) (*Sociology of Literature*, trans. Ernest Pick, Lake Erie College Studies, 4 (Painesville, Oh., 1965), 3), while Hans Norbert Fügen claims that in France Louis de Bonald was the first to explore these issues in 1796 (*Die Hauptrichtungen der Literatursoziologie und ihre Methoden*, 6th edn., Abhandlungen zur Kunst-, Musik- und Literaturwissenschaft, 21 (Bonn, 1974), 8–13).

[15] Fügen, *Hauptrichtungen*, 14.

That is, the goal is to trace the function of literature in society, from the role of writers in their social surroundings (production) through the interconnected web of publishers and booksellers (distribution) to reading as a social act (consumption).[16]

Literary sociology has been useful at a number of points in the preparation of this study, for I share with Escarpit and his followers an interest both in reading and in the social setting within which literature operates. There are also, however, a number of fundamental assumptions here that strike me as problematic. For one thing, the focus on writers and readers is sometimes not so much on concrete individuals as on types that express themselves through regular behaviour. To be sure, there is value in studying the social phenomena that are the conditions for various possible means of literary activity,[17] but such studies tend to end up in a level of abstraction that is too high to be helpful in this study. What is more, the discipline itself seems to call for detailed studies of the book trade and of publishing history as part of its focus on distribution, but as John Sutherland has pointed out, such

[16] Escarpit, *Sociology of Literature*, 21–96. While the focus of the present study is on consumption rather than on production or distribution, it is worth noting that a number of scholars have analysed the writing process and the effort to stabilize its textual product in ways that reinforce some of the points I am trying to make. In *A Critique of Modern Textual Criticism* (Chicago, 1983), Jerome J. McGann argues that 'the fully authoritative text is ... always one which has been socially produced' as a result of negotiations between the author and his or her editor, publisher, public(s), and so forth. See also D. F. McKenzie, 'Typography and Meaning: The Case of William Congreve', in Giles Barber and Bernhard Fabian (eds.), *Buch und Buchhandel in Europa im achtzehnten Jahrhundert*—*The Book and the Book Trade in 18th-Century Europe*, Wolfenbütteler Schriften zur Geschichte des Buchwesens, 4 (Hamburg, 1981), 81–125; and id., *Bibliography and the Sociology of Texts: The Panizzi Lectures, 1985* (London, 1986). This approach has proved quite controversial; see e.g. the essays in *Analytical and Enumerative Bibliography*, NS I (1987), by David Nordloh, 'Socialization, Authority, and Evidence: Reflections on McGann's *A Critique of Modern Textual Criticism*', 3–12, and Craig S. Abbott, 'A Response to Nordloh's "Socialization, Authority, and Evidence"', 13–16. One merit of McGann's approach, however, is that it has encouraged textual critics to integrate their discipline into a broader theoretical framework; D. C. Greetham, 'Textual and Literary Theory: Redrawing the Matrix', *Studies in Bibliography*, 42 (1989), 1–24, for example, offers a comprehensive overview of how textual criticism can interact with writer-, text-, and reader-based theories of literature. See also David Gorman, 'The Worldly Text: Writing as Social Action, Reading as Historical Reconstruction', in Joseph Natoli (ed.), *Literary Theory's Future(s)* (Urbana, Ill., 1989), 181–220. While G. Thomas Tanselle's 'Textual Criticism and Literary Sociology', *Studies in Bibliography*, 44 (1991), 83–143 may be seen to a large extent as a defence of traditional methods, his *The History of Books as a Field of Study*, The Second Hanes Lecture (Chapel Hill, NC, 1981) is open to the opportunities offered by the newer approaches—a welcome gesture in the currently polarized world of textual criticism.

[17] Fügen, *Hauptrichtungen*, 19, 27–9.

studies have not appealed to sociologists of literature.[18] Finally, a more serious problem emerges from the way in which reading is approached within the sociology of literature. Escarpit, for example, focuses on the relationship between the author and his or her original public, for he believes that future readers do not have direct access to the work and are therefore inclined to find in it what they want rather than what the author put there—a process that Escarpit labels 'treason'.[19] This strikes me as a dangerously essentialist view of reading, one that cannot account for the variety of responses to the same literary works among both contemporary readers and those in the generations that follow them.

This variety of responses has been discussed with considerably more sympathy in reader–response criticism, whose origins can be traced to the 1920s but which, like the sociology of literature, did not come into its own until after World War II.[20] The model against which reader–response criticism reacts asserts that meaning is located in the literary text, in 'what the author put there'. Reading is thus a passive process in which the audience lays aside its own ideas and values to receive what is contained in the text, and misreading (Escarpit's 'treason') results when the reader finds what he or she wants in the text rather than what the author put there. The reader–response critic, however, recognizes that interpretation

---

[18] 'Publishing History: A Hole at the Centre of Literary Sociology', in Philippe Desan, Priscilla Parkhurst Ferguson, and Wendy Griswold (eds.), *Literature and Social Practice* (Chicago, 1988), 267–82. See also G. Thomas Tanselle, 'Response to John Sutherland', 283–7 of the same vol.

[19] *Sociology of Literature*, 77–8, 83–5.

[20] Jane P. Tompkins, 'An Introduction to Reader-Response Criticism', in ead. (ed.), *Reader-Response Criticism: From Formalism to Post-Structuralism* (Baltimore, 1980), 10. Although now a little dated, this vol., along with Susan R. Suleiman and Inge Crosman (eds.), *The Reader in the Text: Essays on Audience and Interpretation* (Princeton, 1980), provides a useful survey of the groundbreaking earlier work. Perhaps the most influential Anglophone scholar working in this area has been Stanley Fish; see his *Surprised by Sin: The Reader in Paradise Lost* (London, 1967), and *Is there a Text in This Class? The Authority of Interpretive Communities* (Cambridge, Mass., 1980). I should note here that the methods being discussed in this section are not mutually exclusive, but rather tend to lead into one another. For example, Donald McKenzie, whose *Bibliography and the Sociology of Texts* has proved influential in the scholarly reorientation being described here, writes, 'it seems to me that it would now be more useful to describe bibliography as the study of *sociology of texts*. ... [D]*ifferences in readings constitute an informative history*. What writers thought they were doing in writing texts, or printers and booksellers in designing and publishing them, or readers in making sense of them are issues which no *history of the book* can evade' (5, 10; my emphasis).

always includes in some way or other the ideas and values of the reader. Interpretation still begins with the text, but the text functions rather like an orchestra score, a prestructuring that triggers one potential actualization in each reader. Reading thus becomes an active process in which the audience shares in the creation of meaning.[21]

This approach has been extremely useful in the present study. Venetian Renaissance readers did not interpret Virgil's poetry as we do today—a point to which I shall return periodically—and once we agree that neither our interpretation nor theirs can be labelled 'right' or 'wrong' by reference to a timeless, objective standard, we are free to explore any and all responses for what they can tell us about the ideas and values that readers bring to the texts they read.

Again, however, I find myself parting company with the reader-response critics on several points. The first of these points arises from a consideration of one of the seminal treatments of reader-response criticism, Wolfgang Iser's *The Act of Reading: A Theory of Aesthetic Response*. Since Iser is primarily interested in aesthetic response, it is important for him that the predispositions necessary for a literary work to exercise its effect not be fixed beforehand by any particular historical situation. Iser therefore distinguishes the reader whose aesthetic responses he studies (the 'implied reader') from the individual who actually read and responded to a book (the 'real reader').[22] This distinction makes sense within Iser's system, but I find myself more curious about what real readers actually said about a text than what Iser thinks an implied reader should say.

The work of Hans Robert Jauss, which can be viewed as a branch of reader-response criticism, appears to offer greater promise for the present study, for Jauss's 'Literary History as a Challenge to Literary Theory' explicitly postulates the experiences of real readers as the foundation for literary history. His interest

[21] Wolfgang Iser, *The Act of Reading: A Theory of Aesthetic Response* (Baltimore, 1978), 3–85. Similar observations on the importance of the audience have been made in other fields as well; for example, Brian O'Doherty has observed that the artist 'has limited control over the content of his or her art. It is its *reception* that ultimately controls its content' (*Inside the White Cube: The Ideology of Gallery Space*, 89, qtd. in Timothy W. Luke, *Shows of Force: Power, Politics, and Ideology in Art Exhibitions* (Durham, NC, 1992), 231; emphasis by the author).

[22] *Act of Reading*, 28–38.

remains with aesthetic response, but Jauss is specifically concerned with the historical progression of this response—an 'aesthetics of reception and influence', in his terms[23]—a progression that is bound, as his essay on Baudelaire shows, to historically identifiable readers.[24]

Again, however, I find myself on occasion asking different kinds of questions. For example, Jauss is not particularly interested in the way in which the reception of a text is shaped by its material form, for as Roger Chartier has observed, reception theory tends to postulate an immediate relationship between text and reader.[25] Authors and publishers, however, attempt to impose prescribed readings on texts through prologues, commentaries, and so forth, so that attention to the actual books used by actual readers can provide clues to interpretation that cannot be recovered in any other way. That is, what Gérard Genette calls the 'paratext'—such textual accompaniments as prefaces, illustrations, and commentaries[26]—gives to the particular edition being read a key role in influencing how the potential meanings latent in the text are ultimately actualized.

Fortunately for those of us interested in earlier periods, records of these actualizations survive in concrete form, for just like readers of our day, readers of the Renaissance wrote in their books. Until quite recently, marginalia in printed books have received

[23] *Toward an Aesthetic of Reception*, trans. Timothy Bahti, Theory and History of Literature, 2 (Minneapolis, 1982), 20.

[24] Ibid. 170–85. Robert C. Holub, *Reception Theory: A Critical Introduction* (London, 1984), 134–46, however, notes that the study of actual readings within reception theory has tended toward statistical analyses that go to great lengths to confirm the obvious, while Jonathan Rose, 'Rereading the English Common Reader: A Preface to a History of Audiences', *Journal of the History of Ideas*, 53 (1992), 49–50, notes that in practice even reception theory prefers generalizations about 'implied' or 'informed' readers to the study of real readers. Georg Jäger, 'Historische Lese(r)forschung', in Werner Arnold, Wolfgang Dittrich, and Bernhard Zeller (eds.), *Die Erforschung der Buch- und Bibliothekgeschichte in Deutschland* (Wiesbaden, 1987), 485–507, has also commented on the need to integrate theoretical models with the behaviour of actual readers.

[25] 'Texts, Printings, Readings', in Lynn Hunt (ed.), *The New Cultural History* (Berkeley and Los Angeles, Calif., 1989), 157–8, 161; see also Parker, *Commentary and Ideology*, 26, 46–7.

[26] 'Introduction to the Paratext', *New Literary History*, 22 (1991), 261, picking up on a term used in *Palimsestes* (Paris, 1981), 93. Peter W. Cosgrove, 'Undermining the Text: Edward Gibbon, Alexander Pope, and the Anti-Authenticating Footnote', in Stephen A. Barney (ed.), *Annotation and its Texts* (New York, 1991), 138–9, also notes that commentary can become considerably more than an 'objective' way to clarify meaning as it intervenes between text and reader.

surprisingly little systematic study[27]—a striking contrast to the marginalia in manuscript books, which are frequently discussed by modern scholars, even catalogued by such projects as the *Catalogus translationum et commentariorum*. Yet as information about such features as marginalia and provenance notes, along with information on binding and paste-downs, finds its way into more and more manuscript catalogues, the tendency to apply techniques developed in describing manuscripts to the study of printed books means that incunabulists in particular are becoming more sensitive to such things.[28] This in turn brings us back full circle to the history of the book, as Paul Saenger and Michael Heinlen note:

In the history of the book, evidence based on the perception of the individual artifact is inextricably related to the articulation of valid

[27] This lack of systematic study rests on the mistaken notion, still surprisingly prevalent, that printed books were not glossed by their readers—as Mary and Richard Rouse put it, '[w]ith the growth of print as the normal medium of the page, the main medieval vehicle for relating new thought to inherited tradition disappears—namely, the gloss and the practice of glossing' (*Authentic Witnesses: Approaches to Medieval Texts and Manuscripts* (Notre Dame, Ind., 1991), 465). As my research has shown, this generalization is simply not true; indeed, as Brian Richardson has noted, the editors of early printed books even invited their readers to make changes in ink in their texts (*Print Culture in Renaissance Italy: The Editor and the Vernacular Text, 1470–1600* (Cambridge, 1994), 25). Among scholars who have begun to study marginalia seriously, several merit special attention: Anthony Grafton and Lisa Jardine, *From Humanism to the Humanities: Education and the Liberal Arts in Fifteenth- and Sixteenth-Century Europe* (Cambridge, Mass., 1986), 184–96, with n. 82 containing references to earlier work on the marginalia of Gabriel Harvey; Kristian Jensen, *Rhetorical Philosophy and Philosophical Grammar: Julius Caesar Scaliger's Theory of Language*, Humanistische Bibliothek, Texte und Abhandlungen, Reihe 1, Abhandlungen, 46 (Munich, 1990); Peter Burke, *The Fortunes of the Courtier: The European Reception of Castiglione's Cortegiano*, Penn State Series in the History of the Book, 1 (University Park, Penn., 1995), 75–80; Sherman, *John Dee*, 65–100; James A. Riddell and Stanley Stewart, *Jonson's Spenser: Evidence and Historical Criticism*, Duquesne Studies, Language and Literature Series, 18 (Pittsburgh, 1995); Anthony Grafton, 'Is the History of Reading a Marginal Enterprise? Guillaume Budé and his Books', *Papers of the Bibliographical Society of America*, 91 (1997), 139–57; id., *Commerce with the Classics: Ancient Books and Renaissance Readers*, Thomas Spencer Jerome Lectures, 20 (Ann Arbor, 1997); and Bernard M. Rosenthal, *The Rosenthal Collection of Printed Books with Manuscript Annotations: A Catalog of 242 Editions mostly before 1600 annotated by Contemporary or Near-Contemporary Readers* (New Haven, 1997).

[28] Ian R. Willison, 'The Treatment of Notes of Provenance and Marginalia in the Catalogue of Books printed in the XVth Century now in the British Museum (BMC)', in Lotte Hellinga and Helman Härtel (eds.), *Buch und Text im 15. Jahrhundert / Book and Text in the Fifteenth Century*, Proceedings of a Conference Held in the Herzog August Bibliothek Wolfenbüttel, 1–3 Mar., 1978 (Hamburg, 1981), 169–77, makes a persuasive case for doing this. An exemplary catalogue of Venetian books prepared in accordance with this principle is James E. Walsh, *A Catalogue of the Fifteenth-Century Printed Books in the Harvard University Library*, ii. *Books Printed in Rome and Venice* (Binghamton, NY, 1993).

interpretations of general historical developments. ... It is ... very often the copy-specific attributes of the codices containing incunables that make them of potential interest to scholars.[29]

What is true for fifteenth-century books is true for sixteenth-century ones as well. I have therefore recorded copy-specific data for the books in which I am interested, and I shall rely heavily on this material to show how the ideological responses of readers are bound to the material form in which the text was consumed.

As we move from general considerations of method to the specifics of this study, something should be said immediately about the chronological and geographical parameters of the investigation. The study begins in 1469, when Giovanni da Spira introduced the new art of printing into Venice[30] and effected a revolution in how books were made and disseminated. The concluding date, 1600, is also determined by the way in which printing history is traditionally studied, for special attention is generally devoted to early printed books in two categories: incunabula, or books printed up to 1500, and what the Italians call *cinquecentine*, or books printed during the sixteenth century.[31] In this case at least, the end of the sixteenth century coincides with a well-known decline in Venetian printing,[32] so that it makes sense to end this study around 1600. This terminal point also has the advantage of bringing a key chronological division in the history of printing into line with the division by centuries that still dominates literary and political

---

[29] 'Incunable Description and its Implication for the Analysis of Fifteenth-Century Reading Habits', in Hindman (ed.), *Printing the Written Word*, 226–7. Robert Darnton, 'First Steps toward a History of Reading', in *Kiss of Lamourette*, 154–87, provides support for a number of points made in this section.

[30] On the introduction of printing into Venice, see Carlo Castellani, *La stampa in Venezia: Dalla sua origine alla morte di Aldo Manuzio Seniore* (Trieste, 1973; repr. of Venice, 1889 edn.), 9–15; and Neri Pozza, 'L'editoria veneziana da Giovanni da Spira ad Aldo Manuzio', in *La stampa degli incunaboli nel Veneto* (Venice, 1983), 9–35, esp. 18–19.

[31] Incunabula have long been the subject of loving study by bibliophiles; modern scholarship on them might be said to begin with L. F. T. Hain, *Repertorium bibliographicum, in quo libri omnes ab arte typographica inventa usque ad annum MD typis expressi ...*, 2 vols. in 4 (Stuttgart, 1826–38), with the *Catalogue of Books printed in the XVth Century now in the British Museum*, 12 vols. (London, 1908–), remaining a model of how these books should be treated. *Cinquecentine* are only now beginning to attract similar attention; for example, a project to catalogue books published in Italy during the 16th cent. is still in its early stages.

[32] Basic information about this decline may be found in Paul F. Grendler, *The Roman Inquisition and the Venetian Press, 1540–1605* (Princeton, 1977), 225–33; and Richardson, *Print Culture in Renaissance Italy*, 140–54.

history of the Renaissance. Such divisions, however, should never
be taken as absolute, and relevant evidence from the first few years
of the next century will also find its way into the discussion that
follows.

For an investigation like this one, Venice offers an unusually
fertile field of study. For one thing, its printers produced a disproportionate number of books during the Italian Renaissance: at least
a third, perhaps as many as one half of the approximately 8,000
Italian incunabula, as many as 60 to 70 per cent of all books printed
in Italy during the third quarter of the sixteenth century, and still
almost half of the total in 1600.[33] Secondly, this massive quantity
of books is unusually open to an analysis that goes beyond the
technicalities of printing history, for Venetian printers specialized
in supplementary and interpretive material, the added prefaces and
commentaries that facilitate the identification of the cultural norms
through which texts were being prepared for the press and
brought into print.[34] And finally, the cultural norms of
Renaissance Venice have been seen as unusually distinct and cohesive for hundreds of years. As the great Swiss historian Jacob
Burckhardt wrote, 'The keynote of the Venetian character was,
consequently, a spirit of proud and contemptuous isolation',
within which a set of values and ideals clearly identifiable as
'Venetian' evolved.[35] This is not to say, of course, that each of
these values and ideals was exclusively Venetian, but that there was
a set that is recognizably Venetian as a whole.[36] However,
geographical divisions resist reification as stubbornly as chronological ones: during the fifteenth and sixteenth centuries, for example, Venetian power was also exercised on the mainland,[37] so that

[33] Richardson, *Print Culture in Renaissance Italy*, 39, 140. Precise figures remain elusive,
but there is no question that Venice produced far more incunabular edns. than any other
city in Europe. Figures provided by Paul Needham at the 1991 Rare Book School at
Columbia University suggest that Venice produced about 41 per cent of the Italian
incunabular edns. and about 15 per cent of the total for all of Europe.

[34] Richardson, *Print Culture in Renaissance Italy*, 37, 139, 183.

[35] *The Civilization of the Renaissance in Italy*, introd. by Benjamin Nelson and Charles
Trinkaus, 2 vols. (New York, 1958; repr. of New York, 1929 edn.), i. 87.

[36] Patricia Fortini Brown, *Venice and Antiquity: The Venetian Sense of the Past* (New
Haven, 1996), p. xii, makes a similar point.

[37] An account of Venetian expansion onto the mainland can be found in any good
political history of the period. An accessible, reliable narrative is that of Frederic C. Lane,
Venice: A Maritime Republic (Baltimore, 1973), 202–49; and especially thoughtful analysis
of the impact of this expansion on the culture and psyche of Renaissance Venice may be
found in D. S. Chambers, *The Imperial Age of Venice 1380–1580* (New York, 1970).

the discussion that follows will also take into account selected *terraferma* manifestations of Venetian cultural life.

In the language of reader-response criticism, Venetians of this period constitute an interpretive community, a group of people who read books with a common set of cultural norms through which they interpreted texts and agreed on meaning.[38] Particularly in the Renaissance, this common set of cultural norms derived from what has been traditionally labelled the 'myth of Venice'. The history of this myth is still very much under debate, with different historians emphasizing different phases in its evolution; there is general agreement, however, that the definitive form of the myth is that of the fifteenth and sixteenth centuries.[39] Here, as in so many other areas, Petrarch foreshadows what will be articulated more clearly by those who follow him. After an important military victory in 1364, he wrote from Venice to Pietro da Muglio:

Augustissima Venetorum urbs quae una hodie libertatis ac pacis, et iustitiae domus est, unum bonorum refugium, unus portus, quem bene vivere cupientium tyrannicis undique, ac bellicis tempestatibus quassae rates petant, urbs auri dives, sed ditior fama, potens opibus, sed virtute potentior, solidis fundamenta marmoribus, sed solidiore etiam fundamento civilis concordiae stabilita, salsis cincta fluctibus, sed salsioribus tuta consiliis.

---

[38]   This concept has been popularized by Stanley Fish, with what is probably the fullest explanation available in *Is there a Text in This Class?* This is not to claim, of course, that Venice existed in a vacuum: her commercial interests brought her citizens into contact with an unusually broad range of other cultures, and Venetian printers certainly worked with one eye on the foreign markets in which they expected to sell many of their products. By beginning with Venetian books, however, and focusing on the responses of Venetian readers, I have attempted to close the hermeneutic circle in an especially significant way.

[39]   Gina Fasoli, 'Nascita di un mito', in *Studi storici in onore di Gioacchino Volpe*, 2 vols. (Florence, 1958), ii. 445–79, examines the early history of the myth, claiming that by the Quattrocento the key terms are fixed and what comes afterward is restricted to more examples of the same themes. Edward Muir, *Civic Ritual in Renaissance Venice* (Princeton, 1981), 21–2, argues that the 14th cent. is crucial, for this is the time when Venice turned from a traditional orientation toward Byzantium to a new, more western outlook, seeing herself as a 'new Rome' and clothing the myth of Venice in the neoclassical dress of humanism. Franco Gaeta, 'Alcuni considerazioni sul mito di Venezia', *Bibliothèque d'humanisme et Renaissance*, 23 (1961), 58–75, stresses the importance of the War of the League of Cambrai as a catalyst for the decisive fashioning of the myth; other scholars like Federico Chabod, Alberto Tenenti, Felix Gilbert, Gaetano Cozzi, and Oliver Logan have pursued similar arguments. For references, see Muir, *Civic Ritual*, 27–30; and David Robey and John Law, 'The Venetian Myth and the "De republica Veneta" of Pier Paolo Vergerio', *Rinascimento*, ser. 2, 15 (1975), 6–8.

(The august city of Venice rejoices, the one home today of liberty, peace and justice, the one refuge of honorable men, the one port to which can repair the storm-tossed, tyrant-hounded craft of men who seek the good life. Venice—rich in gold but richer in fame, mighty in her resources but mightier in virtue, solidly built on marble but standing more solid on a foundation of civil concord, ringed with salt waters but secured by even saltier counsels.)[40]

There have already been a number of attempts to sort through the themes expressed in passages like this.[41] I would like to sort through them once more, not in order to attempt an original contribution to the historical study of the myth of Venice, but to organize the material in a somewhat different way that will be useful for the discussion to follow.

A key part of the myth was that Venice was *potens opibus, sed virtute potentior* ('mighty in her resources but mightier in virtue'), as Petrarch put it; in Burckhardt's rather hyperbolic words, 'no state, indeed, has ever exercised a greater moral influence over its subjects, whether abroad or at home'.[42] Venetians were supposed to cultivate wisdom, courage, temperance, and justice with unusual diligence, and to comport themselves with dignity at all times. Both nobles and commoners generally wore funereal-looking black clothing, as did religious, although there were some variations in the dress of civic officials, those celebrating holidays, and well-born young men. Governing councils regularly sought to curb indecency, the regulations of the pious fraternal organizations called *scuole grandi* were strikingly puritanical, and the city functioned essentially as a gerontocracy run by an unusually severe

---

[40] The passage is part of *Epist. sen.* 4. 3. The Latin is quoted in Ellen Rosand, 'Music in the Myth of Venice', *Renaissance Quarterly*, 30 (1977), 512 n. 2, with the English version adapted from *Letters from Petrarch*, trans. Morris Bishop (Bloomington, Ind., 1966), 234. These sentences have been widely quoted elsewhere as well, beginning with Francesco Sansovino, *Venetia* (1581), and continuing into most modern discussions of the myth of Venice.

[41] In addition to the works cited above in n. 39, see Oliver Logan, *Culture and Society in Venice 1470–1790: The Renaissance and its Heritage* (London, 1972), 1–19; Charles J. Rose, 'Marc Antonio Venier, Renier Zeno, and "The Myth of Venice"', *Historian*, 36 (1974), 479–97; and Franco Gaeta, 'L'idea di Venezia', in *Storia della cultura veneta*, iii. Girolamo Arnaldi and Manlio Pastore Scocchi (eds.), *Dal primo Quattrocento al Concilio di Trento* (Vicenza, 1981), pt. 3, 565–641. An unusually thoughtful analysis of the complex nuances of the myth and its effect on Venetian historiography may be found in James S. Grubb, 'When Myths lose Their Power: Four Decades of Venetian Historiography', *Journal of Modern History*, 58 (1986), 43–94.

[42] *Civilization of the Renaissance*, 89.

older generation. Indeed, the mood often matched the climate—not the hazy sunlight of Canaletto, but the cold, wet, foggy days spent inside the gloomy stone buildings of a Tintoretto painting.[43]

Hand in hand with the cultivation of moral rectitude went the cultivation of religious piety. Venice offered an enormous number of churches, sacred objects, and religious processions that created an air of sanctity that struck both residents and visitors alike. The number of prelates in fifteenth- and sixteenth-century Venice was discernibly larger than in other Italian cities of the period, the *scuole grandi* offered special opportunities for pious living and charitable acts, and several generations of patricians devoted strenuous efforts toward the regeneration of Christianity.[44] As a result, Venice seems to have resisted many of the inroads of secularism in Renaissance life: Lorenzo de Monacis's *Oratio elegantissima in laude et edificatione alme civitatis Venetiarum*, for example, elevates a panegyric of the city onto a providential plane that contrasts strikingly with the laicizing treatment of Leonardo Bruni's *Laudatio florentine urbis*, which Lorenzo probably knew.[45] Venice, according to her admirers, was specially chosen and esteemed by God, so that her citizens regularly attributed her political failures to sinful behaviour and the need for religious reform, something that a Florentine like Machiavelli—who was outspokenly critical of the Venetian system—could not understand or accept.[46]

Indeed, it was the Venetian state and its perceived organizational merits that lay at the centre of the myth of Venice; as

[43] Chambers, *Imperial Age*, 144–5.

[44] Ibid. 109–22; and Muir, *Civic Ritual*, 16. William J. Bouwsma, *Venice and the Defense of Republican Liberty: Renaissance Values in the Age of the Counter Reformation* (Berkeley and Los Angeles, Calif., 1968), 64, offers a curious contrast to the general consensus on this point, describing the spirit animating the Venetian government as showing a 'secular bias'. He cites as evidence the willingness to charge interest, and especially government restrictions on the activity of clerics; however, it seems to me that the name applied to families of Venetians holding ecclesiastical positions (*papalisti*) suggests that the source of legislation limiting their activities was fear of divided loyalties that would bring them in line with the political aims of the Papacy, not hostility to religion per se. Bouwsma's first analysis is counterbalanced to a certain extent, however, by the description on 70–83 of how church and state became intertwined in Renaissance Venice, a description that ends up being considerably more conventional than his initial approach to the question.

[45] Gaeta, 'Idea di Venezia', 575.

[46] Ibid. 598–615. Most treatments of Machiavelli that go into any detail at all also touch on his anti-Venetianism. On anti-Venetian propaganda in general, see Nicolai Rubinstein, 'Italian Reactions to Terraferma Expansion in the Fifteenth Century', in J. R. Hale (ed.), *Renaissance Venice* (Totowa, NJ, 1973), 197–217.

Petrarch had put it, Venice was *una hodie libertatis ac pacis, et iusti-tiae domus est … solidis fundamenta marmoribus, sed solidiore etiam fundamento civilis concordiae stabilita* ('the one home today of liberty, peace and justice … solidly built on marble but standing more solid on a foundation of civil concord'). The stability, freedom, and cooperative spirit of the Venetian state were generally attrib-uted to two causes. First was her peculiar form of government. Venice was a republic, but her constitution set up a form of government that was generally described as 'mixed' in the Aristotelian sense and praised as the ideal combination of democ-racy, represented by the Great Council; aristocracy, represented by the Senate; and monarchy, represented by the Doge, her elected ruler.[47] According to Gasparo Contarini's *De magistratibus et repu-blica Venetorum libri quinque*, this system led to the avoidance of factional disputes by offering some element of participation in the common enterprise to each part of the body politic.[48] The second cause of Venetian stability was a unified, rigidly hierarchical, status-conscious social order that at the beginning of the fifteenth century replaced the earlier maze of shifting relationships among members of different classes.[49] To explain the stasis that came into existence at this time, Contarini develops an analogy in which the state is compared to a living creature, all of whose parts obey the eyes, which alone have the capacity to see:

Non dissimili ratione in republica Veneta summa rerum gubernatio patri-cio ordini est demandata, veluti quibusdam oculis civitatis, ignobiliora officia caeteris ex populo: sicque tamquam bene compactum corpus Veneti felicissime vivunt, cum oculi reipublicae non sibi tantum, sed universis membris prospiciant, caeterae vero civitatis partes, non tantum sui habeant rationem, verum etiam hisce oculis, veluti potioribus membris reipublicae libentissime obtemperent.

(In a similar way, in the republic of Venice the greatest governmental power has been given to the patrician order, as being, so to speak, the eyes of the state, while the less noble offices are given to the remaining

---

[47] As Franco Gaeta has noted, the Aristotelian associations of Venice's mixed consti-tution as described by Enrico da Rimini, Pier Paolo Vergerio, and Lauro Quirini were challenged in the middle of the Quattrocento by George of Trebizond and Francesco Barbaro, who tried to link the Venetian constitution to Plato ('Idea di Venezia', 591–2).

[48] On Contarini's *De magistratibus*, see Myron Gilmore, 'Myth and Reality in Venetian Political Theory', in Hale (ed.), *Renaissance Venice*, 431–3.

[49] On the historical background to this change, see Dennis Romano, *Patricians and Popolani: The Social Foundations of the Venetian Renaissance State* (Baltimore, 1987), 11, 152–8.

popular orders. Thus just like a well-ordered body, the Venetians live happily since the eyes of the republic provide for not only themselves, but also all the members, and the remaining parts of the state take into account not only themselves, but also freely obey these eyes, as the better members of the republic.)[50]

The patricians lead and everyone else follows, but all work toward the common good. As Margaret L. King has noted in a similar context, the Venetian hagiographers worship at the altar of unanimity, from which 'they subordinate the individual to the group, and place both in a timeless hierarchical universe, inherited from their ancestors and sanctioned by the authority, as they knew it, of Aristotle and Christ'.[51]

The mythical origins of this state were obscure, with one legend tracing the founding of Padua and the Venetian state to Antenor of Troy,[52] and another dating it to the time when a group of patricians fled across the lagoon to escape the barbarian invaders. This second legend fixed the precise date at 25 March 421, which has the advantage of implying the providential replacement of one civilization with another, since the year was not long after Alaric's invasion of Rome and the month and day were that of the Annunciation to the Virgin Mary. In either case, however, the citizens of Renaissance Venice constructed their identity in reference to the culture of antiquity: 'the Venetians are called new Romans', Bernardus Bembus wrote in his commonplace book, and by the end of the fifteenth century Venice was regularly called a new Rome. Venetian families with similar-sounding names claimed direct descent from Roman families, so that the Cornaro clan traced its origins to the Cornelii and the Barbaro clan claimed descent from Ahenobarbus, the Roman founder of Parma. The Loredan, Cornaro, and Grimani families built houses on the Grand Canal in which Roman architectural orders were adapted to a

[50] The passage from Contarini is quoted by Gaeta, 'Idea di Venezia', 640. Context for this passage is provided by the points developed in Muir, *Civic Ritual*, 16–21, 38–44.

[51] *Venetian Humanism in an Age of Patrician Dominance* (Princeton, 1986), 175. As James S. Grubb has observed, this tendency to subordinate the individual to the group affects the full range of Venetian culture, explaining phenomena ranging from the failure to keep single-family memoirs (*ricordanze*) to a preference for group pictures over individual portraits ('Memory and Identity: Why Venetians didn't keep *Ricordanze*', *Renaissance Studies*, 8 (1994), 375–87).

[52] The legendary founding by Antenor is noted in Vergerio, *De republica Veneta*, 40, ll. 39–42; see also Chambers, *Imperial Age*, 13.

Venetian setting, and public architecture followed suit: the decorations added to the Palazzo Ducale in the 1480s contained reliefs of shields, helmets, and other paraphernalia with such transparent mottoes as 'SPQV', and the monumental tombs of the doges from the same period began to resemble Roman triumphal arches.[53] To be sure, there was disagreement about the exact nature of the relationship, with Marc'Antonio Sabellico claiming that Venice could surpass the achievement of Rome, while Paolo Paruta used part of his official history to show where Venice failed to overcome its Roman model and why.[54] Nevertheless, when the ceiling of the Sala del Maggior Consiglio in the Palazzo Ducale was repainted after the fire of 1577, the climactic position was given to Veronese's *Apotheosis of Venice*, and it is no accident that Venice is personified as a woman who bears a striking resemblance to the goddess Rome.[55]

By this point it is probably beginning to sound as if Renaissance Venice must have existed far away from the world of flesh-and-blood people, where no one cheated on tax obligations, missed an appointed church service, manœuvered for personal political advantage, or forgot the lessons of the past. Our cynical age is not likely to accept this, and indeed postwar social and economic historians have thoroughly explored how the myth of Venice disguises the reality of a people who, like most others, regularly failed to live up to their ideals. Guido Ruggiero, for example, has documented violent behaviour and sexual lapses among the nobles,[56] and Donald Queller has shown how some of these same nobles embezzled money, sold their votes to the highest bidders, and regularly evaded their responsibility to hold office.[57] In the

---

[53] Chambers, *Imperial Age*, 13, 26–8, 126, 169, and 173; Deborah Howard, *Jacopo Sansovino: Architecture and Patronage in Renaissance Venice* (New Haven, 1975), 1–7, 26–8; Barbara Marx, *Venezia—altera Roma? Ipotesi sull'umanesimo veneziano* (Venice, 1978); and ead., 'Venedig—"Altera Roma"', Transformationen eines Mythos', *Quellen und Forschungen aus italienischen Archiven und Bibliotheken*, 60 (1980), 325–73. The fullest study to date of how the powerful families of Renaissance Venice defined themselves in relation to ancient Rome is Brown, *Venice and Antiquity*.

[54] Chambers, *Imperial Age*, 25, 194; and Gaeta, 'Idea di Venezia', 594.

[55] David Rosand, 'Venetia Figurata: The Iconography of a Myth', in id. (ed.), *Interpretazioni veneziane: Studi di storia dell'arte in onore di Michelangelo Muraro* (Venice, 1984), 179–80.

[56] *Violence in Early Renaissance Venice* (New Brunswick, NJ, 1980); and *The Boundaries of Eros: Sex Crime and Sexuality in Renaissance Venice* (New York, 1985).

[57] *The Venetian Patriciate: Reality versus Myth* (Urbana, Ill., 1986).

discussion that follows, the subversive forces of this 'reality' also creep in around the margins of the myth. The myth, however, remains the central text, for it was powerful enough to ensure remarkable stability in Renaissance Venice, with the patricians retaining a striking degree of internal cohesion and the populace an unusual willingness to defer to their authority even though they were effectively disenfranchised.[58] And even when its members were not living up to the ideals they espoused, the Venetian interpretive community still struggled to make sense of what it experienced by fitting those experiences into the myth by which its collective identity was constructed. For this community, ethical, religious, and political values were interconnected in a vision of the state that rivalled ancient Rome as a model of human civilization.

In the other major cities of Italy, a discussion relating fifteenth- and sixteenth-century culture to that of antiquity would lead naturally into a discussion of humanism, the effort to develop the human creative and artistic potential, especially in the disciplines of grammar, rhetoric, poetry, history, and moral philosophy, in accordance with models from the ancient world.[59] Such an analysis is appropriate here as well, but some additional explanation is required.

In one of his less insightful moments, Burckhardt wrote a description of Venice in which he claimed that 'the literary impulse in general was here wanting, and especially that enthusiasm for classical antiquity that prevailed elsewhere'.[60] We might be tempted to dismiss one such judgement, given that its author, although still acknowledged as a great historian, wrote so long ago and hardly claimed to be a Venetian specialist. William Bouwsma, however,

---

[58] Muir, *Civic Ritual*, 8, 34–8; and Romano, *Patricians and Popolani*, 1–11.

[59] I am relying here primarily on the basic definition of Paul Oskar Kristeller, perhaps most accessible in his essay on 'The Humanist Movement', in *Renaissance Thought: The Classic, Scholastic, and Humanist Strains* (New York, 1961; repr. of Cambridge, Mass., 1955 edn.), 3–23. A good general overview of recent work may be found in Albert Rabil Jr. (ed.), *Renaissance Humanism: Foundations, Forms, and Legacy*, 3 vols. (Philadelphia, 1988); and Jill Kraye (ed.), *The Cambridge Companion to Renaissance Humanism* (Cambridge, 1996).

[60] *Civilization of the Renaissance*, i. 93. Burckhardt's treatment of Venice appears in the same chapter as his treatment of Florence (i. 82–106), and it seems to me that his assessment of Venice as generally stagnant derives from an unfortunate, and unnecessary, comparison to the active dynamism of Renaissance Florence.

wrote a much more recent, six-hundred-page book specifically on Renaissance Venice, and he came to a strikingly similar conclusion. Venetian humanism, he observed, is marked by 'relative shallowness' and an 'absence of perspective on antiquity'; what is more, 'their peculiar vision of the past excluded the Venetians from any general participation in this positive estimate of antiquity, especially of ancient Rome'.[61] The teaching of Guarino da Verona and the humanists of the chancery school, the studies of the Bembus and Barbaro families and their patronage of others, the position of Ciceronian rhetoric in Venetian literary and musical culture, the printing of the classics, especially Greek, by Venetian publishers[62]— these do not seem to qualify as real 'enthusiasm for classical antiquity'.

The problem here, I believe, is not that Renaissance Venice displayed an 'absence of perspective on antiquity', but that Venetian humanism existed in a form that was unique to Venice and therefore remains difficult to appreciate for scholars more accustomed to, say, the Florentine or Roman models. The difference, I believe, has to do with what kinds of first principles were adopted as axiomatic, and what principles in turn were allowed to follow from them.

To clarify this difference, we might turn again to a non-Venetian humanist, Petrarch, and see how he handled a question that also interested Venetians of the period: to what form of government should allegiance be given? As a Florentine, Petrarch might be expected to favour a republic, and among the modern scholars who have surveyed his writings on this subject, Carlo Steiner, Thomas Bergin, and Alice Wilson believe that this was in fact his preference.[63] There is, however, no consensus on the issue.

---

[61] *Venice and the Defense of Republican Liberty*, 87–8. This approach still appears with some frequency among those who write about the period; Rona Goffen, for example, takes it as axiomatic that Quattrocento Venice was unsympathetic to humanism and bases her discussion of artistic patronage on this idea (*Giovanni Bellini* (New Haven, 1989), 222 ff.).

[62] In addition to the specific studies cited below, see the following articles on Venetian humanism in *Storia della cultura veneta*, vol. iii, pt. 1: Manlio Pastore Stocchi, 'Scuola e cultura umanistica fra due secoli', 93–121; Vittore Branca, 'L'umanesimo veneziano alla fine del Quattrocento: Ermolao Barbaro e il suo circolo', 123–75; and Agostino Pertusi, 'L'umanesimo greco dalla fine del secolo XIV agli inizi del secolo XVI', 177–264, with accompanying bibliography. On Ciceronian rhetoric in Renaissance Venice, see Martha Feldman, *City Culture and the Madrigal at Venice* (Berkeley and Los Angeles, Calif., 1995).

[63] Steiner, 'La fede nell'Impero e il concetto della patria italiana nel Petrarca', *Il giornale dantesco*, 14/1 (1906), 8–34; and *Petrarch's Africa*, trans. and annotated by Bergin and Wilson (New Haven, 1977), p. x.

Bonaventura Zumbini, Giulio Augusto Levi, and Rodolfo De Mattei argue that Petrarch was an ardent believer in the empire and admirer of its founder Julius Caesar,[64] and Hans Baron claimed that his position evolved over time, that he was a republican as a young man and an imperialist in his later years.[65] Just for good measure, Janet Smarr has suggested that Petrarch was basically indifferent to the whole question.[66]

As I have shown elsewhere, I believe the explanation for this confusion comes from Petrarch's willingness to argue almost any question *in utramque partem*—that is, to use one of the humanistic disciplines, rhetoric, to adjust his attitude to particular circumstances and to see both sides of complicated political issues.[67] Thus when he was writing an epic poem in praise of Scipio Africanus, the great hero of republican Rome, he could drift toward a republican stance, but when he was exhorting Charles IV to return to Rome and govern there, he could provide a generally pro-imperial argument.[68] The political position, in other words, was only temporary because it followed from a rhetorical first principle that required constant re-evaluation and adjustment. As a result, Petrarch was able to move freely from state to state in Renaissance Italy, transferring his political allegiance from republic to tyranny and back again.

---

[64] Zumbini, *Studi sul Petrarca* (Florence, 1895), 161–255; Levi, 'Il concetto monarchico del Petrarca', in *Da Dante al Machiavelli* (Florence, 1935), 105–17; and De Mattei, *Il sentimento politico del Petrarca* (Florence, 1944), 67–84, 103–28.

[65] 'Cicero and the Roman Civic Spirit in the Middle Ages and the Early Renaissance', *Bulletin of the John Rylands Library*, 22 (1938), 72–97; *The Crisis of the Early Italian Renaissance*, 2nd edn. (Princeton, 1966), 47–61, 119–20; and id., 'The Evolution of Petrarch's Thought: Reflections on the State of Petrarch Studies', in *From Petrarch to Leonardo Bruni: Studies in Humanistic and Political Literature* (Chicago, 1968), 7–50.

[66] 'Petrarch: A Vergil without a Rome', in P. A. Ramsey (ed.), *Rome in the Renaissance: The City and the Myth* (Binghamton, NY, 1982), 135. There is a large bibliography on Florentine historiography in general during this period; especially important as background are Nicolai Rubinstein, 'The Beginnings of Political Thought in Florence', *Journal of the Warburg and Courtauld Institutes*, 5 (1942), 198–227; and Eric Cochrane, *Historians and Historiography in the Italian Renaissance* (Chicago, 1981), 3–33.

[67] Kallendorf, 'Virgil, Dante, and Empire in Italian Thought, 1300–1500', *Vergilius*, 34 (1988), 52–61. The importance of the ability to argue *in utramque partem* is discussed in Victoria Kahn, *Rhetoric, Prudence, and Skepticism in the Renaissance* (Ithaca, NY, 1985).

[68] The republican drift is discernible in the epic poem *Africa*, ed. Nicola Festa, Edizione nazionale delle opere di Francesco Petrarca, 1 (Florence, 1926), 2. 228–37, 2. 263–5, 3. 773–4. The exhortation to Charles IV is *Familiares* 10. 1, the standard edn. being that edited by Vittorio Rossi and Umberto Bosco, Edizione nazionale delle opere di Francesco Petrarca, 10–13 (Florence, 1933–42). As I have shown in 'Virgil, Dante, and Empire', however, Petrarch's stance is not fully consistent even within these works.

Among Venetian humanists, I would argue, the process was reversed: Lauro Quirini, Paolo Morosini, and Domenico Morosini began from the belief that the best form of government was a republic—more specifically, the Venetian republic—and that the rhetorical principles learned in humanist study should be directed in praise of that republic.[69] In other words, the political position was the constant, the first principle, and the specific humanist discipline, or rather the relevant parts of the specific humanist discipline, were drawn in afterward for support.

I do not want to overstate the distinction here: there is good reason to believe, for example, that Pier Paolo Vergerio, whose praise of the Venetian government marked a significant contribution to humanist historiography, was not consistently pro-republican in his politics,[70] and even the notoriously Protean Petrarch held beliefs for which his devotion did not waver. Venetian humanism, however, does have a discernibly different flavour, and the distinction being developed here does explain some of what is most puzzling about it. To take another example, Petrarch's devotion to poetry, another of the humanist disciplines, is well known. The object of his poetry, Laura, constantly threatened to lead him away from God, but he admitted that he could not leave her, or his humanistic studies in general, behind, even when he felt his religious principles were threatened.[71] For the Venetian humanist Ermolao Barbaro, the process worked the other way: he began with what he believed to be morally right, politically desirable, and theologically true and examined the discipline of poetry in relation to that. When he concluded that poetry posed a threat to God and country, he wrote two orations against it.[72] The result was a humanism hostile to an entire humanist discipline.

Barbaro, to be more precise, began his enquiry from within the interpretive paradigm typical of an upper-class Venetian of his day, the myth of Venice, and accommodated his humanist studies to

---

[69] These three humanists and their approaches to the Venetian republic are discussed by King, *Venetian Humanism*, 118–50.

[70] Robey and Law, 'Venetian Myth', 32–3.

[71] This struggle forms the basis for his *Secretum*, which may be read in the edn. of Enrico Carrara, in Francesco Petrarca, *Prose*, ed. Guido Martellotti *et al.*, La letteratura italiana, Storia e testi, 7 (Milan, 1955), 22–215.

[72] Barbaro's *Orationes contra poetas* has been edited (along with his *Epistolae*) by Giorgio Ronconi, Facoltà di Magistero dell'Università di Padova, 14 (Florence, 1972), 81–142, and discussed briefly by King, *Venetian Humanism*, 157–61.

the myth. Margaret L. King has noted that something like this is typical of Venetian humanism in general, for the Venetian patriciate appropriated humanism at the beginning of the fifteenth century and saw to it that the humanist studies it patronized reflected its interests.[73] The result was a humanism of moral severity, pronounced piety, and committed republicanism—a humanism, in other words, that privileged certain traditional, fixed beliefs over disciplinary modes of enquiry. Its peculiar character comes through clearly in a paragraph of King's that is devoted not to what is discussed by Venetian humanist authors, but what is not:

This review of the literary production of Venetian humanists may close by a look at the nonexistent. What kinds of works did they not author? What problems did they conspicuously fail to address? The Venetian corpus includes, to my knowledge, no works challenging economic or social assumptions: none, that is, like Poggio Bracciolini's discussion of alternative models of just economic behavior, or assessment of the notion of hereditary claims to nobility. It contains, to my knowledge, no works critically examining received religious or philosophical traditions: none, that is, analogous to Valla's challenge to ecclesiastical authority and medieval systems of thought, or Bruni's reevaluation of Aristotle as a philosopher of civic existence, or Pico's or Ficino's generous eclecticism, which incorporated academic philosophy as part of a broader intellectual vision. It contains, finally, to my knowledge, no works elevating the human being: none celebrating the dynamic will or the profundity of the intellectual life, or the heroic struggle of the individual against the malicious whims of fortune, or contrasting human freedom and creativity with the passive and circumscribed natures of beast, stone, or angel. The distinctive themes of Venetian humanism are found elsewhere.[74]

These writers, in other words, did not allow the disciplines of humanistic enquiry to lead them away from their paradigmatic myth, for 'the task of Venetian humanism was to affirm, not challenge, Venetian culture'.[75]

One of the consequences of this approach is that when compared to, say, the Florentine model, Venetian humanism can appear somewhat truncated. Moral, religious, and political matters

---

[73] *Venetian Humanism*, pp. xix–xx, 25, and 174. Patricia Labalme has made a similar observation: 'Humanism, that Protean concept, was, in fifteenth century Venice, no more nor less than this: an education, a social standard, a service to the state' (*Bernardo Giustiniani: A Venetian of the Quattrocento*, Uomini e dottrine, 13 (Rome, 1969), 15).

[74] *Venetian Humanism*, 172.   [75] Ibid. 187.

are fully, if sometimes timidly, treated, but other parts of the
humanist curriculum, it is often said, are not. Thus Margaret L.
King has noted that in Venetian humanism, a subordinate place is
occupied by several areas that take centre stage in humanist studies in general, especially commentary on classical texts and the
study of literature.[76]

There is certainly a measure of truth in this last observation, but
the evidence suggests that with one author at least, the study of
Roman literature played a larger part in the development of
Venetian humanism than previous scholars have thought. To
pursue this point, I would like to turn to some information that
was not widely available until after King published her analysis.
After a few Protestant teachers were discovered in Italy, Pope Pius
IV drafted a bull, *In sacrosancta beati Petri*, in which all teachers were
ordered to profess their Catholic faith to their bishop or his representative. Venetian teachers were first ordered to obey this bull in
1567–8, but the records of their responses do not survive; the first
available records date from 1587–8, and they include the responses
of 258 teachers.[77] The records provide information about the
teachers themselves—name, age, birthplace, and civil or ecclesiastical status—along with a declaration that they conformed to
orthodox Christian doctrine, placed Christian images on the walls
of their classrooms, and did not own or read prohibited books.
Many of them also provided information about the location and
enrolment of their schools, and most listed the texts they taught.
These records have been thoroughly studied by Paul Grendler,
and they provide an invaluable record of what was being taught in
the schools of Renaissance Venice.[78]

In general, Renaissance education was designed to instruct the
student in the key disciplines of humanistic studies. After learning
basic grammar, the student moved on to the other disciplines,
most often learning rhetoric from Cicero, poetry from Virgil, and
history from Caesar, Valerius Maximus, or Sallust, with moral

---

[76] *Venetian Humanism*, 173.

[77] These records, preserved in the Archivio della Curia Patriarcale, Venice, are found
in a bundle of 331 folios, 'Professioni di fede richiesta agli insegnanti 1587'. A detailed
summary may be found in Vittorio Baldo, *Alunni, maestri e scuole in Venezia alla fine del XVI
secolo* (Como, 1977).

[78] My discussion of these documents is based on the analysis of Grendler, *Schooling in
Renaissance Italy: Literacy and Learning, 1300–1600* (Baltimore, 1989), 42–7.

philosophy being absorbed from constant attention to the moral content of all the texts under study. The schools of Renaissance Venice conformed to this basic pattern: in 1567, for example, the Senate ordered the humanists teaching in the publicly supported *sestiere* schools to teach Cicero in the morning and Virgil, Terence, or Horace in the afternoon. The 1587–8 documents referred to previously indicate in turn that more Venetian teachers of the period (ninety-four) selected Virgil than the other two choices combined (eighty-two).[79]

In other words, in the educational system of Renaissance Venice a privileged position was occupied by the Roman poet Publius Vergilius Maro (70–19 BC). Virgil was once believed to have authored a group of shorter poems, the *Appendix Vergiliana*, but most modern scholars would challenge the attribution of most of these poems to Virgil, leaving three major works securely assigned to him: the *Eclogues*, the *Georgics*, and the *Aeneid*. The *Eclogues* were modelled on the *Idylls* of the Greek poet Theocritus, but they infused new Italian elements into Theocritus' pastoral themes, resulting in ten delicately crafted poems combining an idealized Arcadian setting with references to the history and politics of Virgil's day. The four books of the *Georgics* are ostensibly devoted to farming—Book 1 to the cultivation of crops, Book 2 to the raising of fruit trees, especially vines, Book 3 to the raising of animals, and Book 4 to the cultivation of bees. Like the *Eclogues*, however, the *Georgics* strains at the limits of its genre, for its set pieces, on such topics as mythology, the effects of the plague, and the power of love, make it considerably more than the didactic poem it may first appear to be. The third poem, the *Aeneid*, is an epic modelled on the Homeric poems; it recounts the founding of Rome by Aeneas and his group of followers fleeing the destruction of Troy. The *Aeneid* became the Roman national epic, thought to encapsulate the values of its culture and to have helped create the ideology of Augustus, the emperor who patronized Virgil and supported the development of the poem.

Neither the *Eclogues* nor the *Georgics* proved unusually popular with Venetian teachers: only four masters in the 1587–8 documents specifically reported teaching the former, and only one the latter.[80] To be sure, both poems played a role at key places in the

[79] Ibid. 203–12, 235–55.   [80] Ibid. 206.

development of the ideology of Renaissance Venice: the fourth *Eclogue*, as we shall see, offered intriguing religious connotations, and maxims and sayings consonant with the myth of Venice were extracted from both the *Eclogues* and the *Georgics*.[81] Both poems, however, were set in the countryside, and the Venetians were at heart an urban people. What interest there was in these two poems was probably related to the Venetian expansion onto the mainland and to the ensuing fashion among Venetian nobles of building country estates, but during this period interest in things pastoral was often mediated through contemporary poetry like that of Jacopo Sannazaro rather than being taken directly from Virgilian models.

Renaissance Venetians still felt that their livelihood rested primarily in their political and commercial activities, and these activities tended to draw them to the *Aeneid*, which was presumably the centre of attention for most of the teachers using Virgil in the 1587–8 documents. Venetian ships travelled the same seas as the ships of Aeneas and his men, and as an epic the poem offered an explicit treatment of serious themes that would appeal to a serious, pragmatic people: moral themes, like the proper relationship between love and duty; religious themes, like the nature of divinity and its concern for human affairs; and political themes, like how to lead a people destined for greatness toward their preordained place in world history. Indeed, Virgil's Venetian readers made explicit the link between Aeneas and his modern descendants living on the lagoon. The twelfth-century *Origo civitatum Italie seu Venetiarum* explained that the name of the Veneti or Eneti was derived from Aeneas, since Venice had been founded by Trojan exiles.[82] What is more, in Act II, Scene ii of *Didone*, a tragedy written by Lodovico Dolce and published in Venice in 1547, Aeneas is recounting Mercury's command that he leave Carthage in order to secure a glorious future for his son and his descendants. Dolce adds some lines not in Virgil, in which the descendants of Aeneas are traced through Roman history to the Venice of Dolce's day:

> E i cui tardi nipoti, dopò molto
> Girar di cielo, et lungo spatio d'anni,
> A un'altra gran città daranno initio

---

[81] See below, Chs. 2 and 3.   [82] Brown, *Venice and Antiquity*, 13.

Con piu felice augurio in mezzo l'acque
Ove la pace sempre, ove l'amore,
Ove virtude, ove ogni bel costume
Terranno il pregio in fin che duri il mondo.
Quivi la bella Astrea regnerà sempre
Coronata i bei crin di bianca oliva:
Quivi ne tempi turbidi e aversi
A travagliati sia tranquillo porto.[83]

(And their late offspring, after many a revolution of the heavens and a long extent of years, will give a most auspicious beginning to another great city amidst the waves, where peace and love, where virtue and every good custom will always be held in esteem so long as the world endures. There beautiful Astraea, with lovely locks crowned by the gleaming olive, will always rule, and there in contrary and turbulent times those in travail should find a safe harbour).

Venice had become the new Rome, and its humanist scholars and teachers ensured that the *Aeneid* in particular provided a significant part of its ideological underpinnings.

This can be confirmed by a brief examination of Virgil's place in Venetian Renaissance art. This subject has not been thoroughly explored yet, but enough information is available so that the basic outlines can be sketched out. A painting of Aeneas and his father Anchises by Giorgione (*c.*1478–1510), for example, was in the house of Taddeo Contarini in Venice in 1525; its fate is uncertain, although it may be the painting in London's National Gallery that is also known as *Landscape at Sunset*.[84] Uncertainty also complicates the Virgilian work of Andrea Mantegna (1431–1506), the Paduan painter much admired by humanistically inclined Venetians of the Renaissance. The grisaille of Dido now in Montreal may in fact

[83] *Didone, Tragedia di M. Lodovico Dolce* (Venice: Aldus Manutius, 1547), fos. 11^v–12^r. As Frances A. Yates has observed, the reference to Astraea from Virgil's *Ecl.* 4 was understood elsewhere in Europe as foreshadowing the arrival of Augustus, giving the image imperial overtones (*Astraea: The Imperial Theme in the Sixteenth Century* (London, 1975), 33–8, 69, 115–17). Virgil's association with Augustus more generally made the *Aeneid* especially congenial to a long succession of Holy Roman Emperors, as Marie Tanner has shown (*The Last Descendant of Aeneas: The Hapsburgs and the Mythic Image of the Emperor* (New Haven, 1993)). While we should probably remind ourselves that anti-Venetian propaganda regularly accused Venice of acting like an imperial power in its *terraferma* expansion (Rubinstein, 'Italian Reactions', 197–217), it is perhaps more fair to note that Venetian readers simply emphasized those parts of the *Aeneid* that fit most easily into their republican ideology.

[84] Cecil Gould and Pietro Zampetti, *The Complete Paintings of Giorgione* (New York, 1968), nos. 18 and 88 in the catalogue.

not be by the hand of the master himself, although Berenson
thought that it was,[85] and the sketch of a statue now in the Louvre
may or may not be Mantegna's direct response to Isabella d'Este's
desire to erect a statue to Virgil in his home town of Mantua.[86]

Other works by artists from Venice or the surrounding area,
however, can be discussed with more certainty. The chest with
pictures of Dido now in London's National Gallery, for example,
is securely attributed to Liberale da Verona (*c.*1445–1526),[87] and
there are a series of *placchette* with Virgilian themes that were
executed in the Veneto. One with the arms of Aeneas derives
from Padua at the beginning of the sixteenth century, and two
showing the death of the Carthaginian queen Dido from *Aeneid*
4, one in Venice's Museo Correr and the other now in Rome but
formerly in a Venetian collection, were executed by Andrea
Briosco, known as Il Riccio (1470–1532).[88] Illuminators like the
Master of the London Pliny decorated both manuscripts and early
printed texts of Virgil, in several cases anchoring a book produced
in Venice into the visual style of the region.[89] Finally, there is a
group of paintings on Virgilian themes by Jacopo Tintoretto
(1518–94). One, showing Aeneas telling his story to Dido, has
been lost, but another, painted in 1555–6 and showing Aeneas
taking leave of her, is in the Herzog Anton Ulrich Museum in
Braunschweig.[90] Tintoretto also made several paintings of Venus
at the forge of Vulcan, illustrating the request for arms from
Aeneid 8. One, painted in 1544–5, is now in the North Carolina

[85] E. Tietze-Conrat, *Mantegna: Paintings, Drawings, Engravings* (London, 1955), 190,
fig. 35. Though it is by no means complete, the best single source of information on Virgil's
role in Venetian art is the catalogue of the exhibition held at Rome's Biblioteca Nazionale
Centrale from 24 Sept. to 24 Nov. 1981, Marcello Fagiolo (ed.), *Virgilio nell'arte e nella
cultura europea* (Rome, 1981), with the Montreal grisaille noted on 212.

[86] Paul Kristeller, *Andrea Mantegna*, trans. S. Arthur Strong (London, 1901), 211,
402–3. The project was to have been entrusted to Mantegna, but in any case it was never
executed.

[87] Fagiolo (ed.), *Virgilio nell'arte*, 212.

[88] Ibid. 239–41.

[89] The Virgil decorated by the Master of the London Pliny is now London, British
Library, C.19.e.14; see Brown, *Venice and Antiquity*, 192–3 with frontispiece and pl. 208.

[90] Erich von der Bercken, *Die Gemälde des Jacopo Tintoretto* (Munich: R. Piper, 1942),
no. 45 in the catalogue with pl. 62; Carlo Bernari and Pierluigi De Vecchi, *L'opera completa
del Tintoretto* (Milan: Rizzoli, 1970), no. 119 in the catalogue; and Fagiolo (ed.), *Virgilio
nell'arte*, 212. As Bernari and De Vecchi note, there is some uncertainty about the title of
the painting in Braunschweig, given that Aeneas is clearly descending from the boat rather
than departing in it, but perhaps he is intending to help Dido in some way.

Museum of Art in Raleigh;[91] another is in the Pitti Palace in Florence.[92]

Through material like this, Virgil entered the official iconography of the Venetian state, for in 1576 Tintoretto painted *Venus at the Forge of Vulcan* as part of a group of pictures originally painted for the Atrio Quadrato and moved in 1713 to the Sala dell'Anticollegio in the Palazzo Ducale. The theme of the group is unity or concord, an appropriately Venetian subject.[93] The Sala dell'Anticollegio, which served as a waiting room for those having business with the Doge, also contains a sculptural depiction on the same theme by Tiziano Aspetti.[94] The monumental Scala dei Giganti contains a relief with a winged Victory accompanied by the inscription *Astrea duce* ('with Astraea as leader'), a reference to Virgil's *Eclogue* 4 that urges the Venetian republic to follow its Doge into a new golden age.[95] What is more, the Palazzo Ducale, the centre of Venetian governmental life, contains one more unmistakable appropriation of Virgilian values. On the walls of the Sala del Consiglio dei Dieci, the meeting room for the powerful Council of Ten charged with preserving the security of the state, is a painting by Marco Vecello. In place by 1604, this painting shows the peace concluded in 1529 at Bologna between Pope Clement VII and Emperor Charles V. On the left, in the Piazza di San Petronio, is the meeting between the Venetian legates and the Bolognese Gonfalionere di Giustizia, with the caption *ad Italiae securitatem firmandam accessit prisca Venetorum pietas* ('for confirming the security of Italy, the ancient *pietas* of the Venetians is added').[96] *Pietas* resists translation into English; it certainly includes 'piety' toward the gods, but also suggests all the duties owed to others, to family, friends, and fellow citizens. It is a key value in the *Aeneid*,

[91] Bernari and De Vecchi, *L'opera completa*, no. 30 in the catalogue; and Fagiolo (ed.), *Virgilio nell'arte*, 219.

[92] Von der Bercken, *Die Gemälde*, no. 100 in the catalogue.

[93] Ibid. no. 508 in the catalogue with pl. 294; Hans Tietze, *Tintoretto: The Paintings and Drawings* (New York, 1948), 364 and fig. 226; Bernari and De Vecchi, *L'opera completa*, no. 221D in the catalogue; and Fagiolo (ed.), *Virgilio nell'arte*, 219 with illus. on 220.

[94] *Venezia e dintorni*, Guida d'Italia del Touring Club Italiano, 2nd edn. (Milan, 1969), 131; and Giulio Lorenzetti, *Venezia e il suo estuario* (Trieste, 1974), 253. The Sala dell'Anticollegio was redecorated after a fire in 1574, according to the plan of A. Palladio and G. Rusconi, under the direction of A. Da Ponte.

[95] Brown, *Venice and Antiquity*, 168–9. Astraea also appears in a relief on the base of the central flagpole in the Piazza San Marco, dedicated in 1506 (ibid. 266–7).

[96] *Venezia e dintorni*, 134; and Lorenzetti, *Venezia e il suo estuario*, 261.

and would have been recognized as such by any schoolchild of Vecello's day.

The study that follows is designed to show how the poetry of Virgil came to take this central place in the civic and intellectual life of Renaissance Venice. At the heart of the study lie 251 copies of Virgil's poetry that were printed in the Veneto, annotated almost exclusively by local readers, and left in the libraries of the area—our best evidence for how this Roman poet was understood in the culture of Renaissance Venice.[97] The organization of the following chapters derives from the ideological environment in which the poetry of Virgil was read in this particular time and place. The three core chapters are organized around morality, religion, and social hierarchy—key components of the myth of Venice through which Venetians of this period interpreted the world around them. In each case, we shall see that the poetry of Virgil was, as Daniel Javitch would put it, 'domesticated'; that is, the poetry's 'objectionable or problematic aspects are suppressed or ignored so that it can be shown to conform not only to conventional ethical and religious values, but to artistic ones as well'.[98] Accordingly each chapter will detail both accommodation, the process by which the parts of the Virgilian vision consonant with the myth of Venice were identified and highlighted by readers of this period, and resistance and containment, whereby the 'objectionable or problematic aspects' of that poetry were brought into line with the dominant ideology. The resulting picture is one in which the interpretation of literature does not merely reflect 'reality', but rather becomes a part of the process by which people who read books decide what they believe in and use those beliefs to construct the world in which they live.

---

[97] Since Venetian books were sold throughout Europe, these same edns. were annotated by non-Venetians as well. A survey of the catalogues of, say, the British Library and the Bibliothèque Nationale would undoubtedly lead to interesting discoveries, but it would also break the closed hermeneutic circle of the present project and lead to a study of the reception of Venetian cultural values abroad.

[98] *Proclaiming a Classic: The Canonization of Orlando Furioso* (Princeton, 1991), 6. William Kennedy analyses how similar forces functioned in the canonization of Petrarch (*Authorizing Petrarch* (Ithaca, NY, 1994)).

2

Morality, Schooling, and the Printed Book in Renaissance Venice

Accommodation: The Press and the Schools as Purveyors of Values

Just four years after the first Venetian edition of Virgil's works came off the newly established printing press of Vindelinus de Spira, a copy of the *Eclogues, Georgics,* and *Aeneid* was prepared in the traditional handwritten fashion in Ferrara. By around 1540 this manuscript (now Princeton University Ms. 36) had travelled the hundred kilometres north to Venice, where it entered the library of one Marco Michiel.[1] Michiel's manuscript was a luxury production, written on vellum with illuminated initials, but a series of pointing hands and *Nota* ('note this') markers shows us that its owner had clearly bought this book to use as well as to enjoy.

These pointing hands and *Nota* markers in fact appear frequently enough to let us see how Michiel used his book. On fo. 81^r, for example, he has marked off *Aeneid* 2. 354, *una salus victis, nullam sperare salutem* ('the lost have only this one deliverance: to hope for none'). A few lines later he has tagged *quondam etiam victis redit in precordia virtus* ('at times new courage comes to beaten hearts'; *Aen.* 2. 367, fo. 81^v). In Book 8, Michiel has marked off *attulit et nobis aliquando optantibus etas* ('at last, in answer to our prayers, time brought help to us'; *Aen.* 8. 200–1, fo. 157^r), and in Book 10 he has tagged such lines as *audentes fortuna iuvat timidosque repellit* ('fortune helps those who dare and drives away the timid';

---

[1] The ms contains 214 folios, 22 × 15 cm. in size; Michiel's name appears on fos. 62^v and 140^v. The ms has been examined by Albinia C. de la Mare, whose notes on it may be found in the file on this ms in the Princeton University Library.

Aen. 10. 284, fo. 184^r)[2] and *stat sua cuique dies breve et inreparabile tempus* ('each has his day; there is, for all, a short, irreparable time of life'; *Aen.* 10. 467, fo. 187^r). That is, Michiel has mined his book for *sententiae*, memorable lines whose moral content makes them useful guides amid the confusions and setbacks of daily life.

This same procedure was followed by the owner of a copy of Vindelinus de Spira's *editio princeps*, a Vicentine student named Bartolameus Ghellinus who used pointing hands to mark off such verses from the *Georgics* as *labor omnia vincit | improbus* ('toil conquers everything, unrelenting toil'; *Georg.* 1. 145–6, fo. [16]^r) and *optima quaeque dies miseris mortalibus aevi | prima fugit* ('life's fairest days are ever the first to flee for hapless mortals'; *Georg.* 3. 66–7, fo. [28]^r).[3] Two copies of the second edition printed in Venice by Adam de Ambergau and still to be found there today have been read for the same purpose, as the pointing hands in one next to *improbe amor, quid non mortalia pectora cogis?* ('voracious love, to what do you not drive the hearts of men?'; *Aen.* 4. 412), and in the other next to *discite iusti-tiam moniti et non temnere divos* ('be warned, learn justice, do not scorn the gods'; *Aen.* 6. 620), show.[4] Thus in this regard, Renaissance readers in the Veneto approached printed books and manuscripts with the same expectations, and they continued to do so throughout the sixteenth century.[5] Indeed, even their *probationes*

---

[2] *Aen.* 10. 284 is actually a half-line, with the words *timidosque repellit* ('and drives away the timid') added by a later reader. The ancient lives report that the *Aeneid* was left unfinished at Virgil's death, and the half-lines scattered throughout the poem would presumably have been filled out had Virgil lived to see his project completed. Efforts to 'complete' the *Aeneid* range from these modest additions of less than a line to full-blown supplements of up to two full books, the most famous of which is the thirteenth book of Maffeo Vegio printed regularly in the Venetian Renaissance edns. of Virgil. See F. W. Shipley, 'Vergil's Verse Technique: Some Deductions from the Half-Lines', *Washington University Studies*, 12 (1924), 115–51; Bernd Schneider (ed.), *Das Aeneissupplement des Maffeo Vegio* (Weinheim, 1985), 12–13; and Craig Kallendorf, *In Praise of Aeneas: Virgil and Epideictic Rhetoric in the Early Italian Renaissance* (Hanover, NH, 1989), 204 n. 19. Translations of brief passages from the *Aeneid* are adapted from *The Aeneid of Virgil*, trans. Allen Mandelbaum (New York, 1971).

[3] This book is now Vicenza, Biblioteca Bertoliana, shelf mark RN 1.V.144. For a modern discussion of the importance of precepts in the *Georgics*, see Christine Perkell, *The Poet's Truth: A Study of the Poet in Virgil's Georgics* (Berkeley and Los Angeles, Calif., 1989), 139–90. Translations of the *Georgics* are adapted from *Virgil*, trans. H. Rushton Fairclough, Loeb Classical Library (Cambridge, Mass., 1965).

[4] These books are both in the Biblioteca Nazionale Marciana, Inc. V.152 and Inc. 426.

[5] Although Elizabeth Eisenstein argued in *The Printing Press as an Agent of Change: Communications and Cultural Transformations in Early Modern Europe*, 2 vols. (Cambridge,

pennae, the 'doodlings' inked into the front and back of their books, confirm what was on the minds of these early readers as they opened their copies of Virgil, for we find *virtus quae* ... ('virtue which') on the title-page of a 1574–5 edition of Joannes Maria Bonellus and *amando la virtu aquista honore* ('one acquires honour by loving virtue') at the back of a 1572 edition by the same printer.[6]

A book that was underlined with unusual thoroughness, the 1563 Aldine now in the Biblioteca Civica in Verona,[7] highlights enough passages to suggest the key reference points for the moral filter through which Virgil's poetry was being read in the Veneto of the Renaissance. To begin with, there are general exhortations to virtuous living: *disce, puer, virtutem ex me* ... ('from me, my son, learn valor'; *Aen.* 12. 435, fo. 234ʳ), *macte nova virtute puer, sic itur ad astra* ('a blessing on your young courage, my child; this is the way to scale the stars'; *Aen.* 9. 641, fo. 188ʳ), and so forth. Such virtuous living should bring its rewards, in the expectation that divine power presides over a just universe: *di meliora piis erroremque hostibus illum* ('heaven grant a happier lot to the good, and such madness to our foes'; *Georg.* 3. 513, fo. 50ᵛ), echoed by *at sperate Deos memores fandi*

1979) that printed books led to a decisive departure from the world of handwritten mss, an increasing number of scholars have been emphasizing the continuities in both production and reception between the two. See Curt Bühler, *The Fifteenth-Century Book: The Scribes, the Printers, the Decorators* (Philadelphia, 1960); Lotte Hellinga and Helmar Härtel (eds.), *Buch und Text im 15. Jahrhundert / Book and Text in the Fifteenth Century*, Proceedings of a Conference held in the Herzog August Bibliothek, Wolfenbüttel, 1–3 Mar. 1978, Wolfenbütteler Abhandlungen zur Renaissanceforschungen, 2 (Hamburg, 1981); J. B. Trapp (ed.), *Manuscripts in the Fifty Years after the Invention of Printing*, Some Papers read at a Colloquium at the Warburg Institute on 12–13 Mar. 1982 (London, 1983); Hans Bekker-Nielsen *et al.* (eds.), *From Script to Book: A Symposium*, Proceedings of the Seventh International Symposium organized by the Centre for the Study of Vernacular Literature in the Middle Ages, held at Odense University on 15–16 Nov. 1982 (Odense, 1986); and Sandra Hindman, 'Introduction', in ead. (ed.), *Printing the Written Word: The Social History of Books, circa 1450–1520* (Ithaca, NY, 1991), 1–2 and nn. 2–3. This intermingling of scribal and print culture makes it easier to understand how, for example, a substantial number of mss of three poems in the *Appendix Virgiliana* are all derived not from a handwritten *exemplar*, but from the *editio princeps* of 1471; see M. D. Reeve, 'Manuscripts copied from Printed Books', in Trapp (ed.), *Manuscripts in the Fifty Years*, 14.

[6] These two books are now Venice, Biblioteca Nazionale Marciana, 134.d.54 and Venice, Biblioteca del Museo Correr, F 3678.

[7] The book in which the following passages are found, now Aldine 106, is a copy of the 1563 edn. published by Paulus Manutius. References will be placed in the text of this para. It would be interesting to compare the list of virtues discussed here with the one derived by a 20th-cent. American reader who approaches literature with some of the same presuppositions: William J. Bennett (ed.), *The Book of Virtues: A Treasury of Great Moral Stories* (New York, 1993).

atque nefandi ('then still consider that the gods remember right and wrong'; *Aen.* I. 543, fo. 72^r). Interwoven with this sentiment, however, is a pronounced fatalism, a need to accept what cannot be changed: *manent immota tuorum | fata tibi* ('your children's fate is firm'; *Aen.* I. 257–8, fo. 67^v), *desine fata deum flecti sperare precando* ('leave any hope that prayer can turn aside the gods' decrees'; *Aen.* 6. 376, fo. 139^r), and so forth. There is a consistent emphasis on the value of hard work: *omnibus una quies operum, labor omnibus unus* ('all have one season to rest from labour, all one season to toil'; *Georg.* 4. 184, fo. 55^v), *multa dies, variusque labor mutabilis aevi | rettulit in melius* ('time and the varied work of turning years have mended many things'; *Aen.* 11. 425–6, fo. 216^v), and *vocat labor ultimus omnes* ('the final crisis calls all'; *Aen.* 11. 476, fo. 217^v). Other values highlighted prominently include patriotism—*vincet amor patriae, laudumque immensa cupido* ('his love of country will prevail, as will his passion for renown'; *Aen.* 6. 823, fo. 147^r)—and mercy—*parcere subiectis, et debellare superbos* ('to spare defeated peoples, tame the proud'; *Aen.* 6. 853, fo. 147^v)—with love for a woman posing one of the greatest threats to the attainment of these values: *carpit enim vires paulatim, uritque videndo | femina* ('for the sight of the female slowly inflames and wastes his strength'; *Georg.* 3. 215–16, fo. 45^v), *improbe amor, quid non mortalia pectora cogis?* ('voracious love, to what do you not drive the hearts of men?'; *Aen.* 4. 412, fo. 111^r), etc. In short, such readers as this one heard Virgil encouraging them to work hard for God, country, and what they knew to be right, and to accept what could not be changed as part of the ultimate justice of an ordered universe.

On a more personal level, the most poignant example of this approach to Virgil may be found on the back flyleaf of a copy of the 1532–3 Lucas Antonius Junta edition now in the Biblioteca Bertoliana in Vicenza. First we find a poem in elegiac distichs, entitled *Invitus in quodam carcere Patavii* ('Reluctant, in a certain Paduan prison'):

> Non carcer, non vincla viros, non aspera terrent
>   Tormenta, adversus synceritatis opus.
> Ferte, viri, superanda omnis Fortuna ferendo est:
>   Stat dicus hic, mollit ardua longa dies.

(Neither prison, nor chains, nor harsh tortures terrify men against the exercise of integrity. Endure, men, every fortune is to be overcome by enduring: a dyke stands here, a long day lightens adversity.)

Then beside this, in the same hand, we find an explicit link between what was thought in prison and what was read in Virgil:

Quae conformia sunt dicto Maronis, qui solitus erat dicere, nullam asperam acro [*sic*] esse fortunam, quam prudenter patiendo vir fortis non vincat, et in V° Aeneidos inseruit.

(These things are in conformity to the opinion of Virgil, who was accustomed to say that for the man of spirit there is no fortune so harsh that a brave man cannot overcome it by enduring wisely, which he put into the fifth book of the *Aeneid*.)[8]

This unknown prisoner has revealed more about the circumstances of his life than many of his contemporaries did, but the way he read was no different from that of countless other named and unnamed readers of his age.

The real question here, however, is *why* Renaissance readers in the Veneto responded with such consistency to this particular vision of the moral content of Virgil's poetry. To answer this question, I shall move first from handwritten notes to printed commentaries, then from books as marketable commodities to the educational institutions that created the market for those books. As I shall show, these institutions shaped the way the books were read, which in turn shaped the kinds of moral content that Venetian readers were able to see in Virgil's poetry. From this perspective we can come to understand both the interpretive activities we find in the margins of these texts and those we can imagine there but do not, in fact, find.

Why, then, do so many early Venetian editions of Virgil carry handwritten notes and symbols highlighting the moral content of the poetry? To begin to answer this question, let us return briefly

---

[8] The Renaissance book is now Vicenza, Biblioteca Bertoliana, C.15.7.8; the front flyleaf bears two dates, 23 Oct. 1544 (cancelled) and 11 May 1557. The reference is to *Aen.* 5. 710, *quidquid erit, superanda omnis fortuna ferendo est* ('whatever comes, all fortune must be overcome by our endurance'), a line that was also a favourite of the American Peter van Schaack during his exile from 1777 to 1784 (Meyer Reinhold, 'Vergil in the American Experience from Colonial Times to 1882', in Craig Kallendorf (ed.), *Vergil*, Classical Heritage Series, 2 (New York, 1992), 75–6). Literature written in prison constitutes its own sub-genre, and as Raymond A. Anselment points out, Richard Lovelace also turned to a similar Stoicism during his imprisonment 100 years later (' "Stone Walls" and "I'ron Bars": Richard Lovelace and the Conventions of Seventeenth-Century Prison Literature', *Renaissance and Reformation*, NS 17 (1993), 15–34).

to the book owned by our unknown Paduan prisoner. Three lines
in Book I of the *Aeneid* are marked off in the text:

> di tibi, si qua pios respectant numina, si quid
> usquam iustitiae est et mens sibi conscia recti,
> praemia digna ferant.

> (May gods confer on you your due rewards,
> if deities regard the good, if justice
> and mind aware of right count anywhere.)

> (*Aen.* I. 603–5)

In the margin, we find a handwritten note:

Est potius opinio stoica qui ponunt beatitudinem in recta conscientia, et
actione bonorum. Plenius de libro vide ubertinum in epistulis eius, libro
VI° epistula prima.

(It is rather a Stoic opinion that places happiness in an upright conscience
and the action of the good. For more concerning this book, see
Ubertinus in his letters, sixth book, first letter.)

This note complements the poem and gloss on the back flyleaf—
that is, once again this reader was studying Virgil with an eye on
his own situation, highlighting lines in which virtue is linked to
hope for a better future, then interpreting that hope through the
Stoic concept of happiness. In this case, however, the interpretation in this note is not linked directly to Virgil's text. In addition
to the text, this edition also contains a printed commentary by
Jodocus Badius Ascensius on these same lines:

per quod videtur hoc dicere, videmur quidem nobis pii, sed vix
quidquam iustitiae est apud mortales quod in conspectu deorum, satis
pium ac iustum censeatur, mens tamen nobis conscia recti est. ...

(Through this he seems to say that we indeed seem pious to ourselves,
but there is scarcely anything just among mortals that could be judged
sufficiently pious and just in the sight of the gods; nevertheless, there is
in us a mind aware of right.)

Ascensius, too, was concerned with the moral content of these
lines, but he saw in them a distinction between what seems virtuous to men and what is judged virtuous by the gods. Our
unknown prisoner has therefore shifted the focus from this distinction to the connection between virtue and its rewards. That is, the
handwritten note is actually a gloss on the printed commentary of
Ascensius—a gloss on a gloss, as it were.

The existence here of a printed commentary as intermediary between text and marginal note is significant, for most editions of the Venetian Renaissance were printed like this one, with one or more commentaries surrounding the text. Indeed, of the 132 Latin editions published before 1600, 105 have at least one commentary, with several large folio editions offering at least excerpts from as many as eleven different annotators.[9] To be sure, Renaissance commentaries do not always arouse enthusiasm among modern scholars: an examination of early editions of Livy led Anthony Grafton to complain that '[t]he smooth and eloquent lines of Livy's text were disfigured by commentaries that clung and spread like barnacles.'[10] However, as our Paduan prisoner has just shown, printed commentaries regularly provided an early reader with part of his culture, with 'a horizon of latent possibilities—a flexible and invisible cage in which he can exercise his own conditional liberty'[11] to interpret. I would therefore like to shift my focus for a while to these printed commentaries, to explore the extent to which the 'horizon of latent possibilities' for interpreting Virgil in the Renaissance regularly included moral concerns.

The commentary of Jodocus Badius Ascensius, the Flemish scholar-printer read by our Paduan prisoner, is a good place to start, for it was printed more often than any other commentary in Renaissance Venice: twenty-four times, beginning in 1512 and continuing up to the end of the century.[12] Like commentators for

---

[9] Publishing statistics are derived from my *A Bibliography of Venetian Editions of Virgil, 1470–1599*, Biblioteca di bibliografia italiana, 123 (Florence, 1991). Edns. promising eleven commentaries, like the 1543–4 printing of the heirs of Lucas Antonius Junta, in fact provide only excerpts from most of them; five commentaries were common at the end of the 15th and beginning of the 16th cents., and many edns. (esp. octavos) offered only one. The twenty-seven edns. without commentaries are concentrated among the very earliest printings (nine of the first twelve) and among the products of the Aldine press up to 1558, when Paulus Manutius began including his own commentary in the Virgil edns. published under his name.

[10] '*Discitur ut agatur*: How Gabriel Harvey read his Livy', in Stephen A. Barney (ed.), *Annotation and its Texts* (New York, 1991), 109. Given this attitude, it is little wonder that so many humanist commentaries to classical texts remain so little studied, as August Buck has observed ('Die Ethik im humanistischen Studienprogramm', in Walter Rüegg and Dieter Wuttke (eds.), *Ethik im Humanismus*, Beiträge zur Humanismusforschung, 5 (Boppard, 1979), 39–40).

[11] The phrasing is that of Carlo Ginzburg, *The Cheese and the Worms: The Cosmos of a Sixteenth-Century Miller*, trans. John and Anne Tedeschi (New York, 1989), p. xxi.

[12] The basic source on Ascensius' life and works remains P. Renouard, *Bibliographie des impressions et des œuvres de Josse Badius Ascensius, imprimeur et humaniste, 1462–1535*, 3 vols. (New York, 1967; repr. of Paris, 1908 edn.).

hundreds of years before him, Ascensius begins with an *accessus*, an introduction that provides a 'means of approaching' the text.[13] As part of this *accessus*, Ascensius defines the *intentio auctoris* ('intention of the author'), which was *ut et reipublicae et sibi quam plurimum per huius operis editionem prosit* ('that he profit both the state and himself as much as possible through the publication of this work'), for *constituisse videtur simul et iucunda et idonea dicere vitae* ('he is seen to have determined to describe at the same time things both pleasurable and appropriate for living'). To benefit the state, Virgil endowed Aeneas with wisdom, courage, justice, temperance, and all the other virtues as well, then set him up to be imitated by Augustus. Indeed, since he knew that the Romans would not accept a work of literature that did not offer something to the understanding of morality and the preservation of the state, Virgil used the sixth book of the *Aeneid* to establish punishment for the guilty and rewards for the just, to show that service to the state also brings benefits to the individual—an intention he shares with every good author (*haec communis est omnibus bona et bene scribentis intentio*).[14]

Structuring the moral tone of this passage is an explicit reliance on the *Ars poetica* of Horace, whose analysis of the utility and delight of poetry (l. 333) had exercised a continuous impact on criticism since antiquity and which Ascensius himself had commented upon around 1500.[15] As he writes in his notes on Book 4 of the *Aeneid, cum ergo in toto opere, tum hic poeta et delectat et prodest plurimum, nam simul et iucunda et idonea dicere vitae instituit* ('as therefore in this entire work, so here the poet greatly delights and profits, for at the same time he undertook to say things both pleasurable and appropriate for living'; fo. 202ᵛ, on *Aen.* 4. 1–29). The pleasurable things, to be sure, are described with great

[13] On the *accessus ad auctores*, see Edwin A. Quain, SJ, 'The Medieval *Accessus ad Auctores*', *Traditio*, 3 (1945), 215–64; Fausto Ghisalberti, 'Mediaeval Biographies of Ovid', *Journal of the Warburg and Courtauld Institutes*, 9 (1946), 10–59; Konrad von Hirsau, *Dialogus super auctores*, ed. R. B. C. Huygens (Leiden, 1970); A. J. Minnis, *Medieval Theory of Authorship: Scholastic Literary Attitudes in the Later Middle Ages* (London, 1984); and D. Kelly, '*Accessus ad auctores*', in Gert Ueding (ed.), *Historisches Wörterbuch der Rhetorik* (Tübingen, 1992), i. 27–36.

[14] I have used Ascensius' commentary in *Publii Virgilii Maronis poetae Mantuani universum poema* ... (Venice: Joannes Maria Bonellus, 1558). This reference is to fos. 123ᵛ–124ʳ; other references will be placed in the text.

[15] Bernard Weinberg, *A History of Literary Criticism in the Italian Renaissance*, 2 vols. (Chicago, 1961), i. 71–88.

frequency and power, but Ascensius' real concern, as he admits in his commentary on Virgil's description of the Elysian fields, is with the things that profit (fo. 258^{r-v}, on *Aen.* 6. 656–71).

While it is thus true that Ascensius' interest in the moral content of Virgil's poetry came from his adherence to Horatian critical principles, this is not the whole truth, for other ideas also influenced his reading of Horace and propelled him in the same direction. For example, Bernard Weinberg has observed that Ascensius read the *Ars poetica* 'as if it were part of the classical-medieval rhetorical tradition'.[16] By that, he means that Ascensius found explanations for Horace's ideas about decorum, the rhetorical categories of invention, disposition, and style, and so forth in the works of Cicero and Quintilian. This is fine as far as it goes, and it colours the commentary to Virgil as well (cf. fo. 136^r, on *Aen.* 1. 198–207). However, I would add that Ascensius also drew heavily on another part of the rhetorical tradition: the association between epic poetry and epideictic, the rhetoric of praise and blame.

According to Aristotle, whose scheme was passed on to the Roman rhetoricians and then to later ages as well, oratory could be divided into three kinds: deliberative, judicial (or forensic), and epideictic. The third kind, epideictic, relies on praise and blame as its distinctive elements and directs these elements toward highlighting virtue and vice.[17] As O. B. Hardison, Jr. and Brian Vickers have shown, the principles of epideictic rhetoric became entangled with the principles of literary criticism in late antiquity, so that the praise of virtue and condemnation of vice came to be seen as a legitimate goal of poetry and criticism as well as speechmaking.[18] Thus when Coluccio Salutati, the fourteenth-century chancellor of Florence and fervent admirer of the classics, read line 333 of Horace's *Ars poetica*, he immediately interpreted it as part of the praise-and-blame tradition: *Principaliter igitur utilitati vituperatio correspondet, delectationi laus* ... ('Chiefly, therefore, condemnation corresponds to utility and praise to pleasure').[19]

---

[16] Ibid. 84.   [17] Aristotle, *Rhetoric* 1358^{a-b}, 1366^a.
[18] O. B. Hardison, Jr., *The Enduring Monument: A Study of the Idea of Praise in Renaissance Literary Theory and Practice* (Westport, Conn., 1973; repr. of Chapel Hill, NC, 1962 edn.); and Brian Vickers, 'Epideictic and Epic in the Renaissance', *New Literary History*, 14 (1982–3), 497–537.
[19] Kallendorf, *In Praise of Aeneas*, 11. This book examines epideictic readings of Virgil in Petrarch, Boccaccio, Salutati, Vegio, and Landino.

This approach to poetry affects Ascensius' reading of the *Aeneid* from the very first line, for when Virgil 'sings' the deeds of famous men, he praises them by singing, so that *cano* ('I sing') is to be understood in place of *laudo* ('I praise'; fo. 125ʳ, on *Aen.* 1. 1). What is to be praised is the virtue of Aeneas, by which Virgil's readers might be instructed in how to live well (fo. 126ᵛ, on *Aen.* 1. 8–11). From this point on, Ascensius finds a great many opportunities to highlight the virtuous activities of Virgil's hero and the moral lessons of his story. When Aeneas and his men arrive in Carthage, for example, the Trojan leader does not think of resting his weary body, but climbs a rock to see whether anything around him threatens the safety of his crew, an action that is praiseworthy (fo. 135ʳ, on *Aen.* 1. 180–97). And when Aeneas and his men arrive outside the gates of Dis, Virgil arranges for him to learn the punishments of the evildoers confined inside in order to deter the readers of the *Aeneid* from wrongdoing (fo. 255ʳ, on *Aen.* 6. 259–79).

Sometimes the determination to praise Aeneas leads Ascensius to some interesting critical insights. For example, he takes great care to exculpate Aeneas from any charge of treason or cowardice in his flight from Troy:

Docet quomodo ab Hectore excitatus sit, et ad fugam faciendam admonitus, in qua re ingeniosus poeta, miro utitur artificio, nam sic Aeneam a proditione purgat, ut et fugam illi gloriosam faciat. Purgatur quidem a proditione, quod cum ceteris, eadem fraude deceptus, somno indulgebat, et si quaeratur cur non etiam cum ceteris perierit, respondet, quia ab Hectore admonitus, ex[s]urrexit et virtute, qua plurimum potuit, praecipue ducente deo, per tela, per hostes, evasit. Fugam autem, inclytam facit, quia solus ad hoc a diis electus est, ut deos et sacra per fugam servet. ...

(He teaches how he was awakened by Hector and warned to take flight, in which this clever poet uses striking artifice, for he thus clears Aeneas of treason, as he also makes a glorious departure for him. Indeed he is cleared of treason in that it was in the company of the rest, taken in by the same deception, that he was indulging in sleep, and if someone asks why he did not perish with the others, he answers, it was because he was warned by Hector, got up, and chiefly through divine leadership but also through the prowess in which he excelled, made his way forth through the weapons of the enemy. The departure is celebrated because Aeneas alone has been chosen for this by the gods, so that he might preserve the gods and what is sacred through his departure.)

(fo. 169ʳ, on *Aen.* 2. 268–95)

Similarly Aeneas is to be praised for the dalliance at Carthage, since he does not love in a base and vulgar manner, but he was loved (*amatus est*), and not by someone who has cast aside her honour, but by someone who was pursued by Venus and deceived by Cupid (fo. 202^v, on *Aen.* 4. 11; see also fo. 156^v, on *Aen.* 1. 705–22). Even the final scene in which the enraged Aeneas slays Turnus after he surrenders and begs for mercy ends up being interpreted to Aeneas' credit; the entire book recounts the praises of Aeneas, so that this final victory must mark the final attainment of heroic glory (fo. 351^r, on the arguments printed at the beginning of *Aen.* 12; see also fo. 367^r, on *Aen.* 12. 930–52).[20]

In short, a significant part of Ascensius' critical effort is devoted to identifying the virtues of Aeneas and to establishing the rewards that come to such virtuous heroes as this. Such an approach, as we have seen, is the logical application of Ascensius' general approach to poetry, his reading of Horace through the filter of epideictic rhetoric. However, a closer look at Ascensius' procedure in his commentary on the *Aeneid* reveals that in this case, there are even more constraints than usual on how the humanist scholar constructs the commentary he places between Virgil's text and its Renaissance readers.

Ascensius' normal procedure is to break Virgil's text into manageable sections, then to construe each section under the rubric *ordo est* ('the order is'), and finally to add a discussion of whatever he feels needs explanation. This discussion is based overwhelmingly, as he openly acknowledges, on the late fourth-century commentator Tiberius Claudius Donatus, whose work

---

[20] For Ascensius, the moral content of a passage could even determine whether it deserved to remain in the text. For example, when Aeneas told Dido about becoming so angry at Helen that he considered killing her (*Aen.* 2. 559 ff.), Ascensius observed that he became so embarrassed that he had to look away. The passage was of questionable textual authority, and Ascensius used its inappropriate moral content to banish it from further consideration. Modern scholars continue to debate the issue, though generally on other grounds. Henry T. Rowell, 'The Ancient Evidence of the Helen Episode in *Aeneid* II', in Luitpold Wallach (ed.), *The Classical Tradition: Literary and Historical Studies in Honor of Harry Caplan* (Ithaca, NY, 1966), 210-21 considers Servius and Aelius Donatus as sources for the Helen episode. R. G. Austin, 'Virgil, *Aeneid* 2. 567-88', *Classical Quarterly*, NS 11 (1961), 185-98 reviews the controversy surrounding the passage and argues that the lines should be preserved. However, G. P. Goold, 'Servius and the Helen Episode', *Harvard Studies in Classical Philology*, 74 (1970), 101-68 maintains that the contents of these lines cannot be Virgilian; a thorough bibliographical review of the problem can be found in R. G. Austin, *P. Vergili Maronis Aeneidos Liber Secundus* (Oxford, 1964), 219.

had come to light gradually in the fifteenth century but which had only been systematically exploited once before Ascensius prepared his commentary.[21] Even more than Ascensius, Donatus is single-minded in his adherence to the praise-and-blame approach to the *Aeneid*. Virgil's *materiae genus* ('genus of subject matter'), as Donatus notes at the beginning of his commentary, is *laudativum* ('encomiastic'), so that Virgil's goal is to show Aeneas as *vacuus omni culpa et magno praeconio praeferendus* ('free of all guilt and one most worthy to be publicly presented with great commendation').[22] Donatus takes every possible occasion to praise Aeneas' virtues: he is a good leader (on *Aen.* 1. 159–79), pious toward the gods (on *Aen.* 1. 379), chaste (on *Aen.* 1. 310–20), handsome and brave (on *Aen.* 1. 594–5), and so forth. Donatus also exercises his critical ingenuity to highlight what he sees as Virgil's exculpation of Aeneas: Aeneas is blameless in fleeing Troy, for example, because the city had been destined to fall (on *Aen.* 1. 1). According to this approach, Aeneas emerges from Carthage with his good name intact; in fact, Donatus even outlines a defence that Aeneas could have presented had there been time in the story for it to be recounted (on *Aen.* 4. 271). It is easy to hear echoes of Donatus' approach in Ascensius' commentary: indeed, Ascensius' dependence on Donatus is so great that when a lacuna in his source robs

---

[21] Vladimiro Zabughin, *Vergilio nel Rinascimento italiano da Dante a Torquato Tasso*, 2 vols. (Bologna, 1921–3), i. 189, argued that Donatus' commentary had little impact among the humanists, but as Roberto Cardini has pointed out (Cristoforo Landino, *Scritti critici e teorici*, ed. Roberto Cardini, 2 vols. (Rome, 1974), ii. 292–4), subsequent research has revealed that the commentary was known at least to a number of prominent Quattrocento humanists, among whom were Angelo Poliziano, Battista Guarino, Poggio Bracciolini, Niccolò Niccoli, and Giovanni Pontano. According to Remigio Sabbadini (*Le scoperte dei codici latini e greci ne' secoli XIV e XV*, 2 vols. (Florence, 1967; repr. of Florence, 1905–14 edn.), i. 132 and n. 25, i. 194 n. 53, i. 206 n. C, ii. 220), the ms of the first five books was in Florence by 1438, and the ms containing the later books had arrived in Italy by 1466. An epitome was published in the late 15th cent. by Cristoforo Landino and reprinted at least twenty times by the turn of the century; see Luigi Valmaggi, 'La biografia di Virgilio attribuita al grammatico Elio Donato', *Rivista di filologia e d'istruzione classica*, 14 (1886), 31–4; and Sabbadini, 'Tib. Claudio Donato in Vergilium', in *Storia e critica di testi latini* (Padua, 1971; repr. of Catania, 1914 edn.), 147–51. However, Donatus' commentary does not seem to have been widely used in the late 15th and early 16th cents., and the *editio princeps* did not appear until 1535.

[22] Citations from Donatus are to *Interpretationes Vergilianae*, ed. Henricus Georgii (Leipzig, 1905–6), and will be placed in the text. Although modern scholars have generally held Donatus' judgements in low regard, Marisa Squillante Saccone has argued that Donatus captures a good number of readings that are worth considering (*Le Interpretationes Virgilianae di Tiberio Donato* (Naples, 1985), 119).

him of his normal borrowings, he feels compelled to acknowledge the fact (e.g. on *Aen.* 4. 388–436 and 6. 1–39).[23]

While such a heavy level of borrowing may be due to a scholarly laziness of sorts, there are a couple of other factors at work here as well. For one thing, as Rita Copeland has pointed out, 'commentaries themselves become texts to be appropriated by later exegetes and to be incorporated in later commentaries',[24] so that in fact Ascensius' borrowings from Donatus reflect a common manœuvre among commentators who, after all, feel little inclined to reinvent the proverbial wheel when a body of notes already exists for their text. What is more, as a good humanist, Ascensius believed not only that the literature of antiquity should occupy a privileged place in the culture of his day, but that the interpretation of this literature should be grounded as much as possible in the culture in which it had been produced.[25] The humanists never found a commentary from the Augustan age, of course, but they felt particularly fortunate to have recovered a commentary like Donatus' that was written not too much later than the poem itself. Thus when Ascensius worked through the *Aeneid* as a guide to moral life,[26] he could be confident that this interpretation was

[23]   Modern texts are still based on the same mss that became available in the 15th cent., so that there are still a good number of lacunae in the text. Peter K. Marshall, however, has found some previously unknown ms material, which holds out hope that textual progress may still be possible; see 'Tiberius Claudius Donatus on Virgil *Aen.* 6. 1–157', *Manuscripta*, 37 (1993), 3–20.

[24]   *Rhetoric, Hermeneutics, and Translation: Academic Traditions and Vernacular Texts*, Cambridge Studies in Medieval Literature (Cambridge, 1991), 65, reviewed at length by L. G. Kelly, *Allegorica*, 14 (1993), 83–92. Tracing lines of influence among commentaries is difficult when so much basic work remains to be done; with Virgil, the task should be eased considerably when Virginia Brown and her team complete their work for the *Catalogus translationum et commentariorum*. One example of such influence that has received full discussion is the appropriation of Servius by the annotators of Basel, Öffentliche Bibliothek der Universität, MS F II 23, in Virginia Brown and Craig Kallendorf, 'Two Humanist Annotators of Virgil: Coluccio Salutati and Giovanni Tortelli', in James Hankins, John Monfasani, and Frederick Purnell, Jr. (eds.), *Supplementum Festivum: Studies in Honor of Paul Oskar Kristeller* (Binghamton, NY, 1987), 65–148.

[25]   Eugenio Garin, *Italian Humanism: Philosophy and Civic Life in the Renaissance*, trans. Peter Munz (Oxford, 1965), 1–17.

[26]   Relying on the ancient critics (e.g. Suetonius, *Augustus* 89. 2), modern scholars continue to stress the connection between poetic production and moral ideals in Augustan Rome; see Karl Galinsky, *Classical and Modern Interpretations: Postmodern Architecture, Multiculturalism, Decline, and Other Issues* (Austin, Tex., 1992), 99. It is worth noting that the other great commentator from late antiquity, Servius, was also esteemed as a representative of Virgil's culture, but that his commentary was much less open to moralizing use. However, as Julian Ward Jones, Jr., has noted, there are some twenty-two notes

authorized by a great critic who was speaking to him across the centuries from the very culture in which Virgil himself had lived and worked.

Given the consistent moral flavour of Ascensius' commentary, we could conclude that the handwritten notes of Renaissance readers in the Veneto responded to the moral content of Virgil's poetry at least in part because they were following the cues from a printed commentary like this one. That conclusion, however, simply raises another question: why was Ascensius' commentary with its consistent moral flavour printed more often than other commentaries with other emphases? Why, that is, did Pierio Valeriano's textual annotations appear only eight times in editions of Virgil printed in the Venetian Renaissance? For that matter, why was Pomponio Leto's more narrowly philological commentary not printed at all in this group of books?[27] In other words, what forces—economic, ideological, institutional—made a moralizing commentary the most attractive option to the printers of Renaissance Venice?

As a first step toward answering this question, I would like to take a preliminary look at who was most likely to use a Latin edition of Virgil in Renaissance Venice. First I shall examine some of the prefaces and dedicatory letters in these editions, in order to isolate one group of intended readers. Then I shall look at some

containing moral allegory, mostly concentrated in Bk. 6; Jones's findings are summarized in 'Allegorical Interpretation in Servius', *Classical Journal*, 56 (1961), 220–1, and presented at length in 'An Analysis of the Allegorical Interpretations in the Servian Commentary on the *Aeneid*', Ph.D. thesis (Univ. of North Carolina, 1959). Now and again, a 16th-cent. reader looking for moral guidance picks up on this. The most extensive example known to me is a book now in the Newberry Library in Chicago, shelf mark WING fZP 535 / .G436, a 1536–7 Junta edn. in which a reader has extracted such pithy sayings from Servius as *premia non debentur eventui sed voluntati* ('rewards are not owed to an occurrence, but to the will'; fo. 272[r]).

[27] Considerable confusion surrounds Leto's Virgil commentary, with the attributions in Vladimiro Zabughin, 'L'autografo delle chiose vergiliane di Pomponio Leto', *Arcadia*, 3 (1918), 135–43, challenged in a 1975 exhibition catalogue, R. W. Hunt *et al.* (eds.), *The Survival of Ancient Literature* (Oxford, 1975), 12–15. The commentary was published, but again amid considerable confusion. The unauthorized edn. printed by Daniele Gaitano from 1487–90 was promptly repudiated by Leto, and Zabughin considers the corrected reprint by Giovanni Oporino (Basel, 1544) the 'true *editio princeps*' (*Vergilio*, i. 189–92). Presumably Leto remained tainted by his association with the Roman academy and its controversy with Pope Paul II, as described by John D'Amico, *Renaissance Humanism in Papal Rome: Humanists and Churchmen on the Eve of the Reformation* (Baltimore, 1983), 91–102, but Leto's work on Virgil should be re-examined.

ownership notes and handwritten marginalia, in order to determine how often those intended readers actually bought these
books.

Two dedicatory letters generally accompanied Ascensius'
commentary. The first, in which he explains that Virgil put forth
Aeneas as a *speculum atque exemplar perfecti viri* ('mirror and pattern
of the perfect man'), is addressed to one Lodovicus de Flandria,
who is described as *adolescenti indulgentissimo* ('the kindest of
youth').[28] The other, in which the works of Virgil are praised as
a pathway leading to good character and pious virtue, is
addressed to four *ingenuis optimorum bibliopolarum liberis*
('honourable children of the finest booksellers').[29] That is,
Ascensius assumed that those who would read his commentary
would be young.

Those who printed his commentary made the same assumption.
Georgius Arrivabenus Mantuanus, for example, uses the
colophons of both parts of his 1512 edition to identify his target
audience as *iuventus optima* ('good youth'; Pt. I, fo. 168ʳ, and Pt. II,
fo. AA1ʳ). Three years later, Alexander de Paganinis Brixianus
acknowledges that he has the same audience in mind when he
copies the colophon of the first part (along with the rest of
Arrivabenus' book) into his 1515 edition (Pt. I, fo. 168ʳ). More
specifically, the assumption was that these books would be used by
young readers as school texts. The printer Gregorius de Gregoriis,
for example, uses the colophon of his 1522 edition to make this
clear, for the book is offered to *eminentissimi bonarum litterarum
candidati* ('distinguished candidates in the humanities'; Pt. III, fo.

---

[28] This letter may be found in Renouard, *Bibliographie*, iii. 360–3. As a number of
scholars have recently observed, the prefaces and dedicatory letters in early Venetian books
deserve more systematic study than they have received so far (Conor Fahy, 'The *Index
Librorum Prohibitorum* and the Venetian Printing Industry in the Sixteenth Century', *Italian
Studies*, 35 (1980), 58), since they often provide an interesting middle ground between literary theory and practical criticism (Guido Baldassarri, 'Prefazioni cinquecentesche', in id.
(ed.), *Quasi un picciolo mondo: Tentativi di codificazione del genere epico nel Cinquecento*,
Università degli Studi di Padova, Quaderni dell'Istituto di Filologia e Letteratura Italiana, 1
(Milan, 1982), 13–22). Such prefatory matter has sometimes been slighted on the assumption that the rhetorical excesses of the genre vitiate its reliability, but Claudia Di Filippo
Bareggi has examined the writings of fourteen men who worked as editors for the Venetian
press during the 16th cent. and shown that external evidence regularly confirms the valid-
ity of their observations (*Il mestiere di scrivere: Lavoro intellettuale e mercato librario a Venezia nel
Cinquecento*, 'Europa delle Corti', Centro Studi sulle Società di Antico Regime, Biblioteca
del Cinquecento, 43 (Rome, 1988), 313–14).

[29] Renouard, *Bibliographie*, iii. 363.

43^v), who could be students at any level in school or university studies.[30]

Those who prepared and printed texts of Virgil without commentaries seem to have had the same audience in mind. The 1501 Aldine edition, for example, contains a note from the printer to all students (*studiosis omnibus*) explaining that the obscene poetry attributed to Virgil has been omitted from this edition because Aldus did not consider it worthy of inclusion in an educational handbook (*non censuimus digna enchiridio*; fo. a1^r).[31] Other commentaries were directed to the same school audience. The commentary of Antonius Mancinellus on the *Eclogues* was originally prepared for use in a Roman school, as the dedicatory letter shows (fo. AA2^r), and the commentary by Johannes a Meyen that appeared in Aldine editions at the end of the sixteenth century declares that it has been prepared to accommodate *studiosis adolescentibus* ('youthful students'; fo. +3^v).

I have dwelled on this point a little because a number of scholars have by inference suggested that the bond between Renaissance editions of the Latin classics and the school environment in which they were taught is not so strong as I believe it is. For example, in rightly trying to counter the notion that Aldus pioneered octavo size and italic type to lower book prices and inaugurate some sort of 'paper-back revolution', Martin Lowry argues that books printed in this way were marketed to 'busy men of affairs … [,] secular intellectuals' who could use the new, compact Virgil to 'snatch a few minutes relaxation during a busy day at court'. By printing smaller books in italic type,

---

[30] It is not clear from this expression how old these 'candidates' are or precisely what their candidacy is for. In a personal letter, Paul Grendler suggests that the phrase 'might be a general, somewhat vague statement intended to help sell the book to students at any level', which strikes me as reasonable; at any rate, the key point revolves around the link between commentary and the academic environment for which it was produced, which counters the arguments of Karlheinz Stierle, '*Studium*: Perspectives on Institutionalized Modes of Reading', *New Literary History*, 22 (1991), 123.

[31] This concern is typical of Aldus' publishing programme. In the introduction to his Latin grammar, for example, he says explicitly that his audience is youth (*adulescentuli*), and that while good character and erudition are both proper educational goals, it is better to fall short in the latter area than in the former: *Malo enim eos nullas scire litteras ornatos moribus, quam omnia scire male moratos* (qtd. by Vittore Branca, 'Ermolao Barbaro and Late Quattrocento Venetian Humanism', in J. R. Hale (ed.), *Renaissance Venice* (Totowa, NJ, 1973), 230).

'Aldus was freeing literature from the study and the lecture-room.'[32]

Yet I believe there is more to it than this. A former teacher himself, Aldus also had the needs of teachers in mind as he selected the contents of the 1501 Virgil, which was the first non-religious book to be printed in octavo format and which pioneered the use of italic type. What is more, Aldine editions seem to have been particularly popular among teachers who wanted a good text in which they could enter their own commentary. The Biblioteca Nazionale Marciana, for example, still preserves two Aldine Virgils that had been owned by teachers, one containing three dates from the beginning of the seventeenth century but no name, the other signed and dated 1536 by a Master Caspar B, teacher at the Royal College of St Thomas in Leipzig.[33] Melanchthon's copy of Virgil, now in the New York Public Library, was also an Aldine.[34] To be sure, copies of these editions were undoubtedly sold to Lowry's 'busy men of affairs', who indeed must have used them to while away odd moments at court. However, we should not forget that the taste for Latin poetry was shaped during the school experiences of such men, so that even in cases like this, it strikes me as something of an oversimplification to say that 'Aldus was freeing literature from the study and the lecture-room.'

We must also be careful not to oversimplify the situation with respect to large folio editions. Lowry notes that '[t]he scholar was expected to deploy a large folio on his study lectern',[35] which is certainly true enough. However, the implication is that such a book contained far more than anyone else would need to know. To be sure, it is hard to imagine a student, even one in his early teens, walking through the *calli* of Venice carrying a satchel full of books like this, which is presumably what led Paul Grendler to

[32] *The World of Aldus Manutius: Business and Scholarship in Renaissance Venice* (Ithaca, NY, 1979), 143, 147. Armando Petrucci makes this same point, arguing that the small *libretto da mano* was tied to a new way of reading that moved books out of places where they were used for obligatory study to places where they could be taken up by choice ('Typologie du livre et de la lecture dans l'Italie de la Renaissance: De Petrarque à Politien', in Bekker-Nielsen *et al.* (eds.), *From Script to Book*, 135–8); see also id., 'Alle origini del libro moderno: Libro da banco, libri da bisaccia, libretti da mano', *Italia medioevale e umanistica*, 12 (1969), 306–8.
[33] These two books are copies of the corrected 1514 edn., shelf mark Aldine 628, and the 1505 edn., shelf mark Aldine 687, respectively.
[34] Shelf mark ★ KB 1541, a copy of the 1541 edn.
[35] *World*, 143.

define 'printed editions for school use' as 'inexpensive small octavo or duodecimo imprints with little or no commentary'.[36] Nevertheless, there is no shortage of notices entered into large folio volumes by student owners. In the fifteenth century these volumes were often printed with a plain text surrounded by wide margins in which the student could enter the commentary as it was dictated by the teacher.[37] A copy of the first Venetian edition of Virgil, for example, contains an extensive handwritten commentary with an ownership note in somewhat tentative Latin: *Hic liber est mei Bartolamei Ghellini de Nolilisbus Vicentinae, manet sive habitat Vicetiae descipulus Lodovici Roneoni magister publicus* ... ('This book belongs to me, Bartolameus Ghellinus de Nolilisbus of Vicenza, [who] remains or dwells in Vicenza as a student of Lodovicus Roneonus, the public teacher'), and a copy of the 1476 Antonius Bartholomaei edition contains marginal and interlinear notes interspersed with *non audivi* ('I did not hear [this lesson]'), markers indicating that a section of commentary is missing because the student was absent from class.[38] The crude pictures of bells, faces, and abstract designs entered into the beginning of a copy of the *c.*1488 Liga Boaria edition now in the Biblioteca Comunale, Treviso, suggest that this incunabulum probably belonged to a student as well.[39] Similar notices show that folio volumes continued to be used by young students even after pocket-sized editions appeared, two examples being the 1572 heirs of Joannes Maria Bonellus edition now in the Columbia University Library, on the back flyleaf of which is

[36] *Schooling in Renaissance Italy: Literacy and Learning 1300–1600* (Baltimore, 1989), 240.

[37] As Gerhard Powitz has pointed out, student mss of the late Middle Ages often took this form as well, with the text copied into the middle of the page by a scribe and the commentary entered in the margin by the student as the teacher dictated it ('Text und Kommentar im Buch des 15. Jahrhundert', in Hellinga and Härtel (ed.), *Buch und Text*, 39). Given the close connection between early printed books and the mss from which they were copied, it should not surprise us to find printed edns. replacing ms texts for this market. It is also worth noting, however, that students did not always have their own books; this practice presumably became more common toward the end of the 16th century, but Kristian Jensen observes that most of the surviving printed grammars that contain ms notes seem to be teachers' copies, not ones belonging to students (*Rhetorical Philosophy and Philosophical Grammar: Julius Caesar Scaliger's Theory of Language*, Humanistische Bibliothek, Texte und Abhandlungen, Reihe 1, Abhandlungen, 46 (Munich, 1990), 56–7).

[38] The two books are Vicenza, Biblioteca Bèrtoliana, RN 1.V.144, the 1470 edn. printed by Vindelinus de Spira, fo. [1]ʳ, and Verona, Biblioteca Civica, Incunaboli 856, with the tags indicating absences found on fos. m7ᵛ, m8ʳ, and m8ᵛ.

[39] Shelf mark: Inc. 13716, fo. iv.

written *A di 20 di Maggio 1587 cominciai andare alla scola domini ... Pietro G* ... ('On the twentieth of May, 1587, I began to go to the school of master ... Pietro G'); and the 1578 Petrus Dusinellus edition now in the Biblioteca Comunale, Treviso, whose student owner provided precise details about his study of the *Georgics*: *Lo incominciaremo alli 19 di Aprile 1610 dichiarato da D. Camillo Setti à me Novello Rosen in Ferrara* ('We shall begin on 19 April 1610, [with the text] explained by Master Camillo Setti to me, Novello Rosen[o], in Ferrara'; fo. 43^v).[40]

Two points, I believe, emerge from this discussion. First, the variety of ways in which early owners used their books makes it difficult to generalize about consumption on the basis of size and format. Second, prefaces and dedicatory letters printed in these editions and ownership notes added to them anchor both octavos and folios, both with and without printed commentaries, firmly into the institutional environment of the schools. Virgil was a standard curriculum author in this period, as indeed he had been throughout the Middle Ages. As Paul Grendler has shown, records from the academic year 1587–8 indicate that Virgil was taught more than any other Latin poet by the 258 people teaching in Venice at that time.[41] This situation, which was typical for Italian schools, generated a substantial market—substantial enough to justify an average of one new edition each year throughout this period.

I do not wish to be overly reductive here: obviously, anyone who had the price of the book could buy one, and anyone who could read Latin could read the text privately or in some other

---

[40] Shelf marks are Lodge, 1572 / V5873 (for the Columbia copy) and N.12563 (II.1.B.28) (for the Treviso copy). The student owner of the Treviso copy usually spelled his name *Roseno* in Italian (fos. 59^v, 134^r, 156^r, 212^r), *Rosenus* in Latin (title-page, fo. 176^v). These two edns., like many others of the 16th century, contained illustrations, which provides another possible association with an academic market, for E. P. Goldschmidt felt that those in need of visual reinforcement of the books' contents would have been school-children (*The Printed Book of the Renaissance: Three Lectures on Type, Illustration, Ornament* (Cambridge, 1950), 46–8).

41. *Schooling*, 204–6, 246–7. For a general survey of schools in early Renaissance Venice, see J. Bruce Ross, 'Venetian Schools and Teachers Fourteenth to Early Sixteenth Centuries: A Survey and Study of Giovanni Battista Egnazio', *Renaissance Quarterly*, 39 (1976), 521–36; and two studies by Bruno Nardi, both repr. in his *Saggi sulla cultura veneta del Quattro e Cinquecento*, ed. Paolo Mazzantini (Padua, 1971): 'Letteratura e cultura veneziana del Quattrocento', 3–43, and 'La scuola di Rialto e l'umanesimo veneziano', 45–98.

non-academic institutional context.[42] I am only pointing out that the humanistic schools in Renaissance Venice provided a steady number of Latin-speaking readers with means, motive, and opportunity to procure a copy of Virgil, and that we ought to keep this in mind as we ask ourselves why the moralizing commentary was the most attractive option to printers in this culture.

Behind the classroom practices of the humanist schools in Renaissance Italy lay a coherent philosophy of education, carefully thought out and systematically developed in several treatises that are well known at least to specialists: Pier Paolo Vergerio's *De ingenuis moribus et liberalibus studiis* (*On Noble Character and the Liberal Studies*, c.1393), Leonardo Bruni's *De studiis et litteris* (*On Literary Studies*, c.1405), Aeneas Sylvius Piccolomini's *De liberorum educatione* (*On the Education of Children*, c.1445), Battista Guarino's *De ordine docendi et studendi* (*On the Order of Teaching and Studying*, 1459), and Maffeo Vegio's *De educatione liberorum clarisque eorum moribus* (*On Education and Distinction of Character in Children*, c.1460).[43] From these treatises it is easy to determine what was

---

[42]   Other institutions, of course, also created markets for books—as Mary and Richard Rouse point out, monasteries provided the first market for printed books in Germany and the Low Countries (*Authentic Witnesses: Approaches to Medieval Texts and Manuscripts* (Notre Dame, Ind., 1991), 449–65)—so that the connection between books and schools should not be taken for granted. As a number of modern scholars have observed, however, the relationship between academic institutions and the printing press became closer over time. Severin Corsten, for example, notes that in the case of the University of Cologne, the university as an institution did not promote printing. However, individual professors did pay attention to the new technology, and from c.1485 they tried to ensure that the books on which they were lecturing were available in print. Because of this, Corsten encourages a closer study of how academic teaching affected printing history ('Universität und Buchdruck in Köln: Versuch eines Überblicks für das 15. Jahrhundert', in Hellinga and Härtel (eds.), *Buch und Text*, 189–99). I should also note that printed books like these were purchased for use in an institutional context but were in general owned by individuals. This marks a change from later medieval practices, where corporate ownership of mss was the rule rather than the exception (see Rudolf Hirsch, *Printing, Selling and Reading, 1450–1550* (Wiesbaden, 1967), 12), and it should therefore come as no surprise that private reading came to be an integral part of the development of private life in the early modern period (Roger Chartier, 'The Practical Impact of Writing', in Philippe Ariès and Georges Duby (gen. eds.), *A History of Private Life*, iii. Roger Chartier (ed.), *Passions of the Renaissance*, trans. Arthur Goldhammer (Cambridge, Mass., 1989), 111–59).

[43]   The standard treatment of this material remains that of William Harrison Woodward, *Vittorino da Feltre and Other Humanist Educators*, Renaissance Society of America Reprint Series, 5 (Toronto, 1996; repr. of New York, 1963 edn.), to be supplemented by my 'Ancient, Renaissance, and Modern: The Human in the Humanities', *Journal of General Education*, 39 (1987), 133–51. The text of Vergerio has been edited by Attilio Gnesotto in

supposed to be done with poetry in general and with Virgil in particular.

The basic approach is the same in all five treatises, but it is set forth most clearly in Bruni's *De studiis et litteris*. After learning the essentials of language and composition—what we could call grammar—the student should turn to the two 'master-subjects', divinity and moral philosophy. The second of these, to which Bruni devotes much more attention than the first, will tell us what the various virtues are, whether virtue alone can lead to happiness, and so forth. Other subjects are related to these two, especially to moral philosophy, as they explain or embellish them. History provides examples of outstanding conduct with which to embellish our conversation, rhetoric teaches us to praise good deeds and condemn evil ones, and poets 'have many wise and useful things to say about life and how it should be lived'.[44] These five secular subjects—grammar, moral philosophy, history, rhetoric, and poetry—are, as Paul Oskar Kristeller has shown, the foundation for the *studia humanitatis*,[45] 'those studies which are related to life and behavior ... [and which] become a man and perfect him'.[46]

All five treatises, again, treat Virgil's poetry in essentially the same way, but their common approach this time is developed most clearly in the *De educatione* of Vegio, whose thirteenth book to the

---

Atti e memorie della R. Acc. di Scienze, Lettere ed Arti in Padova, NS 34 (1918), 75–157; Bruni, by Hans Baron in *Leonardo Bruni Aretino: Humanistisch-philosophische Schriften* (Leipzig, 1928), 5–19; Aeneas Sylvius, by Bro. J. S. Nelson in *De liberorum educatione* (Washington, 1940); Battista Guarino, by Eugenio Garin, in *Il pensiero pedagogico dello Umanesimo*, I classici della pedagogia italiana (Florence, 1958), 434–71; and Vegio, by Sisters M. W. Fanning and A. S. Sullivan, *De educatione liberorum et eorum claris moribus* (Washington, 1933–6). English translations may be found in Woodward, *Vittorino da Feltre*, although they are often dangerously loose.

[44] I have used Baron's text with the trans. in Gordon Griffiths, James Hankins, and David Thompson (eds.), *The Humanism of Leonardo Bruni: Selected Texts* (Binghamton, NY, 1987), 241–51; the quotation is on 246.

[45] 'Studies in Renaissance Humanism during the Last Twenty Years', *Studies in the Renaissance*, 9 (1962), 21; and 'Humanism and Scholasticism in the Italian Renaissance', in *Renaissance Thought*, 2 vols. (New York, 1965), i. 92–119. I should note that even the texts from which rudimentary grammar was learned (e.g. the ever-popular *Disticha Catonis*) had a moralizing flavour; see Ruth Morse, *Truth and Convention in the Middle Ages: Rhetoric, Representation, and Reality* (Cambridge, 1991), 38–40; and Paul F. Gehl, *A Moral Art: Grammar, Society, and Culture in Trecento Florence* (Ithaca, NY, 1993), 17.

[46] The phrasing is Bruni's, from his letter to Niccolò Strozzi, in Lorenzo Mehus (ed.), *Leonardi Bruni Arretini epistolarum libri VIII* (Florence: Bernardus Paperinius, 1741), with Eng. trans. in Griffiths *et al.* (eds.), *Humanism*, 252.

Aeneid was included in seventy-nine of the 132 pre-1600 Latin editions of Virgil's works published in the Veneto. Vegio's analysis of the *Aeneid* is therefore of considerable importance and requires quotation at some length:

Nam cum Virgilius sub Aeneae persona virum omni virtute praeditum, atque ipsum nunc in adversis, nunc in prosperis casibus, demonstrare voluerit, ita per Didonem feminas etiam, quibus vitam rationibus instituere deberent vel praemio laudis vel metu infamiae ac tristissimi demum interitus, omni illa sui poematis editione admonere studuit. Quae nam enim audiens illam condendis tantae urbis moenibus intentissime vacantem, iuraque et leges populis iustissime moderantem, marito etiam extincto fidem ac pacta tori conservantem, cum summa laude sua et veneratione finitimorumque omnium timore, non eius exemplo moveatur atque ad virtutis studium magnopere incendatur; contra vero intelligens novi eam hospitis amore insanientem, ab extructione urbis gubernationeque populorum cessantem, lusibus tamen et conviviis indulgentem, derelictamque ab amante demum, dolentemque et affligentem sese, deperditaque omni spe, mortem etiam ultro sibi consciscentem, non animo conquassetur, non exterreatur, non contremiscatur, non pudicitiam licet austeriorem malit amplecti quam blandiorem libidinem, cum huius fructus tandem amarissimi, illius semper suavissimi habeantur.

(For while Virgil in the character of Aeneas wished to show a man endowed with every virtue, now in unfavourable circumstances, now in favourable ones, so also did he take pains throughout his entire poem to admonish women through Dido about the grounds through which they ought to order their lives, either for the reward of praise or in fear of a bad reputation and finally of a wretched death. For who could hear of Dido while she had time to build the walls of such a great city so earnestly, while she was administering laws for her people so justly, while she was preserving the marriage covenant faithfully even though her husband was dead, earning for herself the greatest praise and respect and the fear of all her neighbours—who, I say, would not be moved by her example and greatly aroused toward zealous pursuit of virtue? On the other hand, however, who could become aware of her going mad with love for a newly arrived guest, withdrawing from the construction of her city and the governing of her people, yet giving herself up to dalliance and feasting, and then finally abandoned by her lover, grieving and striking herself, and with all hope lost even inflicting death upon herself— who, I say, could become aware of all this and not be shaken to the depths of her soul, terrified and trembling; who would not prefer to embrace chastity, severe though it is, rather than the allures of lust, since the fruits of the latter are bitter in the end and the fruits of the former are always sweet.)[47]

This passage shows clearly that Dido and Aeneas are to serve as models by which the schoolmaster can inculcate correct behaviour in his students. Dido can serve as either a model of virtue or a model of vice, depending on which part of the *Aeneid* the schoolmaster is explicating. When she founds her city and preserves her chastity, she should move the student to imitate virtue; when she falls in love and abandons first her duties, then life itself, she should move the student to shun vice. Aeneas, by contrast, is 'endowed with every virtue', a consistent positive model for human behaviour.[48] The entire passage is interwoven with the rhetoric of epideictic, through which the *Aeneid* is read as praise of virtue and condemnation of vice.

We have, of course, seen these points before. Like Vegio, Ascensius believed that Aeneas was the perfect hero, the man 'endowed with every virtue'. And like Vegio, Ascensius also believed that the *Aeneid* functioned in accordance with the norms of epideictic rhetoric, praising virtue and condemning vice in an effort to elevate the moral life of the reader. That is, Ascensius' commentary was designed to provide the detailed working out of the critical principles adumbrated in the educational treatises of Bruni, Vegio, and their peers, the *explication de texte* demanded by humanist theory. The humanist schoolmasters wanted such a commentary, so it is little wonder that the printers of Renaissance Venice stepped in to meet the demands of this market.

Ascensius' commentary explicates the moral content of Virgil's poetry, but that is by no means all it does. It also explains the basics of Latin grammar (e.g. fo. 149^r, on *Aen.* 1. 475), calls attention to figures of speech (fo. 255^r, on *Aen.* 6. 559), identifies mythological

---

[47] The passage is sect. 2. 18, taken from the edn. of Fanning and Sullivan. The significance of the passage in relation to Vegio's other writings, esp. his thirteenth book to the *Aeneid*, has been developed in my 'Maffeo Vegio's *Book XIII* and the *Aeneid* of Early Humanism', in Anne Reynolds (ed.), *Altro Polo: The Classical Continuum in Italian Thought and Letters* (Sydney, 1984), 47–56; and *In Praise of Aeneas*, 100–28.

[48] A more detailed analysis of Aeneas as moral example, on both the literal and allegorical levels, may be found in Vegio's *De perseverantia religionis* (Paris: B. Rembolt and I. Waterloes, 1511), fos. 11^v–12^v, 88^r–89^r. That is, in staying with the theme of the treatise, Aeneas is praised as a man who perseveres in both adversity and prosperity, with his travels representing man's journey through life to Latium, the heaven of eternal felicity.

figures (fo. 255^r, on *Aen.* 6. 595), provides cross-references to passages in other authors that could illuminate a point under discussion (fo. 135^{r-v}, on *Aen.* 1. 180–97)—in short, it provides the philological foundation on which the moral interpretation of the text rests, in much the same way as commentaries had since late antiquity.[49]

Humanist educational theorists claimed that there was a close link between this method of reading the classics, which relies heavily on close verbal analysis of the text, and the transferral of the moral precepts contained in the text to the life of the student reader. Recently, however, Anthony Grafton and Lisa Jardine have challenged this 'humanist propaganda claim' by suggesting that there is actually a discontinuity between 'the proliferation of discrete items of literary information, almost entirely without cohesive moral or intellectual comment', and the 'effortless familiarity with antiquity of its literary products, the easy comparisons between authors and works, the critical acumen and moral poise of the ablest scholars and courtiers'. In other words, a gifted teacher like Guarino da Verona 'did include some moral comment in the course of his lectures ... [b]ut these observations inevitably became absorbed into the pedagogical routine—something to be recorded between etymologies and paraphrases, rather than a coherent contribution to a fully articulated moral philosophy'.[50]

Grafton and Jardine's conclusions in fact apply reasonably well to Ascensius' printed commentary, in which the comments on morality are indeed buried among etymologies and paraphrases. From this, we might well wonder whether actual, day-to-day classroom work led to a systematic moral reading of the poem that would have made sense to a student. That is, to what extent did humanist educational practice actually implement humanist educational theory? Without a time machine that would allow us to

---

[49] Indeed, the procedural continuity from the time of Servius to that of Ascensius is striking; see H.-I. Marrou, *A History of Education in Antiquity*, trans. George Lamb (Madison, 1982; repr. of London, 1956 edn.), 279–81.

[50] Grafton and Jardine, *From Humanism to the Humanities: Education and the Liberal Arts in Fifteenth-Century Europe* (Cambridge, Mass., 1986), 22, 27, and 43; see also D. Robey, 'Humanism and Education in the Early Quattrocento: The *De ingenuis moribus* of P. P. Vergerio', *Bibliothèque d'humanisme et Renaissance*, 42 (1980), 38. This argument has led to some vigorous exchanges about the nature of Renaissance education, some of which are summarized by Robert Black in 'Italian Renaissance Education: Changing Perspectives and Continuing Controversies', *Journal of the History of Ideas*, 52 (1991), 315–34.

observe classes in Renaissance Italy, we cannot provide a definitive answer to such a question. However, the handwritten marginalia entered into those copies of Virgil that were used as school texts can guide us at least to some tentative conclusions. In this section, I shall therefore concentrate on marginalia entered into books that can be found at present in the Biblioteca Nazionale Marciana in Venice—books that at least as a group should reflect reasonably well what actually went on in the schools of Renaissance Venice.

In a first group of four books, the dates of publication suggest that the commentaries, records of classroom activity made by students, were entered at different times, although none of them can be dated precisely. The four books with their present Marciana shelf marks are: (1) Inc. 573, published in 1473 by Leonardus Achates (no. 11 in the chronology of editions in Appendix 1); (2) Inc. 418, published in 1476 by Johannes de Vienna in Vicenza (App. 1, no. 125); (3) 147.d.13, published in 1546 by Cominus de Tridino (App. 1, no. 77); and (4) Aldine 664, published in 1558 by Paulus Manutius (App. 1, no. 89).

A number of marginalia reveal evidence of a student struggling to learn basic Latin vocabulary and grammar. For example, we find notes like *ventus est aeris motus* ('wind is a movement of air'; fo. E5^r, in App. 1, no. 11), and *ter denis* ('three sets of ten') at *Aeneid* 10. 213 is glossed as *triginta* ('thirty'; fo. 196^r, App. 1, no. 89).[51] Sometimes the goal is to clarify nuances of correct usage, as in the marginal reference to Servius, *differentia inter totum et omne* ('the difference between "entire" and "every" '; fo. 115^v, App. 1, no. 77). In other places the notes are syntactical, as in the gloss to *Aeneid* 1. 70 that reads *Disice verbum est defectivum non habens nisi imperativum* (' "disperse" is a defective verb, having only an imperative'; fo. h2^r, App. 1, no. 125) and in another that reads *impleo genitivum et ablativum regere* (' "I fill" takes genitive and ablative'; fo. 117^v, App. 1, no. 77). These entries are accompanied by

---

[51] On the teaching and study of grammar in the Renaissance, see W. Keith Percival, 'Renaissance Grammar', in Albert Rabil, Jr. (ed.), *Renaissance Humanism: Foundations, Forms, and Legacy*, 3 vols. (Philadelphia, 1988), iii. 67–83; Grendler, *Schooling*, 162–202; and Jensen, *Rhetorical Philosophy and Philosophical Grammar*. On the relationship between what we now consider grammar and the study of poetry, see Craig Kallendorf, '*Enarratio poetarum*', in *Historisches Wörterbuch der Rhetorik*, ii. 1124–34. To simplify references in this section, particular books will be indicated by bibliographical reference numbers keyed to App. 1 after each group is introduced.

'doodlings'—pictures of a row of faces in one volume (fo. 1^r, App. 1, no. 11), pictures and *probationes pennae* in another (fo. ee8^v, App. 1, no. 125)—that suggest the efforts of fairly young students.

We should note, however, that the instruction proceeded simultaneously on several other, more advanced levels. A teacher's correction of the *addit* ('adds') printed in the Cominus de Tridino edition with *addidit* ('added'; at *Georg.* 1. 129, fo. 47^v, App. 1, no. 77) might well have been accompanied by some discussion of the principles of textual criticism.[52] Etymologies provided both conceptual insights and a way to build vocabulary, so that we find *lepus dicitur quasi levi pes* (' "hare" is referred to as if from "light of foot" '; fo. E5^r, App. 1, no. 11). Geographical references needed identification: *Thomolus est mons Lidie* ('Tmolus is a mountain in Lydia'; fo. E1^v, App. 1, no. 11). Mythological references were marked for future retrieval, as with the *nota fabulam* ('note the myth') beside the story of Ariadne (fo. 51^v, App. 1, no. 77), or explained, as with *Isis in Egypto prima omnium reperit frumentum* ('Isis in Egypt was the first to discover corn'; fo. 24^v, App. 1, no. 89). The identification of rhetorical figures was considered especially valuable for a student trying to cultivate a polished Latin style. The most common marker was *comparatio* ('comparison'; e.g. at *Georg.* 1. 201–3, fo. 50^r, App. 1, no. 77), but others are found as well: *hiberbaton* (at *Georg.* 1. 40, fo. 23^r, App. 1, no. 89), *periphrasis* (at *Georg.* 1. 43, fo. 23^r, App. 1, no. 89), and *anadiplosis figura* (fo. 82^r, App. 1, no. 89). Given the dozens of figures with intimidating names regularly taught by Renaissance schoolmasters,[53] we cannot help but sympathize with the student who wrote and then cancelled *proceusma*, then added *proceleusmasico* (on *Georg.* 2. 180, fo. 35^r, App. 1, no. 89).

Other glosses show various forms of intertextual study. On the most basic level, this involved preparing the text for

---

[52] On textual criticism in the Renaissance, see John F. D'Amico, *Theory and Practice in Renaissance Textual Criticism: Beatus Rhenanus between Conjecture and History* (Berkeley and Los Angeles, Calif., 1988).

[53] Although Renaissance rhetoric remains a largely uncharted morass, some indication of the directions that could be explored may be deduced from James J. Murphy, *Renaissance Rhetoric: A Short-Title Catalogue of Works on Rhetorical Theory ...* (New York, 1981). Representative figures of speech with examples from contemporary documents are described in Lee Sonnino, *A Handbook to Sixteenth-Century Rhetoric* (London, 1968), and examples of where this study might lead may be found in Desiderius Erasmus' *De utraque verborum ac rerum copia* and in Sister Miriam Joseph, *Shakespeare's Use of the Arts of Language* (New York, 1947).

cross-referencing, which produced the 'indexing notes' familiar to anyone who has worked with manuscripts and early printed books. The teacher also helped with this process by providing citations to other authors who conveyed a similar sentiment or explained a difficult point. Among the authors cited in one commentary (App. I, no. 77) are Aulus Gellius (fo. 43^v), Horace (fo. 253^v), Livy (fo. 251^r), Lucretius (fo. 251^v), Pliny (fo. 251^v), and Terence (fo. 46^v).

This first group of commentaries is strictly philological, recording a knowledge of the Latin language and Roman culture on which an understanding of the text could be built. Another group of five commentaries, however, adds observations on the moral content of the poetry to this narrowly philological base. This group of commentaries may be found in the following books: (1) Inc. V.152, published in 1471 by Adam de Ambergau (App. I, no. 2); (2) Inc. 426, another copy of the same book (App. I, no. 2); (3) Rari V.99, published in 1507 by Bernardinus Stagninus (App. I, no. 46); (4) 146.d.18, published in 1543–4 by the heirs of Lucas Antonius Junta (App. I, no. 74); and (5) 134.d.54, published in 1574–5 by the heirs of Joannes Maria Bonellus (App. I, no. 103). Again, although the marginalia cannot be dated precisely, the range of publication dates suggests that any conclusions we might draw should provide some general insight into what schoolmasters had emphasized for their students over the years.

In both copies of the Adam de Ambergau text, which were briefly considered at the beginning of this chapter, a reader has used pointing hands and brackets to mark off lines with an aphoristic quality: *improbe amor, quid non mortalia pectora cogis?* ('voracious love, to what do you not drive the hearts of men?'; *Aen.* 4. 412, App. I, no. 2), and *discite iustitiam moniti et non temnere divos* ('be warned, learn justice and not to scorn the gods'; *Aen.* 6. 620, App. I, no. 2). One of the early owners of another volume (App. I, no. 46), who marked off a number of 'purple passages' in the text (e.g. *Aen.* I. 197–9 and 4. 651), also noted in the margin of Book 4 that Virgil *incontinentiam ostendit Didonis* ('shows the incontinence of Dido'; fo. OO3^v). A reader of the Junta volume cross-referenced St Augustine, providing an explicitly Christian framework for his moral interests:

Augustinus De civitate Dei, superbis Deus resistit, humilibus autem dat gratiam; hoc vero quod Dei est, superbae quoque animae spiritus inflatos affectat, amatque sibi in laudibus dici, 'Parcere subiectis, et debellar[e] superbos'.

(Augustine says in the *City of God* [preface], 'God resists the proud but gives grace to the humble' [Jas. 4: 6]. But that which is of God tries to gain control over the swollen pride of the overbearing spirit and loves it to be said in its praise that it 'spares the subjected and tames the proud'.)

(*Aen*. 6. 853, fo. 361ʳ, App. 1, no. 74)

A particularly interesting version of this same thing may be found in the last volume in this group (App. 1, no. 103), whose owner underlined and recopied moralizing sentiments from the printed commentaries as well as the Virgilian text. On *Eclogue* 2. 70, for example, he highlighted a sentiment from Servius, *tolerabilius est enim non incipere aliquid, quam incepta deserere* ('indeed it is more bearable not to begin something, than to abandon things that have been begun'; fo. 5ᵛ). On *Eclogue* 1. 6–19, he confirmed his reliance on Ascensius by extracting an aphorism from Ascensius' commentary: *res conspecta plus movet quam audita* ('a thing seen is more moving than a thing heard'; fo. 3ᵛ).

What we have seen so far suggests that Grafton and Jardine are at least in good part right, that moral observations tended to get lost in a mass of lexical, syntactical, textual, rhetorical, etymological, geographical, mythological, and intertextual commentary.[54] However, there is one other volume, Aldine 628 (App. 1, no. 52), whose principal commentary suggests that at least now and again, an organized effort was made to effect a transition from the mass of philological detail to the higher values that humanistic study was supposedly designed to foster.

The author of the principal commentary, who is one of several annotators of this volume,[55] never identifies himself, but he does enter dates on three different occasions: *28 Februarius 1601* (fo. 5ᵛ

---

[54] In his discussion of the printed commentaries of the Quattrocento, Vladimiro Zabughin distinguishes four types of commentary, which he labels 'grammatical', 'antiquarian', 'anagogical' (or mystical), and 'comparative historical-literary' (*Vergilio*, i. 186, 202–3). In my examination of the handwritten commentaries in Venetian books, however, I have found it difficult to distinguish among these categories, while on the other hand the way in which moral issues are treated does lead to significant differences of approach.

[55] The presence of notes in several hands in the same book is not unusual. In 'The Books of "Het Suyckerhuis": A Haarlem Bookshop in the Seventeenth Century', a paper delivered at the 1995 conference of the Society for the History of Authorship, Reading, and Publishing in Edinburgh, Scotland, Garrelt Verhoeven noted that 17th-cent. Dutch bookshops intermingled new books with used ones in their stock. This was presumably the case in 16th-cent. Venice as well, suggesting that unlike at present, annotations did not devalue a book in the eyes of potential buyers, which would help explain why so many early books have been annotated by several readers.

of the loose pages bound into the end of the volume), *Nota quod 1606 die 14 Augusti legens hunc locum* ('Note that this place was being read on 14 August 1606'; fo. 74^v), and *1617 die V^a Maii* (fo. a2^v). This reader was if not Venetian, at least Italian, since occasional notes are in this language, e.g. *o avaricia, o crudelta* ('o greed, o cruelty'; fo. 125^r), and *Didone e uno esempio alle vedove di veder quello che fanno* ... ('Dido is an example to widows to watch what they are doing'; fo. 104^r). And he was presumably a teacher rather than a student recording the observations of a teacher, as suggested by the choice of edition, the careful rereading of the text over a period of many years, and the nature of his comments.

These comments indicate a well-read individual who was at home with the classics, vernacular literature like Ariosto's *Orlando Furioso*, and the Bible; at *Aeneid* 12. 887–916, for example, he describes

duellum inter Aeneum [*sic*] et Turnum, sic inter Rugerum et Rudomontem, et inter David et Goliatum, et apud Homerum inter Menelaum et Paridem et inter Aeneam et Diomedem. De hac materia plures scriptae sunt.

(a duel between Aeneas and Turnus, as between Ruggiero and Rodomonte, and between David and Goliath, and in Homer between Menelaus and Paris and between Aeneas and Diomedes. Concerning this material many things have been written.)

(fo. 219^v)

An interest in Christian parallels emerges elsewhere: at *Aeneid* 6. 720–1 the commentator writes *alludere videtur ad resurrectionem corporum* ('it seems to allude to the resurrection of bodies'; fo. 131^r), and at several points in *Aeneid* 6 he labels passages *inferno*, *limbo*, *purgato*, and *paradiso* ('hell', 'limbo', 'purgatory', and 'heaven'; 6. 426 ff., fo. 126^r; 6. 557, fo. 128^v; 6. 617, fo. 129^v; 6. 733 ff., fo. 131^v). These last references suggest that this annotator was reading Virgil with Dante in mind, and this association in turn suggests that the annotator had a special interest in ethics, in using Virgil's text as a guide to salvific action. This is indeed the case. In fact, the moralizing notes entered in this book often present the *bonorum et malorum differentia* ('difference between good and evil things'; *Aen*. 7. 203–4, fo. 137^v) in unusually sharp contrast. On *Aeneid* 8. 387 ff., for example, we find *dolus foemineus* ('female guile') countered by *nota tu vidua casta* ('take note, you chaste widow') shortly afterwards (8. 408 ff., fo. 154ᵛ), and the *nota tu peccator* ('take note, you sinner'; *Aen.* 8. 668–9) is followed immediately by *nota tu pie* ('take note, you pious one'; 8. 670, fo. 159ʳ).

Even more striking, however, are the four additional pages at the end of the book, originally separate sheets but stitched into the volume by a binder in a later period. These pages contain two lists, in the hand of this same commentator, keyed to the text of this volume. (Both lists are transcribed in Appendix 3.) The first list, headed *loca lectorem pium commoventia* ('passages moving a pious reader'), identifies the passages in the *Eclogues*, *Georgics*, and *Aeneid* that are most likely to arouse in the reader the virtues associated with *pietas*, the virtues Virgil was so interested in defining and encouraging. Among the fifty passages signalled here are Aeneas' famous exhortation to his weary troops in *Aeneid* 1. 198 ff. (*O socii* ...), Dido's account of how greed drove her brother Pygmalion to kill her husband Sychaeus (*Aen.* 1. 343 ff.), Polydorus' suffering as a result of the same vice (*Aen.* 3. 41–57), the punishment of the Great Sinners along with Phlegyas' injunction to learn justice and honour the gods (*Aen.* 6. 601–25, esp. 6. 620), the epic simile containing the description of the chaste widow (*Aen.* 8. 407–16), and Evander's lament over the corpse of Pallas (*Aen.* 11. 152–82). The second list, which begins without a title on fo. 4ʳ, sets out the kinds of relationships within which people can help one another, with examples like Orpheus' helping Eurydice in *Georgics* 4 to illustrate each relationship.

In many cases, we can only speculate on exactly what the teacher might have said about these passages. However, if we turn to the sections of the text signalled in this list, we can sometimes find marginal notes containing further clues about where the discussion might have gone.[56] For example, Polydorus and Sychaeus are cross-referenced (fos. 59ᵛ and 81ʳ), since they were both victims of the same vice. *Aeneid* 3. 321 is annotated *ecce fructus belli* ('consider, the fruits of war'; fo. 85ᵛ), suggesting that an

---

[56] Grendler, *Schooling*, 252, provides evidence that in the teaching of Terence, moral lessons were developed orally, for the editor of a new Aldine printing of 1570, Vincenzo Cardato, states that *in locis vitiorum ac virtutum communibus explicandis viva voce apud pueros elaborandum putem* ('I think that where commonplaces of vices and virtues are to be drawn out, one should explain them out loud to the boys'). Grendler speculates that with Caesar as well, moral lessons may have been developed orally (260).

anti-war discussion might have come here. Sections of the Dido story in *Aeneid* 4 contain examples of those driven to extremes of love (4. 412 ff., fo. 99^r), then a moral for the book as a whole: *ecce amor transit in furorem* ('consider, love passes over into madness'; 4. 642–63, fo. 103^r). The discussion of the Great Sinners at *Aeneid* 6. 601–25 (fo. 129^{r-v}) categorizes the sinners being punished—*golosi* ('the gluttons'), *avari* ('the greedy'), *luxuriosi* ('the dissolute'), *perfidi* ('the treacherous'), *luxuriosi seu incestuosi* ('the dissolute or incestuous')—from which a discussion of individual vices with Virgilian examples could easily have been prepared.

If what we find in the margins of this book and the others we have looked at is typical—and there is no reason to assume it is not—then I would be tempted to conclude that many students must indeed have had problems in moving from means to end, from philological minutiae to moral growth and refinement. Only under the guidance of a gifted teacher like the owner of this last book could a student come away from the poetry of Virgil with any sort of 'a fully articulated moral philosophy'.

Without the guidance of a gifted teacher, a student in search of a systematic moral philosophy in the pages of Virgil was forced to rely on the resources offered by the edition he was reading. When that edition included the commentary of Ascensius, as we have seen, a similar situation presented itself: there were indeed a good many moralizing observations, but they tended to get lost in an unstructured mass of detail. The second most commonly printed commentary in the editions of the Venetian Renaissance offers more promise at first glance, for it was both moralizing and systematic. As we shall see, however, it was less successful than we might imagine in imposing a structure on the interpretive strategies of Venetian Renaissance readers.

This second commentary, which appeared in twenty-two pre-1600 Venetian editions,[57] was by Cristoforo Landino, the

---

[57] Strictly speaking Landino's commentary became difficult to find in Venetian edns. published after the 1530s, but its influence was felt through the end of the century. In the 1543–4 Junta edn., for example, the title-page says the book was published *annotationibus Christophori Landini* ('with the notes of Cristoforo Landino'); in fact it contains an abbreviated version of the introduction to the Virgil commentary, along with a few extracts from Landino quoted in the main commentaries accompanying the text. The 1558 Bonellus edn. does not refer specifically to Landino, but another commentator, Ludovicus Caelius

Florentine scholar who also developed his ideas about Virgil in a philosophical dialogue entitled *Disputationes Camaldulenses* and a famous commentary to Dante.[58] In the preface to the Virgil commentary dedicated to Piero di Lorenzo de' Medici, Landino states clearly how he is reading the text:

Quod autem ad bene beateque vivendum pertinet, quis non videat omnia quibus vita humana recte instituatur praecepta ab hoc poeta veluti ex adorandis philosophiae sacrariis promi facile ac percipi posse? Nam ut Cyri vitam Xenophon ita a primis incunabilis producit, ut eius regis exemplo optimus princeps informari possit, sic Maronis poema omne humanae vitae genus exprimit, ut nullus hominum ordo, nulla aetas, nullus sexus sit, nulla denique conditio, quae ab eo sua officia non integre addiscat. Qua obsecro ille acrimonia, quo verborum fulmine metum, ignaviam, luxuriam, incontinentiam, impietatem, perfidiam ac omnia iniustitiae genera reliquaque vitia insectatur vexatque? Quibus contra laudibus, quibus praemiis invictam animi magnitudinem, et pro patria, pro parentibus, pro cognatis amicisque consideratam periculorum susceptionem, religionem in Deum, pietatem in maiores, caritatem in omnes prosequitur! Nam cum hoc in primis sibi proposuisset P. Vergilius, ut generi humano quam plurimum prodesset, eo potissimum consilio in uno Aenea absolutum omnino atque ex omni parte perfectum virum finxit atque expressit, ut omnes illum nobis tanquam unicum exemplar ad vitam degendam proponeremus.

Rhodiginus, seems to be indebted to him in several places (e.g. fo. 136ʳ, on *Aen.* 1. 198–207, and fo. 194ʳ, on *Aen.* 3. 426–8). Landino's commentary got a new lease on life at the end of the century in the vernacular commentary of Johannes Fabrinus, which is so heavily indebted to Landino as to be almost a word-for-word translation in places; see Ch. 3, below.

[58] The basic source for the life and work of Landino remains Angelo Maria Bandini, *Specimen literaturae Florentinae saeculi XV, in quo … Christophori Landini gesta enarrantur* (Florence: Rigaccius, 1747–51), although the main points may also be found in Craig Kallendorf, 'Landino (Cristoforo) (1424–1498)', in Colette Nativel (ed.), *Centuriae Latinae: Cent une figures humanistes de la Renaissance aux Lumières offertes à Jacques Chomarat* (Geneva, 1997), 477–83. To establish the points that interest me here, I have relied on the Virgil commentary for the discussion that follows, but Landino developed the same ideas in his *Disputationes Camaldulenses*, ed. Peter Lohe (Florence, 1980), and in the famous commentary to Dante that was published with great fanfare in 1481. On the Dante commentary, see Manfred Lentzen, *Studien zur Dante-Exegese Cristoforo Landinos* (Cologne, 1971); and Deborah Parker, *Commentary and Ideology: Dante in the Renaissance* (Durham, NC, 1993). On the relationship between Landino's work on Dante and his work on Virgil, see my *In Praise of Aeneas*, 129–65. Landino also lectured on the *Aeneid* during the 1462–3 and 1463–4 academic years at the Florentine *Studio*, and probably again from 1467–9; see Arthur Field, 'An Inaugural Oration by Cristoforo Landino in Praise of Virgil (From Codex '2,' Casa Cavalli, Ravenna)', *Rinascimento*, 2nd ser. 21 (1981), 235–45; id., 'A Manuscript of Cristoforo Landino's First Lectures on Virgil', *Renaissance Quarterly*, 31 (1978), 17–20; and id., 'Cristoforo Landino's First Lectures on Dante', *Renaissance Quarterly*, 39 (1986), 17–24.

(Moreover, as to that which pertains to living well and happily, who could not see that all precepts by which human life is rightly instructed can easily be extracted and grasped from this poet as if from the venerable shrines of philosophy? For as Xenophon brings forth the life of Cyrus from its very infancy, in order that by the example of that king the best prince might be fashioned, so the poem of Virgil expresses every kind of human life, so that there is no class of men, no age, no sex, ultimately no state, which cannot learn its duties in their entirety from him. With what keenness, I implore you, with what verbal thunder does he rail at fear, sloth, dissoluteness, incontinence, impiety, treachery, and every kind of injustice along with the remaining vices? On the other hand, with what praises and rewards does he attend unconquered magnanimity and the calculated undertaking of dangers on behalf of country, parents, relatives, and friends, along with worship toward God, piety toward his elders, and love toward all! For since Virgil first of all resolved to profit the human race as much as possible, above all in accordance with this goal he fashioned and described in Aeneas alone a man fully perfected in every way, so that all of us could propose him for ourselves as an unparalleled example of how to live our lives.)[59]

Like Xenophon in the *Cyropaedia*, Landino's Virgil takes on the role of educator in morality, of teacher of right and wrong to the ruler and, through him, to all his subjects as well. The approach is compatible with Ascensius' in this regard, but unlike Ascensius, Landino takes the individual observations on the various virtues and vices and integrates them into a hierarchy of ethical progress. Aeneas first cultivates the virtues of the civic life, then the virtues of a man trying to move from human to divine affairs, and finally the virtues of a man who has been purified of mortal contagion and achieved heavenly bliss.[60] The ethical progress from civic through purgatorial virtues to the virtues of a spirit at last purified,

---

[59] 'Christophori Landini Florentini in P. Vergilii interpretationes prohemium ad Petrum Medicem Magni Laurentii filium feliciter incipit', in Cristoforo Landino, *Scritti critici e teorici*, i. 215–16. For a discussion that places Landino's views about literature into the general development of humanist commentary and literary theory, see Rainer Stillers, *Humanistische Deutung: Studien zu Kommentar und Literaturtheorie in der italienischen Renaissance*, Studia humaniora, 11 (Düsseldorf, 1988), esp. 91–106.

[60] *Vergilius cum quinque commentariis* (Venice: n.pub., 1492), fo. 230ʳ; references to this edn. will be incorporated into the text. It is difficult to say exactly where Landino found this scheme. It was readily available in Macrobius, *Com. in somn. Scip.* 1. 8. 5–13, where we also find a fourth gradation that exists *in ipsa divina mente* ('in the mind of God'), but whose restriction to the mind of God makes it inapplicable directly to Aeneas' journey (Michael Murrin, *The Allegorical Epic: Essays in its Rise and Decline* (Chicago, 1980), 221 n. 67). See Kallendorf, *In Praise of Aeneas*, 210 n. 28.

which is also the movement from the active to the contemplative life (fos. 122^v–123^r), is Neoplatonic, an effort to develop the key elements of Virgil's thought in accordance with the work of Landino's friends and associates in the Platonic Academy of Florence.[61] The result, as I have shown elsewhere, is the first successful attempt to produce a systematic reading of the *Aeneid* according to the principles of humanist moral philosophy.[62]

Aeneas' journey toward the *summum bonum*, the highest good that consists of knowledge of heavenly affairs, begins in Troy, which is interpreted as bodily pleasure (fo. 225^v). Landino is careful to exculpate Aeneas from any unpraiseworthy action here: he withdraws from battle not from cowardice, but in obedience to the command of the gods (fo. 170^r); he loses Creusa not from carelessness, but because he has properly subordinated his personal interests to his responsibilities toward his countrymen (fo. 172^v); and so forth. Thrace and the Strophades represent wealth, which Aeneas leaves behind when he realizes that the *summum bonum* is not to be found there (fo. 225^v). He then goes to Carthage, which stands for the active life (fo. 225^v), so that Dido takes on a double moral significance: sexual in the passage from temperance to intemperance and political as a representative of the *vita activa et civilis* ('active and civic life'; fos. 192^r–193^v). Thus in leaving Dido and moving on toward Italy, Aeneas attempts to progress from the active life to the contemplative.

[61] On Landino and the Florentine Academy, see Arthur Field, *The Origins of the Platonic Academy of Florence* (Princeton, 1988), 231–68; this discussion is first-rate, although I must disagree with Field's argument that Landino's movement from the active life to the contemplative one marked only a progress of soul or mind without any literal renunciation of worldly life. Indeed, as Jill Kraye has pointed out, both Platonists and Aristotelians in the Renaissance agreed that contemplation was the highest goal of a human being ('Moral Philosophy', in Charles B. Schmitt and Quentin Skinner (eds.), *The Cambridge History of Renaissance Philosophy* (Cambridge, 1988), 349). Basic information on the Florentine, or Platonic, Academy can be found in Kristeller, 'The Platonic Academy of Florence', in *Renaissance Thought*, ii. 89–101; A. della Torre, *Storia dell'Accademia Platonica* (Turin, 1968; repr. of Florence, 1902 edn.); Nesca A. Robb, *Neoplatonism of the Italian Renaissance* (London, 1935); and for a revisionist review of the evidence, James Hankins, 'The Myth of the Platonic Academy of Florence', *Renaissance Quarterly*, 44 (1991), 429–75.

[62] 'Cristoforo Landino's *Aeneid* and the Humanist Critical Tradition', *Renaissance Quarterly*, 36 (1983), 519–46. As Antonie Wlosok has shown, the practice of associating Virgil's poetry with philosophical truths goes all the way back to Servius and extends forward into some interesting practices of ms illumination in the Renaissance ('*Gemina pictura*: Allegorisierende Aeneisillustrationen in Handschriften des 15. Jahrhunderts', in Robert M. Wilhelm and Howard Jones (eds.), *The Two Worlds of the Poet: New Perspectives on Vergil* (Detroit, 1992), 408–32).

On his arrival in Italy, Aeneas is ready for the *descensus ad inferos*, a key point in his moral progress. Landino recognizes five types of descent, the last of which applies to Aeneas:

Quintus in contemplationem vitiorum descendimus, ut illorum pernitie cognita ab eis abstineamus, qua ratione et Virgilius nunc Aeneam descendisse fingit, duce Sibylla ... ut primo in infernum, id est in contemplationem vitiorum descendat, deinde illorum pernitiae [*sic*] cognita in purgatorium assurgat, id est purgatoriis virtutibus animum ab omni labe mundum reddat, atque inde in ipsos caelos penetret, id est earum virtutum quae animi iam purgati dicuntur alis divinas res contemplandas elevetur.

(The fifth [descent takes place] when we descend into the contemplation of vices, so that after we have recognized their destructiveness, we might abstain from them, which is the reason Virgil now fashions Aeneas' descent under the guidance of the Sibyl ... so that he might descend first into the underworld, that is into the contemplation of vices, then with their destructiveness understood, he might ascend into purgatory, that is render his spirit pure from every contagion through the purgatorial virtues, and finally arrive to the heavens proper, that is, he might be elevated to contemplating divine affairs on the wings of those virtues that are called 'virtues of a purified spirit'.)

(fo. 230ʳ)

The details of *Aeneid* 6, as we would expect by now, are subjected to a moral interpretation that can be systematically integrated into this larger framework. Misenus, for example, stands for empty glory, the desire for which must be killed by anyone who wants to attain true knowledge of human and divine affairs (fo. 232ᵛ). That knowledge is represented by the golden bough, which lies hidden in the forest and represents in turn the contagion of the body that prevents us from understanding anything correctly (fo. 231ʳ). Aeneas is led to the golden bough by two doves because according to the Florentine Neoplatonists, there are two kinds of love, divine and human, which correspond to the contemplative and active lives (fos. 232ᵛ–233ʳ).[63] The evil suffer in lower hell, or Tartarus, which stands for the habit of vice, a place one reaches with the aid of Charon, or deprivation of joy. The virtuous exist

---

[63] The doctrine of the two kinds of love, or the two Venuses, was developed by Marsilio Ficino in his commentary to Plato's *Symposium* and disseminated widely in late Quattrocento Florence; see Edgar Wind, *Pagan Mysteries in the Renaissance* (New Haven, 1958), 100–28.

happily in the Elysian Fields (fos. 244^v–247^v), so that *optimus autem poeta huiusmodi narrationibus homines et a vitiis absterret et ad virtutes allicit* ('with stories of this kind, the best of poets frightens people away from vices and allures us to virtues'; fo. 247^v).

The commentary of Landino is detailed, systematic, and relentlessly moralizing. Although it does not develop the moral allegory of the *Aeneid* in quite the detail of the *Disputationes Camaldulenses*, the key points from that work are here as well, and the commentary has the added benefit of philological observations that would aid the teacher in his preliminary work with the text. It offered great potential for the schoolmaster, and its frequent reprintings confirm that its utility was recognized in the educational market of the day.

However, a closer look reveals that Renaissance schoolmasters often failed to take advantage of the potential this commentary offered for inculcating 'a fully articulated moral philosophy' in their students. Indeed, we very seldom find marginalia in Venetian Renaissance editions like 'the doves in *Aeneid* 6 represent divine and human love, or the active and contemplative lives'—notes that are distinctive enough to reveal their origins in Landino's commentary. Now and again, to be sure, a reader like the schoolmaster Caspar from Leipzig did write in his text—which did not have any printed commentaries—*de his vide Landinum Christophorum* ('concerning these things see Cristoforo Landino'; fo. 85^r; see also fo. 83^v). But this is the exception rather than the rule. More typical is the reaction of the early reader of the 1504 Pintius edition now in the Biblioteca Civica in Verona, who drew freely from Servius in his efforts to construe the literal meaning of *Aeneid* 4 but ignored almost completely the interpretive options offered by Landino's commentary.[64] This suggests that there was obviously enough interest in Landino's commentary to justify its reprinting, but not enough so that it was worked through in the classroom with the same care as, for example, Ascensius'.

There are, I believe, a couple of reasons why this was so. To begin with, as scholars like Annabel Patterson and Arthur Field

---

[64] This commentary (now shelf mark Cinq. B.429) is surprisingly modern in its approach, concentrating on sections like *Aeneid* 4 that did not always attract appreciative interest from Renaissance readers and showing what might be considered an unusually sensitive approach to the beauties of Virgil's poetry (e.g. fos. 193^v, 195^r, 196^r).

have recently reminded us, Landino was very much a Florentine.[65] The introduction to his Virgil commentary, for example, was addressed explicitly to Piero di Lorenzo de' Medici, and Landino at least seems to align himself with his patrons.[66] To be sure, the Venetian printers who were publishing this introduction *in toto* in the late 1480s were publishing a condensed version by 1512, when the Georgius Arrivabenus Mantuanus edition presented a version in which the Medici associations were tempered. Nevertheless as Venice shifted into and out of alliance with Florence in the sixteenth century, the Florentine flavour of this commentary must have turned a bit rancid with some regularity.

A more fundamental problem, however, must have arisen from the Neoplatonic framework, the very source of the commentary's systematic approach. This approach made perfect sense in the city of Ficino and the Platonic Academy, but it was an import, something always at least a little foreign, in a city whose humanism was more traditional, and more practical, than that of Florence.[67] What is more, the complexities of this Neoplatonic framework must have presented a real challenge to the Venetian schoolmaster who, we should remember, was still trying to reinforce the basics of Latin grammar at the same time as he was trying to extract a moral lesson from the text. In some places, Landino's commentary helped, but for understandable reasons it did not provide a systematic approach to the moral content of the poems for Virgil's readers in the Venetian Renaissance schools.

As we have thus seen, most students of the Venetian Renaissance would not have taken from their reading of Virgil 'a coherent contribution to a fully articulated moral philosophy', and I believe it would be worthwhile to speculate a little more on why this was so and what the consequences of this failure might be. First I shall

[65] Patterson, *Pastoral and Ideology: Virgil to Valéry* (Berkeley and Los Angeles, Calif., 1987), 62–81; and Field, *Origins*, 231–68.

[66] As Patterson, *Pastoral and Ideology*, 74, points out, the preface to the Virgil commentary links the work to the Medici and places it into the context of Florentine politics, but she argues (74–8) that Landino was not in fact an unequivocal supporter of the Medici.

[67] As Vittore Branca has observed, both the humanist scholar Ermolao Barbaro and the humanist printer Aldus Manutius distrusted Florentine Neoplatonism ('Ermolao Barbaro', 229, 234), and Margaret L. King, *Venetian Humanism in an Age of Patrician Dominance* (Princeton, 1986), esp. 244–51, has stressed the close connection of Venetian humanism to the city in which it developed.

try to reach some basic conclusions about how teachers and students in the Renaissance classroom read a book, in order to provide an underlying explanation for why their observations on Virgil remained so persistently unsystematic. Then I shall explore how these Renaissance strategies of reading led naturally to several of the most distinctive uses of the moralized Virgil in Renaissance print culture.

Although it is not Venetian, or even Italian for that matter, the prologue to Fernando de Rojas's *Celestina* (printed in the 1507 Saragossa edition) offers a remarkably clear and self-conscious description of the different ways in which a book could be read during this period. There were three possibilities. First, a reader could focus not on the story as a whole, but on certain detached episodes. Second, the text could be used as a source for easily memorized formulas, proverbs, maxims, and ready-made expressions. And finally, a reader could work to grasp a text in its totality without reducing it to episodes or maxims, to develop a plural reading that recognizes diversity of interpretation and adapts whatever lessons the book contains to individual needs.[68]

As both Landino's commentary and the 'list of passages moving a pious reader' in Marciana Aldine 628 show, some Renaissance readers did try to deal with the texts of poems in their entirety. Most, however, did not; indeed, even a cursory examination of the records of teaching activity left in the margins of student texts shows that it was unusual for a teacher to read a poem straight through from beginning to end. More common by far was to dip in at certain key episodes, such as the descent to the underworld in *Aeneid* 6.[69] And as we have seen repeatedly, much of the marginal activity in Renaissance texts involves the identification of maxims, proverbs, and moralizing 'tags'. Thus for those studying Virgil in Venetian Renaissance schools, the first and second of the

[68] The importance of this passage is signalled by Roger Chartier in 'Texts, Printings, Readings', in Lynn Hunt (ed.), *The New Cultural History* (Berkeley and Los Angeles, Calif., 1989), 155. General background on reading practices in the Renaissance may be found in William H. Sherman, *John Dee: The Politics of Reading and Writing in the English Renaissance*, Massachusetts Studies in Early Modern Culture (Amherst, Mass., 1995), 59–65.

[69] As Zabughin points out, this preference carries over into those writing imitations of the *Aeneid* as well, for Bk. 6 is the source for the most interesting and courageous imitative work during this period while even the Dido story in Book 4 is used only rarely (*Vergilio*, i. 302).

three modes of reading described in the prologue to the *Celestina* were common, but the third was not.

Both detaching episodes and extracting aphorisms, of course, are ways of reading that fragment the text. There were a number of factors in Renaissance culture that encouraged such fragmentation, one of which was the way the text was normally presented on the page. In many manuscript copies of Virgil, the text was accompanied by a commentary, and when this procedure was carried over into printed editions, as Ruth Morse has pointed out, it affected how the text was read. That is, the eye went back and forth from small units of text to what are normally larger units of analysis and interpretation, units whose placement in the margins forced the reader repeatedly to suspend interaction with the text itself (Plate 1).[70] Continuous reading was discouraged, while a focus on discrete units of plot (episodes) or thought (aphorisms) arose naturally.

Behind the physical layout of the book is a general approach to reading that also encouraged the fragmentation of texts up until the eighteenth century. As Roger Chartier has pointed out, the modern style of reading involves passing freely and casually through a large number of texts. The older style, however, was based on a reverential attitude toward a relatively small number of books, which were recited, memorized, and studied collectively as a way of inculcating a common set of references and quotations.[71] This older style of reading privileged slow, attentive study

---

[70] Morse, *Truth and Convention*, 24–6 and pl. 1, a page from the 1507 Paris edn. of Virgil's works with commentary edited by Ascensius. See also Parker, *Commentary and Ideology*, 40. Renaissance readers generally maintained a distinction between text and marginalia, but as Raymond Cormier points out, 12th-cent. readers sometimes incorporated marginal comments into their creative reworking of a text ('Wild Margins, Tame Text: Inventing the Vernacular in the Gutters of Virgil's *Aeneid*', *French Literature Studies*, 20 (1993), 1–10).

[71] Chartier, *The Cultural Uses of Print in Early Modern France*, trans. Lydia G. Cochrane (Princeton, 1987), 221–5; see also Gehl, *Moral Art*, 135. Elizabeth Eisenstein tries to associate the modern style of reading with the spread of printing (*Printing Press as an Agent of Change*, i. 72), but while there may well be a measure of truth to this association, the older style of reading was preserved when the printed page reproduced the juxtapositioning of text and commentary from ms books. Rolf Engelsing, in turn, situates the 'reading revolution' at the end of the 18th cent., which strikes me as more reasonable, but here again, as Robert Darnton reminds us, we should remember that people read for many reasons and that the older way of reading intensively did not necessarily die out completely when technology produced so many books that people were tempted to read faster ('First Steps toward a History of Reading', in *The Kiss of Lamourette: Reflections in Cultural History* (New York, 1990), 165–6).

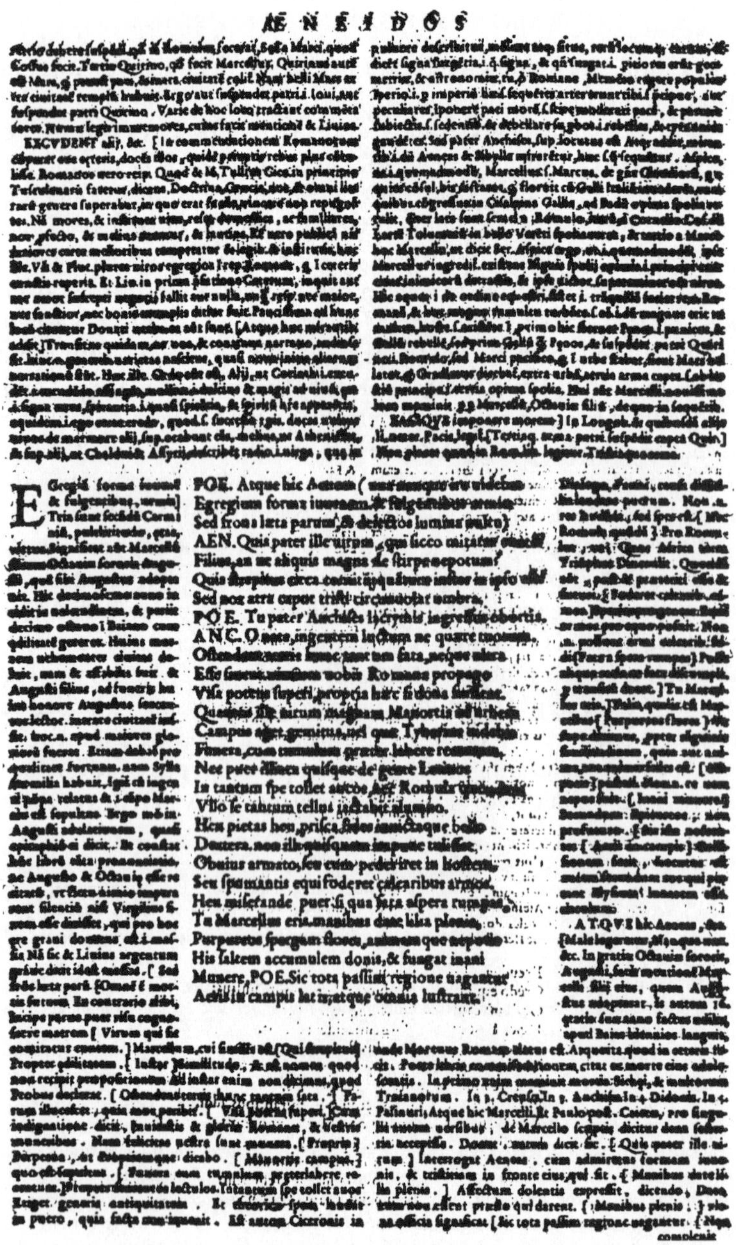

AENEIDOS

POE. Atque hic Aeneas (una namque ire videbat
Egregium forma iuvenem, & fulgentibus armis:
Sed frons læta parum, & deiectos lumina vultu)
AEN. Quis pater ille virum, qui sic comitatur euntem?
Filius, an ne aliquis magna de stirpe nepotum?
Quis strepitus circa comitum? quantum instar in ipso est?
Sed nox atra caput tristi circumvolat umbra.
POE. Tu pater Anchises lacrymis ingressus obortis.
ANC. O nate, ingentem luctum ne quære tuorum.
Ostendent terris hunc tantum fata, neque ultra
Esse sinent. nimium vobis Romana propago
Visa potens superi, propria hæc si dona fuissent.
Quantos ille virum magnam Mavortis ad urbem
Campus aget gemitus, vel quæ Tyberine videbis
Funera, cum tumulum præter labere recentem.
Nec puer Iliaca quisquam de gente Latinos
In tantum spe tollet avos, nec Romula quondam
Ullo se tantum tellus iactabit alumno.
Heu pietas, heu prisca fides, invictaque bello
Dextera. non illi quisquam se impune tulisset
Obvius armato, seu cum pedes iret in hostem,
Seu spumantis equi foderet calcaribus armos.
Heu miserande puer, si qua fata aspera rumpas,
Tu Marcellus eris. manibus date lilia plenis,
Purpureos spargam flores, animamque nepotis
His saltem accumulem donis, & fungar inani
Munere. POE. Sic tota passim regione vagantur
Aëris in campis latis, atque omnia lustrant.

Plate 1. Text and commentary from *P. Virgilii Maronis … universum poema* (Venice: Petrus Dusinellus, 1585–6), fo. 240^{v}. (Author's copy.)

of language and meaning. Such thorough study drastically increased the odds that a work of any length would be broken into sections, some of which would be read and some of which would not.

Finally, fragmentation was compatible with the educational theory of the Italian Renaissance. Battista Guarino, for example, explains that the maxims and *sententiae* collected by the student were to be entered into notebooks, one of which was to focus on rhetorical forms and idioms (*methodice*), the other on content, especially moral content (*historice*). From these notebooks, the results of the students' reading could be applied to their own compositions and, presumably, to their lives as well.[72]

Sometimes these notebooks themselves were published, as was the case with the *Osservationi ... sopra l'opere di Virgilio* of Orazio Toscanella, who taught in the mainland areas dominated by Venice until he moved to the city proper around 1566, where he earned his living by producing works on the standard curriculum authors for the Venetian presses. Toscanella organizes his *Osservationi* under topics such as *bontà* ('goodness') or *consiglio* ('counsel'), with a summary of Virgil's approach to each topic and relevant extracts from his poetry ranged out below. Thus under *difficoltà* ('difficulty'), Toscanella explains that in adverse circumstances Virgil always makes intellect prevail over force, as in Hercules' triumph over Cacus (*Aen.* 8. 231–3, pp. 145–6). Under *pericolo* ('danger'), he explains that the brave always face death courageously; here the references are to Aeneas at the fall of Troy and again to Hercules (*Aen.* 8. 256–7, pp. 337–8). The entry for *offesa* ('offence') leads to the observation that Virgil always brings to ruin those like Nisus (*Aen.* 9. 324–8) who trust exclusively in their own capacities (pp. 304–5). The book in effect becomes an index to the moral content of Virgil's poetry, with the poems themselves shattered into moralizing fragments in accordance with

---

[72] Battista Guarino, *De ordine docendi et studendi*, in Woodward, *Vittorino da Feltre*, 163–72; see also R. R. Bolgar, *The Classical Heritage and its Beneficiaries* (Cambridge, 1954), 270; and Ann Moss, *Printed Commonplace-Books and the Structuring of Renaissance Thought* (Oxford, 1996). Grafton, '*Discitur ut agatur*', 117–18, notes that in his *Methodus ad facilem historiarum cognitionem* (1566), Jean Bodin outlined a similar method of reading, which is derived ultimately from pedagogical practices in antiquity (see Quintilian 1. 9. 1). The method described here is referred to by James Hankins as 'imitative reading' (*Plato in the Italian Renaissance*, 2 vols., Columbia Studies in the Classical Traditions, 17 (Leiden, 1990), i. 21–3).

the strategies for reading applied in the schools of Toscanella's day.[73]

Another product of these same strategies is the emblem book, which had its beginnings in the sixteenth century and ultimately came to generate some one thousand titles issued in over two thousand editions.[74] Each book contains a collection of individual emblems, with each emblem consisting of a *pictura*, a symbolic picture, an *inscriptio*, a pithy motto or title, and a *subscriptio*, a passage of prose or verse, with commentaries sometimes added as well. The genre derives from the same impulse as the epigrams written by the ancients to accompany works of art and collected in the *Greek Anthology*, the *tituli* or poetic labels affixed to ecclesiastical art in the Middle Ages, the heraldic crests of the Middle Ages and Renaissance, and the Egyptian hieroglyphs interpreted as visual symbols of moral and spiritual truth by Renaissance human-

---

[73] Toscanella's importance emerges clearly from Grendler, *Schooling*, 222–33 (on Cicero) and 240 (on Virgil), with a list of his writings on curriculum authors at 222 n. 51. On Toscanella's life and works, see Salvatore Bongi, *Annali di Gabriel Giolito de' Ferrari*, 2 vols., Indici e cataloghi, 11 (Rome, 1890–5), ii. 219–25; Luciano Artese, 'Orazio Toscanella, un maestro del XVI secolo', *Annali dell'Istituto di Filosofia dell'Università di Firenze*, 5 (1983), 61–95; Lina Bolzoni, 'Le "parole dipinte" di Orazio Toscanella', *Rivista di letteratura italiana*, 1 (1983), 155–86; and Di Filippo Bareggi, *Mestiere di scrivere, passim*. I have used the Venetian edn. published in 1566 by Gabriel Giolito De' Ferrari; references will be placed in the text. Toscanella's treatment of Virgil parallels that of later 16th-cent. editors of Castiglione, who marked aphorisms in the margin of the text and provided indexes that treated the work as a collection of such aphorisms; see Peter Burke, *The Fortunes of the Courtier: The European Reception of Castiglione's Cortegiano*, Penn State Series in the History of the Book, 1 (University Park, Penn., 1995), 37–45.

[74] This count was provided by Peter M. Daly (ed.), *The European Emblem: Towards an Index Emblematicus* (Waterloo, Ont., 1980), 1. The study of emblems has turned into an industry in itself over the last couple of decades, but indispensable works include William Heckscher and Karl-August Wirth, 'Emblem, Emblembuch', in L. H. Heydenreich and K.-A. Wirth (eds.), *Reallexicon der deutschen Kunstgeschichte* (Stuttgart, 1959), v. 85–227; Mario Praz, *Studies in Seventeenth-Century Imagery*, 2nd edn., Sussidi eruditi, 16 (Rome, 1964), with *Addenda et corrigenda* (Rome, 1974); Robert J. Clements, *Picta Poesis: Literary and Humanistic Theory in Renaissance Emblem Books*, Temi e testi, 6 (Rome, 1960); Arthur Henkel and Albrecht Schöne (eds.), *Emblemata, Handbuch zur Sinnbildkunst des XVI. und XVII. Jahrhunderts* (Stuttgart, 1967), with the review by Heckscher in *Renaissance Quarterly*, 23 (1970), 59–80; Peter Daly, *Literature in Light of the Emblems* (Toronto, Ont., 1979); and the articles in *Emblematica: An Interdisciplinary Journal for Emblem Studies*, which began in 1986.

Plate 2. (*Opposite*) Emblem CXCV, in Andrea Alciati, *Emblemata cum commentariis amplissimis* (Padua: Petrus Paulus Tozzus, 1621), 828. (Used by permission of the Harry Ransom Humanities Research Center, the University of Texas at Austin.)

diu corpus suum cædendum opposuit, multisque ita vulneribus acceptis, eorum saluti consulere non potuit, sed vna cum ijs est miserrimè confossa. Legimus in expeditione Cyri minoris apud Xenophontem lib. 4. à puero quodam, Dracontio nomine, per imprudentiam puerum interemptũ fuisse, quamobrē in exilium pulsus quanquã puer & imprudens. Sed iudices

non tã quidem iniuriã, quę non potest esse sine animo nocēdi, quàm parentũ incuriã in filio vindicauerunt. Posset idem Emblema multis exemplis insignis parentum amoris illustrari, quæ quia peti possunt ex Val. Maximo lib. 5. Sabel. lib. 3. Æliano, & alijs, nolo longiori sermóne lectorem detinere, sed pium Æneam filijs exemplum statuere pietatis in parentes paro.

Pietas filiorum in parentes.

EMBLEMA CXCV.

PER medios hosteis patria cum ferret ab igne
  AEneas humeris dulce parentis onus:
Parcite, dicebat: vobis sene adorea rapto
  Nulla erit, erepto sed patre summa mihi.

COMMENTARII.

PIvs Æneas armatus patrem Anchisen senio confectum, humeris suis exceptum baiulat, & per mediam flammam

incensæ Troiæ ereptum defert.

AENEAS potissimum commendatur ob summam in patrem Anchisen pietatē,
                            Ilio

ists.[75] For the emblem as well, this impulse sought to connect verbal and symbolic design to teach morality in such a way that it would enter the memory and serve as a guide to understanding and conduct.[76]

The genre had its beginning in the *Emblemata* of Andrea Alciati, whose Emblem CXCV is a good example of how the items in the collection work (see Plate 2).[77] The *inscriptio* in this case is a title: *Pietas filiorum in parentes* ('Piety of children toward their parents'). The *pictura* is a depiction of a warrior carrying an old man on his back away from a burning city. The *subscriptio* is four lines of verse:

> Per medios hosteis patriae cum ferret ab igne
> Æneas humeris dulce parentis onus:
> Parcite, dicebat: vobis sene adorea rapto
> Nulla erit, erepto sed patre summa mihi.

(When Aeneas carried his father, a sweet burden, on his shoulders from the flames of his country through the midst of the enemy, he said, 'Refrain from injuring him; there will be no glory for you in seizing an old man, but the utmost for me in rescuing a father.')

The commentary placed immediately below explains that this is indeed Aeneas carrying his father out of burning Troy, and it goes

---

[75] William S. Heckscher, 'Renaissance Emblems', *Princeton University Library Chronicle*, 15 (1954), 58–9; and Charles Moseley, *A Century of Emblems: An Introductory Anthology* (Aldershot, 1989), 6. This understanding of Egyptian hieroglyphs, of course, is historically inaccurate, but it accords with the humanists' desire to find ancient models for their scholarly activity.

[76] Moseley, *Century of Emblems*, 2; and Clements, *Picta Poesis*, 85–120.

[77] Citations, which will be incorporated into the text, are to *Andreae Alciati emblemata cum commentariis amplissimis* (Padua: Apud Petrum Paulum Tozzum, 1621), but an earlier edn. had been published by Paulus Manutius in Venice in 1546. Indeed, as W. S. Hecksher and A. B. Sherman have shown, Venice is the only city in southern Europe to have published a large number of emblem books, which suggests that we should pay special attention to emblems that appear in Venetian edns.; see their *Emblem Books in the Princeton University Library, Short-Title Catalogue* (Princeton, 1984), 4. The emblem discussed here appears in Jeremias Held's Ger. trans. of Alciati (Franckfurt am Mayn: Georg Raben, 1567), as emblem no. 73; Laurentius Haechtanus, *Mikrokosmos / Parvus Mundus* (Antwerp: Gerardus de Iode, 1579), as emblem no. 25; and Juan de Horozco y Covarrubias, *Emblemas morales* ... (Segovia: Juan de la Cuesta, 1589), as emblem no. 11 of Bk. 3; see Henkel and Schöne, *Emblemata*, col. 1703. As Robert Miola has observed, this Virgilian emblem is also recalled by one of the characters in *The Tragedie of Caesar and Pompey*, a possible source for Shakespeare's *Julius Caesar* ('Vergil in Shakespeare: From Allusion to Imitation,' in Kallendorf (ed.), *Vergil*, 279–80). For further discussion of this emblem, see James Garrison, *Pietas from Vergil to Dryden* (University Park, Penn., 1992), 49–60; and for further examples of Virgilian emblems in other emblem books, see Marcello Fagiolo (ed.), *Virgilio nell'arte e nella cultura europea*, Catalogue of an exhibition held at the Biblioteca Nazionale Centrale, Rome, 24 Sept.–24 Nov. 1981 (Rome, 1981), 253–4.

on to explain that the Greeks were so moved by such a display of *pietas* that they suspended their animosity and allowed Aeneas and Anchises to pass freely wherever they wished (pp. 828–31).

Like other readers of his day, Alciati has approached Virgil's text as a series of episodes that could be mined for their moral content more or less in isolation from one another. Thus Emblem XXXII, to select another Virgilian example, focuses on the Harpies in *Aeneid* 3. The *inscriptio* is *Bonis a divitibus nihil timendum* ('The good have nothing to fear from the wealthy'), and the picture shows two winged angels driving away three Harpies. According to the commentary, 'Harpy' indicates greed, and the emblem shows *quantus thesaurus sit vitae innocentis conscientia, ut quae insultus et iniurias malevolorum rideat* ('how great a treasure is the consciousness of a pure life, that it can laugh at the insults and injuries of the evil'; pp. 179–82). Emblem LXXI, entitled *Invidia* ('Envy'), draws from yet another Virgilian episode to produce a vivid image of a common vice (pp. 316–20). Finally, Emblem CXCVIII, *Nupta contagioso* ('A bride [joined] to a diseased husband'), marks a particularly striking application of the emblematic procedure. The emblem functions as the outcry of an innocent girl who is forced by her father to marry a husband wasting away from syphilis. The marriage, a 'crime' in every sense of the word, is conceived in Virgilian terms, for the picture shows two naked figures being bound together in the same way (as the commentary explains) as the Mezentius of *Aeneid* 8 used to bind together the living and the dead (pp. 842–7).

When emblems, which offered generalized moral guidance, were taken over by individuals, they could serve as *imprese*, devices presenting an illustration and motto that prominent people could use to represent themselves and their values.[78] One of the devices in a mid-sixteenth-century Venetian collection is of particular interest here, for the individual involved chose to present himself in Virgilian terms. The individual was one Scipio Costanzo, a *condottiere* who provided military service to the Venetian state, and his device consists of an architectural border with his coat of arms surrounding a galley and the motto *per tela, per hostes* ('through

---

[78] A helpful discussion on the relationship between the emblem and the device may be found in the introduction by Pierre Laurens to the facsimile edn. of Alciato's *Les Emblèmes* (Paris, 1997), 8–13.

weapons, through enemies'; *Aen.* 2. 527).[79] The discussion that
follows, by Girolamo Ruscelli, identifies the galley with Costanzo
himself and explains that since the motto lacks a verb, the device
applies to past, present, and future actions. In the past, it represents
the thanks that should be rendered to God for bringing Costanzo
safely to port; in the present, it depicts the stormy seas through
which he hopes to arrive in port; and in the future, the device
stimulates him to take courage and overcome the perils that will
arise in whatever voyage he begins. By extension, the motto also
illuminates the past of his family, who rose to prominence in
Naples by living in accordance with these values. An extended
interpretation could also be applied to Costanzo, who gave himself
to the military life at the age of 19, first serving successfully under
Francis I of France, then being elected *condottiere* by the Venetians
to succeed his father Tomasso. In the future, if he finds himself in
troubled waters, *no si riterria d'esporsi & di passar'oltre, per seguir il
viaggio della virtù, & dell'onor suo, overo per servire i suoi Signori et per
far tutto quello, che à valoroso, & onoratissimo Cavaliere & Signore, si
convien fare* ... ('he should not hold himself back from endangering
himself and proceeding onward, in order to follow the journey of
his valour and honour, or to serve his lords and to do everything
that is suitable for a brave and celebrated knight and gentleman to
do'; p. 557). In short, Scipio

con questa Impresa voluto proporre, come per segno e meta, la fortezza
& perseveranza, con la quale un'animo saggio conduce felicemente à fine
ogni giusto disegno suo, & ricordatosi dal cognome della sua Casa, che i
suoi antecessori con la Costanza nel valore, nella prudenza, nelle virtù &
nella bontà condussero felicissimamente in porto la nobiltà & la gloria
loro, mal grado d'ogni travaglio, & d'ogni disturbo della fortuna, & de'
nemici, cosi parimente si convegna sperare & procurare à lui, al qual'
anco è succeduto pur'il medesimo nel passato corso del viver suo. ...

(with this device having wished to propose, as through a goal and target,
the bravery and perseverance with which a wise spirit brings its every just
design to a happy end, and having remembered from the surname of his
house, that his ancestors with constancy brought their noble, glorious
vessel happily into port in valour, prudence, courage, and generosity, in

---

[79]   The collection is *Le imprese illustri con espositioni, et discorsi del S.ᵒʳ Ieronimo Ruscelli, al
serenissimo et sempre felicissimo re catolico Filippo d'Austria* (Venice: Francesco Rampazetto,
1566). Costanzo's *impresa* is illustrated and discussed on 554–6; references to this discussion
will be placed in the text.

spite of every toil and inconvenience of fortune and of enemies, so likewise he himself should expect and bring it about, since the same had
happened to him in the past course of his life.)

(p. 556)

Bravery and perseverance, constancy in prudence and generosity—these are the values that Venetian readers found in Virgil, a
part of the common literary culture explicitly appropriated here by
a military leader serving the state.

Thus Toscanella's *Osservationi*, Alciati's *Emblemata*, and
Costanzo's device are the logical extensions of what goes on in the
margins of Renaissance editions of Virgil, of a way of reading for
moral content that breaks a textual whole into parts according to
either episodic or proverbial needs. Indeed, we might say that
while the pointing hands that Renaissance readers placed in the
margins of these books highlight the moral content of the text, on
another level they also point backward to a theory of reading and
forward to other books that would become in turn the fruits of
that theory.

As we have thus seen, both the commentaries printed in the
margins of Venetian Renaissance editions of Virgil and the handwritten notes entered around them reflect the strategies of reading
through which the moral content of poetry could be most suitably
extracted for use in the schools. There are, of course, other ways
of looking at the moral content of poetry, ways that we can imagine but do not in fact find in the margins of these texts. At this
point I would like to hazard an initial step or two down a couple
of these roads not taken, to suggest that what we do not find in
the margins of these texts is the function of the same institutional
constraints as what we do find.

One of the things we do not find is any significant willingness to
see moral failing in Aeneas. Examples of such moral failing have
been noted by other readers. For example, a number of very influential modern readings of the poem, chiefly those of the so-called
'Harvard' or 'pessimistic' school, dwell less on Aeneas' success in
defining and attaining *pietas* than on his failures to achieve the standards he sets for himself. These readings converge on the climactic
final scene, in which Aeneas' killing of his enemy Turnus is attributed to the very forces of *furor* and *ira* that he has been struggling
so hard to suppress throughout the poem. If we interpret the *Aeneid*

in this way, we are left with a hero who has made very little moral progress indeed since he left Troy, and with the suggestion that there is very little chance for us as readers to do much better.[80] The appeal of these pessimistic readings in the cultural climate of our age is obvious, but we should also note that there is some evidence that at least a few readers of the Renaissance might have seen some of this as well. For example, in a recent article comparing the ending of the *Orlando Furioso* to the ending of the *Aeneid*, Joseph Sitterson, Jr. has argued that Ariosto was one sixteenth-century reader who could have seen the problematic nature of Virgil's ending with its transfer of *furor* and *ira* to Aeneas.[81]

This pessimism, however, is not what we find in the Venetian editions we have been looking at. In the printed commentaries, Landino's Aeneas makes steady progress through the civil and purgatorial virtues to the virtues of a purified soul, and Ascensius' Aeneas, under the influence of Donatus' epideictic approach, is the consistent exemplar of praiseworthy virtue. The handwritten marginalia proceed in a similar way; indeed, I have not seen any notes that suggest that Aeneas' victory over Turnus, for example, is anything but an unequivocal victory of virtue over vice.

The reasons for the prevalence of this uncritical view of Aeneas emerge naturally, I believe, from the way in which the poem was read in the school environment. For one thing, readings that stress Aeneas' failure to progress morally through the poem depend on one's having read the entire poem, so that the recurrence of images and patterns of behaviour from the fall of Troy in Book 2, for example, can be noticed in the final battle scene in Book 12.

---

[80]   For some esp. influential examples of this approach, see Michael C. J. Putnam, *The Poetry of the 'Aeneid': Four Studies in Imaginative Unity and Design* (Cambridge, Mass., 1965); W. Ralph Johnson, *Darkness Visible: A Study of Vergil's Aeneid* (Berkeley and Los Angeles, Calif., 1976), with bibliography of previous work to that date; Andrew Wallace-Hadrill, 'The Golden Age and Sin in Augustan Ideology', *Past and Present*, 95 (1982), 19–36; and Jean-Luc Pomathios, *Le Pouvoir politique et sa représentation dans l'Énéide de Virgile* (Brussels, 1987), 9–14. As Richard Thomas has pointed out, however, the Harvard connection of the pessimists is in fact often tenuous ('Ideology, Influence, and Future Studies in the *Georgics*', *Vergilius*, 36 (1990), 64 n. 1), and Karl Galinsky has warned that the 'pessimistic-optimistic' critical contrast is only one of several unfortunately reductionist antitheses in modern Virgilian criticism (*Classical and Modern Interactions*, 82).

[81]   'Allusive and Elusive Meanings: Reading Ariosto's Vergilian Ending', *Renaissance Quarterly*, 45 (1992), 10–14. See also Craig Kallendorf, 'Historicizing the Harvard School: Pessimistic Readings of the *Aeneid* in Italian Renaissance Scholarship', *Harvard Studies in Classical Philology* (forthcoming).

As we have seen, however, the dominant institutional environment privileged different strategies of reading, so that most teachers and students would not have had the easy control of the entire poem from which an interpretation like this could most naturally emerge.

What is more, acknowledging moral failing in Aeneas would significantly complicate the job of a humanist schoolmaster who approached poetry in order to find 'many wise and useful things to say about life and how it should be lived'. A hero 'endowed with every virtue', as Vegio put it, is the perfect model for discussion and imitation, and it confuses the matter considerably to acknowledge that this model is sometimes a fornicator, or subject to overwhelming surges of anger, or whatever. This is not to say that Renaissance schoolmasters consciously distorted the text. Rather they approached it within a particular interpretive paradigm and found in the text what that paradigm allowed them to see. The capacity to see differently, as Thomas Kuhn might say, would have required a paradigm shift,[82] and in educational theory at least, that shift did not take place during this period.

Now and again other Renaissance readers did manage to see moral ambiguity, the shades of grey in which standards blur and choices become complicated. For example, Karlheinz Stierle has observed a tradition of experimental writing extending from Boccaccio to Montaigne, in which moral standards were problematized and literature offered only a starting point for moral enquiry.[83] More specifically, Giuseppe Mazzotta has argued that in the *Decameron* 'there are no unvarying rules or fixed moral absolutes',[84] Guido Almansi finds in the same work a self-adjusting scale of values that changes to fit character and situation,[85] and Millicent Marcus locates the moral vision of the *Decameron* not through reference to a clearly defined external code, but through the modes of narration by which the stories are told.[86] Reading a

---

[82]   I am referring, of course, to a concept developed in Kuhn, *The Structure of Scientific Revolutions*, 2nd edn. (Chicago, 1970).

[83]   'L'Histoire comme Exemple, l'Exemple comme Histoire: Contribution à la pragmatique et à la poétique des textes narratifs', *Poétique: Revue de théorie et d'analyse littéraires*, 10 (1972), 176–98.

[84]   *The World at Play in Boccaccio's Decameron* (Princeton, 1986), 242, 261.

[85]   *The Writer as Liar: Narrative Technique in the Decameron* (Boston, 1975), 147.

[86]   *An Allegory of Form: Literary Self-Consciousness in the Decameron*, Stanford French and Italian Studies, 18 (Saratoga, Calif., 1979), 8, 24, 108.

work like the *Decameron* presents challenges to familiar ways of thinking about right or wrong—indeed, it raises the most unsettling question of whether there are any fixed standards at all. With Machiavelli and Montaigne, questions of morality are explored in a similar way. As Nancy Struever explains it, '[n]either one denies classical values, and both employ exemplary strategies, but both deny that easy transparency between moral theory and moral practice presumed by the naive exemplary mode that tends to reduce events to a series of instantiations of classical moral-political maxims.'[87]

However, all of these experimental writers have in common a freedom from the constraints of educational institutions. By contrast, reading Virgil in the Renaissance schoolroom meant isolating the events of the story and discussing them as 'instantiations of classical moral-political maxims' which were assumed to hold true for readers of later periods as well. That is, commentary driven by pedagogical needs functioned consistently to efface ambiguity, to level complexity and integrate the text into familiar patterns of thinking about right and wrong.[88] The results may strike us as in some ways naive, but they should not surprise us. After all, at least until recently, education has generally tended to simplify rather than complicate, to focus on the most basic values of a society in order to pass those values on to the next generation.

Thus the pointing hands and *Nota* markers of Virgil's Venetian Renaissance readers reveal their basic personal values, the values compatible with the myth of Venice: 'fortune helps those who dare and drives away the timid' (*Aen.* 10. 284), 'toil conquers everything, unrelenting toil' (*Georg.* 1. 145–6), 'voracious love, to what do you not drive the hearts of men?' (*Aen.* 4. 412), 'be

---

[87] *Theory as Practice: Ethical Inquiry in the Renaissance* (Chicago, 1992), 202. These classical maxims, as Charles B. Schmitt has noted, remained heavily dependent on Aristotle throughout the Renaissance ('Aristotle's Ethics in the Sixteenth Century: Some Preliminary Considerations', in Rüegg and Wuttke (eds.), *Ethik im Humanismus*, 87–112, and *Aristotle and the Renaissance* (Cambridge, Mass., 1983)).

[88] As Janusz Sławiński points out, literary reception at the school level provides the basic point of reference for reactions at all other levels ('Reading and Reader in the Literary Historical Process', *New Literary History*, 19 (1988), 538–9). In 'The Edifying Margins of Renaissance English Books', *Renaissance Quarterly*, 42 (1989), 682, W. W. E. Slights notes that although other procedures are certainly possible, commentary in general often tends to simplify, either by providing an epitome of the text or by setting out one of the possible interpretations of the text as authoritative.

warned, learn justice and not to scorn the gods' (*Aen.* 6. 620),[89] and so forth. These maxims—exhortations to do the right thing, to subordinate the passions to the control of reason, to sacrifice self on behalf of family, friends, and country—do not break much new ground in Renaissance ethical enquiry. Indeed, the interpretations of Virgil derived from the schools of the Veneto are inherently conservative, in that they reinforce both existing values and modes of thinking and stress the need to work for good within existing social institutions.[90] This, however, is what makes them so valuable to us, for in their studies of Virgil, Renaissance schoolmasters demonstrated something of the power that institutions have to shape interpretation, both of books and of life itself.

Resistance and Containment: The Humanist as Pornographer

The Virgil that we have seen so far is the Virgil of the official myth of Venice, the one who reinforced what Venetians in power wanted others to believe about themselves. But there was also another myth of Venice, one that lacked an official sanction but was nevertheless very much alive in the imagination of Renaissance Europe. This counter-myth portrayed Venice as the city of loose living and decadence, the home of courtesans and homosexuals 'on the make', the place where refined elegance was mixed with deception, greed, and hypocrisy.[91] The values on

---

[89] We should not assume that the values extracted from Virgil in the schools of Renaissance Venice are necessarily the ones that will fit in other educational environments. For example, in 1769 John Wilson came to a radically different interpretation, being moved to resign from Friends Latin School in Philadelphia in part because 'the impious Notion Of both the 2d and 8th Eclogues and his representing the Ungrateful Lustful Perfidious Aeneas as the particular Friend and Favorite of heaven are shocking to every System of Morality' (qtd. by Meyer Reinhold, 'Vergil in the American Experience from Colonial Times to 1882', in *Classica Americana: The Greek and Roman Heritage in the U.S.* (Detroit, 1989), 235).

[90] As Paul Grendler has pointed out (*Schooling*, 264), the moral values generally extracted from classical texts in Renaissance Italy fell within a fairly narrow range, focused on working for good within existing social institutions and developing such virtues as discipline, fortitude, and respect. There is obviously much more work to be done in relating this generalization to specific practices in other cities.

[91] On the emergence of a culture of illicit sexuality that existed alongside the licit pattern of marriage and childbirth, see Guido Ruggiero, *The Boundaries of Eros: Sex Crime and Sexuality in Renaissance Venice* (New York, 1985), 10. This counter-myth, as Margaret Rosenthal has observed, has not been thoroughly studied yet, although some early references to it may be found in Gina Fasoli, 'Nascita di un mito', in *Studi storici in onore di*

which the counter-myth rests appear, for example, in the plays of
Pietro Aretino, who wrote three brilliant comedies in Venice in
the early 1540s, *La Talanta*, *Lo ipocrito*, and *Il filosofo*. These plays
are peopled by such traditional characters as parasites and pedants,
braggart soldiers and scheming servants, and as one critic has
noted, they 'all breathe corruption'.[92] The hypocrite, for example,
is a friar who professes *carità* but is actually an unprincipled syco-
phant. Through these plays and other works like them, the values
connected with the official myth of Venice were subverted.

Those who travelled to Italy during the Renaissance were fully
aware of the other Venice that lay behind the officially sanctioned
myth. Thomas Coryat, for example, described St Mark's square in
a way that betrayed considerable unease:

Truely such is the stupendious (to use a strange Epitheton for so strange
and rare a place as this) glory of it, that at my first entrance thereof it did
even amaze or rather ravish my senses. For here is the greatest magnifi-
cence of architecture to be seene, that any place under the sunne doth
yeelde. Here you may both see all manner of fashions of attire, and heare
all the languages of Christendome, besides those that are spoken by the
barbarous Ethnickes; the frequencie of people being so great ... that (as
an elegant writer saith of it) a man may very properly calle it rather *Orbis*
than *Urbis forum*, that is, a market place of the world, not of the citie.[93]

Coryat is obviously impressed by the 'stupendious ... glory' of the
place, but beneath the surface splendour lies a threat, for that which
can 'ravish' the senses threatens the rational restraint and self-
control on which the Venetian state was supposed to rest. What is
more, this 'market place of the world' is open to all languages and
peoples, thereby threatening the *unanimitas* at the centre of the official myth. Shakespeare seems to have caught the contradiction well
in *The Merchant of Venice*. The official myth speaks through
Antonio, 'one in whom | The ancient Roman honour more

Gioacchino Volpe, 2 vols. (Florence, 1958), ii. 445–79, and it certainly received support in
the general anti-Venetian propaganda of the Renaissance (Nicolai Rubinstein, 'Italian
Reactions to Terraferma Expansion in the Fifteenth Century', in Hale (ed.), *Renaissance
Venice*, 197–217). In this section I have followed up on some suggestions provided to me
by Rosenthal and by my colleague Douglas Brooks (personal communications).

[92] Ernest Hatch Wilkins, *A History of Italian Literature*, rev. edn. (Cambridge, Mass.,
1974), 241.

[93] *Coryats Crudities*, qtd. in John Gillies, *Shakespeare and the Geography of Difference*
(Cambridge, 1994), 124. The information in this para. is drawn from Gillies's book, 122–40.

appears | Than any draws breath in Italy' (III. ii. 292–4). Shylock, however, represents everything that challenges the established order from within: the complaint of the politically disenfranchised, the instinct of the market place gone awry, and ultimately the failure to conform to the moral values of the community at large.

For the Renaissance traveller, the other Venice threatened sensual ravishment in several areas, but particularly the sexual. At the beginning of the sixteenth century, the patrician diarist Marin Sanudo noted with disapproval that Venice contained 11,654 prostitutes among the 100,000 people who lived there, and at the beginning of the seventeenth century Coryat claimed that the count had risen to 20,000. Whatever their number, many of these were common prostitutes, but what captured the imagination of Renaissance travellers were the *cortigiane oneste* ('honest or honoured courtesans'). These women were beautiful, to be sure, but they were educated as well, blending sophisticated conversation and artistic accomplishment with skilful navigation through the social labyrinths of the day. Montaigne admired their commercial success, yet others saw in them a symbol of how money had corrupted even basic social relationships in a mercantile society like Venice. Coryat, for example, warns the visitor against the courtesans he would encounter:

As for thine eyes, shut them and turne them aside from these venereous Venetian objects. For they are double windowes that conveigh them to thy heart. Also thou must fortifie thine eares against the attractive inchauntments of their plausible speeches. … [S]o doe thou only breath a few words upon them and presently be gone from them: for if thou dost linger with them thou wilt finde their poyson to be more pernicious than that of the scorpion, aspe, or cocatrice.[94]

Indeed, Sir Henry Wotton, the English ambassador to Venice, is said to have fled the city because he could not trust himself among its prostitutes. To be sure, the *cortigiana onesta* was a far cry from the female icon that represented the official Venice of the sixteenth century as a combination of the Roman goddess of Justice, the Virgin Mary, and Venus Anadyomene, the goddess born from the sea. Yet the state that represented itself officially in this way also recognized and sanctioned its other women, for even

---

[94] *Coryats Crudities*, qtd. in Margaret F. Rosenthal, *The Honest Courtesan: Veronica Franco, Citizen and Writer in Sixteenth-Century Venice* (Chicago, 1992), 20. The information in this para. is drawn from Rosenthal's book, 1–57.

a visitor like Coryat knew that courtesans were specially taxed, bringing them into the economic and political life of the community like any other merchants.

In one of the striking ironies of cultural history, these subversive sexual values are also carried in the pages of many of the very same editions of Virgil through which the official myth was reinforced. If we turn to the back of the folio editions, we generally find a collection of minor poems that Renaissance scholars often attributed to Virgil under the name *Appendix Virgiliana*. One group of minor poems, which is found in sixty-eight of the 132 editions of Virgil published in the Veneto during the Renaissance, is the *Priapea*, a collection of some eighty poems dedicated to Priapus, the Roman god of fertility who was also charged with protecting gardens against thieves. And in contrast to the *Eclogues*, *Georgics*, and *Aeneid*, many of these poems are quite obscene.

The mildest of the group are parodies of religious literature, although even here the size of Priapus' erect member is a regular topic for discussion. About a third of the *Priapea* describe the behaviour of individual Priapuses, rudely carved statues placed in the countryside to scare away birds and thieves. In hopes that their violent language will scare off intruders, these poems threaten rape and sodomistic acts. Poem 35 conveys the flavour of this group:

> Pedicabere, fur, semel; sed idem
> si prensus fueris bis, irrumabo.
> quod si tertia furta molieris,
> ut poenam patiare et hanc et illam,
> pedicaberis irrumaberisque.

> (In your back way I'll go if once you thieve;
> If twice, me in your mouth you will receive;
> And if a third such theft you should attempt,
> Both penalties you'll have to undergo;
> In arse and mouth my potent force you'll know.)[95]

---

[95] *Priapea: Poems for a Phallic God*, trans. and ed. by W. H. Parker, Croom Helm Classical Studies (London, 1988), 122 (text) and 123 (trans.). The analysis in this para. is based on Parker's discussion, 41–4, which should be supplemented in more general terms by Amy Richlin, *The Garden of Priapus: Sexuality and Aggression in Roman Humor* (New Haven, 1983), esp. 57–63, 116–27, 210–13. The reception of the *Priapea* and the attitudes associated with them in the Renaissance are beginning to attract some long-overdue attention now; see e.g. the essays collected in Ingrid de Smet and Philip Ford (eds.), *Eros et Priapus: Erotisme et obscénité dans la littérature néo-latine*, Cahiers d'Humanisme et Renaissance, 51 (Geneva, 1997).

Another third of the collection depict a sexually depraved Priapus functioning like the Roman male at his lowest level of self-indulgent lust, with fornication, pederasty, and irrumation described in much the same tone as Poem 35.

The same humanists who approached poetry as a source for guidance in living an upright life also devoted considerable attention to the *Priapea*. The great teacher Guarino da Verona, whose work formed the basis for the classic of educational theory penned by his son, studied these poems, as did such prominent humanists as Poggio Bracciolini, Giovanni Tortelli, and the members of the so-called Aldine Academy in Venice.[96] Among the eight extant Renaissance commentaries on the *Priapea* are one by a first-rank humanist, Joseph Justus Scaliger, and two by scholars with connections to the Veneto: Lodovico Pretino da Poppi, whose work was printed in Venice around 1500, and Girolamo Avanzi da Verona, who taught in Padua and belonged to the Aldine Academy in Venice.[97] The poems were also imitated in original poetry, beginning with the prehumanist Albertino Mussato and extending to such well-known members of the Venetian cultural scene as Andrea Navagero and Petrus Bembus.[98] In addition, Priapic myths appear along with a series of graphic illustrations in perhaps the greatest of all Renaissance illustrated books, the *Hypnerotomachia Poliphili*, published in Venice in 1499 by Aldus Manutius, and in Giovanni Bellini's famous painting *The Feast of the Gods*.[99]

[96] Frank-Ruther Hausmann, 'Carmina Priapea', in F. Edward Cranz and Paul O. Kristeller (eds.), *Catalogus translationum et commentariorum: Mediaeval and Renaissance Latin Translations and Commentaries, Annotated Lists and Guides*, 7 vols. to date (Washington, 1980–), iv. 426–7; and Edgar Wind, *Bellini's Feast of the Gods: A Study in Venetian Humanism* (Cambridge, Mass., 1948), 32–3.

[97] Hausmann, 'Carmina Priapea', iv. 427–8.

[98] Ibid. 426–7; and Manlio Dazzi, *Il Mussato preumanista (1261–1329): L'ambiente e l'opera* (Verona, 1964), 178–80.

[99] The definitive edn. is Giovanni Pozzi and Lucia Ciapponi (eds.), *Hypnerotomachia Poliphili ubi humana omnia nisi somnium esse docet*, 2 vols. (Padua, 1980; repr. of 1964 edn.). A great deal has been written about this book, with a good overview appearing in Giovanni Pozzi and Giulia Gianella, 'Scienza antiquaria e letteratura: Il Feliciano: Il Colonna', in *Storia della cultura veneta*, iii. Girolamo Arnaldi and Manlio Pastore Stocchi (eds.), *Dal primo Quattrocento al Concilio di Trento*, pt. 1 (Vicenza, 1980), 477–98. Bellini's painting, in which a tumescent Priapus is clearly visible, has a complicated history, some of which is directly relevant to the present study. It was delivered to Alfonso d'Este of Ferrara in 1514 and ultimately retouched by Titian, but the original purchaser of the painting was to have been Alfonso's sister Isabella. Her go-between in the negotiations with Bellini at one point was Petrus Bembus, who had himself shown an active interest in the *Priapea*. See Wind, *Bellini's Feast*, 5, 21–6; Renato Ghiotto and Terisio Pignatti, *L'opera completa di Giovanni Bellini*

Such persistent attention to such obscene poetry was clearly subversive to the values so carefully cultivated through the study of the *Eclogues*, *Georgics*, and *Aeneid*, and the institutional powers of Renaissance Venice developed several strategies to contain this subversion. One such strategy involved the way in which the printers and scholars working with them arranged to present the *Priapea* in the early printed editions. In the smaller octavo editions pioneered by Aldus Manutius, the poems were first banished as *obscoena, quae ... non censuimus digna enchiridio* ('obscene things that ... we do not consider worthy of a handbook'; fo. a1^v of the 1501 edition), then added with reluctance at the end of the book *ut pro uniuscuiusque arbitrio separari possent* ('so that they could be taken out by anyone at will'; fo. 1^v of the 1505 edition), and finally removed and published separately along with the rest of the *Appendix Virgiliana* in 1517 and again in 1534, so that they need not contaminate the purity of the canonical texts. In the larger folio editions, the *Priapea* were banished to the back of the book, where they were generally set in smaller type and published without the commentaries through which attention was drawn to the other poems.

Another strategy for neutralizing these poems was to read them in accordance with the usual paradigm for interpreting literature in the schools of Renaissance Venice. This is the approach taken by Lodovico Pretino da Poppi. In the preface to his commentary, Pretino suggests that these poems offer so much verbal power (*vis dicendi*) and intellectual wisdom (*ingenii sagacitas*) that the reader should delight in such poems (*hoc genere carminis sit ipse oblectatus*) and derive much usefulness (*tantum ... utilitatis*) from them.[100] Then he moves from making the claim that the *Priapea* are in accordance with Horatian dicta to listing other poets who also wrote lascivious works, both Greek (Plato, Pindar, Diogenes the Cynic, Zeno the Stoic, Sappho, etc.) and Latin (Ovid, Catullus, Propertius, Tibullus, and a number of others whose work did not

(Milan, 1969), no. 207 in the catalogue; and Rona Goffen, *Giovanni Bellini* (New Haven, 1989), 222–5 with pls. 164–5. I am grateful to Warren Tresidder for drawing my attention to this painting.

[100] Ludovicus Pretinus de Puppio, *Commentarius in Priapeam Virgilii Maronis* (Venice: Giovanni Tacuino, *c.*1500), fo. a1^r. I have used the copy at the Biblioteca Nazionale Marciana, shelf mark Inc. 466, which seems to be the only copy in Italy of this very rare vol. The preface is found on fos. a1^r–3^r.

survive). Next Pretino fashions a linguistic argument, claiming that obscene words are appropriate when we need to describe obscene activities. Then he observes that one can remain pure in mind while writing lascivious verse, and he concludes by noting that the mind requires some relaxation through less serious activities. The problem with all this is that the general claim that much utility can come from reading the *Priapea* sits uneasily next to the specific observations required by the text, such as the definition of *irrumare* as *hoc est accipies mentulam meam ore tuo* ('that is, you will receive my penis in your mouth').[101] Nevertheless, Pretino's basic strategy is the same one described by Julia Gaisser in her study of sixteenth-century commentaries to Catullus, where we find obscenity either ignored or turned to a virtuous interpretation.[102]

Another way to counter the threat posed by these poems was to challenge their attribution to Virgil, on the assumption that if they could be assigned to another author, they could be more easily marginalized. The attribution to Virgil had a long history, going back to Suetonius, Servius, Donatus, and Pliny in antiquity and picking up again with Boccaccio, who rediscovered the poems and accepted them as Virgilian. However, the editor of the *editio princeps*, Giovanni Andrea Bussi, had some doubts about their authorship, as did such well-known humanists as Angelo Poliziano, Pomponio Leto, Aldus Manutius, and Joseph Justus Scaliger.[103] An especially significant denial of Virgilian authorship came from Petrus Bembus, who grounded his judgement in manuscript authority and the incompatibility of the *Priapea* with Virgil's characteristic modesty; he blamed the attribution to Virgil

---

[101]   Ibid., fo. b5^r.

[102]   'Catullan Imitation from Martial to Marullo', a paper delivered at the first meeting of the International Society for the Classical Tradition, Boston, 24 Mar. 1991. This same strategy was also applied to the *Hypnerotomachia Poliphili*, whose illustrations of Priapic myths show how far the book as a whole is from overt moralization. However, as Lamberto Donati has shown, it was a favourite source for the moralizing emblemist Andrea Alciati, who put into the mouth of the Bacchus from the *Hypnerotomachia* an injunction on how to drink wine in moderation ('Polifilo ed Andrea Alciati (1492–1550)', in Emil van der Vekene (ed.), *Refugium Animae Bibliotheca: Festschrift für Albert Kolb* (Wiesbaden, 1969), 204–24, esp. 224).

[103]   Hausmann, 'Carmina Priapea', 424–7; and Parker, *Priapea*, 32–6. The attribution to Virgil proved appealing in part because of the statement in the life by Donatus-Suetonius that Virgil *fuit ... libidinis in pueros pronioris* ('was ... physically attracted toward boys'), quoted in Zabughin, *Vergilio*, i. 161. Modern scholarship on the question is summarized in Nicolas Horsfall (ed.), *A Companion to the Study of Virgil*, Mnemosyne, suppl., 151 (Leiden, 1995), 10–11 with notes.

on ignorant printers who were eager to increase the size of the Virgilian corpus.[104] These doubts about Virgilian authorship allowed early editors, printers, and teachers a number of options. In the editions of Georgius Arrivabenus (1512) and Alexander de Paganinis (1515), the poems are assigned to Ovid, and since Ascensius came to this same conclusion, this attribution was popularized through the prefatory matter accompanying his works.[105] In the editions of Aldus Manutius (1517 and 1534), Augustinus de Zanis de Portesio (1519), and Guglielmus de Fontaneto Montisferrati (1522), the poems are attributed to 'diverse authors'.[106] Thus by the end of the first quarter of the sixteenth century, any schoolmaster who wanted to could ignore the *Priapea* and the problems they caused simply by labelling them non-Virgilian.

Working in tandem with the educational and political establishments of Renaissance Venice, the church offered another way to control obscenity through various forms of censorship. As early as 1497, the Patriarch Tommaso Donà threatened the printer Lucas Antonius Junta (the elder) with excommunication if he did not modify the nude figures in his new edition of Ovid's *Metamorphoses*, and he complied by retouching the areas around the genital organs and using more modest illustrations in later printings.[107] A number of censorship laws were passed in Venice

---

[104] *Petri Bembi ad Herculem Strotium de Virgilii Culice et Terentii fabulis liber* (Venice: Johannes Antonius de Nicolinis de Sabio and Brothers, 1530), fo. bi[r–v]. The ms on which Bembus relies is presumably the well-known codex of the *Appendix Virgiliana* that he inherited from his father Bernardus, now Vatican City, Biblioteca Apostolica Vaticana, Vat. lat. 3252; other mss containing Virgil's works are known to have been in the family but cannot now be located. It is also worth noting that Bernardus was on good terms with Landino: Bernardus acquired a ms of the *Disp. Cam.* (now Paris, Bibliothèque Nationale, Ms. lat. 3343A) on his own, and Landino sent him a printed copy of his Dante commentary (now Paris, Bibliothèque Nationale, Rés. Yd. 17) in recognition of the monument to Dante erected by Bembus in Ravenna. On the connections between the Bembus family and Renaissance Virgil scholarship, see Nella Giannetto, *Bernardo Bembo: Umanista e politico veneziano*, Civiltà veneziana, Saggi, 34 (Florence, 1985), 261, 263–4, 269, 297–8, 334–5, 356–7.

[105] These judgements are rendered in the colophons of the two edns., Part 1, fo. 168[r] of both edns. (the second is a copy of the first). Ascensius' conclusion is found on fo. 124[v].

[106] Aldus' attribution is found on the title-pages of his two edns. of the *Appendix Virgiliana*, while the other attributions are found in the colophons of the other two edns., Part III, fos. 47[v] and 315[r] respectively.

[107] Paul Grendler, *The Roman Inquisition and the Venetian Press, 1540–1605* (Princeton, 1977), 72; and Bodo Guthmüller, *Ovidio Metamorphoseos Vulgare: Formen und Funktionen der volksprachlichen Wiedergabe klassischer Dichtung in der italienischen Renaissance,*

in 1517, 1526, 1542–3, and 1547 in an effort to control blas-
phemous, scandalous, and obscene books,[108] and in fact there are
records of a suit brought against Zuan Padoan, Francesco
Faencino, and Vielmo da Monferà in 1545 for publishing a work
entitled *Il dio Priapo*.[109] In 1559 the Index of Paul IV specifically
banned books that were immoral, lascivious, or obscene,[110] and
this prohibition was carried over into Rule VII of the Tridentine
Index of Pius IV (1564) and Rule XVI of the Index of Sixtus V
(1590).[111] This provided the grounds for condemning the *Priapea*,
and in the Antwerp appendix to the Tridentine Index (1570), we
find a specific prohibition against reading the *Priapeia false asscripta
Virgilio* ('the *Priapea* falsely attributed to Virgil'). The prohibition
was carried over into the Index of the Spanish Inquisitor General
Quiroga (1583) and the Index of Clement VIII (1596),[112] so that
we find quite a few expurgated sixteenth-century editions from
which the *Priapea* have been removed.[113] As we might expect, the

Veröffentlichungen zur Humanismusforschung, 3 (Boppard am Rhein, 1981), 183–5.
J. P. Sullivan recently tried to extend the term 'censorship' to include all attempts to read
the subversive elements of the Latin classics in accordance with the dominant ideology of
the Renaissance ('Religious Censorship and the Transmission of Latin Classics', a paper
read at the second meeting of the International Society for the Classical Tradition,
Tübingen, Germany, 14 Aug. 1992); in this chapter, however, the term will retain its more
usual, restricted meaning.

[108] Horatio F. Brown, *The Venetian Printing Press, 1469–1800: An Historical Study based
upon Documents for the Most Part unedited* (Amsterdam, 1969; repr. of London, 1891 edn.),
67–82. The magistrates responsible for enforcing obedience to the laws regulating the press,
the *Esecutori contro la bestemmia*, exercised their duties as part of a larger effort to regulate
activities that threatened the social fabric of Venice, such as blasphemy, prostitution,
gambling, etc. On this magistracy, see R. Derosas, 'Moralità e giustizia a Venezia nel
'500–'600: Gli Esecutori contro la bestemmia', in G. Cozzi (ed.), *Stato, società e giustizia nella
Repubblica Veneta (secc. XV–XVIII)*, 2 vols. (Rome, 1980), ii. 430 ff.; and Gaetano Cozzi,
'Religione, moralità e giustizia a Venezia: Vicende della magistratura degli Esecutori contro
la bestemmia (secc. XVI–XVII)', *Ateneo Veneto*, NS 29 (1991), 7–95, with bibliography.

[109] This action is mentioned in Giuliano Pesenti, 'Libri censurati a Venezia nei secoli
XVI–XVII', *Bibliofilia*, 58 (1956), 17.

[110] Grendler, *Roman Inquisition*, 116–17. Specifically condemned were the works of
Aretino, Machiavelli, Rabelais, and Poggio Bracciolini, and Boccaccio's *Decameron* was
ordered expurgated.

[111] These rules are printed by Fr. Heinrich Reusch, *Die Indices Librorum prohibitorum des
sechzehnten Jahrhunderts* (Nieuwkoop, 1961; repr. of Tübingen, 1886 edn.), 249, 456.

[112] Ibid. 299, 426, 572.

[113] Two such copies, for example, may be found in the Biblioteca Comunale, Treviso:
the 1578 Petrus Dusinellus edn., shelf mark N.12563 (II.1.B.28), and the 1588 Joannes
Gryphius Minor edn., shelf mark II.7.E.1. It is worth noting, however, that expurgation of
the *Priapea* was haphazard, even in copies held by clerics: Treviso, Biblioteca del Seminario
Vescovile, shelf mark VII.G.15 (the 1562 Joannes Maria Bonellus edn.), for example, was

Priapic illustrations in the *Hypnerotomachia Poliphili* were also a frequent target for ecclesiastical censors.[114]

Not every copy of every Renaissance edition, however, has been expurgated, and the marginal notes found in some of these unexpurgated copies suggest that here, as in so many other cases, the powers of institutional control never fully succeed. One such unexpurgated book, for example, is found now in the library of the Basilica of St Anthony in Padua, with its current location at least inviting us to speculate about whether its early annotator might have been a cleric. This annotator has lavished loving attention on the *Priapea*, adding titles to some of the poems, correcting the text through collation with another copy, and making explicit some of the implied sexual references.[115] The clerical provenance of a copy of the 1479 edition of Leonardus Achates that has returned at last to its original place of publication in Vicenza is more secure, for an early ownership note places it in the Dominican convent of Santa Maria Gratiarum in Padua. The early reader of this volume, unlike most owners of his day, was primarily interested in the *Appendix Virgiliana*, and on fo. c6^r a section of the *Priapea* is accompanied by a note headed *pedicare* ('to sodomize') and a weeping face.[116] In this case, it seems clear that the officially sanctioned Virgilian values did not prevail. ...

in a convent at least by the middle of the 17th cent., as attested by the ownership note on the title-page (*spectat ad conventum S. Bernardini Collalzi, Ad usum Francisci Ballotti, 1649 XXV Die Junii* ...), yet the pages containing the *Priapea* are intact. We should also note that the removal of the *Priapea* sometimes drove those who wanted to read these poems to curious solutions, such as that found in Verona, Biblioteca Civica, Cinq. C.561, a 1558 Joannes Maria Bonellus edn., in which fos. 385–8 (containing the *Priapea*) were first cut out, then replaced with folios from the 1575 edn. by the same printer. Since the colophon is on the verso of fo. 388, the result is at first glance puzzling from a bibliographical point of view.

[114]   This point is made by Helen Barolini in her study of the *Hypnerotomachia*, *Aldus and his Dream Book* (New York, 1992), 99.

[115]   These notes may be found on fos. 338^v–341^v of the 1500 Junta edn., shelf mark R.VII.12.

[116]   This copy is now in Vicenza, Biblioteca Bertoliana, shelf mark Gonz. 20.8.3 (I.V.65). It is worth noting that there is plenty of evidence that the institutions of the day did attempt to exercise control in this area. For example, as Guido Ruggiero has noted, the authorities in the Veneto were concerned that homosexual advances were often made to young boys in school settings, so that in 1477 a Venetian *parte* directed that all instruction had to take place in groups gathered in public halls, not individually in private rooms (*Boundaries of Eros*, 138). I am grateful to Wayne Rebhorn for drawing my attention to this reference.

3

Virgil, Christianity, and the Myth of Venice

Accommodation: Virgil as poeta theologus

Not long after it came off the presses in 1537, a copy of the large folio edition of Virgil published by Lucas Antonius Junta came into the hands of an unknown scholar whose annotations reveal unusually wide reading,[1] ranging from Diodorus Siculus (Pt. II, fo. 183^r) and Aulus Gellius (Pt. II, fo. 124^r) to Jerome (Pt. II, fo. 38^r) and Lactantius (Pt. II, fo. 195^r) to Boccaccio (Pt. I, fo. 108^v; Pt. II, fos. 195^v, 242^v) and Politian (Pt. II, fo. 54^r; Pt. III, fo. 39^r). This scholar's favourite point of reference in his study of Virgil, however, was Augustine, and his notes show a constant concern with the religious content of the poetry, particularly as it could be used to distinguish the false gods of antiquity from the true God of Christianity. At *Aeneid* 2. 501–2, for example, Servius explained that in the empty prayers of Priam, *latenter ostenditur nihil prodesse religionem* ('it is shown secretly that religion is of no benefit'). For our early reader, this sweeping generalization misses the key point, which he extracts from Augustine, *De civitate Dei* 1. 2: these gods were of no benefit to Priam because they are false gods (Pt. II, fo. 65^r). He makes the same point more forcefully a few folios later, where he writes that *templum junonis sanctissimum non potuit liberare suos troyanos ex manibus grecorum quia vani erant Dii eorum; vid. Aug. lib. j. de c. dei cap. 4* ('the hallowed temple of Juno was not able to

---

[1] The current location of this book (Padua, Biblioteca Antoniana, shelf mark V.VI.15) suggests that the scholar who annotated it may have been a cleric, but whether or not that was the case, it is worth emphasizing that the commentary is among the most learned I have seen in preparing this study. References to this commentary will be placed in the text of this para.

free her Trojans from the hands of the Greeks because their gods were empty; see Augustine, *De civ. Dei* 1. 4'; Pt. II, fo. 74ᵛ, on *Aen.* 2. 761–7). Where one of the printed commentaries drew a parallel between *Eclogue* 1 and the proper Christian God, the reader adds a precise reference in the margin: *David, Psalm 119* (Pt. I, fo. 6ʳ). And when Servius provided an interpretation of *Aeneid* 4. 331 that is consonant with Christian thought, a marginal note indicates satisfaction (*vid. bene*; Pt. II, fo. 123ʳ).

This is not the only Renaissance edition whose handwritten marginal notes suggest that early readers in the Veneto were in the habit of searching for parallels between Virgil and Christianity. A handwritten note added to a copy of the 1543–4 heirs of Lucas Antonius Junta edition, for example, focuses on *Aeneid* 6. 853 to observe that kindness toward the humble is as Augustinian as it is Virgilian:

Augustinus De civitate Dei, superbis Deus resistit, humilibus autem dat gratiam. Hoc vero quod Dei est, superbae quoque animae spiritus inflatos affectat, amatque sibi in laudibus dici, Parcere subiectis, et debellar[e] superbos.

(Augustine says in the *City of God* [preface], 'God resists the proud, but gives grace to the humble' [Jas. 4: 6]. But that which is of God tries to gain control over the swollen pride of the overbearing spirit and loves it to be said in its praise that it 'spares the subjected and tames the proud'.)[2]

A handwritten commentary added to a copy of the 1536–7 edition of Lucas Antonius Junta[3] extends the same process to the *Eclogues*, where a marginal note indicates that in *Eclogue* 4 *Sibylla Augusto divam virginem ostendit* ('the Sibyl reveals the holy maiden to Augustus'; fo. 3ᵛ).

On the one hand, this association of Virgil with Christianity should not come as a great surprise to us. Modern scholarship has generally laid to rest at least the extreme overgeneralizations like

---

[2] Venice, Biblioteca Nazionale Marciana, 146.d.18. Virgil's poetry, of course, played a significant role in Augustine's thought; see the essays collected in John J. O'Meara, *Studies in Augustine and Eriugena*, ed. Thomas Halton (Washington, 1992), 59–87, 103–17.

[3] Vicenza, Biblioteca Bertoliana, C.15.8.8, with a dated note at the end, *MDXXXXIII, Tria antiquissima monumenta nuper reperta cum tribus epitaphiis* ... (fo. 49ʳ), which provides an approximate date for the other annotations. In the context of the present chapter, it is perhaps worth noting that this vol. of Virgilian poetry still has its original binding of boards covered by tooled leather, with a wide variety of religious texts visible as binder's waste—an accommodation of another, but not unrelated, sort.

that of Burckhardt, who wrote that Renaissance 'humanism was, in fact, pagan, and became more and more so as its sphere widened in the fifteenth century'.[4] As a result, a recent exploration of 'humanity and divinity in Italian humanist thought'[5] paves the way toward understanding what we find in the early printed editions of Virgil. Indeed, many of those early readers from the Veneto who encountered the world of humanism through their texts of Virgil were also clerics: *Frater Andreas Nicsil Utinensis ordinis S. Augustini, Giovanni Battista Braccini, Frater Adrianus Leonicenus ordinis predicatorum, Ascanius Varese Patavinus Abbas Generalis Congr. Laterensis, Sig. Cardinale Cosetti, Joannes Petrus Calegarius Presbyter*, etc.[6] And other early possession notes show that copies of Virgil ended up regularly in monastic libraries throughout the Veneto, like those of the Dominican order of the observance of S. Maria del Rosario in Venice, S. Maria del Gesù in Treviso, the Dominican S. Maria

---

[4] *The Civilization of the Renaissance in Italy*, 2 vols. (New York, 1958; repr. of New York, 1929 edn.), ii. 479–80. Burckhardt's analysis of religion was vigorously countered by Giuseppe Toffanin, *History of Humanism*, trans. Elio Gianturco (New York, 1954). Parts of Burckhardt's approach are currently enjoying a revival of sorts in some quarters; see William Kerrigan and Gordon Braden, *The Idea of the Renaissance* (Baltimore, 1989).

[5] Charles Trinkaus, *In Our Image and Likeness: Humanity and Divinity in Italian Humanist Thought*, 2 vols. (Notre Dame, Ind., 1995; repr. of Chicago, 1970 edn.). See also Paul Oskar Kristeller, *Renaissance Thought: The Classic, Scholastic, and Humanist Strains* (New York, 1961; repr. of Cambridge, Mass., 1955 edn.), 70–91; Erich Cochrane, *Italy 1530–1630*, ed. Julius Kirschner, Longman History of Italy (London, 1988), 118–23; and the essays contained in Timothy Verdon and John Henderson (eds.), *Christianity and the Renaissance: Image and Religious Imagination in the Quattrocento* (Syracuse, NY, 1991), esp. pt. 3, 'The World of the Christian Humanist', 445–532. A good bibliography of recent work in this area may be found in the headnote to Charles Trinkaus, 'Italian Humanism and Scholastic Theology', in Albert Rabil, Jr. (ed.), *Renaissance Humanism: Foundations, Forms, and Legacy*, iii. *Humanism and the Disciplines* (Philadelphia, 1988), 344–5, with a useful summary of important trends in the article in the same vol. by John F. D'Amico, 'Humanism and Pre-Reformation Theology', 349–79. Older scholarship is surveyed in Pino Da Prati, 'Il problema religioso nell'Umanesimo', in *Giovanni Dominici e l'Umanesimo* (Naples, 1965), 34–51. Nevertheless, as John Martin recently pointed out, many American and British scholars still sidestep religious questions in their study of the Renaissance ('Recent Italian Scholarship on the Renaissance: Aspects of Christianity in Late Medieval and Early Modern Italy', *Renaissance Quarterly*, 48 (1995), 609).

[6] The books owned by these clerics, along with their present locations, are as follows: the 1507 Bernardinus Stagninus edn., Padua, Biblioteca del Museo Civico, F.7445; 1532–3 Lucas Antonius Junta, Venice, Biblioteca Nazionale Marciana, Rari v.15; 1546 Cominus de Tridino, Venice, Biblioteca Nazionale Marciana, 147.d.13; 1553 Hieronymus Scotus, Padua, Biblioteca Universitaria, 64.a.168; 1562 Joannes Maria Bonellus, Venice, Biblioteca Nazionale Marciana, 134.d.58; and 1566 Joannes Maria Bonellus, Venice, Biblioteca Nazionale Marciana, 19.t.2. One can only wish that the 1543–4 heirs of Lucas Antonius Junta edn., now Padua, Biblioteca del Museo Civico, I.130 but once owned by a *Rabbi Ira Mi* … (fo. +1ʳ), contained annotations.

Gratiarum in Padua, and the Capuchin brothers in Verona.[7] Given the importance of the church in the life and culture of Renaissance Venice, it would seem that in some way or other, the myth of Venice would have to embrace some sort of accommodation between Virgil and the Christian faith.

On the other hand, however, such an accommodation threatens to upset some of our most fundamental assumptions about Renaissance culture. By the end of the sixteenth century, avant-garde Italian scholars had spent two hundred years refining and cultivating 'the critical and historical habit of sizing up authors in their proper dimensions', of studying the classics and trying to 'understand them as a historical phenomenon'. That is, 'it was humanism which placed Virgil back into his historical context; and which tried to explain Aristotle in terms of the problems and sciences of the Athens of the fourth century before Christ'.[8] To suggest that the Christian God favours the same humility as Virgil,

---

[7]   The books owned by these institutions along with their present homes are: 1574–5 heirs of Joannes Maria Bonellus, Venice, Biblioteca Nazionale Marciana, 134.d.54; c.1488 Liga Boaria, Venice, Biblioteca Correr, Inc. E. 233; 1479 Leonardus Achates, Vicenza, Biblioteca Bertoliana, Gonz. 20.8.3 (1.V.65); and 1597 Joannes Baptista and Joannes Bernardus Sessa, Verona, Biblioteca Civica, Cinq. C.583. Venetian books also ended up, of course, in church libraries outside the Veneto: a 1480 edn. published by Petrus de Piasis et al., now Los Angeles, University of California Research Library, Spec. Coll. *A1/V819 1480, ended up at a Franciscan monastery in Fiesole; a 1491–2 Philippus Pintius edn., now Venice, Biblioteca Nazionale Marciana, Inc. V. 134, bears a provenance note Conventus Cracoviensis S. Trinitatis ordinis praedicatorum S. Dominici (fo. Aa2ʳ); a 1544 Hieronymus Scotus edn., now in Rome's Biblioteca Nazionale Centrale, and a 1566 Joannes Maria Bonellus edn. now in the same library, were both once in the library of the Jesuit Collegio Romano; and a 1581 Joannes Baptista Sessa and brothers / heirs of Franciscus Rampazetus edn., now Copenhagen, Det Kongelige Bibliotek, folio 74ˡ–119, was once owned by Loci Immaculatae Conceptionis Mediolani (fo. 318ᵛ). A particularly interesting copy of the 1566 Joannes Maria Bonellus edn., now Rome, Biblioteca Nazionale Centrale, 71.3.E.8, once belonged to the Jesuit Collegio Romano. The reader who entered the marginal notes in this vol. did little beyond an occasional textual emendation until he reached Aeneas' descent to the underworld in Bk. 6 (fos. 241 ff.), but at this point he began interacting vigorously with both the text and the printed commentary, underlining allegorizations (fo. 241ᵛ) and scriptural parallels (fo. 243ʳ) from Ascensius' commentary and even making a cross and falsum ('incorrect') next to a gloss in which Servius notes that Lucretius and other individuals denied the existence of the underworld (fo. 242ᵛ). Romeo de Maio, 'I modelli culturali della Controriforma: Le biblioteche dei conventi italiani alla fine del Cinquecento', in Riforme e miti nella Chiesa del Cinquecento (Naples, 1973), 365–81, calls attention both to the existence of a series of monastic library catalogues from the end of the 16th cent. in Biblioteca Apostolica Vaticana, Vat. lat. 11266–11326 and to the need to study and organize this material so that it can be made useful for historical study.

[8]   Eugenio Garin, Italian Humanism: Philosophy and Civic Life in the Renaissance, trans. Peter Munz (New York, 1965), 6, 14–15.

however, or to read *Aeneid* 6 in connection with Christian ideas about heaven and hell, threatens to do something quite different: to remove the *Aeneid* from its historical context and yoke it arbitrarily to the ideas and values of another, later culture. Such critical assumptions veer dangerously close to making Virgil into a prophet of Christ—a notion that has remained stereotypically 'medieval' since the days of Comparetti.[9]

In the first part of this chapter, I shall attempt to show that the commentaries most frequently published in the Renaissance Venetian editions of Virgil provided their early readers with enough interpretive cues to steer between the Scylla of ahistorical syncretism and the Charybdis of a pure classicism that had little bearing on an everyday life infused with the goals and values of Christianity. To do this, I shall first look briefly at the traditional relationship between poetry and theology as it had been understood in late antiquity and the Middle Ages and modified by the first generation or two of Renaissance humanists. I shall then turn to selected passages in the three most important commentaries printed in Renaissance Venice, to show how the authors of these commentaries forged a progressively tighter link between Virgil and their Christian faith. Finally, I shall examine from this perspective Marco Girolamo Vida's *Christias*, an epic poem whose fusion of the Christian and the Virgilian both draws on Renaissance readings of the *Aeneid* and helps in turn to shape those readings. In this way I hope to show that anyone who read Virgil in an edition of the Venetian Renaissance was forced to confront the relationship between pagan and Christian in ways that our modern habits of approaching the classics threaten to obscure.

From its beginnings, Christianity struggled to develop an appropriate response to the religious content of pagan poetry. For a few of the most pious, prohibition was the only answer, but the famous dream in which Jerome imagines himself being turned away from the heavenly gates because he was more Ciceronian than Christian shows how difficult it was for the intellectual leaders of the early church to turn their backs on the culture in which

---

[9] Domenico Comparetti, *Virgilio nel Medioevo*, ed. Giorgio Pasquali, 2 vols. (Florence, 1981; repr. of Florence, 1943 edn.), i. 118–27.

they had been trained.[10] In theory at least, a type of cultural relativism that allows all peoples their own religious beliefs offered another possible response, but in fact such open-mindedness was almost impossible in an age when many individuals took their religion seriously enough to die willingly for it. The most common response was to view the content of pagan poetry as containing at least some elements of Christian truth, either because the author consciously concealed a hidden truth below a deceptive surface or because the author received unconscious access to that truth through divine inspiration. This made pagan poetry into a kind of prophecy, in need of interpretation to reveal its hidden meanings—a 'poetic theology', or *theologia poetica*.[11]

The tradition of the poet as theologian had a long and venerable history that later writers traced back as far as Aristotle (*Metaphysics* 1. 3. 983^{b}28–30). Allegory allowed almost limitless opportunities for identifying the prophetic statements in ancient poetry that foretold later revealed truth, and medieval authors ranging from Abelard to Innocent III took advantage of these opportunities.[12] The diverse strands of this tradition were collected

----

[10]   A discussion of the letter in which the dream appears (*Epist.* 22), with a thorough analysis of recent bibliography, may be found in Steven M. Oberhelman, *Rhetoric and Homiletics in Fourth-Century Christian Literature*, American Classical Studies, 26 (Atlanta, 1991), 64 n. 5.

[11]   Trinkaus, *In Our Image*, ii. 683–9. Stanley Meltzoff, *Botticelli, Signorelli and Savonarola: Theologia Poetica and Painting from Boccaccio to Poliziano*, Biblioteca di 'Lettere Italiane', Studi e testi, 32 (Florence, 1987), 5–6, provides a broader definition: '*Theologia poetica*, Pico della Mirandola's phrase, is our present summary for a collection of attitudes about the place in the cosmos of a mankind created in the image of God, the ways in which God revealed himself outside the Scriptures in ancient poetry and philosophy, and the means by which this knowledge might be revealed. Poetic theology was the common center of a group of ideas about the dignity of man, his progress and perfectibility.' This definition leads Meltzoff to describe Trinkaus, *In Our Image* as 'a masterful thousand-page summary of the poetic theology' (6), where in fact only the section entitled 'From *Theologia poetica* to *Theologia platonica*' (ii. 683–721) deals with this topic. Meltzoff's definition of *theologia poetica*, in other words, threatens to become so broad as to include most of Renaissance philosophy, which strikes me as less than useful terminologically, but the book as a whole is a fascinating example of how the concept can illuminate the history of art as well as intellectual and literary history.

[12]   Ronald Witt, 'Coluccio Salutati and the Conception of the *Poeta Theologus* in the Fourteenth Century', *Renaissance Quarterly*, 30 (1977), 539–42. As Ernst Robert Curtius points out, modern scholars believe that in Aristotle's system poetry cannot actually be equated to theology (*European Literature and the Latin Middle Ages*, trans. Willard Trask, Bollingen Series, 36 (Princeton, 1953), 218), but this point rests on an understanding of the *Poetics* that would not have been possible in the Middle Ages and early Renaissance. See O. B. Hardison, Jr., 'The Place of Averroes' Commentary on the *Poetics* in the History of

together at the beginning of the fourteenth century by the Paduan prehumanist Albertino Mussato, who presented nine reasons to consider poetry divine: (1) from its earliest manifestations, poetry has been called theology, (2) poetry discusses theological issues, (3) poets are called prophets, (4) poetry was given to us by God, (5) poetry causes wonder and delight for its audience, (6) Moses used poetry to thank God for freeing Israel from bondage, (7) poetry is in accordance with the Bible, (8) the beauty of poetry is eternal, and (9) the Christian faith was announced by means of poetry.[13] Indeed, for Mussato, ancient poetry, like the Bible itself, was inspired directly by God.[14]

From this point on, the theory of the poet as theologian became a cornerstone of humanist poetics.[15] However, as Mussato's arguments were taken up again and refined over the next couple of generations, new complexities were discovered and acknowledged. In his *Invective contra medicum*, for example, Petrarch develops several of Mussato's points with a slightly different emphasis:

Primos nempe theologos apud gentes fuisse poetas et philosophorum maximi testantur, et sanctorum confirmat autoritas, et ipsum, si nescis, poete nomen indicat. In quibus maxime nobilitatus Orpheus, cuius decimoctavo civitatis eterne libro Augustinus meminit. At nequiverunt quo destinaverant pervenire, dicet aliquis. Fatebor. Nam perfecta cognitio veri Dei, non humani studii, sed celestis est gratie. Laudandus tamen animus studiosissimorum hominum, qui certe quibus poterant viis ad

---

Medieval Criticism', in John L. Lievsay (ed.), *Medieval and Renaissance Studies: Proceedings of the Southeastern Institute of Medieval and Renaissance Studies, Summer, 1968* (Durham, NC, 1970), 57–81.

[13] In 1316 Mussato engaged in a debate with the Dominican Fra Giovannino da Mantova over these issues. Mussato's letter to Fra Giovannino does not survive, but in good scholastic fashion his opponent summarizes his arguments before responding to them, and it is from this summary that I have presented Mussato's position. Fra Giovannino's letter (with an Italian trans.) may be found in Eugenio Garin, *Il pensiero pedagogico dello Umanesimo*, I classici della pedagogia italiana (Florence, 1958), 2–13. Mussato's ideas as summarized in this letter are similar to those developed in his *Epist.* IV, VII, and XVIII, which suggests that Fra Giovannino's summary is probably accurate enough; see Garin, *Pensiero pedagogico*, 2, headnote, and Giorgio Ronconi, *Le origini delle dispute umanistiche sulla poesia (Mussato e Petrarca)*, Strumenti di ricerca, 11 (Rome, 1976), 17–59, esp. 34–5. Italian translations of all three letters may be found in Manlio Dazzi, *Il Mussato preumanista (1261–1329): L'ambiente e l'opera*, Collana di varia critica, 22 (Vicenza, 1964), 181–3, 188–95.

[14] Dazzi, *Mussato preumanista*, 14; and Witt, 'Coluccio Salutati', 539–42.

[15] August Buck, *Italienische Dichtungslehren vom Mittelalter bis zum Ausgang der Renaissance*, Beihefte zur Zeitschrift für romanische Philologie, Heft 94 (Tübingen, 1952), 72.

optatam veri celsitudinem anhelabant, adeo ut ipsos quoque philosophos in hac tanta et tam necessaria inquisitione precederent. Credibile est etiam hos ardentissimos inquisitores veri ad id saltem pervenisse, quo humano perveniri poterat ingenio, ut—secundum illud Apostoli supra relatum—per ea que facta sunt, invisibilibus intellectis atque conspectis, prime cause et unius Dei qualemcunque notitiam sortirentur; atque ita deinceps omnibus modis id egisse, ut—quod publice non audebant, eo quod nondum viva veritas terris illuxerat—clam suaderent falsos deos esse, quos illusa plebs coleret.

(Certainly the greatest philosophers testify and the authority of the saints confirms that the first theologians among the gentiles were the poets, and, if you do not know it, the name of poet itself indicates it. Among these Orpheus was especially ennobled, whom Augustine mentions in the eighteenth book of the *City of God*. 'But they failed to arrive at the destination they sought,' someone will say. I shall admit it, for perfect knowledge of the true God is the consequence not of human study but of heavenly grace. Nevertheless the spirit of these most studious men should be praised, because, by what roads they could, they panted after the desired height of truth so that they preceded the philosophers in this very great and necessary inquiry. It should be believed also that these most ardent investigators of the truth did at least reach as far as they were able to go by human powers, so that, according to that principle of the Apostle stated above, invisible things having been known and seen from those things that are made, they attained to some sort of knowledge of the first cause and of the one God; and thus they successively acted in all ways so that, what they did not dare do publicly because the living truth had not yet illumined the world, they might secretly persuade—that the gods were false whom the deluded people worshipped.)[16]

Here Petrarch begins with the basic idea that the first pagan poets were theologians, but he develops the point with a sense of caution not found in Mussato: the poets were forced to conceal their challenge to polytheism, and they did not attain full and perfect knowledge of God, but went as far as they could go in their time and culture. In his *Genealogie deorum gentilium*, Boccaccio concedes a key point of chronology by admitting that

---

[16] Francesco Petrarca, *Invective contra medicum*, ed. Pier Giorgio Ricci (Rome, 1950), 71–2, qtd. in Trinkaus, *In Our Image*, ii. 692. This para. and the one that follows are derived from Trinkaus's masterful discussion, with the translations being adapted from the same source. On Petrarch's relationship to Venetian culture, see P. O. Kristeller, 'Il Petrarca, l'Umanesimo, e la Scolastica a Venezia', in *La civiltà veneziana del Trecento* (Florence, 1956), 149–78; and Manlio Pastore Stocchi, 'La biblioteca del Petrarca', in *Storia della cultura veneta*, ii. Girolamo Arnaldi (ed.), *Il Trecento* (Vicenza, 1976), 536–65.

Moses was the originator of this *theologia poetica* and that the Greeks followed him and the other poet-prophets of the Hebrew Bible.[17] Coluccio Salutati, the third great early Florentine humanist, clarifies in turn what could and could not be done in interpreting poetry in this tradition:

Omnia, inquam, que apud poetas fabulosa videntur, oportet vel ad deum vel ad creaturas aut ad aliquid ad hos pertinens debita expositione reduci. Cumque poetarum abdita misticus interpres aperiet, et ad deum, naturam, vel mores singula referens adaptaverit, sine dubitatione reputet se, quamvis incogitatum ab autore dici queat id quod invenerit, in sententiam tolerabilem incidisse. Quod si ad illa que senserit adaptare poterit propriorum nominum rationem, audacter affirmem ipsum sine controversia veram auctoris elicuisse sententiam, aut si forsitan illa non fuerit, et ad id quod autor intendisset nomina non accedant, longe commodiorem sensum quam cogitaverit invenisse.

(I say that everything that seems fabulous in the poets must necessarily be reduced by due exposition to God or to creatures or to something pertaining to them. When the mystical interpreter reveals the hidden meanings of the poets, and modifies each detail by referring it to God, nature, or customs, he may certainly suppose that he has hit upon an acceptable interpretation, even though what he has found can be said to have been unintended by the author. But if he can fit the significance of the proper names to the meaning he has found, I would boldly assert that he has unquestionably elicited the author's true meaning; or if this is not the case, and the names do not fit what the author has intended, I would assert that he has found a much more fitting sense than that which the author meant.)[18]

In this passage Salutati offers an honest admission that the standard against which pagan poetry is to be measured is Christian truth. If possible, interpretation ought to uncover what the poet-theologian had really meant, but if adapting pagan poetry to Christian truth produces something that violates authorial intention, such a violation is nevertheless an 'acceptable interpretation … a much more fitting sense than that which the author meant'.

Such ideas became the common currency of Italian humanism, with a Venetian version appearing in the *De concordantia poetarum, philosophorum, et theologorum,* written in the middle of the fifteenth

---

[17] Trinkaus, *In Our Image,* ii. 695.
[18] *De laboribus Herculis,* ed. B. L. Ullman (Zürich, 1951), 86, qtd. in Trinkaus, *In Our Image,* ii. 700.

century by Giovanni Caldiera and published in Venice some one hundred years later.[19] The relevant sections are in Book 1, where Caldiera explains that the human perceives the divine in four ways, proceeding from observation and poetic myth-making, to inspired prophecy, then to revelation in the incarnation of Christ, and finally to a direct and final vision of God. The first three stages are earthly, corresponding to non-scriptural philosophical and poetic modes of knowledge, to knowledge about the future revealed through prophets and sibyls, and to theological insight as seen in the incarnation; thus God, according to Caldiera, is perceived by poets, philosophers, and theologians alike (fos. 3^v–4^v). This elaboration of the *theologia poetica* tradition allows Caldiera to find a great many Christian truths, such as the mystery of the Trinity, obscured in the poetry of the ancients (fos. 6^r–9^r).[20]

Given Virgil's continued popularity throughout the Middle Ages and Renaissance, we should not be surprised that his poetry was subjected regularly to this sort of interpretation. Mussato claims that *nostra fides sancto tota est praedicta Maroni* ('our faith was completely prophesied by holy Virgil').[21] Salutati in turn cites *Aeneid* 1. 664–5 as a discussion concerning *unitate scilicet essentie et multiplicitate persone* ('the unity of essence and the multiplicity of person'), a truth that was hidden from Virgil but in conformity with the true God.[22] In his letter to Giuliano Zonarini, Salutati cites this same passage along with others that illustrate Christian doctrines: *Eclogue* 8. 72–4 adumbrates the Trinity; *Aeneid* 3. 409, the institution of the church; *Aeneid* 6. 616–17, the existence of hell; and *Aeneid* 6. 743–4, the existence

---

[19] Biographical and bibliographical information on this humanist-physician may be found in Margaret L. King, *Venetian Humanism in an Age of Patrician Dominance* (Princeton, 1986), 344–5, with a discussion of his ideas in ead., 'Personal, Domestic, and Republican Values in the Moral Philosophy of Giovanni Caldiera', *Renaissance Quarterly*, 28 (1975), 535–74. Trinkaus's discussion is based primarily on his reading of the text in Vatican City, Biblioteca Apostolica Vaticana, Urb. lat. 1178, since the printed edn. (Venice: Cominus de Tridino, 1547) 'constantly makes such misreadings as *diversitas* for *divinitas* and is worse than useless' (*In Our Image*, ii. 868 n. 64). I have used the Vatican ms as well (with references placed in the text), in part by default, since I have not been able to gain access to a copy of the printed edn.; however, given that 'literary works are fundamentally social rather than personal or psychological products' (Jerome McGann, *A Critique of Modern Textual Criticism* (Chicago, 1983), 43–4), one could argue that a poorly prepared printed text is at least as important for the concerns of this book as an accurate ms that was seen by relatively few people.

[20] Trinkaus, *In Our Image*, ii. 704–7.

[21] As qtd. by Fra Giovannino da Mantova, in Garin, *Pensiero pedagogico*, 6.

[22] *De laboribus Herculis*, 82–3, qtd. in Trinkaus, *In Our Image*, ii. 865 n. 42.

of purgatory and paradise. Here he suggests that the poet was directly influenced by God.[23] Other scholars proceeded in much the same way, with the descent to the underworld in *Aeneid* 6 offering the most obvious opportunities for discussion. Francesco da Fiano (d. 1425), for example, cites *Aeneid* 6. 724–5 to show that Virgil is in accord with the Bible, although he speaks with greater stylistic elegance.[24] In the middle of the sixteenth century, as part of the Counter-Reformation flowering, Lamberto Ortensio Monforte turned to *Aeneid* 6. 265 and provided a tissue of parallel citations on chaos from classical authors, although he ultimately concluded that it would be simpler and more accurate to get the same information directly from Genesis.[25]

The most famous application of *theologia poetica* to Virgil, however, is the conversion of *Eclogue* 4 to the *Messianic Eclogue* that prophesies the coming of Christ. The poem in part reads as follows:

> Ultima Cumaei venit iam carminis aetas;
> magnus ab integro saeclorum nascitur ordo.
> iam redit et Virgo, redeunt Saturnia regna,
> iam nova progenies caelo demittitur alto.
> tu modo nascenti puero, quo ferrea primum
> desinet ac toto surget gens aurea mundo,
> casta fave Lucina: tuus iam regnat Apollo.
>
> .   .   .   .
>
> si qua manent sceleris vestigia nostri,
> inrita perpetua solvent formidine terras.
>
> .   .   .   .
>
> ipsae lacte domum referent distenta capellae
> ubera, nec magnos metuent armenta leones;
> ipsa tibi blandos fundent cunabula flores.
> occidet et serpens, et fallax herba veneni
> occidet; Assyrium vulgo nascetur amomum.
>
> (Now hath the last age come, foretold by the Sibyl of Cumae;
> Mightily now upriseth a new millennial epoch.

[23] *Epistolario di Coluccio Salutati*, ed. Francesco Novati, 4 vols. (Rome: Istituto Storico Italiano, 1891–1911), i. 304, qtd. in Witt, 'Coluccio Salutati', 547.

[24] Vladimiro Zabughin, *Vergilio nel Rinascimento italiano da Dante a Torquato Tasso*, 2 vols. (Bologna, 1921–3), i. 116 and 137 n. 50. Basic information on Francesco's criticism may be found in Concetta Carestia Greenfield, *Humanist and Scholastic Poetics, 1250–1500* (Lewisburg, Penn., 1981), 168–77.

[25] Zabughin, *Vergilio*, ii. 77–8.

Justice the Maid comes back, and the ancient glory of Saturn;
New is the seed of man sent down from heavenly places.
Smile on the new-born Babe, for a new earth greets his appearing;
Smile, O pure Lucina; the iron age is departing,
Cometh the age of gold; now reigns thy patron Apollo.
. . . .
Should some lingering traces of old-world wickedness haunt us,
They shall perish, and fear from the earth be banished for ever.
. . . .
Home shall the goats their udders bring with milk heavy-laden,
Willingly, nor great lions affright men's cattle hereafter.
Even thy cradle, O Babe, shall pour forth flow'rs to caress thee,
Snakes shall perish, and plants whose fruit is treacherous poison;
All the whole earth shall be sweet with the breath of Assyrian
    spikenard.)

(ll. 4–10, 13–14, 21–25)[26]

In the fourth century AD, the emperor Constantine delivered an
address to an ecclesiastical assembly in which the parallels between
this passage and Christian doctrine were developed at some length:
the *nova progenies* ('new … seed of man') is Christ, the *virgo* ('maid')
is Mary, the disappearance of human crimes results from the resurrection of Christ and the institution of baptism, the lions no longer
feared by flocks are governmental authorities who persecute the
faithful, the serpent is the one from Genesis who disappears to
symbolize the defeat of Satan, the *amomum* ('spikenard') stands for
the propagation of the Christian faith, and so forth.[27] Not all the
Church Fathers accepted all these details: Lactantius favoured a
Christian interpretation but connected it not to Christ's birth but

[26] Throughout this chapter, hexameter translations of *Ecl.* 4 are from Thomas Fletcher
Royds, *Virgil and Isaiah: A Study of the Pollio* (Oxford, 1918), 74–85. A good close reading
of the text may be found in John Van Sickle, *A Reading of Virgil's Messianic Eclogue* (New
York, 1992); see esp. 117–41.

[27] The address, 'Oratio ad coetum sanctorum', has been ascribed by Eusebius to
Constantine and appended by him to his *Vita Constantinii*; see Timothy Barnes, *Constantine
and Eusebius* (Cambridge, Mass., 1981), 73–6; and Salvatore Pricoco, 'Messianismo', in
Francesco della Corte (ed.), *Enciclopedia virgiliana*, 6 vols. (Rome, 1984–91), iii. 495–8, with
bibliography. Basic sources on the fourth eclogue and its religious context include E.
Norden, *Die Geburt des Kindes: Geschichte einer religiösen Idee*, Studien der Bibliothek
Warburg herausgegeben von Fritz Saxl, 3 (Leipzig, 1924); J. Carcopino, *Virgile et le mystère
de la IVᵉ Églogue*, 2nd edn. (Paris, 1943); P. Courcelle, 'Les Exégèses chrétiennes de la
quatrième Églogue', *Revue des études anciennes*, 59 (1957), 294–319; and S. Benko, 'Virgil's
Fourth Eclogue in Christian Interpretation', *Aufstieg und Niedergang der römischen Welt*, 2. 31.
1 (1980), 646–69, with a full list of potential parallels to Christianity on 662–9, a discussion
of Constantine's address on 671–2, and bibliography on 702–5.

to his promised return, while Jerome ridiculed the entire notion
that Virgil could have known Christian truth before the coming of
Christ.[28] Nevertheless, some form of Christian interpretation was
accepted by Proba, Ambrose, Prudentius, and Augustine, and in
later centuries by Abelard and Dante; indeed, Dante's Statius
explains in *Purgatorio* 22. 64–73 that *Eclogue* 4 induced his conversion to Christianity.[29] Petrarch denied a direct reference to Christ
in the poem but allowed the pious reader to make the analogy if he
or she preferred.[30] Salutati proceeded in a somewhat different way,
arguing that Virgil was a prophet, either as the result of genius, or
ignorance, or some sort of divine inspiration.[31] Leonardo Bruni
noted that the coming of Christ had been prophesied by the Sibyl,
while it was Virgil's achievement to recognize that the promised
time was at hand.[32] Antonio Mancinelli, whose *De poetica virtute*
was written at the end of the fifteenth century and published in the
1519 Venetian edition of his works, continued to refer to the
Christian prophecy of the Sibyl and the importance of *Eclogue* 4 to
this prophecy.[33] The Cumaean Sibyl in the pavement of the cathe-
dral of Siena, finished at the end of the fifteenth century, quotes
Eclogue 4. 4–7,[34] and the Christian interpretation of the poem had
its defenders well past the end of the Renaissance.[35]

[28] Pricoco, 'Messianismo', iii. 497; and Comparetti, *Vergilio nel Medioevo*, i. 101. The
references are to Lactantius, *Div. inst.* 7. 24, and Jerome, *Epist.* 53. 7 (to Paulinus of Nola).

[29] Pricoco, 'Messianismo', iii. 497; and Benko, 'Virgil's Fourth Eclogue', 670–81.

[30] Witt, 'Coluccio Salutati', 543, citing *De otio religioso*, ed. G. Rotondo, Studi e testi,
195 (Vatican City, 1958), 29.

[31] Witt, 'Coluccio Salutati', 548–9; the reference is to Salutati's second letter to
Zonarini, in *Epistolario*, i. 327.

[32] *De studiis et litteris*, in Hans Baron (ed.), *Leonardo Bruni Aretino: Humanistisch-
philosophische Schriften* (Leipzig, 1928), 15–16.

[33] Zabughin, *Vergilio*, i. 125–7.

[34] Carcopino, *Virgile*, 203 n. 1 and pl. opposite title-page.

[35] Don Cameron Allen, *Mysteriously Meant: The Rediscovery of Pagan Symbolism and
Allegorical Interpretation in the Renaissance* (Baltimore, 1970), 147–8, n. 40. In 1712 Pope
could still write *Messiah: A Sacred Eclogue Composed of Several Passages of Isaiah the Prophet,
Written in Imitation of Virgil's Pollio*; see Rosario Portale, *Virgilio in Inghilterra: Saggi* (Pisa,
1991), 100–1. While denying that Virgil forecast either the birth of Christ or the theology
of the incarnation, Royds continued to assert at the beginning of this century that spiritual
affinities bring 'us back to the old view that Virgil, like Isaiah, was a real prophet of Christ'
(*Virgil and Isaiah*, 69). And as one of the anonymous referees engaged by OUP has pointed
out, the popular Christmas carol 'It came upon a Midnight Clear' (composed in 1850) also
alludes to the prophetic nature of *Ecl.* 4: 'For lo, the days are hastening on, | By prophet
bards foretold, | When with the ever circling years | Comes round the age of gold; |
When peace shall over all the earth | Its ancient splendour fling, | And the whole world
gives back the song | Which now the angels sing'.

The longevity of this approach is a point worth stressing, since there are modern scholars who are distinctly uncomfortable with the principles on which it rests. Ciro Trabalza, for example, identifies *theologia poetica* with medieval thought, where fiction served as a means to express a truth to be discovered through allegorical interpretation. Progressive thinkers like the humanist Leonardo Bruni, according to Trabalza, argued that fiction does not leave moral traces in the reader but constitutes itself the value of art. As a result, 'the *poeta theologus* is transformed into the *poeta rhetor et philologus*', which marks progress toward the modern aesthetic conception of art. Trabalza acknowledges that *theologia poetica* was not completely abandoned in the early Renaissance, but he sees the rhetorical-philological approach as the soul of humanist criticism and the theological approach as a holdover from an outdated, medieval mode of thought.[36] Cesare Vasoli proceeds in much the same way, arguing that

the newest and most valid aspect of the humanist arguments in defence of poetry consists in the definitive substitution of the idea of a poetry that is a living and spontaneous expression of man and that narrates his deeds, describes his characteristics, sentiments, and passions, using only the perfect understanding of a refined literary technique and an effective understanding of the human spirit, in place of the medieval conception of the poet as seer and theologian and the theory of doctrinal poetry, which has the unique goal of serving a religious and moral truth.[37]

Such a simple chronological dichotomy, however, will not do; as we shall see, the assumptions of *theologia poetica* remained very much alive in the Venetian Renaissance editions of Virgil.

These assumptions remained alive at least in part, I believe, because the problems raised by this approach had still not received definitive answers in the early Renaissance. For example, one of the most basic questions raised by the concept of *theologia poetica* revolved around how the elements of Christian truth found their way into pagan poetry: did the author attain a truth compatible with Christianity through natural reason, or did that author receive unconscious access to Christian truth through divine inspiration?

[36] *La critica letteraria: Dai primordi dell'Umanesimo all'Età nostra*, ii. *Secoli XV–XVI–XVII* (Milan, 1915), 3–5.

[37] 'L'estetica dell'Umanesimo e del Rinascimento', in *Momenti e problemi di storia dell'estetica*, pt. 1. *Dall'antichità classica al barocco* (Milan, 1959), 333.

The relevant material from Petrarch, Boccaccio, and Salutati has been surveyed several times in the past century, but there is still no consensus on what it means. August Buck suggests that all three authors believed that the *poeta theologus* was inspired by a divine spirit,[38] while Ronald Witt argues that the same three authors all came to believe that any theological truths expressed by pagan poets were accessible to natural reason without any direct divine influence.[39] Trinkaus is less than clear on the entire issue, suggesting in one place, for example, that Boccaccio did not attribute direct divine inspiration to pagan poets and in another place that he did.[40] Such disagreement on the part of three well-established scholars ought to make us suspect that the relevant texts may not offer a clear, consistent approach. The problem under consideration was a complicated one, and changing rhetorical and ideological contexts would naturally have led to changing nuances in a discussion where any 'wrong' assertions could easily lead to a charge of heresy. In at least one case—that of Salutati—the effort to describe the role of the Christian God in the inspiration of pagan poets led to a complete volte-face on the subject.[41]

Thus on the threshold of the age of printing, *theologia poetica* continued to encourage students of the classics to search for parallels to Christian thought and to speculate on how those parallels came into being. And as a central text for the classical tradition, Virgil stimulated his fair share of such analysis.

At the end of the fifteenth century, the most popular Virgilian commentary among the Venetian printers was that of Cristoforo Landino.[42] Landino was a Neoplatonist whose understanding of

[38] *Italienische Dichtungslehre*, 87. As regards Petrarch, Ronconi came to the same conclusion (*Origini*, 146).

[39] 'Coluccio Salutati', 538–9. I have relied in part here on Witt's review of scholarship on this point, which is esp. acute. In 'Dante Theologus-Poeta', in *Studies in Dante*, L'Interprete, 16 (Ravenna, 1980), 83, Robert Hollander also states that the Trecento defenders of the *poeta theologus* do not claim the inspiration of the Holy Spirit for their work.

[40] Trinkaus, *In Our Image*, ii. 695, 713.

[41] Witt, 'Coluccio Salutati', 548–63.

[42] The first Venetian edn. to carry Landino's commentary was published at the end of the 1480s. Over the next twenty-five years, twenty-five Latin edns. of Virgil appeared in Venice, all but six of which contained Landino's commentary. It was still being printed in its entirety twenty years later, and Landino's preface to Virgil along with extracts from his commentary appeared in the popular Junta edns. past the middle of the 16th cent. See Craig Kallendorf, *A Bibliography of Venetian Editions of Virgil, 1470–1599*, Biblioteca de bibliografia italiana, 123 (Florence, 1991).

poetry was rooted in the concept of divine inspiration, or *furor*.[43] Although some of the key Platonic material on this subject had been in circulation for a while, Landino was also able to benefit from the work of Marsilio Ficino, whose study and translation of the *Ion* and *Phaedrus* helped make the concept a commonplace of Renaissance literary criticism.[44] Thus when Landino gets to the word *furenti* at *Aeneid* 6. 100, he stops to explain that this 'frenzy' or 'madness' is the gift of god (*divinitus infunditur*). The only people who truly deserve to be called poets are those 'who have been carried away by this divine madness' (*qui divino furore perciti*), for 'the spirit filled by god is transported to heaven' (*deoque plenus ad caelum trahitur animus*).[45]

When applied to a pagan poet like Virgil, however, this general assertion raises a couple of basic questions. Was Virgil being transported to a Christian heaven by the God of Moses, Abraham, and Jesus? If so, did he understand what happened to him—that is, did he have prophetic knowledge of events and doctrines that would be made clear to most people only after his death?

It is here that the tradition of *theologia poetica* provides Landino with a way to clarify his thinking. In the introduction to his commentary on the *Aeneid*, he writes,

Neque enim alius est magnus verusque poeta quam theologus, quod non solum Aristotelis tanti philosophi auctoritas testimoniumque ostendit, sed ipsorum quoque scripta apertissime docent. Duplex enim theologia est: altera quam priscam vocant, cuius divinus ille vir Mercurius cognomine Trimegistus primus fontem aperuit, alter nostra est, quae non modo

---

[43] 'Comento di Cristoforo Landino fiorentino sopra la Comedia di Dante Alighieri poeta fiorentino', in Cristoforo Landino, *Scritti critici e teorici*, ed. Roberto Cardini, 2 vols. (Rome, 1974), i. 140–53. Landino's basic Neoplatonism is beyond dispute, although good warnings are sounded periodically against overemphasizing this aspect of his thought: e.g. Mario Di Cesare, 'Cristoforo Landino on the Name and Nature of Poetry: The Critic as Hero', *Chaucer Review*, 21 (1986), 155–81, reminds us that Landino was first and foremost a poet; and Arthur Field, 'The *Studium Florentinum* Controversy, 1455', *History of Universities*, 3 (1983), 31–59, notes that Landino was not skilled enough as a professional philosopher to have been able to assume the philosophical part of the teaching duties associated with the vacant chair once held by Marsuppini. I think that even after both of these points have been granted, however, the discussion of Landino's poetic theory must still be anchored in Neoplatonism.

[44] Trinkaus, *In Our Image*, ii. 712–13; 712–21 of this book offer a useful introduction to *theologia poetica* and its Neoplatonic adaptation in Landino. See also Buck, *Italienische Dichtungslehre*, 91–5.

[45] *Vergilius cum quinque commentariis* (Venice: n.pub., 1492), fo. 229[r–v]; references to this edn. will be incorporated into the text.

verior comprobatur, sed ita verissima, ut neque addi quicquam nec imminui inde possit.

(For the great and true poet is none other than the theologian, which is proven not only by the authoritative testimony of so great a philosopher as Aristotle, but also by what is taught openly in the writings of the poets themselves. For theology is twofold: there is one that is called 'ancient', whose source was first opened by the godlike Mercurius Trismegistus, and the other is ours, which is not only esteemed as more true, but as so absolutely true that nothing can either be added to it or taken away from it.)[46]

Theologia prisca, or 'ancient theology', is the traditional *theologia poetica*, the line of reasoning by which Orpheus, Linus, and Musaeus wrote many true things about God and the angels, about the soul and the freedom of the will. *Theologia nostra* ('our theology') carries knowledge about God and his interactions with people from David and Moses to Dante in modern times. The two theologies, in other words, are like two branches of a stream, parallel through much of their course but not through all of it.[47]

Landino's commentary to Virgil's *Eclogue* 4 provides him with the opportunity to work out exactly how much could be known from the *theologia prisca* branch of the tradition. When Landino reaches line 4, the beginning of the section most closely associated with the Messianic exegesis of the poem, he moves immediately to provide both pagan and Christian referents for the passage: the Sibyl, he writes, prophesied many things about the Roman world, but as Augustine wrote, she also prophesied many things about Christ. Virgil, however, was ignorant of that latter theology (*verum Maro istius theologiae ignarus*), so that in fact he refers to Octavian and the events of his rule (fo. 12ʳ). At line 7, on the *nova progenies* ('new ... seed of man'), Landino again insists on having it both ways, stating that *quod sibylla de Christo praedixit, hic ad Octavianum refert* ('what the Sibyl foretold about Christ, here

---

[46] 'Christophori Landini Florentini ad Petrum Medicem Laurentii filium in P. Vergilii interpretationes prohemium incipit feliciter', in Landino, *Scritti critici e teorici*, i. 230. Cardini's commentary on this passage (ii. 303–6) is very helpful, while a more general overview of Landino's critical prefaces may be found in Frank La Brasca, ' "Scriptor in Cathedra": Les Cours inauguraux de Cristoforo Landino au "Studio" de Florence (1458–1474)', in Charles Adelin Fiorato and Jean-Claude Margolin (eds.), *L'Écrivain face à son public en France et en Italie a la Renaissance*, Actes du colloque international de Tours (4–6 Décembre 1986), De Pétrarque a Descartes, 53 (Paris, 1989), 107–25.

[47] Landino, *Scritti critici*, ii. 230–2.

refers to Octavian'). This shifting focus allows Landino to interpret *nova* in reference to *nova progenies* in three different ways, as
a 'new' kind of child who is both divine and human, as a 'new'
political wonder who will bring peace to the entire Roman
world, and as a 'new' power that can transform the human race
(fo. 12ᵛ).⁴⁸

Thus on the one hand *Eclogue* 4 illustrates the claim Landino
had made in his preface to the *Aeneid*, that the pagans had written
many true things about God and the angels, so it is perfectly
reasonable for him to search out these true things in the rest of the
Virgilian corpus. We would expect this search to be particularly
successful in *Aeneid* 6, the descent to the underworld, and so it is.
The underworld is located in the centre of the earth, as
Christianity teaches, since *dominus dixit quod filius hominis esset futu-
rus in corde terrae tribus diebus et tribus noctibus, centrum enim ita
novimus esse in medio terrae, ut cor est in medio corporis* ('God said that
the Son of Man would be in the heart of the earth for three days
and three nights, for we know that the centre is in the middle of
the earth, as the heart is in the middle of the body'; fo. 230ʳ, on
Aen. 6. 126).⁴⁹ There are five kinds of descent to the underworld,
the fifth one being a contemplation of vice so that we can recognize evil and abstain from it; this is the descent that Virgil made
under the guidance of the Sibyl, and Dante made under the guidance of Virgil (fo. 230ʳ). To be sure, before we pass from the active
life to the safe harbour of contemplation, we are tossed about by
so many storms that many of us never reach the *summum bonum*.
For this reason, at line 692 Landino cites Christ's comment to
Martha in Luke 10: 41, *Martha, Martha, sollicita es et versaris circa
plurima* ('Martha, Martha, you are troubled and concerned about
many things'), for Martha, interpreted as the active life, can teach
us that the soul that is distracted in daily affairs is rendered unfit for
the contemplation of the divine (fo. 248ᵛ). Other citations from
the Bible, ranging from Job and the Psalms to the beginning of the
Gospel of John, remind us continually that for Landino, there was

---

⁴⁸ Zabughin, *Vergilio*, i. 195–6, discusses this passage briefly; these two pages constitute
the best introduction I have seen to the relationship between the Christian religion and
Virgil's poetry in Landino's thought. See also James Garrison, *Pietas from Vergil to Dryden*
(University Park, Penn., 1992), 26–8 for an approach to this problem through Landino's use
of the Virgilian word *pietas*.

⁴⁹ The biblical reference is to Matt. 12: 40.

a deep and fundamental agreement between these two kinds of sacred texts.[50]

On the other hand, however, *theologia prisca* is ultimately not the same as *theologia nostra*. As Landino puts it in explicating *Eclogue* 4, Virgil was 'ignorant of that latter [Christian] theology', so that sometimes, as with the sibylline prophecies embedded in his bucolics, he simply did not understand the full significance of what he wrote. At other times, what he wrote turned out to be wrong. For example, the passage in *Aeneid* 6 where Anchises explains to Aeneas how human souls are cleansed and then reborn (ll. 724–51) was a difficult one, for Landino believed that Platonic reincarnation was not compatible with Christian orthodoxy. Landino explains what he sees as the plain sense of the passage, then continues

Huiuscemodi igitur ratione putavi hos versus interpretandos, non quia haec crederem, aut illis assentirer, nam de animis nostris sine ulla haesitatione eadem omnino sentio quae Christiana perhibet religio, eas esse nihilo a deo creatas et eodem tempore creatas et corporibus infusas, et pleraque alia quae nos in nostris de anima dialogis prolixius scripsimus, sed Platonem [*sic*, for Poetam?] nostrum quoniam nostrae religionis ignarus fuerit, et platonicus omnino ex[s]titerit, ad Platonicum dogma eius sententias traducendas censui.

(I thought that these verses were to be interpreted along this line of reasoning, not because I believed these things or consented to them, for concerning our souls I assert completely and without any hesitation the very same things that the Christian religion maintains, that souls are created by God out of nothing, and that they are created and put into bodies at one and the same time. I also assert a great many other things that I have written about more fully in my dialogues on the soul,[51] but as regards our Plato, I decided that since Virgil was ignorant of our religion and since he was a Platonist in all things, his ideas should be referred to Platonic doctrine.)

(fo. 250ᵛ)

Here the Christian reader has no choice but to pull back, to acknowledge that a pagan poet 'ignorant of our religion' has

---

[50]   e.g. fo. 230ᵛ, on *Aen.* 6. 126, cites Job 33; fo. 231ᵛ, on *Aen.* 6. 162, cites Ps. 115: 17–18; and fos. 249ᵛ–250ʳ, on *Aen.* 6. 724, cite John 1: 1. In 'Sacred Eloquence: Humanist Preaching and Lay Piety in Renaissance Florence', in Verdon and Henderson (eds.), *Christianity and the Renaissance*, R. Weissman points out that Landino also preached in the Florentine confraternities, and that his sermons there reconciled traditional penitential practice with the newer Neoplatonic themes he was developing in his 'secular' writings (264).

[51]   The reference is to *De nobilitate animae libri tres*, composed *c*.1471.

written something that cannot be accepted. As Landino repeatedly says in his commentary to Dante's *Divina Commedia*, one can follow Virgil and the other ancient poets only so far as Christian theology allows.[52]

Thus for Landino, a Platonizing version of the traditional *theologia poetica* provided the guidance he needed for bringing Virgil into conjunction with the Christian faith. So long as *theologia prisca* and *theologia nostra* could be brought into agreement—and they usually could—it was right and proper for a reader of Virgil to point out parallels with the Bible and with Christian authors like Augustine. On occasion, however, *theologia prisca* failed to flow in parallel with *theologia nostra*. On such an occasion, Landino was not prepared to do violence to the literal level of his text or to contort the basic chronology of the past. At that point he could only acknowledge the divergence, secure in the knowledge that with this author at least, the two theological streams would quickly flow in parallel once again.

The Virgil commentary of Jodocus Badius Ascensius, the Flemish scholar-printer, received its first Venetian printing in 1512, but it captured the market almost immediately and retained its position for the next seventy-five years as the commentary of choice among those who wanted a detailed, full-blown analysis of the text.[53] Ascensius freely acknowledged his debt to Landino,[54] so it should not surprise us to find that this new commentary resembles Landino's both in its search for parallels between the Bible and Virgilian poetry, and in its recognition of the limitations that must be placed on this search.

Ascensius does not develop a detailed theory regarding *theologia*

---

[52] In the Dante commentary as printed in *Cantica del divino poeta Danthe Alighieri fiorentino* (Venice: Bernardinus Stagninus, 1536), representative references may be found at fo. d7ʳ, on *Inf.* 4. 67–75; fo. g1ʳ, on *Inf.* 8. 67–75; and fo. g6ʳ, on *Inf.* 9. 89–90.

[53] Kallendorf, *Bibliography of Venetian Editions*. Ascensius' commentary was published in twenty-five of the sixty-seven Venetian edns. that appeared between 1512 and 1586; given that a great many of the Virgil texts published during this period were octavos without any commentary at all, it is clear that Ascensius dominated the Venetian market in Latin commentaries during this period.

[54] I have studied Ascensius' commentary in *Publii Virgilii Maronis poetae Mantuani universum poema ...* (Venice: Joannes Maria Bonellus, 1558). References to this edn. will be placed in the text. Ascensius acknowledges his debt to Landino on fo. 139ᵛ, at *Aen.* 1. 267–85; fo. 141ʳ, on *Aen.* 1. 286–96; fo. 151ʳ, on *Aen.* 1. 532; fo. 164ʳ, on *Aen.* 2. 122, etc.

poetica. It is difficult to say why this is so. As a non-Italian, he may not have had the intimate familiarity with the early humanist texts on the subject that were Landino's birthright as a Florentine. What is more, as a former schoolmaster, Ascensius tended to aim his commentary at younger students than the university audience Landino normally dealt with. He may therefore have felt that working out the intricacies of a subject like this would carry him too far afield from the principal interests of his commentary.[55] At any rate, Ascensius' practice in this area is similar to Landino's, but less subtle and intellectually rigorous.

Toward the beginning of *Eclogue* 4, for example, Ascensius acknowledges that the announcement of the final age and the newborn child indeed corresponds to the coming of Christ, but at the same time he insists that Virgil did not understand the lines in this way but rather referred them to the offspring of Caesar (fo. 21^r, on *Ecl.* 4. 1–17). Here, as elsewhere, Ascensius advocates searching for parallels between Scripture and Virgil—he later refers to the practice as 'confirming the secular through the sacred' (*prophana sacris confirmare*; fo. 258^v, on *Aen.* 6. 656–71)—but as with Landino there are limits on how far this process can go. When he comments on *Aeneid* 6. 724–51, the same passage on the reincarnation of souls that troubled Landino, Ascensius clarifies this point:

Plurima autem horum ex Orpheo et Platone efficta sunt, qui quia ex prophetarum libris et Aegyptiaea disciplina, didicerant animas immortales aliquando in corpore redituras, putabant in eadem corpora, post putre-factionem et consumptionem redire non posse, unde in alia redire dice-bant, ut asserit Divus Augustinus. Verum cum haec fere erronea sunt, licet quae ad purgationem pertinent, non penitus reprobentur, ideo altiore indagatione supersedens. ...

(A great many of these things, moreover, have been produced out of Orpheus and Plato. Since they had learned from the prophetic books and

---

55 See Paul Gerhard Schmidt, 'Iodocus Badius Ascensius als Kommentator', in August Buck and Otto Herding (eds.), *Der Kommentar in der Renaissance*, Deutsche Forschungsgemeinschaft, Kommission für Humanismusforschung, 1 (Boppard, 1975), 63–71. Ascensius also worked under tremendous time constraints: as Fred Schreiber indicated in 'The French Scholar-Printer of the Renaissance', a lecture given at Columbia Univ. on 16 and 17 July 1991, Ascensius prepared commentaries for some 110 different texts by more than seventy authors at the same time as he was supervising the printing of more than 750 different edns. The basic source on Ascensius' life and work remains P. Renouard, *Bibliographie des impressions et des œuvres de Josse Badius Ascensius, imprimeur et humaniste, 1462–1535*, 3 vols. (New York, 1967; repr. of Paris, 1908 edn.).

the wisdom of the Egyptians that the immortal souls will return at last in the body, they thought that the souls could not re-enter the same bodies after those bodies had decayed and withered away, from which they claimed that the souls returned into other bodies, as St Augustine asserts. But although these things are in general untrue, there is no reason to reject completely those things that are relevant to purgation, provided that a deeper investigation prevails.)

Here are the basic features of *theologia poetica* as developed by Landino: the association of Virgil with Plato and with a prophetic knowledge that can be traced back to Orpheus and then to the secret wisdom of Egypt, the acknowledgement that sometimes the *theologia prisca* goes astray, and the final need to correct such errors through reference to the revealed truth of *theologia nostra*, the Christian faith that Virgil did not have.

Nevertheless, even though he does not use the terms, Ascensius seems to agree that *theologia prisca* as it is found in Virgil is usually compatible with *theologia nostra*. For example, the Roman custom of *devotio*, whereby heroes like the Decii willingly sacrificed their lives for their country, is easy to transfer to a Christian value matrix, where the saints willingly sacrifice their lives for their faith (fo. 157^r, on *Aen*. 1. 712).[56] The entire sixth book presents *multa Christiano non indigna* ('many things not unworthy of a Christian'; fo. 237^r, on the arguments preceding *Aen*. 6): the eternal punishment of the guilty, the purgation of those souls only slightly defiled, the type and order of punishments meted out to sinners, and so forth. First we find the infants who died without baptism, then those who are in purgatory because of a venial sin or because they have not yet finished doing penance, then those who brought an everlasting death to their body or their soul; one and the same fire torments them all, yet they suffer in accordance with the gravity of their sin (fo. 251^v, on *Aen*. 6. 424–39).[57] Paradise, by

---

[56] The reference is to a father and son, both named Publius Decius Mus, who were popularly believed to have consecrated themselves to the gods and charged into the enemy ranks to their deaths, the father as consul in a battle against the Latins (340 BC), the son at the battle of Sentinum (295 BC). See Livy 8. 9, 10. 28.

[57] In *The Fear of Hell: Images of Damnation and Salvation in Early Modern Europe*, trans. Lucinda Byatt (University Park, Penn., 1991), 11–12, Piero Camporesi notes that the Celtic conception of the underworld as undefined open space was replaced by a Dantesque hell as a structured, hierarchical city, which was replaced in turn by a Baroque sewer without order or shape. Writing within the second of these three paradigms, Ascensius appears to view Virgil's underworld in the same basic terms.

contrast, is inhabited first by those who died for what they believed in, then by priests and prophets, then by those whose learning and actions benefited others (fo. 258ᵛ, on *Aen*. 6. 656–71).

In most cases, Ascensius has little trouble accommodating Virgilian values to those of Christianity. That is not to say that he thought Virgil had a full understanding of the Christian truths contained in his poem—or even that Ascensius troubled himself a great deal about exactly how Virgil had come to the understanding he did have. What is important, however, is that as we proceed through the sixteenth century, those who bought and read a large folio edition of Virgil published in Venice would continue to find that in the major commentary to their text, the poetry of Virgil was interpreted in line with the basic principles of their Christian faith.

As we have seen, both Landino and Ascensius were careful to balance the interpretive potential of *theologia poetica* against what they saw as limitations in the extent to which pagan poetry could be brought into line with the Bible. Two other commentators of the later sixteenth century, however, tipped the balance away from the analysis of limits toward the positing of a greater affinity between Virgil and Christian truth.

The first of these commentators, the Spaniard Juan Luis Vives, wrote a discussion of *Eclogue* 4 that was first printed in Venice in 1544 and became a standard offering in the large folio editions of Virgil published there up to the end of the century.[58] Vives's innovation was quantitative: as he put it, *omnia sunt de Christo* ('everything refers to Christ'; on l. 1) in this poem, and his explication provides a fuller analysis than any previous edition had carried. The commentary to lines 4–17 exemplifies the detail in which Vives develops his ideas. The Sibyl had foretold the coming of Christ, but Virgil discovered when he would arrive (on l. 4), as part of the golden age foretold by Isaiah (on l. 6). No Christian, according to Vives, could ever explain the coming of Christ more eloquently than Virgil did in line 7 (*iam nova progenies caelo demittitur alto*, 'new

---

[58] Vives's commentary on *Ecl*. 4 was printed a dozen times in Venice between 1544 and 1586. I have used once again the 1558 Bonellus edn., *Universum poema*; the commentary to *Ecl*. 4 is found on fos. 23ᵛ–24ʳ.

is the seed of man sent down from heavenly places'), while lines
13–14 (... *si qua manent sceleris vestigia nostri,* | *inrita perpetua solvent
formidine terras,* 'should some lingering traces of old-world wicked-
ness haunt us, | they shall perish, and fear from the earth be
banished for ever') describe how Christ cancels out the effects of
original sin in mankind. If we have faith, we have nothing to fear
(on l. 14), for the faithful will see Christ both physically and spir-
itually (on l. 16), as the Bible says: *beati oculi qui vident, quae vos vide-
tis* (Matthew 13: 16–17). This level of detail, which continues
throughout the commentary on the rest of the poem, recalls the
explication presented as part of Constantine's ecclesiastical address,
which is in fact cited here (on l. 4). The cumulative impression,
which Vives encourages at the beginning of his commentary, is
that of an ever closer fit between *Eclogue* 4 and Christianity:
*Taceant impii, nam vel simplici verborum sensu, absque ullis omnino alle-
goriis, de nullo prorsus alio potest intelligi, quod hic dicitur, quam de
Christo.* ('Let the impious be silent, for even by the straightforward
sense of the words, completely without any allegorization, what is
said here cannot be understood with reference to anything else at
all other than Christ'; on l. 1.)

The other commentator who expanded the range of Christian
readings of Virgil was Giovanni Fabrini, who began teaching in
Venice around the middle of the sixteenth century and published
a commentary in Italian to accompany the Latin text of the *Aeneid*
in 1575–6. This commentary, which was reprinted regularly into
the middle of the eighteenth century,[59] is significant not so much
for the number of parallels it presents between Virgil and the

---

[59] Actually Fabrini's commentary ends with Book 7 of the *Aeneid*, with the commentary to Books 8–12 provided by Filippo Venuti. This commentary was reprinted separately
in 1581, then as part of a book containing commentaries to the *Eclogues* (by Carlo Malatesta)
and the *Georgics* (by Venuti) in 1588 and 1597. Zabughin, *Vergilio*, ii. 372–3, cites an edn.
from as late as 1741, while Giuliano Mambelli, *Gli annali delle edizioni virgiliane*, Biblioteca
di bibliografia italiana, 27 (Florence, 1954), 111, cites one of 1751. However, the bibliographical record for this commentary is unusually chaotic. The title-page is in Italian, which
has misled some cataloguers into considering it a translation; this in turn has led to the
recording of ghost edns. (e.g. a 1588 Italian 'translation' of the text of the *Aeneid*, in
Mambelli, *Annali*, 195 (no. 804)). In addition, the edns. containing commentaries to all
three major works were often broken apart, so that ghost edns. of the separate parts also
enter the record (e.g. again the 1588 edn. cited by Mambelli as his no. 804, which he lists
here as an edn. of the *Aeneid* only). After several years of searching, I have been unable to
locate a copy of the 1568 edn. listed by Mambelli (76, no. 233), which is commonly cited
in the secondary literature as the *editio princeps* but never with an indication of where a copy
may be found.

Bible, as for the way in which it ultimately ends up reshaping the reader's understanding of *theologia poetica*.

The importance of this theme is established immediately in the letter to Cardinal Zaccaria Delfino that precedes Book 1 in the earliest editions of the commentary: [*v*]*edrà parimente teologia antica in molte parti celata dal presente poeta sotto oscuri velami di cose et scoperta dal Fabrino con fino et purgato giudicio* ('you will see as well the theology of the ancients hidden in many sections by the present poet under obscure veils and revealed by Fabrini with a refined and purified judgement').[60] Early on in the commentary proper, Fabrini moves to the relationship between Virgil and Christianity, first addressing Virgil in a way that sounds conventional enough:

O divino ingegno, o poeta degno veramente del nome di poeta, il quale non essendo Christiano, non dice cosa, che non sia simile a la dottrina Christiana. Leggi San Paolo, che tu vederai, che non attende ad altro, che a voltar gl'huomini a questa vita. Perche, cosa è, che San Paolo scrive diffusamente, che questo poeta non la confermi con parlari brevissimi e chiarissimi? E cosa veramente mirabile, che tutte le sue parole, espriminò le sententie di Platone et di Aristotele ne la Republica. ...

(O divine intelligence, o poet truly worthy of the name of poet, who although not Christian, does not say anything that is not similar to Christian doctrine. Read St Paul, who you will see does not concern himself with anything that does not turn men to this kind of life. On this account, is there anything St Paul writes about at length that this poet does not confirm with brevity and clarity? It is truly wondrous that all his words express the ideas of Plato and Aristotle in the *Republic*.)[61]

The wisdom of the Greeks passes into the *Aeneid*, which is 'similar to' Christian doctrine. The ideas sound like Landino's, and a closer look reveals that the words are his, too, taken directly from the *Disputationes Camaldulenses* and translated loosely into Italian:

O divinum ingenium! O virum inter rarissimos viros omnino excellentem et poetae nomine vere dignum! qui non Christianus omnia tamen Christianorum verissimae doctrinae simillima proferat. Lege apostolum

---

[60] The letter appears in *L'Eneide di Virgilio mantuano* ... (Venice: Joannes Baptista Sessa et fratres, 1576), fo. +2^r-v, and in the 1581 edn. of the same book, but was dropped in the series of edns. beginning in 1588 that contain commentaries to all three major works of Virgil.

[61] For the commentary to the *Aeneid*, I have used *L'opere di Virgilio mantoano* ... (Venice: Joannes Baptista and Joannes Bernardus Sessa, 1597), fo. 14^r; further references will be to this edn. and will appear in the text.

Paulum! Libet enim unum hunc ex omnibus veluti nostrae religionis caput nominare, qui vitam humanam ad huiuscemodi normam dirigit, ut neque corporis necessaria subtrahenda et vero investigando semper vacandum censeat. Quid enim ille fuse lateque describit, quod hic poeticis angustiis non coactet? Mira profecto res, ut singula paene verba longissimas e Platonica et Aristotelicaque re publica sententias amplecti valeant.

(O divine intelligence! O man completely remarkable among the rarest of men and truly worthy of the name of poet, since he, although not a Christian, nevertheless puts forth all things similar to the true Christian doctrine. Read the Apostle Paul! It pleases us to call this man alone among all men the head, as it were, of our religion, who directs human life to this sort of standard, that one might think both that bodily necessities are not to be taken away and that there should always be leisure for study and contemplation. For what does he describe at copious length, that Virgil does not tighten up with poetic concision? It is truly wondrous that long thoughts from what Plato and Aristotle have said about the republic can almost be embraced by individual words.)[62]

Since this discussion of *theologia poetica*, along with a great many other things in Fabrini's commentary, comes straight from Landino,[63] we might expect that Fabrini would continue to take his ideas on this subject, along with his examples, from his predecessor.

For a while he does just this. When he gets to *Aeneid* 6. 125–35, for example, Fabrini follows Landino in observing that the underworld is in the centre of the earth (fo. 149ʳ; see also Landino's commentary, fo. 193ᵛ). Fabrini quotes the same passages from Scripture as Landino does and justifies the references by observing that Virgil's description of the underworld *si assomiglia molto à l'opinione de' Christiani* ('is much like the ideas of the Christians'; fo. 149ʳ). However, as he proceeds further and further into *Aeneid* 6, his explanations get longer and longer. They slowly begin to strain against the limits of his source, until he finally makes a statement about *theologia poetica* that cannot be squared with what Landino wrote:

[62] *Disputationes Camaldulenses*, ed. Peter Lohe (Florence, 1980), 175.

[63] Paul Grendler, *Schooling in Renaissance Italy: Literacy and Learning, 1300–1600* (Baltimore, 1989), 248, notes that Fabrini took his civic-life allegory from Landino as well. Grendler's treatment of this commentary in general (244–50) is most welcome; seventy years ago Vladimiro Zabughin singled it out as 'of the highest importance for the history of pedagogy' (*Vergilio*, ii. 373), and I am glad to see that it is finally beginning to receive the attention it deserves.

Et considerate come questo poeta procede quasi Christianamente, che è forza, ò che lo spirito divino lo facesse parlare, conciosia che la Maestà sua molte volte s'è servito di peccatori, e de animali in scoprirsi la voluntà sua; overo che egli havea letto (come è facile da creder) i nostri libri sacri del Testamento vecchio, volesse dichiararlo quì; che egli fosse levato a questo ragionamento da spirito divino, non è gran fatto, perche la poesia è un furor divino, come benissimo prova il divin Platone. ...

(And consider how this poet proceeds like a Christian, which must be either because the Holy Spirit made him say what he did, given that God often uses sinners and animals to make known his will, or—something that is easy to believe—because he had read our holy books in the Old Testament and wanted to say here what he had read there. That he was led to this line of reasoning by the Holy Spirit is not remarkable, because poetry is a divine frenzy, as the godlike Plato so convincingly establishes.)

(fo. 167^r, on *Aen.* 6. 426–39)

Landino did not say that the Holy Spirit led Virgil, nor did he say that Virgil was familiar with the Old Testament.

This statement was not an idle slip of the pen, for Fabrini continues to develop the points raised here as he progresses through Book 6. For example, when he gets to *Aeneid* 6. 548–58, Fabrini describes the three walls that surround the city of Dis as the disposition toward sin, the act of sin, and the habit of sinning, all of which are glossed with a reference to Psalms 1: 1. Landino interpreted the passage in the same way and cited the same Bible verse. However, Fabrini adds a key sentence that is not found in Landino, but that is consistent with his belief that Virgil might have read the Old Testament: [*q*]*uesto medesimo dice Davit, in modo, che pare, che Virgilio habbia tolto questo da lui* ('David says the same thing in such a way that it appears that Virgil has taken it from him'; fo. 173^v; see also Landino's commentary, fo. 206^v, and *Disp. Cam.*, p. 248).[64] Elsewhere Fabrini picks up the idea that the *poeta theologus* might have been divinely inspired and carries it one step further. At *Aeneid* 6. 595–607, Fabrini interprets a fable from Plato in accordance with the Christian account of the creation and

[64] It is worth noting that some scholars today still believe Virgil may have had direct contact with Jewish ideas through association with Pollio, or knowledge of the Jewish versions of the Sibylline oracles, or even contact with a Septuagint version of Isaiah, although the consensus is that the more directly the contact is postulated, the less likely it was to have existed. See Benko, 'Virgil's Fourth Eclogue', 682–7, and Royds, *Virgil and Isaiah*.

redemption of man, with the explanation that *Platone nel Sinfosio, volendo mostrare l'avvenimento di Christo, fa questa mirabile et santissima favola* ('wanting to show the coming of Christ, in the *Symposium* Plato makes this wondrous and holy fable'; fo. 177ᵛ). The key point here is the claim that Plato consciously (*'wanting* to show'; emphasis mine) crafted a myth with Christian significance, something that follows logically from the attribution of direct inspiration to the *poeta theologus* but that runs directly counter to Landino's belief that Virgil was not aware of any Christian significance *Eclogue* 4 might have.

Fabrini's efforts to tighten the link between Virgil and Christianity receive an interesting kind of support from one set of illustrations that accompanied his commentary to *Aeneid* 6. In the 1588 edition, the illustrations derived from the Grüninger woodcuts give way in *Aeneid* 6 to another set of illustrations in a different, more modern style. In one of these woodcuts, a figure labelled 'D' is running toward another figure labelled 'V', with a leopard, a lion, and a wolf in hot pursuit. In another woodcut labelled *carnali cerchio secondo* ('carnal, second circle'), the figures 'D' and 'V' are conversing with two other figures who have detached themselves from a swirling mass of naked, fleeing people. 'D', of course, is Dante and 'V' is Virgil, with these woodcuts being adapted from the illustrations to Alessandro Vellutello's 1544 commentary to the *Divine Comedy*.[65] There is no reason to assume that Fabrini himself had anything to do with the transfer of these illustrations to his commentary on *Aeneid* 6, but the systematic visual allusions to the *Divine Comedy* certainly serve to tighten the link between Virgil's underworld and the Christian hell.[66]

This is not to say that Fabrini effaces all difference between the theology of the ancients and the Christian faith. In the same passage in which he suggests that Virgil either wrote under the influence of the Holy Spirit or read the Old Testament, Fabrini acknowledges that the author of the *Aeneid* was not a saint and did

---

[65] These illustrations are discussed by John Kleiner, 'Mismapping the Underworld', *Dante Studies*, 107 (1989), 1–31, esp. 30–1. I have considered the effect of these illustrations on our usual, unidirectional understanding of literary history in 'The Reader and the *Nachleben* of Classical Texts', *Modern Philology*, 92 (1994), 146–51, with the two relevant woodcuts reproduced on pp. 148–9 as pls. 2 and 3.

[66] On the relationship between the *Divine Comedy* and the *Aeneid* in the Virgil criticism of the Italian Renaissance, see Craig Kallendorf, *In Praise of Aeneas: Virgil and Epideictic Rhetoric in the Early Italian Renaissance* (Hanover, NH, 1989), 129–65.

not write his poem to reveal everything about the underworld. Nor is everything Virgil wrote in complete agreement with Catholic doctrine (fo. 167ʳ, on *Aen.* 6. 426–39): Virgil failed to place children who have died without exercising their free will in limbo, for example, but original sin directs this judgement for a Christian, *et questo si debbe credere* ('and we ought to believe this'; fo. 166ᵛ, on *Aen.* 6. 426–39). Usually Virgil and Holy Scripture tell us the same thing, but if Virgil is not enough for us, seeing that his poem is only a 'poetic fiction' (*una fintione poetica*), we can go directly to the first and principal source of truth, which is God himself (fo. 174ᵛ, on *Aen.* 6. 570–2).

Nevertheless, the similarities between Virgil and Christian doctrine overwhelm the handful of differences acknowledged in Fabrini's commentary. This is so, I believe, because Fabrini has made some significant changes in the understanding of *theologia poetica* that had governed the interpretation of Virgil up to this point. To say that an ancient poet was directly inspired by the Holy Spirit and conscious of the Christian meaning contained in his poem, and to say that a *poeta theologus* like Virgil may well have read the Old Testament, threaten to eliminate the most fundamental distinctions between *theologia poetica* and what Landino called *theologia nostra*, the Christian religion. The two streams are not yet united, but for Fabrini, the waters are very close indeed to a final union.

A final union of *theologia poetica* and Christianity does occur around Virgil—not in the commentaries themselves, but in a Christian epic composed in imitation of the *Aeneid*: the *Christias*, written by a poet named Marco Girolamo Vida.

The *Christias* was by no means the first attempt at Christian epic in the Renaissance; in the fifteenth century, Girolamo delle Valli wrote a *Gesuide*, Maffeo Vegio an *Antonias*, and the monk Ilarione da Verona a *Crisias*.[67] Yet these poems were not very popular even in their own day, so that humanistically inclined churchmen continued to feel a need for a grand epic on the life of Christ that would definitively unite the worlds of learning and faith. The Lutheran heresy made this need more urgent, so that in 1518 Pope Leo X commissioned Vida to write the long-awaited epic. The

[67] Zabughin, *Vergilio*, ii. 179–81.

finished poem was delivered to Leo's successor Clement VII in
1532, and the *editio princeps* was published three years later in
Cremona.[68] The *Christias* was an immediate success: there were
thirty-six more editions printed all over Europe—including five in
Venice—before 1600, and it was popular enough in the seventeenth century for Milton to have known and admired it.[69]

The prevailing assumption in modern criticism has been that
Vida's goal was 'to combine Christian material with pagan adorn-
ment'.[70] This is obviously true in a certain sense, but it has
produced discussions of the *Christias* that tend to leave content and
form essentially unintegrated. That is, one line of reasoning shows
how Vida uses his biblical material, beginning with Christ's journey to Jerusalem (Book 1) and his arrest there (Book 2), then
moving to the narration before Pilate of past events by Joseph
(Book 3) and John (Book 4), and concluding with the crucifixion
(Book 5) and resurrection (Book 6).[71] Another line of reasoning
concentrates on Vida's control of Virgilian devices like diction,
characterization, narrative structure, and thematic design.[72] The
temptation is then to consider the analysis finished, to pronounce
the poem a 'baroque confusion' of Christian content and pagan
form and the poet a second-rate talent who lacks a feeling for 'the
harmonious proportion of the whole'.[73] However, I believe that
content and form are in fact integrated in this poem, and that this
integration results from the way in which Vida situates himself
within the tradition of *theologia poetica* as it had been applied to the
works of Virgil.

Vida was well aware of the long association between poetry and
religion in the Latin tradition. One could certainly use the word
poeta for 'poet', but the alternative *vates* was at least as likely a

[68] Mario Di Cesare, *Vida's Christiad and Vergilian Epic* (New York, 1964), 25–8. This
book is by far the best modern treatment of the *Christias*.
  [69] Id., *Biblioteca Vidiana: A Bibliography of Marco Girolamo Vida*, Biblioteca bibliografica
italica, 39 (Florence, 1974). The *Christias* was also translated into Spanish and Italian during
the 16th cent. and received its own commentary by Bartolomeo Botta.
  [70] Hazel Alberson, 'Lo Mio Maestro', *Classical Journal*, 32 (1937), 196.
  [71] Vincenzo Cicchitelli, *Sulle opere poetiche di Marco Girolamo Vida* (Naples, 1904),
296–377; and Bonaventura Zumbini, 'Dell'epica cristiana, italiana e straniera, e particolar-
mente dei poemi del Vida e del Sannazaro', in *Studi di letteratura comparata* (Bologna, 1931),
39–62.
  [72] Gaetano Moroncini, *Sulla Cristiade di M. G. Vida* (Trani, 1896), 19–24, 50–63;
Alberson, 'Mio Maestro', 193–208; and Di Cesare, *Vida's Christiad*.
  [73] Zabughin, *Vergilio*, ii. 192; cf. Cicchitelli, *Sulle opere*, 284, 318, 321, 377–84.

choice, and *vates* meant both 'prophet' and 'poet'. Apollo and the Muses presided over poetry, and the poet would turn to them for poetic inspiration. As Vida himself reminds us in his *Ars poetica*, the traditional language for this has both religious and literary over-tones. The poet becomes a *sacerdos* ('priest')[74] of the Muses, and he approaches their *templa* ('sanctuaries'; 2. 3) *sacra ferens* ('as a sacra-ment bearer'; 2. 4) and asks that they *inspirate* ('inspire'; 2. 3) him. That is, the poet *supplicibus poscit votis, facilesque precatur* ('makes appeal in suppliant prayers, and implores godspeed'; 2. 10). The power of inspiration is certainly divine (*deus certe*; 1. 547), and it carries the inspired mind out of itself into the heavens (*afflatasque rapis super aethera mentes*; 1. 548).

Since Vida was a passionate admirer of Virgil, he concludes his *Ars poetica* with a paean to the poet of poets that makes Virgil himself the source of inspiration:

> Te colimus: tibi serta damus, tibi tura, tibi aras,
> Et tibi rite sacrum semper dicemus honorem
> Carminibus memores. salve, sanctissime vates.
> Laudibus augeri tua gloria nil potis ultra,
> Et nostrae nil vocis eget. nos aspice praesens,
> Pectoribus tuos castis infunde calores
> Adveniens, pater, atque animis te te insere nostris.

(To you we give our reverence; to you give garlands; yours is this incense, and yours the altars we make: to you we shall ever duly sing a sacred litany, remembering you in our songs. Hail, holiest of poets! Your glory cannot be increased by praise, nor does it need my voice. Be present, and look with favor upon us; come, father, pour into our pure minds your fire, and infuse yourself through our souls.)

(3. 586–92)

This is passionate admiration, to be sure, yet in a sense it does not seem all that unusual. The link between religion and poetry is built into the Latin language and confirmed by the tradition of *theologia poetica*, and there is nothing particularly inappropriate about invok-ing a pagan author at the end of a poetry-writing manual that stresses the importance of imitating classical models.

It would, however, be inappropriate to invoke a pagan poet or

---

[74] Text and translations (modified slightly) are taken from *The De arte poetica of Marco Girolamo Vida*, ed. with trans. and commentary by Ralph G. Williams (New York, 1976). References to this book will be incorporated into the text.

the pagan gods in a Christian poem, so when Vida begins his
Christias, he calls upon the Holy Spirit instead:

> Qui mare, qui terras, qui coelum numine comples
> Spiritus alme, tuo liceat mihi munere regem
> Bis genitum canere, e superi qui sede parentis
> Virginis intactae gravidam descendit in alvum,
> Mortalesque auras hausit puer, ut genus ultus
> Humanum eriperet tenebris, et carcere iniquo
> Morte sua, manesque pios inferret Olympo.
> Illum sponte hominum morientem ob crimina tellus
> Aegra tulit, puduitque poli de vertice Solem
> Aspicere, et tenebris insuetis terruit orbem.
> Fas mihi te duce mortali immortalia digno
> Ore loqui, interdumque oculos attollere coelo,
> Et lucem accipere aetheream, summique parentis
> Consilia, atque necis tam dirae evolvere causas.

(Cherishing Spirit, you who fill with godhead the sea and land and sky,
may it be given me to sing, with your help, of the twice begotten King
who from the throne of his heavenly Father descended into the chaste
virgin's womb and as a child drew human breath that as avenger he might
rescue mankind by his death from darkness and the bondage of sin and
bear the souls of the faithful to paradise. Sorrowing earth received him
who willingly died for the sins of man, and the sun, feeling shame to gaze
thereon from the zenith of the sky, terrified the world with unaccus-
tomed darkness. Under your guidance may I, a mortal, speak worthily of
things immortal, and raise the while my eyes to heaven and apprehend
celestial light, and unfold the designs of the supreme Father, and the
causes of a death so dire.)[75]

(1. 1–14)

On the level of content, this is the kind of invocation we might
well expect in a Christian epic. However, in an age when the
works of Virgil were commonly required school reading in a
process by which poetry was subjected to painstaking, word-for-
word analysis, a reader would be hard pressed not to notice some
verbal parallels to the *Aeneid* and the *Eclogues*:

l. 1   *qui mare, qui terras* omnis dicione   (*Aen.* 1. 236)
         tenerent

---

[75] I have used the text and translations (modified slightly) by Gertrude C. Drake and
Clarence A. Forbes, *Marco Girolamo Vida's The Christiad* (Carbondale, Ill., 1978).
References to this edn. will be incorporated into the text.

l. 6   dispiciunt clausae *tenebris et carcere* caeco   (*Aen.* 6. 734)
ll. 11–12 *te duce*, si qua manent ...   (*Ecl.* 4. 13)
           sit *mihi fas* audita *loqui* ...   (*Aen.* 6. 266)
           mortaline manu factae *immortale*   (*Aen.* 9. 95–6)
           carinae | *fas* habeant?

Now, one could look at this as just another example of the Christian content–Virgilian form dichotomy so often observed in modern discussions of the *Christias*. However, I believe there is more going on here than this. The tradition of *theologia poetica* had long recognized that Virgil's poetry had theological content, limited to a greater (Landino) or lesser (Fabrini) extent by the fact that Virgil was not a Christian. Imitation of Virgil's words by a Christian poet, however, creates the opportunity to remove any and all sense of limits. The Holy Spirit speaks directly through Vida, and when he speaks in Virgil's words, he does so without any partial or erroneous knowledge. The result is a fusion of Christian and pagan in the *Christias*.

The effects of this fusion are striking in Vida's allusions to *Eclogue* 4. As we have just seen, there are two allusions to the *Messianic Eclogue* in the first dozen lines of the *Christias*, and the echoes continue throughout the poem. When Joseph thinks back over the prophecies of Christ's coming, he thinks in Virgilian terms of a time when *toto surgat gens aurea mundo* ('a golden race would arise in the whole world'; *Christias* 3. 312; see also *Ecl.* 4. 9). Joseph's hopes that he would live to see the birth of Christ were tied up to his hopes for a new golden age (3. 534–8), the same Virgilian golden age that John the Baptist had foretold: *seclaque mutato succedent aurea mundo* ('a golden age shall follow when the world has been transformed'; 3. 198; see also *Ecl.* 4. 9). When Vida needs another breath of poetic inspiration, he reinvokes the Holy Spirit, once again with an echo of *Eclogues* 4. 51 (*Christias* 5. 201). Indeed the poem ends after Pentecost, when the spirit-filled followers of Christ go out into a transformed world where *toto surgit gens aurea mundo* | *Seclorumque oritur longe pulcherrimus ordo* ('a golden race arose upon all the earth, and by far the fairest succession of the ages began'; 6. 985–6).[76] The poem ends

---

[76] Di Cesare, *Vida's Christiad*, 117–18, 157–8, 160–1, 271, and 356 n. 74 signals the parallels between *Ecl.* 4 and the *Christias*. Di Cesare, however, feels that in Vida's hands the Virgilian golden age becomes a mirage, that the closing allusions are too pat, too far removed from the difficult demands placed on the church by the Reformation (282–5).

the same way it began, with an allusion to the Virgilian poem that had been linked for so many centuries to the coming of Christ.

Thus throughout the *Christias*, Virgil's words carry an unambiguous expression of Christian faith—that is, under the guidance of the Holy Spirit who is reinvoked throughout the poem, Vida used the words and images of *Eclogue* 4 to describe the golden age inaugurated by Christ. The association, as we have seen, is not an arbitrary one; the major commentaries of his day had already linked Virgil's poetry to Christian truth through the concept of *theologia poetica*.[77] Vida's achievement lay in seeing that moving from commentary on Virgil to the creation of a new poem allowed a definitive tightening of the link, in which the language of the *Messianic Eclogue* could refer unequivocally to the Messiah without doing violence to either literary history or religious dogma. Form and content become one as *theologia poetica* finally becomes *theologia nostra*, our Christian theology.

Resistance and Containment: Piety, Censorship, and the Politics of Printing

While the scholars, critics, and poets whose work we have been examining up to this point favoured an accommodation between the *theologia poetica* of the ancients and the Christian theology of their contemporaries, this was not the only option available to Virgil's Renaissance readers. As Evelyn Tribble notes, the margins of a humanist text are often the site of resistance as well as accommodation.[78] Thus for the remainder of this chapter, I would like to examine the resistance to the Virgilian theological synthesis on

---

[77]   As Di Cesare notes, we can only speculate about exactly which Virgilian commentaries Vida had studied (*Vida's Christiad*, 279). However, as I have suggested, either Landino or Ascensius, major commentators in both Venetian and non-Venetian Italian editions of Virgil, would have led him in the same general direction. We should also note, as Di Cesare does, that the process worked both ways—that is, '[i]n major ways he [Vida] shaped and influenced the *fortuna* of Vergil' (*Biblioteca Vidiana*, 7), and it is interesting (though highly speculative) to consider whether Fabrini had read the *Christias*. David Quint, *Origin and Originality in Renaissance Literature: Versions of the Source* (New Haven, 1983), 69–80, suggests that the poet Jacopo Sannazaro grappled with some of the same problems in his *De partu virginis* as Vida did. I am grateful to an anonymous reader of an earlier draft of this material for bringing this reference to my attention.

[78]   *Margins and Marginality: The Printed Page in Early Modern England* (Charlottesville, Va., 1993), 6.

the part of those who lived in Renaissance Venice or whose works were published there. First I shall look at several treatises in which challenges to the principles of *theologia poetica* led to a real ambivalence toward Virgil and his poetry. Then I shall return to the early editions of Virgil's works, to show how the religious scruples of some powerful Counter–Reformation readers helped to alter the publishing history of Virgil in Renaissance Venice.

The Dominican Giovanni Dominici, who had presided over the theological school at SS. Giovanni e Paolo beginning in 1388, was exiled from Venice in 1399 and returned from there to his native Florence. There he was drawn into a dispute with Coluccio Salutati over the nature and value of ancient literature, with his side of the controversy developed in a long book entitled *Lucula noctis*, or 'The Firefly'.[79] Dominici acknowledges that there are a great many things in pagan books that are consonant with the Christian faith—things pertaining to the incarnation, to the suffering and death of Christ, and to the apocalypse. Dominici refers twice to these things as *revelata* ('revealed'), which seems to suggest that he would attribute these passages to the actions of the Holy Spirit. Such revelations, however, were directed toward the salvation of the Gentiles, so that they would have no excuse if they failed to accept Christianity. For those who already believe and can read about matters of faith in the Bible, the revelations to the Gentiles are unnecessary (p. 189); indeed, these revelations are actually a threat to their faith, for in pagan literature the Holy Spirit shares co-authorship with the devil (*auctore dyabolo*, p. 338). Thus even Virgil often mixes false things in with the true (*sepiusque*

---

[79] Basic information on Dominici and his relevant works may be found in P. Augustin Rösser, *Cardinal Johannes Dominici, O. Pr., 1357–1419: Ein Reformatorenbild aus der Zeit des grossen Schisma* (Freiburg im Breisgau, 1893), esp. 14–40 (on Dominici's years in Venice); B. L. Ullman, *The Humanism of Coluccio Salutati*, Medioevo e umanesimo, 4 (Padua, 1963), 63–70, 201–2; Da Prati, *Giovanni Dominici e l'Umanesimo*, 233–42 with bibliography; B. L. Ullman, 'The Dedication Copy of Giovanni Dominici's *Lucula Noctis*: A Landmark in the History of the Italian Renaissance', in *Studies in the Italian Renaissance*, 2nd edn., Storia e letteratura, Raccolta di studi e testi, 51 (Rome, 1973), 255–75; and Ermolao Barbaro (il Vecchio), *Orationes contra poetas, epistolae*, ed. Giorgio Ronconi, Facoltà di Magistero dell'Università di Padova, 14 (Florence, 1972), 13. An excellent treatment of Dominici's expulsion from Venice and its relation to the myth of Venice is in Daniel Bornstein, 'Giovanni Dominici, the Bianchi, and Venice: Symbolic Action and Interpretive Grids', *Journal of Medieval and Renaissance Studies*, 23 (1993), 143–71. The edn. used is *Johannis Dominici lucula noctis*, ed. E. Hunt (Notre Dame, Ind., 1940); references will be placed in the text.

veris falsa permiscet, p. 338), like the claim in *Aeneid* 6. 730–3 that vice comes from the body, not from original sin (p. 364). This approach allows Dominici to summarize his position by turning two lines of Virgil against the reading of pagan authors:

> Qui legitis flores et humi nascentia fraga,
> Frigidus, o pueri, fugite hinc, latet anguis in herba.

(Ye who cull flowers and low-growing strawberries, away from here, lads; a chill snake lurks in the grass.)[80]

(*Ecl.* 3. 92–3, qtd. on p. 250)

Not even allegory can save such texts, for in pagan poetry the hidden content is as empty and putrid as the allegorical veil that hides it (p. 383). Thus for Dominici, *theologia poetica* must yield to the theology of Christ, in which the truth of the Holy Spirit remains pure and unadulterated.

A similar line of reasoning was developed in the *Orationes contra poetas* of Ermolao Barbaro il Vecchio, the Venetian-born, humanist bishop of Verona whose response in 1455 to an epistolary defence of poetry by a certain Fra Bartolomeo amounts to a frontal assault on *theologia poetica*.[81] Barbaro begins at the beginning, with Orpheus, the legendary pre-Homeric poet to whom the origins of *theologia poetica* were generally assigned. Barbaro, however, describes an Orpheus whose associations with Dionysus and with pederasty were found revolting by the ancients—and how can we call someone a 'theologian' whose rites were unacceptable even in his own culture? (p. 87). The equation of poetry and theology had found support in the Church Fathers, as we have seen, but Barbaro cites Paul, Jerome, Augustine, and Athanasius on the deficiencies of poetry (p. 100).[82] Poetry tells lies, that Jove is first changed into a bull to assault Europa, then into a golden rain to assault Danae, then into Amphitryon to assault Alcmena (p. 113). And allegory does not provide any defence, for removing the shell only reveals clearly that the kernel of ancient poetry is a Jove who commits adultery and rape (pp. 136–7). Barbaro then uses the immoral

---

[80] The translation is by H. Rushton Fairclough, from the Loeb Classical Library edn. of *Virgil*, revised edn. (Cambridge, Mass., 1965).

[81] Basic information on the work and its background may be found in *Orationes*, ed. Ronconi, 3–22; references are to this edn. and will be placed in the text.

[82] Barbaro is relying on I Cor. 8: 9–11; Jerome, *Epistle* 21. 13. 4, 7, and 8; Augustine, *De civitate Dei* 1. 32 and 2. 8; and Athanasius, *Contra gentes* 15 (25. 32c).

content of poetry and its association with false gods to separate it from theology:

Sed cum recti mores, ut ab initio ostendi, bene vivendique ratio et, quod maximum est, vera Dei cognitio semper defuerit, ut qui in vanis quibusdam religionis studiis fuerint versati, non video profecto cur abs te theologi aut divini sint appellandi, cum theologia ex veri Dei ratione divinarumque rerum cognitione proficiscatur et ex virtutis operatione divinitas comparetur.

(But since good character, as I have shown from the beginning, a rationale for living well, and (what is most important of all) a true understanding of God were always lacking, seeing that they spent their lives in commitment to various false notions of religion, I do not see at all why you should call them 'theologians' or 'divines', since theology proceeds from a reasoned understanding of the true God and the understanding of sacred matters, and divinity is obtained by the practice of virtue.)

(p. 116)

Barbaro admits that ancient poetry also contains some truth compatible with Christianity, but this, he insists, is the result of natural understanding (*cognitio nobis adeo insita sit a natura*, p. 140), not divine inspiration, and as St Paul observes in Romans 1: 21–3, the authors of ancient poetry are among those who recognize God not to glorify and thank him, but to vanish into their own foolish thoughts (pp. 140–1).

Virgil's position within this humanized poetics is problematic. On the one hand, epic poets like Virgil are spared the worst of Barbaro's wrath, which is directed against the unbridled lasciviousness of the dramatists (p. 91). Virgil and Horace, but especially Virgil, are singled out as well for the dignity and elegance of their language. However, Barbaro cannot resist closing the passage praising Virgil's language by observing that even the best of poets like Virgil failed to find a useful and honoured place in society (p. 97). A little later Virgil takes a direct hit when Barbaro asks derisively who are the grave and venerable followers of poetry—surely not Virgil, whom *scribit Servius rusticana facie fuisse et adeo exarsisse libidine ut nec pepercerit maribus* ('Servius writes was of rustic complexion and so inflamed with lust that he did not spare males'; p. 125). Nor will it work to point out that lines like *at pater omnipotens, rerumque aeterna potestas* ('O father, o eternal king of men and things'; *Aen.* 10. 18) help us recognize God, since such recognition does not require knowledge of ancient poetry and since any Christian truth found there is always tainted with suspicion of error (pp. 121–2).

The same issues were taken up in a somewhat different context by the Dominican friar Girolamo Savonarola. As Stanley Meltzoff has shown, such works from the early 1490s as the *Panepistemon* and *Lamia* of Angelo Poliziano and several letters of Marsilio Ficino returned to the ideas of Petrarch, Boccaccio, and Salutati and developed an updated version of *theologia poetica*.[83] In response to this development, Savonarola contributed his *Apologeticus de ratione poeticae*, his only work to deal specifically with literary criticism.[84] His ideas found greater favour with Venetian printers than with the Florentine intellectual community in which they were nurtured, reminding us once again that the Venetian Renaissance often developed differently from the dominant Florentine model.

The *Apologeticus* is a general classification of all knowledge in which poetry holds the lowest position among all the branches of speculative knowledge (fo. +5^r). The treatise does not quote poetry or cite poets (except David), and pagan learning in general is denigrated, since the Bible and the sacraments are all a Christian needs.[85] Savonarola acknowledges that some people consider poetry and theology to be one and the same thing, but such people are wrong. The object of poetry is the *exemplum*, he explains, but the object of theology is God, and the *ars poetica* is not an essential part of the writings of the prophets (fo. +5^r). The passage continues:

Nec tamen prophete usi sunt versibus Virgilianis aut Ovidianis, sed his quos non vana hominum superstitio et diabolica instigatio ad colenda idola invenit, sed spiritus sanctus qui vult hominem de se ipso humilia non alta sentire. Inter versus enim poetarum gentilium et prophetarum nostrorum infinita distantia est. In illis enim magnus diaboli laqueus

---

[83] *Botticelli*, 21–32, 37–59.

[84] Meltzoff (ibid. 393–4) records four Venetian edns. (1513, Lazarus de Soardis; 1534, Aurelli [?]; 1542, heirs of Lucas Antonius Junta; and 1543, heirs of Lucas Antonius Junta), along with the 1492 Pescia *editio princeps* and a 1596 Wittenberg edn. by Andreas Hoffman. There is a rare Sienese trans. by V. Mattei (1864), and a text with Eng. trans. has been promised by E. Wirshbo, which will, I hope, facilitate the further study this treatise deserves. References to the copy I have used in the Biblioteca Apostolica Vaticana, shelf mark Barberini L.V.35(5), which unfortunately lacks title-page and colophon, will be incorporated into the text.

[85] Meltzoff, *Botticelli*, 37–43. See also Buck, *Italienische Dichtungslehre*, 113–15.

absconditus est. Sicut enim diabolus ad sui cultum et superstitionem hominum nutriendam ea carmina docuit, ita et in eis superbissimam vanitatem inanisque glorie intolerabilem fetorem reliquit.

(Nevertheless the prophets did not use verses of Virgil or Ovid, but verses that have not been crafted by the empty superstition of man and the instigation of the devil for the worship of idols, but by the Holy Spirit who wishes man to think humbly, not proudly, of himself. Infinite is the distance between the verses of the pagan poets and those of our prophets, for hidden in pagan poetry is a great diabolical snare. As the devil teaches these poems to encourage worship of himself and superstition in mankind, so in them he also leaves proud vanity and an intolerable stench of empty glory.)

(fo. +5^r)

Both pagan poetry and theology use metaphor, but this is not enough to make them the same thing (fo. +6^r), for 'infinite is the distance between the verses of the pagan poets and those of our prophets'.

The same attitude continues into the Cinquecento, as we see in a rare little work by Cesare Delfini entitled *Civis Parmensis artium et medicinae doctoris clarissimi in carmina sexti Aeneidos digressio*, published in Venice in 1523.[86] Delfini acknowledges Virgil's skill as a poet and his learning in many areas, but he insists that much of what is contained in the descent to the underworld in the *Aeneid* is absolutely incompatible with Christian dogma. God is not a world spirit, angels are not composed of matter and form, the spirit is not corporal, there is no 'great year' of 49,000 years, metempsychosis does not take place, and so on. As Zabughin puts it, Delfini in essence calls Virgil before the tribunal of the Inquisition and condemns him to the stake.[87]

From these assaults on *theologia poetica* in general and on Virgil in particular, a number of points emerge. First, a significant minority of readers, especially clerics, continued to resist the reading of pagan poetry well into the sixteenth century, and this minority included a number of influential individuals. We can perhaps question the importance and impact of Delfini's work, but when Barbaro and Savonarola challenge the doctrine of *theologia poetica*

---

[86] The work, in six folios, was published by Bernardinus de Vianis de Laxona Vercellensis and was studied by Zabughin, *Vergilio*, ii. 94–5, on whose summary I rely.

[87] *Vergilio*, ii. 94–5.

and express ambivalence toward the poetry of Virgil, we are forced to take notice of what is being said.

Second, we must not be tempted by the easy dichotomy in which anti-humanist, reactionary, and pious challengers to *theologia poetica* stand in stark contrast to progressive humanists whose attraction to the classics was complemented by a relative indifference toward Christianity. According to one modern scholar, Dominici, for example, was not hostile to humanism in general but only to its paganizing excesses,[88] while it is generally acknowledged that Salutati, his humanist opponent, adhered to many aspects of scholastic thought and piety.[89] One of the most recent students of Savonarola's sermons declared herself 'surprised to find their content to be more humanistic than is usually acknowledged'.[90] And the case of Barbaro in particular resists easy generalization, for here Fra Bartolomeo is resting his case in *theologia poetica* and Barbaro is attacking him in the rolling periods of Ciceronian Latin.[91]

For most humanists of the Venetian Renaissance, eloquence could be successfully joined to religion most of the time. As Vittore Branca has pointed out, this attitude can be traced all the way back to Petrarch, who was living on the Riva degli Schiavoni in Venice when he wrote his *De ignorantia*, which stressed that Christianity complements and completes ancient culture.[92] We have seen, however, that the strain of piety characteristic of Venetian humanism was sufficiently pronounced that it often led to conclusions that seemed peculiar to non-Venetians.[93]

---

[88] Da Prati, *Giovanni Dominici e l'Umanesimo*, 28–33, 164–201. See also Daniel R. Lesnick, 'Civic Preaching in the Early Renaissance: Giovanni Dominici's Florentine Sermons', in Verdon and Henderson (eds.), *Christianity and the Renaissance*, 210.

[89] The standard biography of Salutati, from which these themes emerge clearly, is Ronald Witt, *Hercules at the Crossroads: The Life, Works, and Thought of Coluccio Salutati*, Duke Monographs in Medieval and Renaissance Studies, 6 (Durham, NC, 1983).

[90] Marcia B. Hall, 'Savonarola's Preaching and the Patronage of Art', in Verdon and Henderson (eds.), *Christianity and the Renaissance*, 494.

[91] On Barbaro's Latinity, see *Orationes*, ed. Ronconi, 20–2. Zabughin, *Vergilio*, i. 120–2, comments on the irony of the positions taken by monk and humanist in this controversy, and Toffanin, *History of Humanism*, goes so far as to claim that in the disputes between mendicants and humanists, 'the Curia, almost constantly, sided with the latter' (241).

[92] 'Ermolao Barbaro and Late Quattrocento Venetian Humanism', in J. R. Hale (ed.), *Renaissance Venice* (Totowa, NJ, 1973), 226.

[93] King, *Venetian Humanism*, 31–7. In 'L'umanesimo veneziano alla fine del Quattrocento: Ermolao Barbaro e il suo circolo', *Storia della cultura veneta*, iii. Girolamo Arnaldi and Manlio Pastore Stocchi (eds.), *Dal primo Quattrocento al Concilio di Trento*, pt. 1 (Vicenza, 1980), 137–8, Vittore Branca notes as well that the Christian element is especially strong in Venetian humanism.

Sometimes, therefore, religion and secular learning seemed to pull in opposite directions, so that the occasional resistance to Virgil in Renaissance Venice turns out to be both longer in duration and broader in scope than we might expect.

So far the resistance we have encountered to Virgil as *poeta theologus* has emerged in a number of more general treatises written by Venetians or published in Venice during the fifteenth and sixteenth centuries. However, we can also find the effects of this resistance in the pages of several Renaissance Venetian editions of Virgil's poetry.

As we have seen, the ranks of those who bought and read these editions included clerics. Among the copies of Virgil with a clerical provenance in the collection of the Biblioteca Nazionale Marciana in Venice is one published in 1566 by Joannes Maria Bonellus, now shelf mark 19.t.2. The title-page (Plate 3) shows that this book once belonged to *Joannes Battista Visconte*, then to *Joannes Petrus Calegarius Presbyter*. In addition, the title-page also shows that Calegarius' book had two other readers: *Frater Dominicus de Suneo Inquisitor Papiensis vidit et concessit* ('Brother Dominic de Suno, Inquisitor of Pavia, has examined and authorized'), followed by [*q*]*ue expurganda erant ex hoc volumine Iodoci Vilichii expurgata fuere, Dominus Joannes Franciscus Cayrus deputatus etc.* ('the things that were to be expurgated from this volume of Iodocus Vilichius have been expurgated, Lord John Francis Cayrus the deputy and so forth').[94] Iodocus Vilichius (or Willichius) wrote a commentary on the *Georgics* printed in this edition. But

---

[94] Since the first name is cancelled and since Calegarius was connected to the church, I assume he is the one who took the book in for expurgation and added the marginal glosses, which range from corrections to the text (e.g. fo. 157ʳ, on *Aen.* 1. 702) and brief explanations of key terms (e.g. fo. 162ʳ, on *Aen.* 2. 57) to displays of Greek grammatical knowledge (e.g. fos. 171ʳ and 172ᵛ) and observations on Roman religious practices (e.g. fo. 158ʳ, on *Aen.* 1. 731 ff., and fo. 192ʳ, on *Aen.* 3. 360). An interesting parallel to the points developed here may be found in the efforts of church censors to come to terms with Castiglione's *Courtier*, as analysed by Peter Burke in *The Fortunes of the Courtier: The European Reception of Castiglione's Cortegiano*, Penn State Series in the History of the Book, 1 (University Park, Penn., 1995), 99–106. Expurgation could also be effected, however, by the bookseller, as was the case with a copy of the 1558 Joannes Maria Bonellus edn. now at Princeton Univ. (shelf mark: VRG 2945 1558q), whose title-page was inscribed in a 16th-cent. hand, *Espurgato per me Cingi Forcathini* (?) *librero*. Willich's name, again, is inked out on the title-page and in those places in the *Georgics* commentary where it was written out in full.

P. VIRGILII MARONIS,

POETAE MANTVANI,

VNIVERSVM POEMA:

CVM ABSOLVTA SERVII HONORATI MAVRI, GRAMMATICI,
& Badij Afcenfij interpretatione: Probi, & Ioannis Viuis in Eclogas allegorijs:
Iodocíque eruditis fuper Georgica commentarijs.

QVIBVS ACCESSERVNT LVDOVICI COELII RHODIGINI,
Ioannis Scoppæ Parthenopæi, Iacobi Conftantij Fanenfis, Francifci Campani Colenfis, Iacobi
Crucij Bononienfis, necnon alterius, docti hominis, lucubrationes,
& annotationes in loca difficiliora:

*ELEGANTISSIMAE PRAETEREA LIBRORVM OMNIVM
figura, argumenta, lectionum denique varietates, quas & Ioannes Pierius, &
alij doctiffimi viri hactenus obferuarunt.*

QVAE NON, VT ANTEA, PLVRIMIS FOEDATA MENDIS, SED
acri ftudio emendata, atque omni, quantum licuit, ex parte expolita, emifimus.
quod, alios libros cum noftro conferentibus, patebit.

VENETIIS,

APVD IOANNEM MARIAM

BONELLVM.

M. D. LXVI.

Plate 3. Title-page with censors' notes, *Universum poema* (Venice: Joannes Maria Bonellus, 1566). (Used by permission of the Biblioteca Nazionale Marciana, Venice.)

this raises an obvious question: what could he have said about Virgil that would have aroused the ire of a clerical censor?

Willich (also spelled Wilcke or Wild) was born in Prussia in 1501. He studied in Frankfurt and became in 1524 Professor of Greek at Frankfurt an der Oder, then in 1540 Professor of Medicine. At his death on 12 November 1552, Willich left a substantial body of work, ranging from a *Compendium artium* and *De formando studio in quolibet profanarum artium genere* to medical treatises like *Exercitationes et probationes de urinis* and *Consilia medica*. He also prepared commentaries to a wide variety of texts, from the biblical letters to the Thessalonians, Timothy, and Titus, to classical authors like Tacitus and Horace, with an especially important Latin translation of and commentary on Hippocrates' *De genitura*. His interest in Virgil was longstanding: he had begun his commentary on the *Eclogues* in his youth, and his commentary on the *Georgics* was published in the edition owned by Calegarius.[95]

In accordance with standard practice of the day, the censor has gone through Willich's commentary and inked out the author's name (e.g. fos. 44ʳ, 46ʳ) and the individual passages that he found objectionable. In order to determine what the censor was objecting to, I have compared this copy to another, unexpurgated text containing Willich's commentary. There are three cancelled passages:

1. On *Georgics* 1. 31, Willich wrote,

> Tria commoda manent Augustum quoniam in classe marinorum deorum futurus esset. Primum est, quod a nautis coletur, non aliter ac Neptunus, atque vulgo apud Christianos Divus Nicolaus.

> (Three pleasant things await Augustus, seeing that he would be in the category of sea gods. First is that he will be worshipped by sailors, no differently from Neptune, and commonly among Christians, St Nicholas.)

The censor has obliterated the last phrase, *atque ... Nicolaus* ('and ... Nicholas').

⁹⁵ J. H. Zedler, *Grosses vollständiges Universal-Lexicon aller Wissenschaften und Künste* (Graz, 1962; repr. of Halle, 1732–50 edn.), lvii. 241–3; and C. G. Jöcher, *Allgemeines Gelehrten-Lexicon* (Hildesheim, 1961; repr. of Leipzig, 1750–1 edn.), iv. 1996–7. I have not been able to find M. Hostus, *De vita Jodoci Willichii* (Franckfurt, 1607), which Jöcher mentions in his biography.

2. On *Georgics* 2. 390, Willich wrote,

Hinc. Ex his sacris magnum numerum vini sperabant, cum iisdem Bacchus fit propitius. Nam ad eos sacrificantes respicit tanquam opitulaturus, quod hic hypotyposi exprimitur. Heu quanta superstitio, cuius adhuc similis est apud quosdam, sed alicuius divi nomine.

(*From here.* From these sacred rites they were hoping for a large amount of wine, when Bacchus becomes propitious to them. For he looks to those sacrificing to him as a gift-giver, which is expressed here in *hypotyposis*. Oh how great a superstition, to which there is still something similar among certain others, but in the name of another god.)

The censor has obliterated the last sentence, *Heu ... nomine* ('Oh ... god').

3. On *Georgics* 3. 313, Willich wrote,

Usum in castrorum. Ut fierent Cilicia, quae iuxta Asconium tecta sunt in usum castrorum ac nautarum. Conficiebantur autem ex pilis tam hircorum, quam caprarum. Non desunt religiosuli, qui tunicas imas Cilicinas sibi parant.

(*For the use of the camp.* So as to be made into 'Cilicia', which according to Asconius [Ps.-Asc. on Cic. 2 *Verr.* 1.95] are coverings for military and naval use. Moreover they were made from the hair of male and female goats. Nor are there lacking certain little religious, who prepare long Cilician tunics for themselves.)

The censor has obliterated the last sentence, *Non ... parant* ('Nor ... themselves').

In each obliterated passage, Willich has brought Virgil's world into contact with the world of contemporary Christianity in a way that made the censor uncomfortable. In the first case, the suggestion that the worship of St Nicholas is like the worship of the pagan Neptune and of a deified Augustus is simply too much for the censor.[96] In the second case, he objected to the suggestion that

---

[96] It is worth noting that associating characters from Christianity with pagan deities seemed to present greater problems when the author was suspected of Protestant leanings than it did for someone whose orthodoxy was not in question. For example, in the commentary to his Italian trans. of the *Georgics*, Bernardino Daniello wrote, *Ritrovò Noè (il quale sotto il nome di Bacco e di Lieo celebrò l'antica età e per Dio adorò* ... ('It was found by

Christian worship could be a 'superstition' resembling pagan worship of Bacchus, the god of drinking and debauchery. And in the third case, the problem was the anticlericalism behind the gratuitous observation that 'certain little religious' (*religiosuli*—the suffix is derogatory) affected coarse garments like those originally made of Cilician goats' hair.[97]

I would like to suggest that these three strokes of the censor's pen are important enough to suggest a solution to a puzzle in the annals of Virgilian publishing. Willich's commentary on the *Georgics* was printed six times in Renaissance Venice, first in 1544 by Hieronymus Scotus, then by Bartholomaeus Cesanus in 1551 and 1551–2, and finally three times by Joannes Maria Bonellus, in 1558, 1562, and 1566. Given that the basic conservatism of Venetian printers provided commentators like Landino and Ascensius with a shelf-life of decades, we cannot help but wonder at the relatively sudden appearance and disappearance of this commentary. The disappearance becomes even more striking when we look at later editions put out by the three printers who introduced Willich. Cesanus did not print any more Virgils, but when Scotus returned to this text in 1555, he reset it completely and removed Willich's commentary. Bonellus' heirs likewise reset the text without Willich when they brought out new editions in 1572 and 1574–5, although their resetting retains the commentaries of Lucius Johannes Scoppa and Ludovicus Caelius Rhodiginus that had originally accompanied Willich. Bonellus' partners Petrus Dusinellus and Joannes Gryphius (the younger) put out four editions from 1578 to 1586 that likewise retain Scoppa and Rhodiginus but delete Willich.[98]

The statement by Calegarius' censor on the title-page of the

Noah, whom antiquity celebrated under the name of Bacchus and Lyaeus and adored as God'); *La Georgica di Virgilio, nuovamente di latina in thoscana favella per Bernardino Daniello tradotta e commentata* (Venice: Giovanni Farri and Brothers, 1545), fo. a2ᵛ, and this did not require expurgation.

[97] As Kristian Jensen has shown, Julius Caesar Scaliger encountered similar problems with anticlerical remarks in his commentary on Theophrastus, which was placed on several indexes among books that needed correction before they could be read (*Rhetorical Philosophy and Philosophical Grammar: Julius Caesar Scaliger's Theory of Language*, Humanistische Bibliothek, Texte und Abhandlungen, Reihe 1, Abhandlungen, 46 (Munich, 1990), 30–1).

[98] On this partnership, see E. Pastorello, *Tipografi, editori, librai a Venezia nel secolo* XVI, Biblioteca di bibliografia italiana, 5 (Florence, 1924), 14, 79.

Marciana copy of the 1566 Bonellus edition, I believe, explains the disappearance of Willich's commentary from mid-century Venetian editions. Willich's works, the censor explains, 'were to be expurgated'—that is, they contained statements contrary to the faith and were to be corrected by a church official before they could be read. Indeed, Willich's works had appeared on the list of books condemned by the Venetian Index of 1549, and the prohibition continued in the Venetian Index of 1554, the Index of Paul IV (1559), the Tridentine Index of Pius IV (1564), and the Index of Sixtus V (1590).[99] This commentator, in other words, was suspect, and the censor was reflecting the belief that heresy could even creep into a commentary on Virgil.[100]

As Paul Grendler has observed, Venice's role as legendary defender of the faith was a part of the myth of Venice, and that role required her to combat heresy and to suppress the ideas of those in opposition to the faith.[101] In this case, however, Venice's role as defender of the faith came into conflict both with the desire

---

[99] F. H. Reusch, *Die Indices Librorum prohibitorum des sechzehnten Jahrhunderts* (Nieuwkoop, 1961; repr. of Tübingen, 1886 edn.), 39, 59, 163, 192, 225, 268, 322, 415, 492; and Paul Grendler, 'Introduction historique', in *Index des livres interdits*, iii. J. M. De Bujanda (ed.), *Index de Venise (1549), Venise et Milan (1554)* (Sherbrooke, 1987), 306–7. See also Horatio F. Brown, *The Venetian Printing Press, 1469–1800: An Historical Study based upon Documents for the Most Part Hitherto Unpublished* (Amsterdam, 1969; repr. of London, 1891 edn.), 122–34; and Brian Richardson, *Print Culture in Renaissance Italy: The Editor and the Vernacular Text, 1470–1600* (Cambridge, 1994), 140–54. A good study of how the Venetian Inquisition dealt with heterodox ideas is John Martin, *Venice's Hidden Enemies: Italian Heretics in a Renaissance City* (Berkeley and Los Angeles, Calif., 1993); printers with heretical leanings are discussed on 81, 132, and 135–7. Mere possession of prohibited books could lead to denunciation and trial before the Inquisition; as E. William Monter and John Tedeschi have noted, almost 10 per cent of the Inquisition's cases between 1570 and 1592 involved prohibited books, although prosecutions seem to have declined beginning with Venice's quarrel against the Papacy ('Toward a Statistical Profile of the Italian Inquisitions, Sixteenth to Eighteenth Centuries', in Gustav Henningsen *et al.* (eds.), *The Inquisition in Early Modern Europe: Studies on Sources and Methods* (De Kalb, Ill., 1986), 137, 144). Interesting material for comparison may be found in Henry Kamen, *Inquisition and Society in Spain in the Sixteenth and Seventeenth Centuries* (Bloomington, Ind., 1985), ch. 5, 'Silence Has Been Imposed'.

[100] Of course, commentaries on other classical authors could also come under suspicion. For example, a copy of Herodotus with commentary by Joachim Camerarius, published by Johann Herwagen in Basel in 1541, made its way to Naples, where an ecclesiastical censor gave permission for the book to be read (*lege potest*) and entered the date, 20 June 1587, on the title-page. The names of the commentator and the printer, both of whom were Protestant sympathizers, have been inked out. The book is described as no. 66 in Catalogue 22 of the book dealer Phillip J. Pirages (McMinnville, Ore., 1992); it is now in the Department of Special Collections, Sterling B. Evans Library, Texas A&M University.

[101] 'Introduction historique', 42.

of the government to exert its authority against the Papacy in Rome and with the commercial interests of those of its citizens who printed and sold books of questionable orthodoxy. As a result, the period from the middle of the sixteenth century through the ascendancy of Paolo Sarpi at the beginning of the seventeenth century was marked by repeated changes in censorship practices as first the church, then the state gained the upper hand.[102]

However, within this general flux I believe we can discern some very specific changes in what a printer of Virgil felt he could and could not print. The commentary of Willich was first published in 1544, in the middle of a decade that Paul Grendler has characterized as unusually open to the printing of new books and new ideas, including those connected to Protestantism. It continued to be published in Venice after the works of Willich were banned, but it finally disappeared at a time when Counter-Reformation tensions made everyone associated with the Venetian book trade more sensitive to what was being printed and what the consequences of printing might be.[103] In this changed climate, the printers who had introduced Willich into the Venetian market found it safer to withdraw this one commentary by a heretical author so they could continue publishing what was otherwise an uncontroversial, and potentially profitable, text.

It is worth noting here as well that once we have been alerted to this course of events, several parallel examples present themselves. The closest one involves the edition of Virgil's works

[102] On the role of censorship in the general development of Venetian policy during this period, see William J. Bouwsma, *Venice and the Defense of Republican Liberty: Renaissance Values in the Age of the Counter Reformation* (Berkeley and Los Angeles, Calif., 1968); Paul Grendler, *The Roman Inquisition and the Venetian Press, 1540–1605* (Princeton, 1977); and Andrea Del Col, 'Il controllo della stampa a Venezia e i processi di Antonio Brucioli (1548–1559)', *Critica storica*, 17 (1980), 457–510. Grendler's 'The Tre Savii sopra Eresia, 1547–1605: A Prosopographical Study', *Studi Veneziani*, NS 3 (1979), 283–340, shows how closely control of heresy was tied to political life in Renaissance Venice.

[103] Grendler, *Roman Inquisition*, 225–33. See also Horatio Brown, 'The *Index Librorum Prohibitorum* and the Censorship of the Venetian Press', in *Studies in the History of Venice*, 2 vols. (London, 1907), ii. 44–5; Paolo Ulvioni, 'Stampa e censura a Venezia nel Seicento', *Archivio veneto*, 106 (1975), 50; and Conor Fahy, 'The *Index Librorum Prohibitorum* and the Venetian Printing Industry in the Sixteenth Century', *Italian Studies*, 35 (1980), 53–6. Willich's commentary, of course, continued to appear in edns. printed in Protestant cities; the best source for tracing the publishing history of this commentary remains C. G. Heyne and G. P. E. Wagner (eds.), *Publius Virgilius Maro varietate lectionis et perpetua adnotatione*, iv. *Carmina minora, quaestiones Virgilianae et notitia literaria*, 4th edn. (Leipzig, 1832), 476 ff.

printed in 1539 by Johannes Antonius de Nicolinis de Sabio and Federicus de Torresanis and containing commentaries by, among others, Leonard Culmann, Eobanus Hessus, and Philip Melanchthon. These three commentaries were not reprinted, again leading us to seek an explanation for their sudden appearance and disappearance when other commentaries were reprinted for decades. A survey of sixteenth-century indexes confirms that like Willich, Culmann, Hessus, and Melanchthon were regularly condemned.[104] Again it would seem that the Venetian printers found it safer to remove these commentaries and to print only the works of those classical scholars whose thinking had remained untainted by heresy.

Two expurgated Virgils now in the Biblioteca Universitaria in Padua raise a more complicated series of questions. Neither bears a signature either of a previous owner or of the censor himself, and in both cases the expurgated commentaries were written by good Catholics whose works had been used by most readers of the day to reconcile Virgil and their Christian faith. The first book has Vives's name on the title-page and his commentary to *Eclogues* 1–5 cancelled along with a section of Ascensius' commentary to *Eclogue* 4; in the second book, the commentary of Ascensius in general is the target.[105] We can only speculate about why those who censored these two books objected to material that passed the scrutiny of their colleagues, but a comparison of the contents of the expurgated passages in the first volume to what has been removed in Calegarius' book suggests a tentative answer. The cancelled section of Ascensius' commentary on *Eclogue* 4 is a discussion of how the three Fates, Clotho, Lachesis, and Atropos, determine the course of each human life, a discussion that might well raise troubling questions about fate and free will in a doctrinally troubled age (fo. 22^v). Vives's commentary on *Eclogues* 4 and 5 relentlessly traces parallels first to Christ's birth, then to his death and resurrection (fos. 23^v, 27^{r-v}). This process of establishing parallels between pagan culture and Christianity was precisely what troubled the official who censored Calegarius' book, and it appears that the clerics who expurgated these two volumes found

[104]   F. H. Reusch, *Indices*, *passim*.
[105]   The first of these two books is a copy of the 1562 Joannes Maria Bonellus edn., shelf mark 80.b.45; the second is a 1585–6 Petrus Dusinellus, now 175.c.106 (*olim* 45.d.1). References to these books will appear in the text.

that even in the hands of a good Catholic, this process was more likely to undermine the faith than to support it.

What goes on in the margins of these expurgated books is thus a concrete demonstration of the exchange of power in the world of Renaissance Venetian publishing. The commentaries printed in these books, like all commentaries, are an attempt at 'controlling audience consumption of the text',[106] at imposing a reading on the reader. The responses of the Venetian censors, however, confirm an observation of Roger Chartier that '[e]very textual or typographic arrangement that aims to create control and constraint always secretes tactics that tame or subvert it.'[107] In these cases, readers backed by sufficient institutional power have not only resisted the reading advanced by the commentary, but have even helped to force the removal of some printed commentaries in favour of others that advance a reading more in line with the dominant ideology of their institutions. Once this is done, however, the Virgil who came forth from the presses of Venice again supports the myth by which her citizens lived their lives.

---

[106] Ralph Hanna III, 'Annotation as a Social Practice', in Stephen A. Barney (ed.), *Annotation and its Texts* (New York, 1991), 181.

[107] 'Texts, Printings, Readings', in Lynn Hunt (ed.), *The New Cultural History* (Berkeley and Los Angeles, Calif., 1989), 173.

4

Class, Gender, and the Virgilian Myth

Accommodation: Books and Social Unification

As we have seen, those who bought and read a Latin edition of
Virgil in Renaissance Venice tended to approach the text with
several concerns uppermost in their minds. When their interest in
Virgil came from the institutional environment of the schools,
they tended to concentrate on the moral content of the poetry, to
hear in it exhortations to work hard for God, country, and what
they knew to be right and to accept what could not be changed as
part of the ultimate justice of an ordered universe. As Christians,
Virgil's Venetian readers also struggled throughout the
Renaissance to integrate his poetry into their own religious life
through the concept of *theologia poetica*. These moral and religious
concerns emerged naturally as Virgil was read in accordance with
the prevailing intellectual and political paradigm of the day, such
that in this time and place Virgil can only be understood in relation to the myth of Venice.

One problem that remains, however, is to determine
precisely who in Renaissance Venice bought a Latin edition of
Virgil and read it in this way. If we turn for guidance to recent
work in the history of printing, we find two radically different
approaches to the dissemination of the classics in Renaissance
Europe. The first of these approaches is developed by Miriam
Usher Chrisman in her study of printing in Renaissance
Strasbourg. Here

[t]he evidence from the study of book publication ... revealed that two
cultures were present in a sixteenth-century city: a Latin culture dominated by the universities and the churches and a vernacular culture rooted
in the interests of ordinary men and women. This division was hardly

new. The development of printing, however, served to increase or formalize the distance between them.[1]

That is, not only were there two cultures in Renaissance Strasbourg, but the evidence from what was printed there suggests that the two cultures were quite distinct: 'From these disparate sources each culture developed its own system of values and beliefs: the Latin culture was based on the ethics and philosophy of ancient Rome, the Bible, and the Church Fathers; the lay culture was based on the laws and commandments of Scripture.'[2] Thus, since *savant* and *populaire* moved in two different worlds, well-educated members of the social elite would not have seen the printing press primarily as a tool to disseminate a thinner, diluted version of classical culture to the masses.

Roger Chartier, however, has challenged some of the assumptions of the currently fashionable studies of popular culture, that exclusive relationships exist between specific cultural forms and specific social groups, and that terms like *populaire* and *savant* can be opposed with clarity and rigour. These assumptions rest on cultural cleavages and social hierarchies, but Chartier 'instead found evidence of fluid circulation, practices shared by various groups, and blurred distinctions'.[3] An examination of records in Amiens, Grenoble, and Paris shows that from the beginning, a variety of printed books reached readers at the lower end of the social scale, readers who did not read all that the nobles read but who nevertheless had neither distinct reading matter of their own nor distinct expectations with which they approached a book.[4] In other words, popular culture was not completely divorced from the upper-class interest in the culture of antiquity.

As we might expect, scholarship on the history of printing in Renaissance Venice has developed within this broader disagreement about the dissemination of the classics. For example, in his study of the great pioneer printer Nicholas Jenson, Martin Lowry has confirmed that the classics played a significant part in Jenson's publishing programme, but he also reminds us that this same

---

[1] *Lay Culture, Learned Culture: Books and Social Change in Strasbourg, 1480–1599* (New Haven, 1982), pp. xix–xx.

[2] Ibid. p. xx.

[3] *The Cultural Uses of Print in Early Modern France*, trans. Lydia G. Cochrane (Princeton, 1987), 7.

[4] Ibid. 145–52, 180–2.

printer produced five small devotional tracts in quarto. These were early products of Jenson's press formerly understood to have been directed toward a popular market, but a recently discovered Bodleian manuscript shows that these editions can be traced directly to the interest of Francesco Trevisan, prior of the Carthusian S. Andrea and confidant of several members of the same humanist patrician group who patronized the printing of the classics. Since the influence of this same group on Jenson and his competitors became more noticeable through the early 1470s, Lowry warns against approaching the history of printing in early Renaissance Venice with rigid ideas about new classes of readers and the power of a mass market.[5]

In *Printing and Publishing in Fifteenth-Century Venice*, however, Leonardo Gerulaitis proceeds much like Chrisman and insists that different social groups moved in different worlds, although his social groups are not defined in exactly the same way as Chrisman's. Gerulaitis first distinguishes the goals of the humanist scholars of the classics from the goals of the professional people and bourgeoisie, then argues that printed books should be associated with the latter group. He then concludes 'that humanism, as such, never became a dominant, or even a really widespread cultural movement in the fifteenth century, and printed books represent the prevailing culture of the bourgeoisie'.[6] In other words, Gerulaitis believes that a new class of readers and the development of mass markets for the press created a division between vernacular culture and the humanist readers of the Latin classics.

Which approach we accept has significant implications for the concerns of this study. If humanism never became a widespread cultural movement in Renaissance Venice and if vernacular readers moved in a completely different world from that in which the Latin editions of Virgil were found, we could still argue that the ideas developed so far are important because of the disproportionate influence exercised by a small, elite group. If, however, *populaire* and *savant* were fluid categories in Venice and if there was significant contact between the Latin and vernacular worlds, then the study of Virgil's place in the history of printing can provide a

---

[5] *Nicholas Jenson and the Rise of Venetian Publishing in Renaissance Europe* (Oxford, 1991), esp. 59–60.
[6] *Printing and Publishing in Fifteenth-Century Venice* (Chicago, 1976), 161.

broader corroboration for the social and political unity that is at the foundation of the myth of Venice. Accordingly in this chapter, I shall try to determine as precisely as possible who in Renaissance Venice was likely to be thinking about Virgil's poetry and the extent to which that poetry was understood differently by different groups of readers. First I shall use the evidence from the Latin editions, ranging from ownership notes and records of cost to bindings and illustrations, to clarify which groups of people bought and used these books. Then since there were a considerable number of translations of Virgil published in Renaissance Venice, I shall ask the same questions of this second group of books. Next I shall extend the analysis to the translations themselves, to determine the extent to which those reading Virgil in Italian were seeing the same Virgil as those reading in Latin. Finally I shall focus on one group of readers in particular—women—to suggest how gender issues in Virgil's poetry are bound up with gender issues in the ideology of Renaissance Venice. In short, this chapter is designed to explore the role of class and gender in crafting a vision of Virgil compatible with the myth of Venice.

One of the copies of the edition of Virgil's poetry published in Venice by Liga Boaria around 1488 has ultimately found its way into the Biblioteca del Museo Correr, where it now rests under the shelf mark Inc. E 233. A bookplate pasted into the front identifies the man who donated this book to the library as Emanuele A. Cicogna (1789–1868), a well–known scholar of Venetian history. Cicogna loved his books and did considerable research on them, from which we can follow the peregrinations of this volume in precise detail.[7] A note on fo. ii^r identifies its first owner as ... *Francisci Malapellensis not. ... Tarvisini*, i.e. Francesco Malapellense, a notary who lived on the mainland near Venice in the city of Treviso around 1500. A second note on the same page, *Bibliotheca*

---

[7] The book was rebound in the 19th cent., at which point the pages containing Cicogna's notes were stitched into the binding. In addition to the information contained in this para., Cicogna's notes include information collected from the bibliographies of his day and from correspondence with various Italian libraries, all of which serves as a valuable record of how this kind of research was conducted prior to such landmark works of scholarship as the *British Museum Catalogue of Printed Books* and the *Indice generale degli incunaboli delle biblioteche d'Italia*.

Tarvisii Sanctae Mariae de Jesu, records the donation of the book to the monastery of S. Maria del Gesù in Treviso, of which Malapellense was founder and patron. Stamped ownership notes on fos. ii[r] and C5[v] record the next owner as the Venetian patrician Alessandro Semitecolo, who received the book when the monastery was suppressed.[8] In the 1820s Cicogna records that he saw the volume in the possession of Vincenzo Grimani, a Venetian patrician living in Treviso, and it was obtained next by a bookseller in Treviso, Giuseppe Antonio Molena, who recorded it in a catalogue of 1845. It was bought by Giovanni Massocchi, whose fiscal difficulties led him to approach several collectors, one of whom was Cicogna, who bought it for 175 lire *per quell'amor patrio* ('for love of country'). This book, along with many others owned by Cicogna, eventually ended up in the Correr library.

Thanks to Cicogna's careful research, we know more details than usual about the early possessors of this volume, but the general pattern of ownership established here is also typical of other Venetian editions of Virgil that were bought and used near home. For example, the early buyer of another one of these books was the Venetian patrician Alvise Moresini, who signed his name in the 1539 edition of Joannes Antonius de Nicolinis de Sabio and Federicus de Torresanis de Asula now in the Biblioteca Comunale, Treviso (shelf mark N.1194 [L.2.30.H]). In a number of other cases, books passed from the larger private libraries formed by wealthy Venetians, usually nobles, into the Biblioteca Nazionale Marciana. Two copies of Virgil, for example, came to that library from branches of the Contarini family. One (1566, Franciscus Laurentinus: 219.c.161), donated by Alvise 2° Girolamo, was part of the library of the Contarini of S. Trovaso until it entered the Marciana in 1843.[9] The front flyleaf of this same book indicates that it once belonged to *Thoma Contareni* (1562–1614), who added considerably to the well-stocked library in his family home near the church of the Madonna dell'Orto.[10] The other copy (1507,

---

[8] Semitecolo's ownership of a rare edn. of Virgil has been previously noted; see Rinaldo Fulin, 'E. A. Cicogna: Festa letteraria nel Regio Liceo Marco Polo', *Ateneo Veneto*, 3–4 (1872), 24; and Marino Zorzi, 'Le biblioteche a Venezia nel secondo Settecento', *Miscellanea Marciana*, 1 (1986), 283 and n. 263.

[9] Zorzi, 'Biblioteche a Venezia', 272.

[10] G. Benzoni, 'Tomaso Contarini', *Dizionario biografico degli Italiani* (Rome, 1960–), xxviii. 316.

Bernardinus Stagninus: Rari V.603) belonged to one *Andreas Contarenus* (fo. RRR4^v) before passing to Apostolo Zeno. Zeno's library in turn, which contained several other copies of Virgil, entered the Marciana between 1823 and 1827.[11]

Three other Virgils were among the two thousand volumes bequeathed to the Marciana in 1814 by Girolamo Ascanio Molin, the last member of the S. Stin branch of the family.[12] About two of these (1501, Aldus Manutius: 396.d.244,2; and 1563, Paulus Manutius: 388.d.283) we know very little, but the third (1552, heirs of Lucas Antonius Junta: 390.d.21) at least hints of its earlier history. On the title-page is *Ex libris Francisci Ferri Veneti*, and it is tempting to speculate about an association with Girolamo Ferro (d. 1562), the translator of Cicero and Demosthenes whose library of 270 books was, of course, rich in the classics.[13] Another hint of an illustrious history may be found in an incunabulum printed by Baptista de Tortis in 1483 (Inc. V.265). On fo. K10^r of this book there are several lines of writing, cancelled in ink and now virtually illegible, but the passage begins *Nicola Mocenigo* and ends *Domenego Bragadin*. The Mocenigo family of S. Stae, of whom Alvise IV became librarian of the Marciana and later Doge, had a notable library that included many *cinquecentine* and that was kept together until it was bought by the bookseller Adolfo Cesare in 1811.[14]

The links between wealthy buyers and their books can also be traced through the bindings added to their volumes. A great many books in Italy—perhaps more than in most other parts of Europe—were sold without expensive bindings, with simple parchment covers being especially common for the smaller octavos toward the end of the sixteenth century.[15] A buyer of means, however, could

[11] On the libraries of various members of the Contarini family, see Zorzi, 'Biblioteche', 272–3, and id., 'La circolazione del libro a Venezia nel Cinquecento: Biblioteche private e pubbliche', *Ateneo Veneto*, NS 28 (1990), 131 and 144–8. On Zeno's library, see id., 'Biblioteche', 258–9. A copy of the 1501 Aldine Virgil, now Paris, Bibliothèque Nationale, Rés. p. Yc. 1265, also has an ex-libris of Apostolo Zeno.

[12] Id., 'Biblioteche', 278, and id., *La libreria di San Marco: Libri, lettori, società nella Venezia dei Dogi*, Ateneo Veneto, Collana di studi, 1 (Milan, 1987), 367.

[13] Id., 'Circolazione', 119.

[14] Ibid. 146, and id., 'Biblioteche', 278.

[15] E. P. Goldschmidt, *Gothic and Renaissance Bookbindings, exemplified and illustrated from the Author's Collection* (London, 1928). Much useful information can also be found in Tammaro De Marinis, *La legatura artistica in Italia nei secoli XV e XVI*, 3 vols. (Florence, 1960); and a useful bibliographical survey of the field is available in B. H. Breslauer, *The Uses of Bookbinding Literature* (New York, 1986).

demonstrate his wealth and prominence by having his books bound in leather, often with blind and gold tooling in various designs: fleurs-de-lis (1483, Baptista de Tortis: Venice, Biblioteca Nazionale Marciana, Incun. V.265), rectangular boxes with floral designs and interlocking vines (c.1488, Liga Boaria: Treviso, Biblioteca Comunale, Inc. 13716), diamonds, rectangles, and circles (1536–7, Lucas Antonius Junta: Padua, Biblioteca Antoniana, V.VI.15; and 1566, Franciscus Laurentinus: Padua, Biblioteca Universitaria, 121.c.161), and so forth. An especially important binding is the one on the copy of Nicholas Jenson's 1475 Virgil now in Darmstadt, Landesbibliothek, Inc. IV.25, which was probably commissioned in Venice in an effort to imitate the new orientalizing binding style of the late fifteenth century. This style in general is associated with the libraries of the patricians; in this case the owner was Peter Ugelheimer, Jenson's partner,[16] so that we can see in tangible form the relationship between books, the men who made them, and the wealthy individuals who supported the printers and received their products in Renaissance Venice.

The same relationship is also evident in the painting and illumination added to the earliest printed books by those who could afford it. Most books from the first decades of printing did not receive any hand-painted additions, surviving today either with empty spaces where initials should be or with rubrication only— that is, with initials and chapter headings added in red and / or blue ink. Some books, however, received hand-painted and gilded initials in one or more empty spaces after they had been rubricated, as in the 1473 Leonardus Achates edition of Virgil now in Venice (Biblioteca Nazionale Marciana, Inc. 573) and the 1501 Aldine now in Los Angeles (University of California at Los Angeles Research Library, Special Collections Z233/A4V819/1501). A buyer who wanted to spend more money could purchase a book with an attractive but relatively standardized border to which a coat of arms could be added; among Virgilian examples still to be found in the Veneto are two copies of an edition published in 1476 by Antonius Bartholomaei (Venice, Biblioteca Nazionale Marciana, Inc. V.414; and Treviso, Biblioteca Comunale, Inc. 12113, painted by the Master of the Pico Pliny—see Plate 4) and a copy of the edition published by Baptista de Tortis around 1482 (Venice,

---

[16] Anthony Hobson, *Humanists and Bookbinders: The Origins and Diffusion of Humanist Bookbinding 1459–1559* (Cambridge, 1989), 51 and n. 65; and Lowry, *Nicholas Jenson*, 87–8.

Biblioteca Correr, Inc. E 225).[17] At the top of the hierarchy of hand illumination are elaborate, original frontispieces and painted initials, sometimes by named artists. Since these hand-painted additions often added considerably to the cost of the book—Leonardo Sanudo paid the artist Zorzi Tedesco in Ferrara 1.5 ducats, or as much as three times the cost of the book, to add 300 small letters to his copy of Virgil[18]—they made a mass-produced volume into an individual work of art capable of celebrating the wealth and status of its owner. Such additions often reflected the precise instructions of the buyer,[19] so that the classicizing vocabulary of triumphal arches and antique armour, medallions and acanthus, and cameos with scenes from antiquity shows that wealthy buyers were

[17]   A number of early incunabula also have a printed woodcut border, added as a guide so that the illuminator could work more quickly; see Frederick R. Goff, 'Illuminated Woodcut Borders and Initials in Early Venetian Books (1469–1475)', *Gutenberg Jahrbuch* (1962), 380–9; and Lowry, *Nicholas Jenson*, 86–7. The hierarchy used in this para. to describe the degree of finish for Venetian incunabula is that of Lilian Armstrong, 'The Impact of Printing on Miniaturists in Venice after 1469', in Sandra Hindman (ed.), *Printing the Written Word: The Social History of Books, circa 1450–1520* (Ithaca, NY, 1991), 180–92. A good bibliographical survey of recent work in this area may be found in the notes to Armstrong's article, from which the following should be singled out: Giordana Mariani Canova, *La miniatura veneta del Rinascimento* (Venice, 1969); and Lilian Armstrong, *Renaissance Miniature Painters and Classical Imagery: The Master of the Putti and his Venetian Workshop* (London, 1981). I would also like to acknowledge my debt here to Professor Armstrong, to whom I owe the identification of the painter of the vol. illustrated in Pl. 4 and much of the information in this para. Illustrations of work by the Master of the Pico Pliny may be found in L. Armstrong, 'Il Maestro di Pico: Un miniatore veneziano del tardo Quattrocento', *Saggi e memorie di storia dell'arte*, 17 (1990), illus. 215–53, and 'Impact of Printing', figs. 6.2–6.5, 6.8. The 1476 edn. seems to have been a favourite of early owners interested in illuminating their books, for it was also decorated by the Master of the London Pliny for the Agostini, a wealthy Venetian family of merchant-bankers; see Patricia Fortini Brown, *Venice and Antiquity: The Venetian Sense of the Past* (New Haven, 1996), 192–3 with frontispiece and pl. 208.
[18]   Lowry, *Nicholas Jenson*, 35–7 and nn. 26–8. Another interesting case involves Andrea Navagero, whose efforts to have a copy of Virgil (presumably from one of the edns. he had prepared) bound and illuminated led to disputes over prices with the binder; in this case we know that the illuminator was Benedetto Bordone, a famous master in this genre. I am grateful for this information to Lilian Armstrong, who in turn received from Dr Gabriele Mazzucco of the Biblioteca Nazionale Marciana the reference to Navagero's letter in Emanuele Antonio Cicogna, *Delle iscrizioni veneziane* (Bologna, 1970; repr. of Venice, 1853 edn.), vol. vi, pt. 1, 323–5. Additional information on the costs of rubricating and illuminating an early printed book may be found in Konrad Haebler, *Handbuch der Inkunabelkunde* (Leipzig, 1925), 156. Such hand-painted additions to incunabula were also valued as objects of art in their own right, such that they were sometimes removed from the books in which they were painted, as happened with material from Venice, Biblioteca Nazionale Marciana, Inc. 426, a copy of the 1471 Adam de Ambergau edn.
[19]   Haebler, *Handbuch der Inkunabelkunde*.

Plate 4. Illumination by the Master of the Pico Pliny in Treviso, Biblioteca Comunale copy of *Opera omnia* ([Venice]: Antonius Bartholomaei, 1476), fo. a2ʳ. (Used by permission of the Biblioteca Comunale, Treviso.)

also sophisticated enough to match decorative style to the content of their books according to *au courant* humanistic norms.[20]

The Latin editions of Virgil are also linked to the Venetian patriciate through the dedicatory letters and prefaces they contain. In his 1514 edition, for example, Aldus Manutius addressed a prefatory letter to Petrus Bembus in which he acknowledged taking the octavo format of his book from a manuscript in the library of Petrus and his father Bernardus.[21] Some forty years later

[20] Ibid. 82–7; and E. P. Goldschmidt, *The Printed Book of the Renaissance: Three Lectures on Type, Illustration, Ornament* (Cambridge, 1950), 60–88. As Michael Camille points out, these architectural frames and illusionistic vignettes are more serious in style than their medieval predecessors, where scatological sporting and bawdy play were common (*Image on the Edge: The Margins of Medieval Art* (Cambridge, Mass., 1992), 153–60). Such illuminations gradually disappear as woodcuts gain in popularity (see below), but efforts to dress up a book continue sporadically when a wash is added to the printed pictures. This process begins as soon as wood-cuts appear (e.g. 1507 Bernardinus Stagninus edn.: New York, Columbia University Library, Lodge 1507/V587) and continues up to the end of the 16th cent. (e.g. Venice, Biblioteca Nazionale Marciana, 134.d.54, a copy of the 1574–5 edn. published by the heirs of Joannes Maria Bonellus); see Goldschmidt, *Printed Book*, 54. Indeed, sporadic illumination of early printed books has continued up to modern times; for example, the paintings in Florence, Biblioteca Riccardiana, Ed. Rara 74, a copy of the 1472 'Printer of Ausonius' incunabulum, have been dated to the 19th cent. by Lilian Armstrong (private communication).

[21] This letter may be found in G. Orlandi, *Aldo Manuzio editore: Dediche, prefazioni, noti ai testi*, 2 vols. (Milan, 1975), i. 152. The edns. in which the letter first appears are both dated 1514, with one containing correction sheets and one having the corrections incorporated into the text; however, on the basis of the style of the printer's device used here, H. G. Fletcher III has recently argued that the second of these edns. should be redated to *c.*1520 (*New Aldine Studies: Documentary Studies on the Life and Work of Aldus Manutius* (San Francisco, Calif., 1988), 120–2). The letter was reprinted in the Aldine edns. of 1527, 1541, 1545, 1573, 1580, and 1587. On Bernardus Bembus, see Margaret L. King, *Venetian Humanism in an Age of Patrician Dominance* (Princeton, 1986), 335–9, with bibliography. On the Bembus library, see Nella Giannetto, *Bernardo Bembo: Umanista e politico veneziano*, Civiltà veneziana, Saggi, 34 (Florence, 1985), with the additional bibliography contained there. What is intriguing here, given Aldus' pioneering work with octavos, is his reference to *parvam hanc enchiridii formam* ('this small format for the handbook'), which is quite precise. As Silvia Rizzo has noted (*Il lessico filologico degli umanisti*, Sussidi eruditi, 26 (Rome, 1973), 47–8), *forma* was in regular use as a technical term for the size of a ms and *parva* was one of the adjectives regularly coupled to it for mss ranging in size from 260 × 165 cm. to 175 × 120 cm. One candidate for the ms in question has recently emerged at the Princeton University Library. Ms. 104, which contains forty-nine pen-and-wash drawings copied from the Vatican Virgil of the 4th or 5th cent. along with relevant accompanying text, is of the appropriate size (230 × 170 cm.) and has recently been attributed to the scribe Bartolomeo Sanvito, working in Padua in 1507 or later, by Albinia de la Mare (private communications of 13 June 1988 to Jean Preston and of 5 Jan. 1993 to me). The ms is described by Rosalie B. Green, 'Mirrors of the Mediaeval World: Illuminated Manuscripts from the Princeton Collections', *Princeton University Library Chronicle*, 27 (1966), 189 (no. 61). The connection between Bartolomeo Sanvito and Aldus' octavo books is discussed in Armando Petrucci, 'Alle origini del libro moderno: Libro da banco, libri da bisaccia, libretti da mano', *Italia medioevale e umanistica*, 12 (1969), 306–8; and Nicolas Barker, 'The Aldine Italic', in Robin Myers and Michael Harris (eds.), *A Millennium of the Book: Production, Design & Illustration in Manuscript & Print 900–1900* (Winchester, 1994), 54–9.

Aldus' son Paulus addressed a dedicatory letter to the patrician Antonius Callierges, and shortly after that he addressed to Petrus Bembus' son Torquatus another prefatory letter in which he discussed the relationship between fable, verse, and philosophical truth in poetry.[22] In explaining in turn how his editorial efforts would facilitate the use of Virgil by those aiming to perfect their Latin style, the scholar Nicolaus Erythraeus dedicated his efforts to the humanist patrician Franciscus Contarenus, at the same time offering a rhetorical flourish by which Virgil became an adopted Venetian: *Tibi igitur amicorum antistiti Patricio Veneto Venetum Virgilium poetarum facile antistitem Venetus ego nuncupo.* ('Therefore I, a Venetian, pronounce Virgil, easily the most accomplished of poets, a Venetian, before you, Venetian patrician and the most accomplished of friends.')[23]

Dedications like these have often been dismissed as empty flattery, reflecting more the desire for patronage on the part of printers than real interest on the part of patricians. However, recent research indicates that patrician patrons were tied more closely than once thought to the early printers of the classics in Venice. As Martin Lowry has shown, a small group of Venetian patricians whose studies in Padua during the 1430s and early 1440s contained a heavy dose of the classics obtained a series of important political posts in the 1440s and 1450s, where they used their polished Latin style and knowledge of classical jurisprudence to advance their own political interests. The election of Christoforo Moro as doge in 1462 gave these humanist patricians a secure power base, from which they sought to strengthen public education, to arrange for the donation of a first-rank classical library to the state, and to patronize the new art of printing in Venice. Although much of this patronage was indirect, Bernardo Giustiniani provided significant

[22]   The first letter is found on fos. 1ʳ–2ʳ of the 1553 edn. and fos. 2ʳ–3ʳ of the 1555 edn. The second letter was first printed in the 1558 edn. (fos. [2]ʳ–4ᵛ) and reprinted in the Aldine edns. of 1560, 1563, 1565, 1570, 1573, 1576, 1580, and 1587. On the relationship of Paulus Manutius with the publishing plans of the Accademia Veneziana, see A.-A. Renouard, *Annales de l'imprimerie des Alde, ou histoire des trois Manuce et de leurs éditions* (New Castle, Del., 1991; repr. of Paris, 1834 edn.), 267–81; and Pietro Pagan, 'Sulla Accademia "Venetiana" o della "Fama" ', *Atti dell'Istituto Veneto di Scienze, Lettere ed Arti* (Classe di scienze morali, lettere ed arti), 132 (1973–4), 359–92.

[23]   This letter was first printed in the 1538–9 edn. of Johannes Antonius de Nicolinis de Sabio and reprinted in the edns. of Franciscus Rampazetus and Melchior Sessa and their heirs in 1555–6, 1565, 1582–3, 1586, and 1597, and in the edns. of Franciscus Laurentinus, 1566, and Damianus Zenarus, 1587. The quotation is taken from the 1582–3 edn., fo. a3ʳ.

assistance to the printer Nicholas Jenson, Pierfrancesco Barbarigo invested both capital and the influence of his family name in the Aldine company, and members of the Bragadin and Giustiniani families pioneered the printing of Hebrew in Renaissance Venice.[24] In return, patrician patrons often received special presentation copies of the books they had helped finance, sometimes (though by no means always) on vellum.[25] In short, the often-quoted but self-interested judgement of the Florentine scribe Vespasiano da Bisticci, that printed books dared not show their faces among the elegant manuscripts of the Duke of Urbino's library, has led to too much misleading scholarship about aristocratic disdain for early printed books.[26]

What we have seen so far tends to confirm an association, much written about of late, between humanist study of the classics and high social and economic status.[27] However, it would be a mistake to oversimplify this point. For one thing, the nature of the surviving evidence often raises as many questions as it answers. Ownership notes, for example, can be difficult to analyse, given that after five hundred years it is often difficult to determine the social and economic status of individuals whose families are not so well known as the Contarini and Bragadin. Among the owners of books now in

[24] Lowry, *Nicholas Jenson*, 1–25, 48–75, 99–100, and id., *The World of Aldus Manutius: Business and Scholarship in Renaissance Venice* (Ithaca, NY, 1979), 84–5. In 'A Theory of the Early Italian Printing Firm, Part I: Variants of Humanism', *Harvard Library Bulletin*, 33 (1985), 341–77, and 'Part II: The Political Economy of Patronage', 34 (1986), 294–332, M. Feld examines the role of patronage and Curial politics in the early development of printing in Rome, and some good general comments on the positive effects of patronage on literary culture may be found in Robert Escarpit, *Sociology of Literature*, trans. Ernest Pick, Lake Erie College Studies, 4 (Painesville, Oh., 1965), 38–9.

[25] Lowry, *Nicholas Jenson*, 70–1. This may also explain the unusual blue-paper copy of the 1514 Aldine Virgil now in Los Angeles, University of California Research Library, Spec. Coll. Z233/A4V819/1514, which Lawrence Witten considered a kind of presentation copy, somewhere between regular paper and vellum; the book is illustrated as the frontispiece of Nicolas Barker *et al.*, *A Catalogue of the Ahmanson-Murphy Aldine Collection at UCLA*, fascicle I. *The Publications of Aldus Manutius the Elder* (Los Angeles, Calif., 1989) and described as item 110, 154–5.   [26] Lowry, *Nicholas Jenson*, 70.

[27] Lauro Martines, for example, writes that 'all humanists ... made a candid alliance with power' (*Power and Imagination: City-States in Renaissance Italy* (London, 1980), 271). It is easy to extend this observation to other areas, such that Wolfgang Reinhard argues in general that humanism was allied to the colonialist enterprise through an ideological affinity with Roman imperialism ('Missionaries, Humanists and Natives in the Sixteenth-Century Spanish Indies—A Failed Encounter of Two Worlds?' *Renaissance Studies*, 6 (1992), 360–76), and Richard Waswo argues in particular that Virgil's poetry guided the power relationships between 16th-cent. Europeans and Americans ('The History that Literature makes', *New Literary History*, 19 (1988), 541).

the Marciana, for example, is also one Paulo Cisonato, whose ownership note asks that anyone finding his beloved copy of Virgil (1552, heirs of Lucas Antonius Junta: 390.d.21) restore it to its place in his bookcase; we know nothing about him, nor about Flaminius Graspa and Angelus de Lazaris, whose books (1507, Bernardinus Stagninus: Rari V.99; and 1562, Joannes Maria Bonellus: 134.d.58) have ended up in the same library. Once we move to the cities on the mainland that passed in and out of Venetian control in the Renaissance, the problems of identification become even greater. The name *Urbanus Vendraminus* tempts us to link this book owner to the Venetian patrician family that produced a doge at the end of the fifteenth century; on the other hand, the adjective *Tarvisinus* ('of Treviso') that accompanies this name and the fact that the book (1555–6, Franciscus Rampazetus and Melchior Sessa: N.2162) has been in the Biblioteca Comunale in Treviso for almost two hundred years raise as many questions as they answer. The painstaking researches of local historians in the cities of the Veneto have not shed any light on the Maximius Gadius whose copy of Virgil (1542, heirs of Lucas Antonius Junta: Cinq. B.270) is now in the Biblioteca Civica in Verona, or on the Franciscus di Luriana whose book (1588, Joannes Gryphius Minor: C.15.5.5) is now in the Biblioteca Bertoliana in Vicenza. While we know in general that many of the books in the collection of the Biblioteca del Museo Civico in Padua came from the old families of some prominence in that city, that does not tell us anything specific about those who bought a Venetian edition of Virgil and signed their names in their books: *Georgius Regi* ... (1522, Lucas Antonius Junta and Gregorius de Gregoriis: G.4596), *Antonius Gonnella* (1552, heirs of Lucas Antonius Junta: M.681), *Clement Martinus Nicoeoensis* (1562, Joannes Maria Bonellus: F.10008), *Bernardinus Cedinus* (1574–5, heirs of Joannes Maria Bonellus: G.8173), *Michaelis Simonus* (1580, Aldus Manutius Minor: F.6386), or *Laurentius Pignoria Patavinus* (1582–3, heirs of Franciscus Rampazetus and Melchior Sessa: I.413). And when one of these Paduan books (1534, Petrus de Nicolinis de Sabio: M.1886) signed by Daniel Brascus is also annotated in Hebrew, the lack of information becomes frustrating indeed.[28] The odds suggest that Urbanus Vendraminus was a noble and that Daniel Brascus was not;

---

[28] Padua, Biblioteca del Museo Civico, I.130, a copy of the 1543–4 heirs of Lucas Antonius Junta edn., was owned by *Rabbi Ira Mi ... uo ... Se ...*, about whom again it

about the others, and about many like them, we simply cannot say for sure.

It is equally difficult to speak with precision about the owners of books that ended up in religious communities. We find a wide variety of orders possessing one or more copies: the Dominican Convent of S. Maria Gratiarum in Padua (1479, Leonardus Achates de Basilea: Vicenza, Biblioteca Bertoliana, Gonz. 20.8.3 (I.V.65)), the Carthusians of Montello (1536, Aurelius Pintius: Padua, Biblioteca Universitaria, 74.b.142), the Congregation of the Lateran Canons in Padua (1553, Hieronymus Scotus: Padua, Biblioteca Universitaria, 64.a.168), the Theatines of Ferrara (1575–6, Joannes Baptista Sessa and Brothers: Ferrara, Biblioteca Ariostea, L.11.11.30), the Capuchin brothers in Verona (1597, Joannes Baptista and Joannes Bernardus Sessa: Verona, Biblioteca Civica, Cinq. C.583), and so forth, with a noticeable concentration among Jesuit houses—no surprise, given the emphasis on liberal arts teaching within the order.[29] As we might expect, the movement of books between the secular and religious worlds confirms that a copy of Virgil in Latin was often associated with the upper classes. One copy that had been in the patrician Corradini family, for example, passed to the Dominican order of the observance of S. Maria del Rosario or of the Gesuati in Venice (1574–5, heirs of Joannes Maria Bonellus: Venice,

would be nice to know more. On the general topic of Judaism in the Veneto during this period, see Pier Cesare Ioly Zorattini, 'Gli Ebrei a Venezia, Padova e Verona', in *Storia della cultura veneta*, iii. Girolamo Arnaldi and Manlio Pastore Stocchi (eds.), *Dal primo Quattrocento al Concilio di Trento*, pt. 1 (Vicenza, 1980), 537–76.

[29] Two books now in the Biblioteca Ariostea, for example, belonged to the Jesuit college in Ferrara (1507, Bernardinus Stagninus: M.5.4.41; and 1536–7, Lucas Antonius Junta: M.1.11.9), and two others now in the Biblioteca Nazionale Centrale in Rome once belonged to the Collegio Romano (1544, Hieronymus Scotus: 36.12.E.5; and 1566, Joannes Maria Bonellus: 71.3.E.8). On Jesuit education in general, see Aldo Scaglione, *The Liberal Arts and the Jesuit College System* (Amsterdam, 1986); and John W. O'Malley, *The First Jesuits* (Cambridge, Mass., 1993), 200–42. As my colleague Daniel Bornstein has pointed out, a disproportionate number of the religious groups in this list are among the more stringent, newer orders, which may reflect in part the support for classical learning within certain quarters of the Counter-Reformation Church; see also Erich Cochrane, *Italy, 1530–1630*, ed. Julius Kirschner, Longman History of Italy (London, 1988), 118–23. The libraries of newly founded orders, of course, would also be more likely to have a standard text like Virgil in a printed edn. than in a ms, since they would not have the resources of an old library at hand. It is worth noting here that the number of printed copies held by religious institutions is large enough to make me a bit hesitant about the often-repeated generalization (e.g. Goldschmidt, *Printed Book*, 60–1) that the medieval book was an institutional possession, but the printed book of the Renaissance became the property of individuals.

Biblioteca Nazionale Marciana, 134.d.54), and another copy was donated by Count Joannes Montanarus to the Discalced Carmelites in Vicenza (1522, Lucas Antonius Junta: Treviso, Biblioteca Comunale, N. 19284 [R.2.23.A]). A third copy of Virgil now in Padua (1534, Petrus de Nicolinis de Sabio: Biblioteca del Museo Civico, M.1881) followed the path of Cicogna's Virgil and moved from a notary to a cleric, in this case Giovanni Abitantius Bassarisius. More frequently the name of an individual clerical owner appears alone, and these cases are more difficult to analyse. Sometimes we can deduce that the individual—the Paduan Ascanius Varese, Abbot General of the Congregation of Lateran Canons, for example (1553, Hieronymus Scotus: Padua, Biblioteca Universitaria, 64.a.168)—was of some prominence. This is less likely the case, however, for someone who signed his book (1507, Bernardinus Stagninus: Padua, Biblioteca del Museo Civico, F.7445) simply *frater Andreas Nicsil Utinensis ordinis S. Augustini*, and we know nothing about the man who indicated possession merely with *Carlo Margignon Chierico* (1581, Joannes Baptista Sessa and Brothers, and heirs of Franciscus Rampazetus: Ferrara, Biblioteca Ariostea, S.20.7). Given that religious communities in the Renaissance contained people from a variety of social and economic backgrounds, however, it would be reasonable to assume that as with secular readers, there is at least some social and economic diversity among the clerics who owned a copy of Virgil.

While the absence of precise information about these early owners at least leaves open the possibility that some copies of Virgil in Latin entered the libraries of people who lacked great wealth and prominence, the copies associated with the environment of the schools establish that here, this was certainly the case. To be sure, the majority of the 47 per cent of Venetian students enrolled in Latin as opposed to vernacular schools in 1587–8 were children of nobles, professional men, and merchants of at least middling rank, in training to obtain the humanistic education necessary for advancement within the church or the government. It is difficult to estimate how much schooling the other 90 per cent of the population, ranging from smaller merchants to artisans and labourers to servants and the destitute, obtained, but Paul Grendler has estimated that a substantial minority of the men and a few women in these groups could at least read and write.[30] Communal schools regularly made provisions for instructing a few students on scholarship, and the communal *sestiere* schools, which were by statute free of charge, included among the children of nobles and citizens at least a few commoners,[31] who must have written some of the dozens of *recordationes* entered by anonymous Venetian students into early printed texts of Virgil. What is more, teachers themselves illustrate the spread of Latin books into the classes below the rich and famous. Technically teachers were included in the same professional class as lawyers, notaries, government secretaries, university professors, and physicians, but they ranked at the bottom of this group, sometimes rising from the artisan class below and sometimes falling back into poverty again.[32] Moreover, there is no question that teachers owned printed copies of the texts they taught—as evidenced by the extensive commentary entered by an anonymous teacher into the Marciana Aldine discussed in Chapter 2.

This discussion raises the question of precisely how great an investment an early edition of Virgil was in the economic terms of Renaissance Venice. I know of three copies still in the Veneto whose buyers recorded the price they paid for their books. The first (Venice, Biblioteca Correr, Inc. E 241) is a copy of the 1493 folio edition of Bartholomaeus de Zanis whose buyer, one Johannes Proger, indicated that he bought it in Italy the year it was published for £6 s15, a price that may have included the elegant leather binding in which the book is still covered. The second (Vicenza, Biblioteca Bertoliana, C.15.7.8), a copy of the 1532–3 Lucas Antonius Junta edition, also in folio, was sold twice within twenty–five years after its publication. The first buyer, whose cancelled name can be read in part as *Joannes à Pre ... gensis*, paid £4 s16 on 23 October 1544; the second, who did not leave his name, paid £5 s2 when he bought it on 11 May 1557. The third book (Venice, Biblioteca Nazionale Marciana, 58.d.197) is an octavo, the 1587 Damianus Zenarus edition, that was bought by Gregorius Bartadicus in Venice for £3 s10.

Comparison of these prices to booksellers' catalogues of the

---

[30] *Schooling in Renaissance Italy: Literacy and Learning, 1300–1600* (Baltimore, 1989), 42–7, 61.

[31] Ibid. 16, 61–70.   [32] Ibid. 37–9, 51–6.

period suggests that there were also less expensive options. The record book of the Venetian bookseller Francesco de Madiis indicates that a folio copy of Virgil with Servius sold at £3, then at £2 during the 1480s, while the early Aldine price lists show that one of the new octavos cost £1 s10 at the turn of the century (although the five folio volumes of Aristotle cost a hefty 11 ducats).[33] The Aldine price list of 1592 offers the 1580 edition for £3 s10 and the 1585 edition for £1 s10; the stockbook of Bernardus Junta confirms that a text of Virgil in octavo could be had for only £1 s4 in 1600.[34] Thus successful negotiation with a bookseller, fluctuations in prices, and the appearance of plain texts in the smaller octavo format made it possible in the course of the sixteenth century to buy at least a text of Virgil without commentary for considerably less than Bartadicus paid.

The key question, of course, is how these prices compared to incomes in Renaissance Venice. The annual incomes of patricians and wealthy merchants could run into thousands of ducats, with skilled craftsmen earning between fifty and two hundred ducats per year and unskilled workers less. A privileged intellectual like

[33] The record book of de Madiis is printed as doc. VIII in Horatio F. Brown, *The Venetian Printing Press, 1469–1800: An Historical Study based upon Documents for the Most Part Hitherto Unpublished* (Amsterdam, 1969; repr. of London, 1891 edn.), 431–52, and analysed by Lowry, *Nicholas Jenson*, 128, 178–98. The three Aldine catalogues of 1498, 1503, and 1513 may be found in G. Orlandi, *Aldo Manuzio editore* (Milan, 1975), with discussion in Rudolph Hirsch, 'The Art of Selling Books: Notes on Three Aldine Catalogues', *Studies in Bibliography*, 1 (1949), 83–101; and Martin Davies, *Aldus Manutius: Printer and Publisher of Renaissance Venice* (London, 1995), 25–6. A good overview of this topic may be found in Martin Lowry, *Book Prices in Renaissance Venice: The Stockbook of Bernardo Giunti*, Occasional Papers, 5 (Los Angeles, Calif., 1991), esp. 8–12. In the discussion that follows, the plotting of prices given by de Madiis provides an approximate orientation: 1 ducat = 6.4 lire, and 1 lira = 20 soldi.

[34] The Aldine price list is found at the end of the 1592 edn. of *Demonomania de gli stregoni ... di Giovanni Bodino francese, tradotta dal K. R. Hercole Cato*, fos. ★★★★7ʳ–8ᵛ. Two folios bound at the end of *Essame de gl'ingegni de gl'huomini ... di Giovanni Huarte tradotto dalla lingua spagnuola da M. Camillo Camilli* (1590) contain another price list; there is a *Virgilio con Annotationi, & Tavole, 8. £3 s.10*, but the entry does not specify exactly which edn. is meant. The 1592 catalogue, along with several earlier ones (mostly lacking prices), is reprinted in Renouard, *Annales de l'imprimerie des Alde*, 328–45. On Bernardus Junta's price list, see Lowry, *Book Prices*, 16–30. See also Paul Grendler, 'Printing and Censorship', in Quentin Skinner and Eckhard Kessler (eds.), *Cambridge History of Renaissance Philosophy* (Cambridge, 1988), 31; and Fletcher, *New Aldine Studies*, 88–91. As Rudolf Hirsch has observed, the prices of early books fluctuated significantly in ways that often elude explanation today (*Printing, Selling and Reading, 1450–1550* (Wiesbaden, 1967), 69–72), a warning repeated in slightly different form by Haebler, *Handbuch der Inkunabelkunde*, 146, so that any conclusions reached here must remain tentative.

Giorgio Merula might earn 120 ducats per year and a schoolmaster perhaps seventy-five to one hundred; in short, four to five ducats per month was adequate, and anything over ten was relative affluence. Thus a book was a substantial investment, with the cost of an octavo equivalent to perhaps 5 or 10 per cent of the basic cost of living for a month and a Greek folio equivalent to a month's wages for the compositor who set it—expensive, but not completely out of reach for someone of at least middling economic status.[35] This would suggest that a literate artisan could own a few books, a schoolteacher a few more, a well-paid university teacher a hundred or more, and a patrician collector several thousand, and the surviving records seem to confirm this pattern.[36] The buyers of the 119 copies of Virgil sold by Francesco de Madiis between 1484 and 1488 were largely other booksellers, nobles, and priests, with a few professional people and a large group of unknown social status.[37] This continues a trend from the century before the introduction of printing, in which a manuscript copy of Virgil often found its way into the smaller private libraries of physicians and humble priests as well as the larger patrician collections in Venice,[38] and the researches of Christian Bec have shown that Florentine owners of the classics included merchants as well.[39]

[35] Lowry, *Nicholas Jenson*, 186–8; Grendler, *Schooling*, 18; and Shifra Z. Baruchson-Arbib, 'The Prices of Hebrew Printed Books in Cinquecento Italy', *Bibliofilia*, 97 (1995), 149–61.

[36] Grendler, 'Printing and Censorship', 31. Calculating independently, Martin Lowry came to essentially the same conclusion: 'When a skilled workman was earning around 3 ducats—say 20 lire per month—he would have to think twice before spending 10 per cent of his wages on a book; but at least he could think, rather than merely yearn' (*Book Prices*, 9). We should not, however, overestimate the effect of printing per se on lowering the price of books, since Caterina Tristano estimates that a non-illuminated ms owned by the Calabrian humanist Aulo Giano Parrasio would have cost less than we might imagine— about 1 per cent of his university professor's annual salary, which was a little above average for his profession ('Economia del libro in Italia tra la fine del XV e l'inizio del XVI secolo: Il prezzo del libro "vecchio" ', *Scrittura e civiltà*, 14 (1990), 237–41). We should also not forget that books could be borrowed as well as bought, so that readers of more modest means could obtain some books in this way as well: Carlo Ginzburg, for example, notes that of the eleven books in the possession of the Friulian miller Menocchio when he was arrested for heresy, at least six had been loaned to him (*The Cheese and the Worms: The Cosmos of a Sixteenth-Century Miller*, trans. John and Anne Tedeschi (New York, 1989), 28–31). Unfortunately, information about lending practices in the 15th and 16th cents. is very difficult to find.

[37] Lowry, *Nicholas Jenson*, 194–8.

[38] Susan Connell, 'Books and their Owners in Venice, 1345–1480', *Journal of the Warburg and Courtauld Institutes*, 35 (1972), 173–4.

[39] *Les Livres des florentins (1413–1608)*, Biblioteca di 'Lettere Italiane', Studi e testi, 29 (Florence, 1984), 124–7.

An examination of the woodcuts in these early Venetian editions of Virgil provides evidence that those who used these books included some individuals even further removed from the humanistically educated members of the upper classes. After the first illustrated Venetian edition of Virgil came off the presses of Philippus Pintius in 1505, over half the Latin editions printed during the sixteenth century contained woodcuts.[40] The artist who designed the woodcuts for the Pintius edition, a somewhat bizarre Venetian known only by his initial 'L', produced a simplified set of illustrations that often inclined toward a classicizing humanist taste (see Plate 5). However, another popular set of designs was based on 'L''s recutting of the woodcuts taken from the Sebastian Brant–Johannes Grüninger Strasbourg edition. First printed in Venice in 1519 and reprinted there as late as 1586,[41] these designs were decidedly old-fashioned in style (see Plate 6), with a heavy reliance on the crowded layout, serial presentation, and anachronistic fashions typical of medieval art. Such features would have been discordant to a taste moulded by humanist principles, which expected events from antiquity to be presented so as to acknowledge the differences between this earlier world and that

[40] Basic information on these early illustrated edns. may be found in V. M. Prince d'Essling, *Études sur l'art de la gravure sur bois à Venise: Les Livres à figures vénitiens de la fin du XVe siècle et du commencement du XVIe* ..., 3 pts. in 4 vols. (Florence, 1907–14); Max Sander, *Le Livre à figures italien depuis 1467 jusqu'à 1530: Essai de sa bibliographie et son histoire*, 4 vols. (Milan, 1942); and Arthur M. Hind, *An Introduction to a History of the Woodcut*, 2 vols. (New York, 1963). It seems that the percentage of Renaissance edns. of Virgil in Latin that contained illustrations was higher than for other classical authors.

[41] Vladimiro Zabughin, *Vergilio nel Rinascimento italiano da Dante a Torquato Tasso*, 2 vols. (Bologna, 1921–3), ii. 389–92; Goldschmidt, *Printed Book*, 46–8 with fig. 14, pl. 5; T. K. Rabb, 'Sebastian Brant and the First Illustrated Edition of Vergil', *Princeton University Library Chronicle*, 21 (1960): 187–99; Martine Gorrichon, 'Sebastien Brant et l'illustration des œuvres de Virgile d'après l'édition strasbourgeoise de 1502', in P. Tuynman, G. C. Kuiper, and E. Kessler (eds.), *Acta Conventus Neo-Latini Amstelodamensis*, Proceedings of the Second International Congress of Neo-Latin Studies, Amsterdam 19–24 Aug. 1973 (Munich, 1979), 440–52; Eleanor Winsor Leach, 'Illustration as Interpretation in Brant's and Dryden's Editions of Vergil', in Sandra Hindman (ed.), *The Early Illustrated Book: Essays in Honor of Lessing J. Rosenwald* (Washington, 1982), 175–210; Bernd Schneider, ' "Virgilius pictus"— Sebastian Brants illustrierte Vergilausgabe und ihre Nachwirkung: Ein Beitrag zur Vergilrezeption im deutschen Humanismus', *Wolfenbütteler Beiträge: Aus den Schätzen der Herzog August Bibliothek*, 6 (1983), 202–62; Ruth Mortimer, 'Vergil in the Light of the Sixteenth Century: Selected Illustrations', in John D. Bernard (ed.), *Vergil at 2000: Commemorative Essays on the Poet and his Influence* (New York, 1986), 159–84; Alexander G. McKay, 'Book Illustrations of Vergil's *Aeneid* AD 400–1980', *Augustan Age*, 6 (1987), 227–37 and pls. following 269; and Annabel Patterson, *Pastoral and Ideology: Virgil to Valéry* (Berkeley and Los Angeles, Calif., 1987), 92–106.

Plate 5. Woodcut of the council of the gods in *Opera omnia* (Venice: Philippus Pintius, 1505), fo. 289ʳ. (Biblioteca Casanatense, Rome; used by permission of the Ministero per i Beni Culturali ed Ambientali.)

of the present,[42] yet these illustrations were reprinted for sixty-five years.

This suggests that the audience for the woodcuts was not always the same as the audience for the humanist commentaries accompanying the Latin text. Indeed, a number of modern scholars have

[42] It is now a commonplace to note that Renaissance humanists recovered the ability to set aside their own cultural perspective in order to envision the past in its own terms; see e.g. Jean Seznec, *The Survival of the Pagan Gods: The Mythological Tradition and its Place in Renaissance Humanism and Art*, Bollingen Series, 38 (Princeton, 1972), 322; and Eugenio Garin, *Italian Humanism: Philosophy and Civic Life in the Renaissance*, trans. Peter Munz (New York, 1965), 6, 14–15. There is a certain irony, however, in the fact that the illuminations painted by hand into Virgilian incunabula—the holdovers from medieval book production—reflect a humanist aesthetic more consistently than the woodcuts printed according

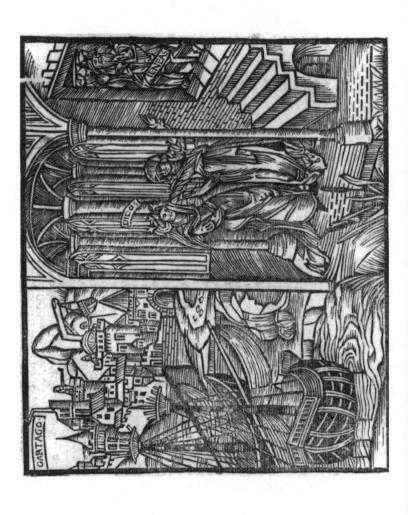

suggested that the illustrations in sixteenth-century books served as a way to instruct those who could not read the text, in this case either because they could not read Latin or because they could not read at all, so that the same book ended up serving different functions for different audiences.[43] Brant himself acknowledged this at the end of his edition:

> Virgilium exponant alii sermone diserto
> Et calamo pueris tradere et ore iuvent.
> Pictura agresti voluit Brant atque tabellis
> Edere eum indoctis rusticolisque viris.

(Let others explain Virgil in eloquent speech and be pleased to hand him down to boys both by pen and speech; Brant wished to publish him for unlearned and peasant folk in rustic pictures and drawings.)[44]

---

to the new technology in 16th-cent. Venetian edns. As Elizabeth Eisenstein has pointed out, these woodcuts were often used and reused in ways that challenge the integration of classical form and spirit generally said to characterize the Renaissance ('The Advent of Printing and the Problem of the Renaissance', *Past and Present*, 45 (1969), 74–5).

[43] Goldschmidt, *Printed Book*, 50; Lucien Febvre and Henri-Jean Martin, *The Coming of the Book: The Impact of Printing 1450–1800*, trans. David Gerard (London, 1990), 98–9; Chrisman, *Lay Culture*, 105–6; and Miriam Rothstein, 'Disjunctive Images in Renaissance Books', NS 14 (1990), 101–20. As Mario Praz has observed, the emblem books discussed in Ch. 2 also combine illustrations and text so that different groups of readers might use the same book (*Studies in Seventeenth-Century Imagery*, 2nd edn., Sussidi eruditi, 16 (Rome, 1964), 168). In 'Form and Function in Italian Renaissance Popular Books', *Renaissance Quarterly*, 46 (1993), 470, Paul Grendler shows that although it is in Latin, the format of *Officium Beatae Mariae* marks it as a popular work aimed at a target audience, especially of women, who were not likely to have known enough Latin to read the book comfortably. This example serves as another warning against overly hasty generalizations about who might have used a particular Renaissance book.

[44] Quoted in Patterson, *Pastoral and Ideology*, 104–5, from which the trans. is adapted; Patterson's emphasis on Brant's approach to the *Eclogues* as a version of pastoral appropriate to the common people supports the argument developed here. The identification of two different audiences for the same book is also found in other 16th-cent. writing, e.g. in an adaptation of the popular *Ars moriendi*: 'But so that his matter may be fruitful and of value to all, and that no one be excluded from its speculations, but in it all people of whatsoever estate may learn that they must die well, I have treated and deduced this book in two manners corresponding one to the other. First in sermons, [citations of] authorities, and parables to serve the clergy and lettered people, second in figures and images showing figuratively and before their eyes what is meant speculatively by letters. And I have done so to serve the laity and the illiterate.' Qtd. from *Art et science de bien vivre et bien mourir* (Paris, n.d.), fo. Kiiiʳ, in Roger Chartier, 'Texts and Images: The Arts of Dying, 1450–1600', in *Cultural Uses of Print*, 59.

Plate 6. (*Opposite*) Woodcut of Aeneas arriving in Carthage, *Opera* (Venice: Cominus de Tridino Montisferrati, 1546), fo. 205ᵛ. (Foto Biblioteca Vaticana.)

Those who came to these illustrated Virgils to study the pictures—poorly educated, humble folk—stayed faithful to the Gothic illustration style,[45] so that once we have identified them as the audience for the Brant–Grüninger designs, the persistence of the older style of illustration serves to broaden the consumption base for these books.

There is one final indication that a Latin edition of Virgil could be used in different ways by different audiences. On the back of the title-page of a copy of the 1551 Bartholomaeus Cesanus edition now in the Biblioteca Civica in Verona (Cinq. C.698), we find the following notice:

Memoria quando morse la venerabile signora gridonia filio primo del signor conte Gaihes [?] conte de Sartero qual fu molier del venerabile signor conte aurelio Becaria conte di la pieve morse alle 16 die novembre a hore 10 de note del ano 1579.

(A memorial of the death of the venerable Signora Gridonia, first child of Gaihes, count of Sartero, who was the wife of the venerable Count Aurelio Becaria, count of the parish; she died on 16 November, at 10 at night in the year 1579.)

This copy of Virgil was being used like a family Bible, an object whose mystical significance made it appropriate for recording key events in the lives of its owners.[46] Those owners may have been titled, but like the humble reader who studied the woodcuts in the Brant Strasbourg edition, they remind us that a Latin edition of Virgil could meet a wider range of needs in a wider range of consumers than we might at first imagine.

---

[45] Febvre and Martin, *Coming of the Book*, 98–9. Lilian Armstrong, 'The Illustration of Pliny's *Historia Naturalis* in Venetian Manuscripts and Early Printed Books', in J. B. Trapp (ed.), *Manuscripts in the Fifty Years after the Invention of Printing*, Some Papers read at a Colloquium at the Warburg Institute on 12–13 Mar. 1982 (London, 1983), 97–106, notes that a new *all'antica* cycle of figurative initials failed to displace a traditional ms cycle that became the basis for the woodcut versions predominating in Pliny incunabula of the 1470s, so that on this level as well, we do not find linear 'progress' in pictorial representation. On figurative initials in general, see Giuseppina Zappella, 'Incisione, illustrazione, figura: (L'iniziale)', *Miscellanea Marciana*, 2–4 (1987–89), 221–66; and Franca Petrucci Nardelli, *La lettera e l'immagine: Le iniziali 'parlanti' nella tipografia italiana (Secc. XVI–XVIII)*, Biblioteca di bibliografia italiana, 125 (Florence, 1992).

[46] The use of books like a family Bible in which events like births and deaths were recorded has been noted before, but as an activity of the semi-literate who would have known little or no Latin and would therefore have had little reason to own a book of Roman poetry like this one; see Armando Petrucci, 'Introduzione', in id. (ed.), *Libri, editori e pubblico nell'Europa moderna: Guida storica e critica*, Biblioteca Universale Laterza, 291 (Bari, 1989), pp. xx–xxi.

In addition to the Latin volumes on which our attention has been focused so far, Virgil was also published in Italian some seventy times in Renaissance Venice.[47] Since many people either could not read Latin at all or would not choose a Latin text when a vernacular translation was available, the existence of a sizeable selection of translations is an obvious extension of the market beyond the well-educated teachers, students, and churchmen whose professional activities drew them temporarily or permanently to Latin. Nevertheless before pursuing the obvious, I would like to suggest that the Italian translations are more closely bound to their Latin originals and those who read them than it might at first appear—in other words, that *volgare* editions of Virgil remained anchored in the world of the educated elite at the same time as they opened up access to that world to those below it.

To begin with, the translations of Virgil published in Renaissance Venice were consciously designed so that the physical appearance of the book resembled a Latin edition of the same size and format.[48] The title-pages, for example, were regularly designed to evoke the cultural milieu of antiquity rather than that of contemporary vernacular culture, although some of the earlier attempts (e.g. that of the 1544 Giovanni Padovano *et al.* edition; see Plate 7) were less consistently successful than the later ones (e.g. the 1597 Giovanni Battista Ciotti edition; see Plate 8). Almost all of these translations were small octavos, and the typeface in which they were printed was almost invariably the same one that Aldus Manutius had developed for his new octavo editions of the Latin classics: italic, based on the humanist cursive handwriting pioneered by Niccolò Niccoli and widely used in contemporary

---

[47] R. R. Bolgar, *The Classical Heritage and Its Beneficiaries* (Cambridge, 1954; repr. 1973), app. II: 'The Translations of Greek and Roman Classics before 1600', 539 and 541 gives some basic bibliographical information on Italian translations of Virgil, although this list was never intended to be exhaustive and has been treated harshly by reviewers (e.g. Carlo Dionisotti, *Italia medioevale e umanistica*, 1 (1958), 427–31, repr. as the beginning of 'Tradizione classica e volgarizzamenti', in *Geografia e storia della letteratura italiana*, Piccola Biblioteca Einaudi, 163 (Turin, 1967), 125–32). See also Zabughin, *Vergilio*, ii. 358–74. My *A Bibliography of Renaissance Italian Translations of Virgil* (Florence, 1994) includes descriptions of this material. The discussion that follows is concerned with some of the same issues developed by Deborah Parker in *Commentary and Ideology: Dante in the Renaissance* (Durham, NC, 1993), 130–51.

[48] This appears to signal a change from previous practice, for as Paul F. Gehl notes, *volgare* mss of the later Middle Ages preserved a distinctly different look from Latin mss (*A Moral Art: Grammar, Society, and Culture in Trecento Florence* (Ithaca, NY, 1993), 76).

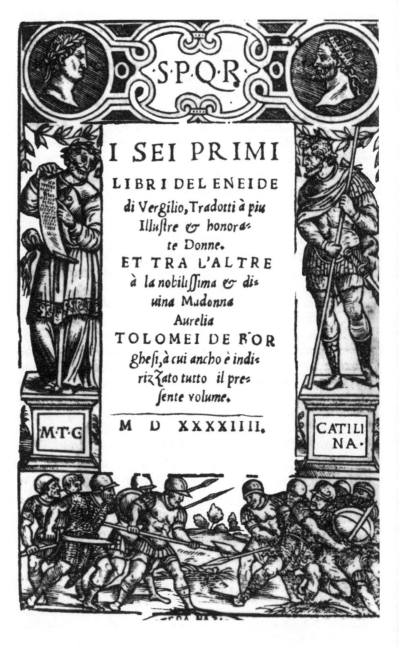

I SEI PRIMI
LIBRI DEL ENEIDE
di Vergilio, Tradotti à piu
Illuſtre & honora:
te Donne.
ET TRA L'ALTRE
à la nobiliſſima & di:
uina Madonna
Aurelia
TOLOMEI DE ɓOR
gheſi, à cui ancho è indi:
rizƷato tutto il pre:
ſente volume.

M D XXXXIIII.

M·T·G

CATILI
NA·

Plate 7. Title-page of *I sei primi libri del Eneide* (Venice: Giovanni Padovano *et al.*, 1544). (Used by permission of the Biblioteca Nazionale Marciana, Venice.)

manuscripts in an effort to reproduce what a copy of the text from antiquity was thought to have looked like.[49] Indeed in one case, the 1534 edition of *Aeneid* 4 published by Giovanni Antonio Nicolini Da Sabbio, the Italian translation was accompanied by a facing-page Latin text that does not seem to have appeared intrusive. That is, the 'feel' of these vernacular translations was almost identical to that of smaller Latin texts of the same author.

Secondly, the notes entered into both sets of books show that in the minds of early readers, the boundary between Latin and the vernacular was permeable, to say the least. To take the Latin books first, the death notice in the back of the Verona Virgil described above is written in Italian. Stray jottings in these books ranging from *Toni magna merda* ('Tony eat shit'; 1483, Baptista de Tortis: Venice, Biblioteca Nazionale Marciana, Incun. V.265, fo. riii[r]) to *amando la virtu aquista honore* ('one acquires honour by loving virtue'; 1572, heirs of Joannes Maria Bonellus: Venice, Biblioteca Correr, F 3678, fo. 389[v]) remind us that for many early readers, the mind wandered in Italian, not Latin. Other early readers left marginalia that allow us to watch their efforts to translate the text into their own language. Often, as in a copy of the 1588 Joannes Gryphius Minor edition now in the Biblioteca Bertoliana in Vicenza (C.15.5.5), these efforts are restricted to an occasional textual difficulty, as when *somnosque petivit* is glossed as *si adormento* ('he slept'; on *Aen.* 7. 88), but in one case (a 1562 edition of

---

[49] B. L. Ullman, *The Origin and Development of Humanistic Script*, Storia e letteratura, Raccolta di studi e testi, 79 (Rome, 1960), 59–77; Carlo Dionisotti, *Gli umanisti e il volgare fra Quattro e Cinquecento* (Florence, 1968), 1–14; Lowry, *Aldus Manutius*, 135–41, with bibliography; and Fletcher, *New Aldine Studies*, 77–87. A series of jottings on the inside front cover of a copy of a miscellany of translations (Venice, Biblioteca Nazionale Marciana, 46.D.221) shows how conscious early readers were of when it was appropriate to use the various script styles. The owner, who was a German speaker, copied the maxim *Cura omnia potest* ('careful attention can accomplish all things') into his text, then translated it into three languages, each time selecting one of the writing styles normally used for that language: *mel[et]e panta dunata*, in Greek; *Die Sorge als Magt*, in *bastarda*; and *La cura puo ogni cosa puolluit* [?], in roman. On this point in general see Febvre and Martin, *Coming of the Book*, 78–83; Hirsch, *Printing, Selling and Reading*, 114–18; Paolo Trovato, *Con ogni diligenza corretto: La stampa e le revisioni editoriali dei testi letterari italiani (1470–1570)* (Bologna, 1991), 32–3; and Gehl, *Moral Art*, 37–8. There are, of course, occasional exceptions to any generalization, but the efforts of Elizabeth Eisenstein (*The Printing Press as an Agent of Change: Communications and Cultural Transformations in Early Modern Europe*, 2 vols. (Cambridge, 1979), i. 205–7) to challenge the basic associations between typefaces and linguistic cultures strike me as ill-advised. That is, Grendler's observation that italic type went with a 'wealthier literary market' seems reasonable on the basis of what I have observed ('Form and Function', 482).

FIDES

L ENEIDE DI VIRGILIO
RIDOTTA IN OTTAVA RIMA, DAL
S. HERCOLE. VDINE.
AL SERENISS. PRINCIPE
IL SIG. DON VINCENZO GONZAGA
DVCA DI MANTVA, DI MON-
FERRATO. ET Z.
Venetia Apresso
Bat. Cioti, 1597.

Plate 8. Title-page of *L'Eneide di Virgilio* (Venice: Giovanni Battista Ciotti, 1597). (Used by permission of the Biblioteca Civica Bertoliana, Vicenza.)

Joannes Maria Bonellus: Treviso, Biblioteca del Seminario Vescovile, VII.G.15) many pages of the *Georgics* are accompanied by a literal, interlinear translation. Sometimes other readers who were making marginal notes in Latin shifted into Italian for a stray explanatory comment, as in the 1514 Aldine in Venice's Biblioteca Nazionale Marciana (Aldine 628): *Didone e uno esempio alle vedove di veder quello che fanno* ... ('Dido is an example to widows to watch what they are doing'; fo. 104ʳ). At other times the marginal notes mark a conscious effort to draw the Latin text into the cultural orbit of Italian literature by cross-referencing key works in the vernacular canon, as when the annotator of this same volume compares the final duel between Aeneas and Turnus to that of Ruggiero and Rodomonte in Ariosto's *Orlando Furioso* (fo. 56ᵛ, on *Aen.* 12. 887–916).[50] The most frequently referenced author, as we might imagine, is Dante, especially since the commentary of Landino and its derivative by Fabrini—which, we should recall, is in Italian even though it was published with a Latin text—often provided guidance here, as we can see in the notes to the 1581 edition of Joannes Baptista Sessa and brothers and the heirs of Franciscus Rampazetus now in the Biblioteca Ariostea in Ferrara (S.20.7; see, for example, fos. 4ᵛ and 6ᵛ).

Conversely the handwritten notes in the Italian translations are often in Latin. For example, while many readers entered their ownership notes in the vernacular, a great many others signed the front of their translations just as they would have signed a Latin text: *Ex Francisci Azzoni libris* ('One of Franciscus Azzonus' books'; 1597, Giovanni Battista Ciotti: Verona, Biblioteca Capitolare, Q.VI.17 [*olim* V.V.21]), or *fratris Antonii Patris Reformatoris, Veronae* ('belonging to brother Antonius of the Reformist Fathers, Verona'; 1564, Grazioso Percaccino: Verona, Biblioteca Civica, Cinq. C.49). Next to ownership notes like these, we find doodlings in Latin, ranging from commonplace sentiments (*Laus Deo virginis Mariae*, 'praise to God, [son of] the virgin Mary'; 1544, Giovanni Padovano *et al.*: Venice, Biblioteca Nazionale Marciana, 69.D.152) to practice in Latin declensions (*mors, mortis, morti, mortem, in morte* ..., 'death, of death, to death, death, in death ...'; 1540, Comin da Trino *et al.*: Venice, Biblioteca Nazionale Marciana, 32.D.248). Marginal commentary was usually in

---

[50] This point is discussed in greater detail above, p. 59.

Italian but sometimes in Latin, and occasionally we can even see the mind of the annotator at work as he shifted back and forth from one language to another in the same note: *perche boni civis est una per ruinar a fine quella cum civitate perire* ('because it is the duty of a good citizen to go completely to ruin at the end and to perish together with that city'; 1544 Giovanni Padovano *et al.*: Verona, Biblioteca Civica, Cinq. F.506, fo. 18ᵛ). And sometimes, as in the citation to *Iliad* 18. 12 in the margins of a copy of the 1597 Giovanni Battista Ciotti translation now in Padua (Biblioteca Antoniana, R.III.35, fo. 64ᵛ), cross-references served to associate the text not with the culture of the language in which it was being read, but with the Graeco-Roman culture from which it originally came.

What is more, many of the Italian translations were bought by the same kinds of people who bought a text in the original. As we might expect, the ownership notices in the translations are often just as enigmatic as the ones in the Latin editions: the identities of the Paulo Marchesi who once owned a copy of the 1539–40 Niccolò Zoppino *et al.* translation (Vicenza, Biblioteca Bertoliana, C.16.2.4 [*olim* H.15.5.35]), and of the Veronese Carmelite brother Bernardus Masius who once owned a copy of the 1597 Giovanni Battista Ciotti translation (Verona, Biblioteca Civica, Cinq. C.451), remain obscure. In some cases, however, the prominence of an early owner is beyond question, a good example being provided by the copy of the 1549 translation of the *Georgics* published by Giovanni Grifisen that entered the University of California at Los Angeles Research Library (Spec. Coll. 115034) through the Royal Society of London. The Royal Society had received it in 1667 from Henry Howard, sixth Duke of Norfolk, who in turn had received it from the Earl of Arundel, who though a foreigner had preferred an Italian translation to a copy in the language universally used by the educated men of his day. One other prominent owner of another book, the patrician Thomas Contarenus, is especially worth mentioning, since he appeared among the owners of the Latin editions as well; indeed, his copy of the 1564 Grazioso Percaccino translation (Venice, Biblioteca Nazionale Marciana, 263.c.82) ultimately ended up in the same library as his Latin text.[51]

---

[51] It is worth noting that interest in these translations persisted among prominent Venetians of later periods: the same Apostolo Zeno whose collection furnished three Latin

A survey of the prefaces and dedicatory letters appearing in editions in Italian indicates that the Venetian patricians who took an interest in the publication of the Latin editions were also viewed as potential patrons for the vernacular translations. The translation of *Aeneid* 11 by Bernardino Daniello is dedicated to Bernardo Zane (1545, Giovanni Farri and brothers, fos. A2^r–3^v), and the same translator's version of the *Georgics*, which became the standard rendering of that poem during the second half of the sixteenth century, is dedicated to Leonardo Mozenigo (1545, Giovanni Farri and brothers, fo. a2^{r-v}).[52] Others of wealth and prominence were approached in a similar fashion. Nicolo Liburnio addressed his translation of *Aeneid* 4 to Georgius de Selva, the French ambassador to Venice (1534, Giovanni Antonio Nicolini Da Sabbio, fos. A1^v–2^v), while Giovanni Giustiniano di Candia went directly to the French king, Francis I, in the prefatory letter he drafted in Venice (1542, Giovanni Antonio and Pietro Da Sabbio and Giovanni Francesco Torresano, fos. A2^r–B3^r). Prominent clerics received their due as well, with Cesare Baccon, vicar of the Patriarch of Venice, being addressed in the prefatory letter to Giovanpaulo Vasio's translation of the *Aeneid* (1538, Bernardino De Vitali, fo. a2^{r-v}; reprint 1538–9).

A particularly striking effort to use a Virgil translation to curry favour with the rich and powerful is afforded by Giovanni Andrea dell'Anguillara's rendering of *Aeneid* 1, published by the Paduan printer Grazioso Percaccino in 1564 (see Plate 9). At the end of the book are found two notices:

—Tutti quelli che ringratieranno l'autore del dono, almeno con parole, ò con lettere, saranno trovati da Enea ne campi Elisi, dove saranno da Anchise lodati; gli altri per aventura si ritroveranno ne l'Inferno non senza colpa loro.

---

edns. of Virgil to the Biblioteca Marciana in the 1820s also had nine different Italian translations in his library (current Marciana shelf marks Misc. 2385, Misc. 2381, 39.D.133, 93.D.148, 69.D.141, 55.D.115, 69.D.152, 32.D.226, and 33.D.237). Eisenstein, *Printing Press*, i. 63, has some incisive remarks on how difficult it is to make correlations between social status and the use of Latin versus the vernacular.

[52] The same letter also accompanied Daniello's trans. in the edns. of 1559, Onofrio Farri and brothers; 1562, Domenico Farri; 1568, Giorgio Cavalli; 1586, Giacomo Cornetti; and 1593, Paulo Ugolini. On the financing of both Italian and Latin edns. by the same group of wealthy Venetians, see Brian Richardson, *Print Culture in Renaissance Italy: The Editor and the Vernacular Text, 1470–1600* (Cambridge, 1994), 30.

IL
PRIMO LIBRO
DELLA ENEIDA
DI VERGILIO,

RIDOTTO DA GIOVANNI ANDREA

DELL'ANGVILLARA

in ottaua rima,

AL MAGNANIMO CARDINAL

DI TRENTO.

IN PADOVA,
Appreſſo di Gratioſo Perchacino
1 5 6 4.

Plate 9. Title-page of *Il primo libro della Eneida* (Padua: Grazioso Percaccino, 1564). (Used by permission of the Biblioteca Nazionale Marciana, Venice.)

(All those who will thank the author for his gift, at least with words or with letters, will be found by Aeneas in the Elysian Fields, where they will be praised by Anchises; the others, perchance, will be found in the Inferno, not without fault of their own.)

—La risposta si indirizzi à Venetia alla libraria della Serena.

(The response should be sent to the bookshop of the Serena in Venice.)

In most of the surviving copies, Anguillara wrote a dedication note on the back of the title-page (*Giovanni Andrea dell'Anguillara dona di propria mano*) along with the name of the recipient (see Plate 10), suggesting that he sent most of the press run out as a sort of sample in hopes of finding a patron to support a translation of the remaining books.[53] Anguillara completed his translation of Book 2, which was published in 1566 by the Roman printer Giulio Accolti, but does not appear to have progressed beyond that point, presumably because he did not succeed in finding a patron. We have here a striking piece of negative evidence: Books 3–12 of Anguillara's translation of the *Aeneid* were apparently never written because the translator failed to find his niche among the powerful, humanistically educated supporters of the arts in Renaissance Italy.

Thus a study of the physical appearance of these early translations, the marginalia and ownership notices entered into them, and the dedications and prefatory letters printed with them tends to link these books to the world of the humanistically educated upper class in the Veneto. In a somewhat different way, the language of these translations also pulls them higher into the social hierarchy than we might at first expect, for while this language is Italian, it is a special kind of Italian, as the title-pages regularly declare: *lingua toscana* (1532, Bernardino De Vitali), or *thoscana* (1552, Nicolò

---

[53] Since copies exist with the dedication notice but no recipient named (e.g. Ravenna, Biblioteca Classense, 25.4.T) and with neither the name of a recipient nor a dedication notice (e.g. Verona, Biblioteca Capitolare, Q.IV.20 [*olim* G.VII.58]), we should probably assume that some copies were sold in the regular way as well. On Anguillara, see M. Pelaez, 'La vita e le opere di G. A. dell'Anguillara', *Propugnatore*, 4 (1891), 40–124; G. Lorini, 'Per la biografia di G. A. dell'Anguillara', *Giornale storico della letteratura italiana*, 53 (1935), 81–93; and C. Mutini, 'Giovanni Andrea dell'Anguillara', in *Dizionario biografico degli Italiani* (Rome, 1960 ff.), iii. 306–9, with bibliography. For a full study of this edn. and the problems it raises, see Craig Kallendorf, 'In Search of a Patron: Anguillara's Vernacular Virgil and the Print Culture of Renaissance Italy', *Papers of the Bibliographical Society of America*, 91 (1997), 294–325.

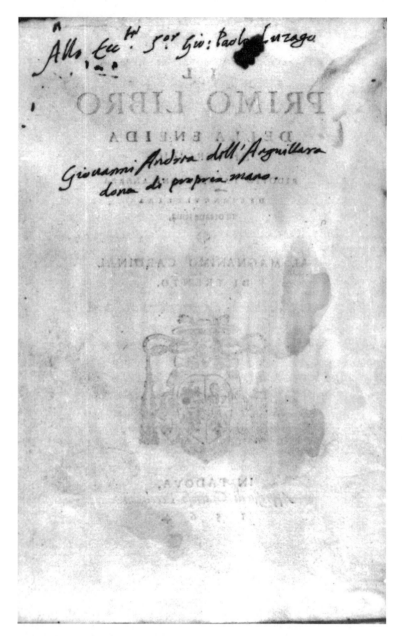

Plate 10. Autograph dedication of Giovanni Andrea dell'Anguillara, *Il primo libro della Eneida* (Padua: Grazioso Percaccino, 1564), fo. 1ᵛ. (Used by permission of the Biblioteca Nazionale Marciana, Venice.)

Bascarini), or *thoscana favella* (1545, Giovanni Farri and brothers; 1549, Giovanni Grifi sen.). To understand what this 'Tuscan' language is and who in Renaissance Venice would read a translation of Virgil written in it, we must look a little at its emergence as a means of literary expression within the changing norms of translation in sixteenth-century Italy.

At the end of the fifteenth century and the beginning of the sixteenth, Virgil's poetry, like other classical literature, was printed in translations made in the Trecento and early Quattrocento. A typical example is the paraphrase of the pre-humanist notary Ser Andrea Lancia, which was translated prior to 1316 from a Latin compendium of an unidentified brother Anastasio; it was printed in Vicenza in 1476 and still being reprinted in Venice a half-century later (1528, Niccolò Zoppino).[54] Like other works of its kind, this translation, or rather paraphrase, was not closely bound to the original. The content was reproduced with considerable freedom, and there were no explicit stylistic or literary goals. There was a pronounced didactic flavour to the whole, and it was aimed at a broad, rather undiscriminating public.[55] Humanists like Petrarch who could have orchestrated a new series of accurate translations did not do so, since for them Latin was not a language that was really open to translation. Typical was the attitude of Guarino da Verona, whose 1429 letter to Cambiatore da Reggio was decidedly cold because he saw no use for the vulgarization of the *Aeneid* that Cambiatore was preparing, even though this was one of the earliest efforts to be based on a direct re-examination of

---

[54] On the early translations of the classics in general, see Cesare Segre (ed.), *Volgarizzamenti del Due e Trecento* (Turin, 1980); 565–637 cover the *Aeneid*, with information on later translations and the edns. in which they were published in Bartolomeo Gamba, *Digeria bibliografica ... intorno ai volgarizzamenti italiani delle opere di Virgilio* (Verona, 1831), 3–28. On treatments of Virgil in particular, see also Antonio Benci, 'Volgarizzamenti antichi dell'*Eneide* di Virgilio', *Antologia*, 2 (1821), 161–200; and E. G. Parodi, 'I rifacimenti e le traduzioni italiane dell'*Eneide* di Virgilio prima del Rinascimento', *Studi di filologia romanza*, 2 (1887), 97–368; 311–32 cover translations, of which 312–22 are devoted to Lancia. A broader perspective is offered in G. Folena, ' "Volgarizzare" e "tradurre": Idea e terminologia della traduzione dal Medio Evo italiano e romanzo all'umanesimo europea', in Centro per lo Studio dell'Insegnamento all'Estero dell'Italiano, Università degli Studi di Trieste (ed.), *La traduzione: Saggi e studi* (Trieste, 1973), 57–120.

[55] Zabughin, *Vergilio*, ii. 357–8; and Bodo Guthmüller, *Ovidio Metamorphoseos Vulgare: Formen und Funktionen der volkssprachlichen Wiedergabe klassischer Dichtung in der italienischen Renaissance*, Veröffentlichungen zur Humanismusforschung, 3 (Boppard, 1981), 116–23, 178–9.

the original.[56] Even in the first decades of the Quattrocento, humanists like Leonardo Bruni conceived the problems of translation for the most part as problems in rendering Greek texts in Latin, so that up to the 1530s there were few vulgarizations of the classics that had a real effect on the course of Italian literary history.[57]

Things began to change in the second half of the Quattrocento with the appearance of the translation of Pliny's *Natural History* by Cristoforo Landino, who favoured enriching the *volgare* with Latin and Greek words. Boiardo became the first great Italian writer since Boccaccio to emphasize translation, and in the last two decades of the fifteenth century, the refined *volgare* spread throughout Italy, gradually ceasing to be narrowly Tuscan and becoming a national literary language.[58] Since the printing of texts in Italian was centred in Venice, Venetian printers played a key role in helping to stabilize this national literary language.[59] Progress in translating the classics stalled in the early sixteenth century, however, when tensions between the two linguistic worlds grew. On the one side, figures in the literary vanguard like Ariosto, Bembo, and Castiglione were struggling to develop a more purely vernacular literary language free of what they considered undue deformation by humanist Latin. On the other side, those sympathetic to Latin tended to see things from the perspective of Nicolo Liburnio, who wrote in his prologue that he could only print the Latin text of *Aeneid* 4 next to his Italian translation so that *e conoscitori di polite lettere latine veggiano subitamente quanto, et in che modo la penuria di loquela volgare possasi avicinare alla copia varia*

[56] Guthmüller, *Ovidio Metamorphoseos*, 139; and Dionisotti, 'Tradizione classica', 141–3. The letter to Cambiatore may be found in the *Epistolario di Guarino Veronese*, ed. R. Sabbadini, 4 vols. (Venice, 1915–19), ii. 76.

[57] Dionisotti, 'Tradizione classica', 148–50; and Leonardo Bruni, *De interpretatione recta*, in Hans Baron (ed.), *Leonardo Bruni Aretino: Humanistisch-philosophische Schriften* (Leipzig, 1928), 81–96, with translation and discussion in *The Humanism of Leonardo Bruni: Selected Texts*, trans. and introd. by Gordon Griffiths, James Hankins, and David Thompson, Medieval and Renaissance Texts and Studies, 46 / The Renaissance Society of America Renaissance Texts Series, 10 (Binghamton, NY, 1987), 197–212, 217–29.

[58] Dionisotti, 'Tradizione classica', 150–74; and Leonardo Olschki, *Bildung und Wissenschaft im Zeitalter der Renaissance in Italien*, Geschichte der neusprachlichen wissenschaftlichen Literatur, 2 (Leipzig, 1922), 199–217, for general background.

[59] W. T. Elwert, 'L'importanza letteraria di Venezia', in *Studi di letteratura veneziana*, Civiltà veneziana, Studi, 5 (Venice, 1958), 19–28.

et infinita del sommo poeta ('the connoisseurs of polished Latinity
may see immediately to what extent and in what way the poverty
of the *volgare* may approach the infinite variety of the greatest of
poets'; 1534, Giovanni Antonio Nicolini Da Sabbio, fo. A3ᵛ). By
around 1540, however, a truly national literary language with its
own rules had become the patrimony of a majority of Italian writers, and from this secure position there was no longer a significant
risk in encountering the classics. Translation of the classics was
therefore taken up again with vigour from 1540 to 1560, this time
as a central part of Italian literary life,[60] and the translations
produced during this period joined those produced in the following decades to supply a steady source of material to Venetian printers.

   Among this material were the translations of Virgil, and it is
significant that they were published in this national literary
language rather than, say, Venetian dialect. This national literary
language was different, a Tuscan import by origin that always
remained a bit rarefied and removed from the banalities of everyday life in Venice. Indeed, even today a visitor to Venice is invariably struck by the distance between Venetian dialect and standard
modern Italian, the heir of the literary language of Petrarch and
Bembo. Yet this literary language was also different from Latin,
the official idiom of institutional wealth and power. It therefore
came to occupy an intermediate position, below Latin but nevertheless associated with a certain level of sophistication and taste.[61]
The prefatory matter of these Virgil translations recognizes this, for
like other renderings of the classics in this period, these books are
addressed to readers described as *virtuosissimi e dottissimi* ('virtuous
and learned'), *discreti e benigni* ('reasonable and well-disposed'),

---

[60]   Dionisotti, 'Tradizione classica', 150–74; Guthmüller, *Ovidio Metamorphoseos*, 236;
and Ettore Bonora, 'I grandi traduttori', in Emilio Cecchi and Natalino Sapegno (eds.),
Storia della letteratura italiana, iv. *Il Cinquecento* (Milan, 1966), 551–61. This period of
increased interest in translation is associated with a general increase in the number of
books aimed at a less learned audience; see Richardson, *Print Culture in Renaissance Italy*,
91.

[61]   Dionisotti, 'Tradizione classica', 158. It is worth noting as well that the publication
of translations of the classics in Venice was fostered by the Accademia Veneziana as part of
a general programme of cultural improvement (Lina Bolzoni, 'L'Accademia Veneziana:
Splendore e decadenza di una utopia enciclopedica', in Laetitia Boehm and Ezio Raimondi
(eds.), *Università, accademie e società scientifiche in Italia e in Germania dal Cinquecento al
Settecento*, Annali dell'Istituto Storico Italo-Germanico, Quaderno, 9 (Bologna, 1980),
129–30).

candidi ('pure'), and *studiosi* ('studious').[62] These were readers who could appreciate connections with other works in the vernacular canon, for even as early as the 1525 translation published by Gregorio De Gregori, the language of *Eclogue* 5 was specifically associated with that of Sannazaro's *Arcadia*. Somewhat later Antonio Mario Negrisoli's translation of the *Georgics* was published along with a generous selection of his lyric poetry (1543, Melchior Sessa sen.; 1552, Nicolò Bascarini), and the two works could only be seen as complementary on stylistic grounds. The readers of such books did not necessarily have to have the same level of learning as someone capable of using the Latin commentaries of Ascensius or Landino, but neither did they include many members of the lowest classes, who would probably have been illiterate and whose linguistic world would have been to a certain extent circumscribed by the dialect they spoke. In other words, even though they were written in the vernacular, these translations were more accessible to some people than to others in Renaissance Venice.

Nevertheless, while the *volgare* renderings remained bound to the upper classes in a number of key areas, we should not let this blind us to the obvious point here: frequent translation of Virgil into Italian—any version of Italian—marked a significant widening of access to the text. Paul Grendler notes that 53 per cent of Venetian students at the end of the sixteenth century attended vernacular schools, where they learned enough Latin to recognize a few words but not enough to read an author of Virgil's complexity.[63] However, once translations into the vernacular were readily available, those literate in Italian only—who outnumbered their friends and neighbours with Latin-school educations—could also read the poems. Sixteenth-century translators, of course, were well aware of this fact. Bernardino Daniello, for example, wrote a preface to his popular translation of the *Georgics* that has been justly highlighted for defending the use of translations by those *i quali da diverse cure e maneggi impediti, non hanno ne la loro primiera età potuto ne a la Greca, ne a la Latina favella dar opera* ('who impeded by various concerns and duties, were not able to devote their efforts in their youth to Greek or Latin literature'; 1545, Giovanni Farri and brothers, fo. b2ʳ).[64] As his prefatory letter indicates, Daniello's

---

[62] Guthmüller, *Ovidio Metamorphoseos*, 122, 247.
[63] *Schooling*, 50.   [64] Febvre and Martin, *Coming of the Book*, 239–42.

translation of *Aeneid* 1 (1551, Paulo Gherardo, fo. a2^{r-v}) is likewise devoted to the utility and satisfaction of those whose ignorance of Latin has deprived them of knowledge of the poetry. By the middle of the sixteenth century, those who were restricted to the linguistic world of the *volgare* would have found it easy to locate a copy of Virgil they could read or have read to them in Italian.

What is more, the copy they found would have cost less than most Latin editions. There were no translations of Virgil in folio published in Renaissance Venice, and very few quartos; almost every edition was an octavo, and editions of (for example) just one book of the *Aeneid* were also common. Since size and length were important determinants of price, most translations were comparatively inexpensive—as Paul Grendler has noted, the prices of vernacular titles, including 'one of the ubiquitous vernacular translations of classical texts' in small formats, went from forty soldi down to as little as four.[65] What is more, such books were seldom finished at any significant expense. The age of hand-painted illuminations was over before 1540, and in almost every case the original bindings I have seen are simple parchment.[66]

Thus an artisan or a merchant with a few extra soldi to spend and a basic grasp of literary Italian could, and did, buy a translation of Virgil, as did a wealthy cleric or noble. The Latin editions were on the whole more expensive, but as we have seen, they, too, could be, and were, used by a broad range of consumers. There was, of course, a difference. If in each case we conceive of all potential readers arranged in a hierarchy by class, beginning with wealthy patricians at the top and descending all the way down to the humblest servant, the greatest concentration of vernacular users undoubtedly clustered further down their continuum than the greatest concentration of Latin users clustered on theirs. Yet this difference should not blind us to the fact that books of Virgilian poetry served to unify the classes in Renaissance Venice: the same book, in Latin or in Italian, had the capacity to affect many people from many different walks of life, and the evidence left in the books themselves suggests that categories were fluid and

---

[65] 'Printing and Censorship', 31, 40. See also John Martin, *Venice's Hidden Enemies: Italian Heretics in a Renaissance City* (Berkeley and Los Angeles, Calif., 1993), 81–4.

[66] The one significant exception known to me is Treviso, Biblioteca Comunale, IV.67.M.18, a copy of the 1559 Onofrio Farri and brothers trans., which has an elaborate tooled leather binding that may be original.

that different linguistic and social worlds intersected regularly in
the margins of Venetian books.

Resistance and Containment: Challenges of Class and Gender

The new Italian translations of Virgil—those produced during the
Renaissance and published from around 1540 on—certainly
widened access to the text. That does not mean, however, that
those who read Virgil in translation necessarily understood his
poetry in precisely the same way as those who read a text in the
original Latin. At this point, then, I would like to examine the
extent to which the Italian translations both reinforced and modified the concerns developed in the Latin editions.

Like the Latin editions, the Italian translations contain handwritten commentaries that record how their readers were responding to the text. Sometimes early readers left indexing notes, names
and key words written in the margin by means of which they
could find their way through the text on a later reading (e.g. 1539-
40, Niccolò Zoppino et al.: University of California at Los
Angeles Research Library, Spec. Coll. 123034; 1540, Comin da
Trino and Niccolò Zoppino: Venice, Biblioteca Querini
Stampalia, R.I.g.1305). In other cases, these readers responded
more fully to the concerns of the text, as when information on the
dates of solstices was entered into a translation of the *Georgics*
(1545, Giovanni Farri and Brothers: Verona, Biblioteca Civica,
Cinq. D.613, fo. 106^v) and cross-references to Pliny and
Theophrastus were entered into another copy of the same book
(Verona, Biblioteca Civica, Cinq. D.521, fos. 34^r, 36^r). A copy of
the 1544 Giovanni Padovano et al. edition of the first six books of
the *Aeneid* now in Verona (Biblioteca Civica, Cinq. F.506)
contains what might reasonably be called a full commentary on the
text. This commentary contains a large number of textual corrections, identifications of figures from mythology (*Iffigenia
Agamemnon figliuola*, 'Iphigenia [was] the daughter of
Agamemnon', fo. 5^r), references to Servius (e.g. fo. 20^r), and even
an effort to work out the relationship between the *Aeneid* and
Christianity by associating the star that appeared over Ascanius
with the one that led the Magi to Christ (fo. 20^v). And like the
readers of the Latin texts, those reading Virgil in translation were

also alert to the presence of *sententiae*, pithy sayings whose moral content made them worth remembering. A representative sampling may be found in the lines marked off in the copy of the 1592 Bernardo Giunta junior edition now in Verona (Biblioteca Capitolare, Q.IV.18 (*olim* R.VII.19):

> ... Un sol rimedio
> A chi speme non have è disperarsi.

> (The lost have only
> This one deliverance: to hope for none.)

> (*Aen.* 2. 354; p. 66)

> Che se ben pregio et lode
> Non s'acquista à punire, o vincer donna.

> (... for although there is no memorable name
> in punishing a woman and no gain of honour in such victory ...)

> (*Aen.* 2. 583–4; p. 80)

> Ah perfido, celar dunque sperasti
> Una tal tradizione? ...

> (Deceiver, did you hope, then, to hide
> such a betrayal? ...)

> (*Aen.* 4. 305–6; p. 150)

For all intents and purposes, these are the same kinds of responses found in the Latin editions, but developed here in Italian.

As we have seen in Chapters 2 and 3, reactions like these are a major source of information on how early readers were responding to the Latin text of Virgil's poetry. Such reactions, however, are much more difficult to recover from the Italian translations—indeed, it is quite unusual to find marginal notes in sufficient quantity that they may be said to constitute a true commentary. It is unusual as well to find a printed commentary in a sixteenth-century translation, with Daniello's vernacular commentary on the *Georgics* being the exception that proves the rule. Since a great many of the Latin commentaries had their origins in some sort of academic environment, the relative absence of commentaries in the Italian translations suggests that they never received widespread adoption as school texts. Recent research on the curriculum in the schools of Renaissance Italy confirms this conclusion, for as Paul Grendler has shown, Virgil was not taught in the vernacular schools that provided the principal alternative to a humanist education in sixteenth-century Venice.[67] Since the Italian translations were in general used differently from the Latin editions, we shall have to rely more heavily on evidence other than commentaries to determine how Renaissance readers understood the *volgare* Virgil.

Fortunately other evidence is available. For example, many vernacular editions of Virgil contain title-pages with illustrations and accompanying mottoes.[68] While a number of these illustrations were printer's devices, reusable at will on the title-pages of many different books, one is striking in its appropriateness—the one from the 1546 Comin da Trino edition of *Aeneid* 7, where a circular scroll surrounds a woman holding a city in her right hand and identified as Dido by the accompanying motto, *semper honos nomenque tuum laudesque manebunt* ('your name and praise and honor shall always last'; *Aen.* 1. 609; see Plate 11), which comes from Aeneas' first speech to the Carthaginian queen. The title-pages, of course, suggest in general terms what the reader might expect to find in the book, and the illustrations on several of them have a common theme. The translation of *Aeneid* 8 published in 1542 by the brothers Da Sabbio and Giovanni Francesco Torresano, for example, contains a picture of a wrecked ship with a figure labelled *Virtus* in the stern and a motto reading *nemo perit hac duce* ('no one perishes with this one as guide'; see Plate 12). The 1545 Giovanni Farri and brothers edition of the *Georgics* is adorned with a hippograph standing on a book that in turn surmounts a winged globe, all of which is accompanied by a motto reading *virtute duce comite fortuna* ('with virtue as guide and fortune as companion'). The rare translation of *Aeneid* 1 published *c.*1551 by Alberto di Gratia detto il Toscano presents a woman holding a sheaf within an oval containing the inscription *virtus est firma possessio* ('virtue is a firm possession'). The translations of the first book of the *Aeneid* published by Cieco and De Franceschi (1569, 1570, and 1572) and of the second book published by Christoforo Cieco da Forlì (1579) contain an elaborate border surrounding a seated

---

[67] *Schooling*, 275–305. As Grendler has observed, roughly half the students in Renaissance Venice were educated in vernacular schools at the end of the 16th cent. ('The Organization of Primary and Secondary Education in the Italian Renaissance', *Catholic Historical Review*, 71 (1985), 199–200).

[68] Goldschmidt, *Printed Book*, 82–8, discusses the emblematic nature of title-pages like these. For a general treatment of title-pages in Italian books of the Renaissance, see Francesco Barberi, *Il frontespizio nel libro italiano del Quattrocento e del Cinquecento*, 2 vols., Documenti sulle arti del libro, 7 (Milan, 1969).

IL SETT'IMO DI
VERGILIO DAL VERO
SENSO IN VERSI SCIOLTI
TRADOTTO PER M. GIV•
SEPPE BETVSSI.
CON VNA ELEGIA D'I AVGVSTO
IN FINE SOPRA L'ENEIDA.

ALLA ILLVSTRE ET
VALOROSA SIGNORA LA
S. COLLALTINA COL•
LALTA ET TRECCHA.

NOMEN Q TVVM LAV•

Vinegia al segno di San Bernardino.

Plate 11. Title-page of *Il settimo di Vergilio* (Venice: Comin da Trino, 1546).
(Used by permission of the Biblioteca Nazionale Marciana, Venice.)

IL LIBRO OTTAVO DE

LA ENEIDE DI VERGILIO,
PER MESSER GIOVANNI
GIVSTINIANO DI
CANDIA.

Con Priuilegio dello Illuſtriſſimo Do. Veneto,
In Vinegia. M D X L I I.

Plate 12. Title-page of *Il libro ottavo de la Eneide di Vergilio* (Venice: Giovanni Antonio and Pietro Nicolini Da Sabbio and Giovanni Francesco Torresano, 1542). (Used by permission of the Biblioteca Nazionale Marciana, Venice.)

queen who is identified in an accompanying motto: *regina virtus* ('queen virtue'). That is, in some way or other, these title-pages suggest that the product of reading Virgil should be virtue.

This same point is made repeatedly in the *ottava rima* translation by the Venetian Lodovico Dolce that provides the most extensive paratext among the Italian translations of the *Aeneid*. The prefatory letter by the publisher Gabriele Giolito De' Ferrari in the 1572 edition explains that in this book, which also contains Dolce's version of the *Iliad*, the reader will find two virtues greatly praised by the ancients, courage in the person of Achilles and *pietà* in Aeneas (fo. a6^r).[69] Among the front matter is a *Tavola delle sentenze, che si contengono nel presente libro* (fos. a1^r–3^v)—that is, a list of memorable maxims indexed by key words like *magnanimo, prudenza, temerità*, and so forth. From this list it is clear that Dolce felt free to highlight and expand upon the *sententiae* already present in Virgil's text, so that we find such pithy sayings as these, with their keyword headings and the pages on which they are found:

[69] On Dolce's life and works, see E. A. Cicogna, 'Memoria intorno la vita e gli scritti di Messer Lodovico Dolce letterato veneziano del secolo XVI', *Memorie dell' R. Istituto Veneto di Scienze, Lettere ed Arti*, 11 (1862), 93–200; and Claudia Di Filippo Bareggi, *Il mestiere di scrivere: Lavoro intellettuale e mercato librario a Venezia nel Cinquecento*, 'Europa delle Corti', Centro Studi sulle Società di Antico Regime, Biblioteca del Cinquecento, 43 (Rome, 1988), *passim*. The first book of Dolce's rendering of the *Aeneid*, entitled *Il primo libro dell'Enea di Messer Lodovico Dolce* ..., appeared in 1566 from the press of Giorgio Cavalli. The entire *Aeneid* appeared as *L'Enea di Messer Lodovico Dolce* ..., published by Giovanni Varisco in 1567–8, and this was combined with the rendering of the *Iliad* as *L'Achille et l'Enea di Messer Lodovico Dolce, dove egli tessendo l'historia della Iliade d'Homero à quella dell'Eneide di Vergilio, ambedue l'ha divinamente ridotte in ottava rima* (1570 and 1572, Gabriele Giolito De' Ferrari). References are to this last edn. and will be incorporated into the text. The extensive paratext in this edn. and its publication in quarto rather than octavo suggests that Giolito intended this book for a mid–level rather than a popular audience (Trovato, *Con ogni diligenza corretto*, 220). On Dolce's trans., see Parodi, 'Rifacimenti', 270–3; and Luciana Borsetto, 'Riscrivere l'historia, riscrivere lo stile: Il poema di Virgilio, nelle "riduzioni" cinquecentesche di Lodovico Dolce', in Giancarlo Mazzacurati and Michel Plaisance (eds.), *Scritture di scritture: Testi, generi, modelli nel Rinascimento*, 'Europa delle Corti', Centro Studi sulle Società di Antico Regime, Biblioteca del Cinquecento, 36 (Rome, 1987), 405–37, where the author points out that the emphasis on moral exemplarity increased markedly between the 1567–8 and 1570 versions. I am grateful to Daniel Javitch for providing me with this reference. On Dolce's relations with the press of Giolito, see S. Bongi, *Annali di Gabriel Giolito de' Ferrari da Trino di Monferrato stampatore in Venezia*, 2 vols., Indici e cataloghi, 11 (Rome, 1890–5), to be supplemented by the works listed in Fernanda Ascarelli and Marco Menato, *La tipografia del '500 in Italia*, Biblioteca di bibliografia italiana, 116 (Florence, 1989), 374–5, esp. Amedeo Quondam, ' "Mercanzia d'honore" / "Mercanzia d'utile": Produzione libraria e lavoro intellettuale a Venezia nel Cinquecento', in Petrucci (ed.), *Libri, editori e pubblico*, 51–104.

bene	Il far bene ad altrui non nocque mai, [p.] 172	(fo. a1ᵛ)
	(Doing good to another never did any harm)	
pietà	La primiera pietà, che dopo Dio	(fo. a3ʳ)
	Par che si debbia in terra a ricercarsi,	
	E verso il Padre in ogni officio pio	
	In vita, e dopo morte dimostrarsi. [p.] 358	
	(The first piety that, after God, one ought to seek	
	out on earth is to show oneself pious to one's	
	father in every duty, in life and after death.)	
vittoria	... Non è maggior vittoria	(fo. a3ᵛ)
	Di quella, quando l'huom vince se stesso. [p.] 39	
	(There is no greater victory than when a person	
	conquers himself.)	

There is no commentary per se in this edition, but in addition to the woodcuts and arguments that begin each canto, there are also allegories that provide moral cues to the reader. These cues are sometimes tinged with a Neoplatonism that reminds us of Landino and his follower Fabrini, as when the doctrine of the two Venuses emerges, with the same goddess appearing *in bono* to show through Aeneas that divine favour is always available to good men (p. 317) and *in malo* to show through Dido that carnal desire is inflamed through earthly beauty (p. 327). As with the Latin commentaries, Dolce's moral allegory is relentless in its positive evaluation of Aeneas. The Aeneas who arms himself for a final defence of Troy is not a rebel against divine will, but a good citizen who refuses to abandon his country, even if it costs him his life (p. 269). The Aeneas who falls in love with Dido, then abandons her, represents the noble soul who in listening to the commands of the gods rather than the tears of his lover, elevates honour over personal pleasure (p. 347). The Aeneas who slaughters indiscriminately to avenge the death of Pallas shows how just anger is conceived from the evil deeds of others (p. 467), and following Maffeo Vegio, Dolce concludes by transferring Aeneas to the stars, giving him his due reward and inviting us to follow his example so that we, too, may earn the rewards of justice and piety (p. 536).[70]

Like the readers of the Latin editions, Dolce also worked to

---

[70] Borsetto, 'Riscrivere', 432–4 observes that Dolce draws here on Vegio and presents 'a continuous sententious "discourse" on the religious virtues, on nobility, on custom, on sexuality, on age'. See also James D. Garrison, *Pietas from Vergil to Dryden* (University Park, Penn., 1992), 162–3, for some trenchant observations on the shifting nuances of *pietas* as it is transferred from a classical Latin to a Renaissance Italian linguistic matrix.

integrate Virgil's poetry into the larger framework of a Christian world-view. Cloanthus, who wins the galley race in *Aeneid* 5 when his prayer for divine aid is answered, reveals the basic operating principle in Dolce's universe: ... *si nota, quanto sia giovevole all'huomo invocar nelle sue imprese l'aiuto e favor divino, peroche quando Dio favorisce le nostre imprese, sempre sortiscono ottimo fine* ('it is observed how profitable it is for man to invoke God's help and favour in his undertakings, since when God favours our undertakings, they always turn out in the best possible way'; p. 357). Aeneas, of course, is the best example of how this principle works itself out in human history. When he carries his father safely out of the burning city of Troy at the beginning of the *Aeneid*, we see how the pious man is protected by God from the dangers that threaten him (p. 279), and when Aeneas gives thanks at the end of the poem for his victory over Turnus, we see the piety of a Christian prince who understands that all his glorious achievements come from God (p. 526). Like the authors of the major Latin commentaries published in Renaissance Venice, Dolce cites verses from the Bible that parallel the points he is trying to develop in his allegory. When Latinus proposes to marry Lavinia to Aeneas rather than Turnus, Dolce cites Solomon to explain that this episode shows the need to prefer virtue in someone unknown over riches in someone whose vices are known (p. 397). At the end of the poem, when Jove forbids any of the gods to intervene in the battle between the Trojans and the native Italians, Dolce explains that this shows the impartiality of divine justice, which should serve as a model for judges on earth, for as Scripture says, *Giudicate giustamente voi che giudicate la terra* ('Judge justly, you who judge the earth', p. 457). In short, *Per Enea ... si comprende, che l'huomo deve in ogni tempo riconoscer' Iddio, così nelle cose prospere, come ancor ne i travagli, adorandolo et pregando sempre la maestà sua, che si degni farne capace de quel ben, che à noi è incomprehensibile* ('in Aeneas ... we understand that man ought at all times to acknowledge God, in both prosperity and in tribulation, adoring him and always beseeching him in his majesty that he may deign to make us capable of doing that good which is beyond our understanding'; p. 466).

The universe presided over by this just God is strikingly hierarchical, with Aeneas himself occupying a middle position in it. On the one hand he is the good prince, the captain who does not miss any opportunity to provide for his subjects, for those below him in the social hierarchy. But on the other hand he is a man, not a god, and men should always be obedient to the divine will that intends only prosperity and success for them (p. 317). Indeed the basic principle on which this hierarchical universe operates is that of obedience, of submission by lesser to greater:

Per Giunon, che essequiesce prontamente i precetti di Giove, si dinota, che i minori non deveno contender mai co i maggiori suoi, ma far tutto quello, che lor vien'imposto, perche cosi acquistano la gratia sua. Il che se vien'osservato ne i Cieli stessi (essendo meglio il prestar'obedianza, che il santificare) perche vogliamo noi esser ritrosi in non essequirlo?

(Through Juno, who executes promptly the commands of Jupiter, it is indicated that the lesser should never oppose their betters, but should do that which is imposed on them, because in this way they enter their good graces. That which is observed in the heavens themselves (offering obedience being better than sanctifying)—why do we want to be found not executing it?)

(p. 525)

That is, Venus defers to her superior Juno (p. 337), Nisus and Euryalus undertake their night raid in support of their commander (p. 436), and Ascanius withdraws from battle under prompting from Apollo to show how obedience can help the young restrain their desires (p. 456).[71]

---

[71]   While this translation was by no means a rarity—it received four printings in its complete form and the number of surviving copies suggests that the press runs must have been fairly large—it did not achieve the popularity of Dolce's rendering of Ovid, and it is interesting to speculate about why this was so. As Daniel Javitch has shown, during his long association with the printer Gabriele Giolito De' Ferrari, Dolce also prepared an edn. of Ariosto's *Orlando Furioso* that was part of an effort by the Venetian publishers to canonize this text by presenting it in large, annotated, illustrated edns.—a format previously reserved for edns. of major Latin authors ('Sixteenth-Century Commentaries on Imitations in the *Orlando Furioso*', *Harvard Library Bulletin*, 34 (1986), 221–50, now in *Proclaiming a Classic: The Canonization of Orlando Furioso* (Princeton, 1991), 48–70). The Ovid edn. was also in this format, and Javitch suggests that it achieved commercial success because readers recognized a certain counterclassical spirit in both texts that made the typographical affinities seem reasonable. That same spirit does not inform Virgil—indeed, Virgilian epic is exactly what Ovid is having fun with in the *Metamorphoses*—which may explain why Dolce's effort to present Virgil in this same format was less successful ('The Influence of *Orlando Furioso* on Ovid's *Metamorphoses* in Italian', *Journal of Medieval and Renaissance Studies*, 11 (1981), 1–9, now in *Proclaiming a Classic*, 74–85). On the related phenomenon of shaping translations of the classics in accordance with stylistic norms derived from *volgare* authors like Petrarch and Ariosto in Cinquecento Italy, see R. Romani, 'La traduzione letteraria nel Cinquecento: Note introduttive', in Centro per lo Studio dell'Insegnamento (ed.), *Traduzione*, 387–402.

In the editions without allegorizing cues to the reader, this hierarchical emphasis also emerges from the translations themselves, as Luciana Borsetto has shown. That is, the voice of Virgil is often blended with the voice of the translator, who has expanded on what Virgil wrote and consciously or not, leaves traces of his own world-view.[72] For example, at *Aeneid* 1. 697–700 and 707–8, Aeneas and his men join Dido for a banquet. In the translation of Anguillara these six lines are expanded to twenty-four, and a Virgilian scene in which the two groups simply sit down to dinner is expanded to one in which social standing and rank are clearly delimited in accordance with Renaissance practice:

> Avea Didone intanto Enea condutto
> Nella più ricca ed onorata sede
> Incontro al seggio ove s'era ella assisa
> E tutti *eran disposti* a questa guisa:
>   *Didone in mezzo alla mensa* si pose,
> E fé seder le *donne dal suo lato*;
> E *presso* al seggio *le più pompose*
> Fé stare *e le più illustri* del suo stato:
> *Di mano in mano* poi *l'altre* dispose,
> E fu *secondo il grado il loco* dato;
> E quella s'intendeva esser preposta
> Che fu *più presso a la reina* posta.
>   Cinquanta donne la reina avea
> Dall'una mano e dall'altra altrettante:
> *Allo incontro* di lei *sedeva Enea*
> Con gli altri uomini tutti a lei davante:
> E chi più *presso al re trojan* sedea,
> *Fra gli uomini* s'intesa *il più prestante.*
> Quivi si collocar *di mano in mano*
> *Un cavalier sidonio* ed *un trojano*
>   In modo ch'ogni frigio cavaliero

---

[72] Luciana Borsetto, *L''Eneida' tradotta: Riscritture poetiche del testo di Virgilio nel XVI secolo* (Milan, 1989). As a discussion of the 16th-cent. Italian translations of Virgil and a preliminary bibliographical survey of them, this is a very valuable book, although Thomas Brückner has pointed out a number of shortcomings in a detailed, trenchant review (*Arcadia*, 26 (1991), 79–83). On the general problems connected with moving between the linguistic worlds of Latin and the *volgare*, see Ann Moss, 'Being in Two Minds: The Bilingual Factor in Renaissance Writing', in Rhoda Schnur (gen. ed.), *Acta Conventus Neo-Latini Hafniensis*, Proceedings of the Eighth International Congress of Neo-Latin Studies (Binghamton, NY, 1994), 61–74; although most of Moss's examples are French, the principles should hold for other vernacular languages as well.

Fra due baroni tirij il lato ottenne,
E così ogni baron del tirio impero,
A star fra due di Frigia venne. ...

(Meanwhile Dido had brought Aeneas into the richest and most ornate place, opposite the throne where she herself sat, and all were seated in this way:

Dido positioned herself in the middle at the table, and made the women sit at her side, and near her throne she placed the most magnificent and distinguished women of her country; one by one then she positioned the others, and place was assigned according to rank, and she who was placed near the queen understood herself to have been preferred.

Fifty women the queen had on one side, and just as many on the other; opposite her sat Aeneas, with all the other men before her, and whoever sat near the Trojan king understood himself the most preferred among the men, with a Sidonian knight and a Trojan one thus arranged one by one,

In such a manner that every Phrygian knight sat beside two Tyrian barons, and so every baron of the Tyrian empire came to stand between two from Phrygia.)

(St. 244, vv. 5–8; st. 245–6; st. 247, vv. 1–4; emphasis Borsetta's)[73]

In the translation of Dolce, only dukes and captains appear, with the women banished completely from the scene, but once again there is a hierarchical arrangement, with those of lesser grade at lesser positions and those of greater preferment at better places. Dido and Aeneas both have thrones of gold, silk and tapestry are disbursed in accordance with rank, and everything was done *non molto differenti a l'uso nostro* ('not much differently from our [i.e. sixteenth-century] custom'; *L'Enea*, st. 207, v. 2).[74]

In a sense, this concern over social hierarchy arises naturally from the same concerns over morality and religion that shaped analysis of the Latin text, for this hierarchy was generally seen as the divinely established referent against which what is right or wrong for a given individual could be measured.[75] This hierarchical structure is

---

[73] Borsetta, *'Eneida' tradotta*, 112–14. Such an expansion of Virgilian narrative in accordance with Renaissance ideas and practices is also consonant with Anguillara's procedures as a translator of Ovid's *Metamorphoses* (Maria Moog-Grünewald, *Metamorphosen der Metamorphosen: Rezeptionsarten der ovidischen Verwandlungsgeschichten in Italien und Frankreich im XVI. und XVII. Jahrhundert*, Studien zum Fortwirken der Antike, 10 (Heidelberg, 1979), 27–112). This trans. has been studied in detail in Kallendorf, 'In Search of a Patron'.

[74] Borsetta, *'Eneida' tradotta*, 114–16.

[75] This association is suggested by Constance Jordan, *Renaissance Feminism: Literary Texts and Political Models* (Ithaca, NY, 1990), 21.

certainly not incompatible with what is found in the Latin commentaries, but it is not developed explicitly there in the way that it is in the Italian translations.

It is worth speculating about why this change in emphasis develops as we move from the linguistic world of Latin to that of Italian. Borsetta has argued that this concern with social and political hierarchy is linked to the world of romance,[76] and there is probably a measure of truth to that argument. But I believe it will be more profitable to approach the problem in terms of readership as it has been analysed in this chapter. Latin was the language of the political and economic elite, those for whom the desirability of the existing social order was generally a given. A book in Italian was accessible to these same people, but to many others as well— probably but seldom to the humblest of servants and artisans, as we have seen, but certainly to those who could have had good reason to wonder why others had so many more advantages than they had, and whether in the right set of circumstances there might be justification for some social reordering.

Dolce's allegorization actually suggests that fear of revolt lurks beneath this concern with defining and clarifying a proper social hierarchy, for Virgil's Rutulians follow Juturna rather than their king in assaulting the Trojan camp, from which Dolce points out how easily the vulgar masses can be deceived by a facile speaker (p. 506). This is precisely what happened in Florence, where the problems the Medici experienced with maintaining control in the 1450s culminated in assassination and revolt in the Pazzi conspiracy of 1478. Among those who celebrated the restoration of Medici power was Cristoforo Landino, who referred to these events at some length in the prologue to his Virgil commentary.[77] This discussion, interestingly enough, is missing from most Venetian editions, especially the later ones. It may be that these

---

[76] 'Eneida' tradotta, 114–16. In Boiardo's Orlando Innamorato: An Ethics of Desire (Cranbury, NJ, 1993), 3–11, 45–6, and 167, Jo Ann Cavallo also suggests ways in which the ethical content of Virgil's poetry entered Boiardo's chivalric world.

[77] The reference may be found in 'Christophori Landini Florentini in P. Vergilii interpretationes prohemium ad Petrum Medicem Magni Laurentii filium', in Cristoforo Landino, Scritti critici e teorici, ed. Roberto Cardini, 2 vols. (Rome, 1974), i. 220. Landino's response to these events is actually a little difficult to interpret; see Cardini's commentary in Scritti critici, ii. 284–5; and Patterson, Pastoral and Ideology, 62–85. For Landino's relations to the Medici in the 1450s, see Arthur Field, The Origins of the Platonic Academy of Florence (Princeton, 1988), 3–51, 231–68.

events were considered irrelevant in a non-Florentine environment, but I suspect that there was also little inclination on the part
of the Venetian authorities to encourage thinking about civil
uprising against republican authority, even when the uprising was
ultimately put down.

Indeed, fear of revolt was very real in Renaissance Venice. The
Tiepolo-Querini conspiracy of 1310 had not been forgotten, and a
variety of problems continued to fester away: discontent among the
large numbers of seamen in the city, a public debt that continued
to rise along with Venice's political ambitions, and oligarchical
scheming within the nobility itself. The nobles made various efforts
to maintain order, ranging from elaborate checks and balances on
the exercise of political power to the staging of pageants in which
rulers and ruled confirmed their allegiance to the political and social
system.[78] Nevertheless, the maintenance of this order could never
be taken for granted, and I suspect it is no accident that the translations of Virgil that broadened access to his poetry did so with a
new emphasis on a social hierarchy that was very much in the
interest of those who financed, patronized, and regulated the press
of the period. After all, as Dolce pointed out, if rebellion can be
contained, religion maintains the republic and exalts those who
govern (p. 426), so that the proper hierarchy can remain intact.

At this point, we might naturally wonder about the status of one
group of readers whose numbers the Italian translations would
have significantly increased: women. As Margaret King has
pointed out, women exercised considerable influence as patrons,
purchasers, and distributors of books, chiefly in the vernacular.
Almost two hundred laywomen have been identified as manuscript owners in the fourteenth and fifteenth centuries, and under
certain restricted conditions women also functioned as printers in
Renaissance Italy. As a reader, Isabelle d'Este complained to
Aldus Manutius himself in 1505 over the high prices of his

[78] The problems referred to here are discussed in any of the standard histories of
Venice; for ease of reference, one might consult Frederic C. Lane, *Venice: A Maritime
Republic* (Baltimore, 1973), 108–9, 173, and 186; and Edward Muir, *Civic Ritual and
Renaissance Venice* (Princeton, 1981). On efforts to control violence and maintain order, see
Gaetano Cozzi, 'Authority and the Law in Renaissance Venice', in J. R. Hale (ed.),
Renaissance Venice (Totowa, NJ, 1973), 293–345; and Guido Ruggiero, *Violence in Early
Renaissance Venice* (New Brunswick, NJ, 1980).

books.[79] Indeed, one of the most frequently reprinted translations of Virgil in the sixteenth century was entitled *I sei primi libri del Eneide di Virgilio, tradotti à piu illustre et honorate donne* ..., and this title unequivocally identifies the target audience as female.[80]

Most women in sixteenth-century Venice did not learn much if any Latin, and their marginal position in the social and political life of the day was determined at least in part by their exclusion from the language of wealth and power. Indeed, as Walter Ong has pointed out, the cleavage between the vernacular world and the world of Latin was essentially one between family life and life outside the family, with the latter world being an almost exclusively male preserve.[81] However, we should note that at least in the Quattrocento, this cleavage was not absolute; Leonardo Bruni's treatise on education, for example, was written for Battista Malatesta of Montefeltro, and this treatise advocated a virtually full programme of humanistic studies for women.[82] What is more, there is a striking concentration of learned women who followed a

[79] King, *Women of the Renaissance*, Women in Culture and Society (Chicago, 1991), 173–5. As King points out, one of the better-known female patrons of learning was Caterina Cornaro, who abdicated the throne of Cyprus to return to the territory of her native Venice, where Petrus Bembus enjoyed her hospitality in Asolo (ibid. 162–3; Horatio F. Brown, 'Caterina Cornaro, Queen of Cyprus', in *Studies in the History of Venice*, 2 vols. (London, 1907), i. 255–92; and Louise Buenger Robbert, 'Caterina Corner, Queen of Cyprus (Venetian, 1454?–1510)', in J. R. Brink (ed.), *Female Scholars: A Tradition of Learned Women before 1800* (Montreal, 1980), 24–35). See also Deborah Parker, 'Women in the Book Trade in Italy, 1475–1620', *Renaissance Quarterly*, 49 (1996), 509–41.

[80] The first Venetian edn. was printed in 1539–40 by Niccolò Zoppino, Giovanni Antonio and Domenico Volpini, and Comin da Trino; it was reprinted by Comin da Trino and Niccolò Zoppino (1540), Comin da Trino, Niccolò Zoppino, and Andrea Arrivabene (1540), Andrea Arrivabene (1540–1), and Giovanni Padovano, Niccolò Zoppino, and Federico Torresano (1544). Since the individual books in this trans. often had individual title-pages, composite edns. were sometimes formed by combining parts of different edns.

[81] In a now-famous essay, Ong argued that the study of Latin was so strongly gendered that it functioned as a rite of passage for boys in the Renaissance ('Latin Language Study as a Renaissance Puberty Rite', *Studies in Philology*, 56 (1959), 103–24; see also id., *Orality and Literacy: The Technologizing of the Word, New Accents* (London, 1982), 113; and King, *Women*, 173, 175).

[82] *De studiis et litteris*, in Baron (ed.), *Bruni: Schriften*, 5–19; Eng. trans. in Griffiths *et al.* (eds.), *Humanism of Leonardo Bruni*, 240–51. Admittedly some concession is made to the fact that the addressee is a woman: the stress on religion is increased, probably reflecting the traditional emphasis in education for women and the fact that many women humanists only found the freedom to study in a convent, and the study of rhetoric is curtailed, since oratorical contests in the forum are the proper province of men. Nevertheless the educational programme developed here is both rigorous and in accordance with the principles developed in the other treatises of the day, although as Ruth Kelso points out, not all of Bruni's contemporaries were willing to allow such latitude to women students (*Doctrine for the Lady*

programme of studies like this in and around the Veneto.[83] Among the better-known humanistically educated women of the area are the Veronese noblewomen Ginevra Nogarola (1417–[1461–8]) and her sister Isotta (1418–66), who devoted herself to study for many years in her mother's house; Costanza Barbaro (born after 1419), the daughter of the humanist Francesco Barbaro; Cecilia Gonzaga (1425–51), the daughter of the sovereign of Mantua who was encouraged in her studies by the Venetian noble Gregorio Correr; Cataruzza Caldiera (d. 1463); Cassandra Fedele (1465-1558), from a Venetian citizen family active in the secretariat of the republic; and Olimpia Morata, the daughter of a court humanist in Ferrara.[84] To be sure, we must wait quite a while for a woman to receive a doctorate from a European university, but the first to do so was Venetian, Elena Lucrezia Cornaro Piscopia, who received her degree from the University of Padua in 1678.[85]

Behind these educational achievements lay a set of social, economic, and ideological conditions that occasionally opened up greater space for women than was customary in Renaissance Europe. Women in Venice, for example, contributed a good deal to the nexus of relationships among the Venetian patriciate by providing capital for business and by creating a system of horizontal ties among families that complemented the vertical lineage ties binding men.[86]

---

of the Renaissance (Urbana, Ill., 1956), 58–77). General information on the education of women in Italian Renaissance culture may be found in Gian Ludovico Masetti Zannini, *Motivi storici della educazione femminile: Scienza, lavoro, giuochi* (Naples, 1982), 7–116.

[83] Margaret L. King, 'Book-Lined Cells: Women and Humanism in the Early Italian Renaissance', in Patricia H. Labalme (ed.), *Beyond their Sex: Learned Women of the European Past* (New York, 1980), 67. Though dated, Eugenio Musatti, *La donna in Venezia*, 2nd edn. (Padua, 1892), still offers a useful introduction to the activities of famous Venetian women.

[84] These women have been the subject of considerable scholarly interest of late. See esp. Margaret L. King, 'Thwarted Ambitions: Six Learned Women of the Early Italian Renaissance', *Soundings*, 59 (1976), 280–304, with a thorough bibliography on 301–4. On the general place of women students in humanist educational theory, see William Harrison Woodward, *Vittorino da Feltre and Other Humanist Educators*, Renaissance Society of America Reprint Texts (Toronto, 1996; repr. of New York, 1963 edn.), 247–50.

[85] Patricia H. Labalme, 'Women's Roles in Early Modern Venice: An Exceptional Case', in ead. (ed.), *Beyond their Sex*, 129–52. Also useful as general background is P. O. Kristeller's essay in the same vol., 'Learned Women of Early Modern Italy: Humanists and University Scholars', 91–116.

[86] Stanley Chojnacki, 'Patrician Women in Early Renaissance Venice', *Studies in the Renaissance*, 21 (1974), 176–203; see also id., 'Dowries and Kinsmen in Early Renaissance Venice', *Journal of Interdisciplinary History*, 5 (Spring, 1975), 571–600; and Donald E. Queller and Thomas F. Madden, 'Father of the Bride: Fathers, Daughters, and Dowries in Late Medieval and Early Renaissance Venice', *Renaissance Quarterly*, 46 (1993), 695–9.

Virginia Cox has recently argued that a crisis in the Venetian marriage market led on the one hand to an increased number of unmarriageable spinsters and reluctant nuns who challenged their traditional subordinate position in society, and on the other hand to a greater sense of self worth in those women whose inflated dowries led to an increased status within their families.[87] The Venetian *corti-giana onesta* in turn challenged the system of gender ideologies defining a woman's position as private and family-oriented, for the courtesan did not fill the traditional role of a woman excluded from the public sphere.[88]

Once women began exercising non-traditional roles, a space was also opened for non-traditional ideas. Indeed, all three authors whom Ginevra Conti Odorisio and Patricia Labalme present as innovative for their time in their treatment of gender roles were Venetian,[89] and a striking preponderance of treatises examined by Constance Jordan as representative of Renaissance feminism were published in Venice. Among these treatises, that of Lucrezia Marinelli has been interpreted by Jordan as showing that interpretations of Aristotelian pronouncements on social and political institutions are themselves historically conditioned, so that the authoritative is replaced with the author, whose truth is contingent and relative.[90] Girolamo Ruscelli argues that the determination of moral worth on which the humanist practice of praise and blame rests is never absolute,[91] and Galeazzo Flavio Capella in turn argues that what was generally considered the 'natural' inferiority of women to men was in fact an image projected by men, in

---

[87] 'The Single Self: Feminist Thought and the Marriage Market in Early Modern Venice', *Renaissance Quarterly*, 48 (1995), 513–81.

[88] Margaret F. Rosenthal, 'Veronica Franco's *Terze Rime*: The Venetian Courtesan's Defense', *Renaissance Quarterly*, 42 (1989), 227–57; and ead., *The Honest Courtesan: Veronica Franco, Citizen and Writer in Sixteenth-Century Venice*, Women in Culture and Society (Chicago, Ill., 1992).

[89] Odorisio, *Donna e società nel Seicento: Lucrezia Marinelli e Arcangela Tarabotti*, Biblioteca di cultura, 167 (Rome, 1979), with excerpts from and analysis of Moderata Fonte's *Il merito delle donne*; and Labalme, 'Venetian Women on Women: Three Early Modern Feminists', *Archivio Veneto*, 112 (1979), 81–109. Of the three women considered here, Jordan, *Renaissance Feminism*, also discusses Fonte (253–7) and Marinelli (257–61).

[90] Marinelli, *La nobiltà et l'eccellenza delle donne co' diffetti et mancamenti de gli huomini* (Venice, 1601), discussed in Jordan, *Renaissance Feminism*, 257–61.

[91] *Lettura ove … si pruova la somma perfettione delle donne* (Venice, 1552), discussed in Jordan, *Renaissance Feminism*, 160–1.

whose interests it was to exclude women from certain activities.[92] Indeed, if Jordan's analysis is on target, such sixteenth-century writers as Fausto da Longiano understood that 'ideas and social practices related to sex and gender are culturally constructed'—a conclusion with potentially earth-shaking consequences.[93]

Once authority was recognized as historically contingent and relevant only to the particular circumstances it addressed, the way was clear to propose non-traditional views of women that challenged the bounds of patriarchy. In his *Discorso della virtù feminile e donnesca*, for example, Tasso faces directly the nature of a woman who is 'heroic'. For her, the wifely virtues are inappropriate; her virtue is *donnesca*, that of a governor who happens to be female but who is judged along with men according to a single standard.[94] In accordance with this definition, real-life women like Joan of Arc and Elizabeth Tudor join literary women like Britomart and Bradamante[95]—and Dido. In his *Lettere di molte valorose donne*, Ortensio Landi purports to have collected letters from noble women around the Veneto in which they imagine themselves in male roles. One of the most interesting of these women is Isabella Sforza, who imagines herself as Virgil's Aeneas, able to reject desire along with her sex so that as a 'Diana-like version of Aeneas', she, too, could become the subject of an eternal paean of praise.[96] Those women with a humanist education could go one step further and use a shared language and a shared literary culture—which included Virgil—to correspond with their male counterparts with a measure of equality. Lodovico Foscarini, for example, wrote a letter to Isotta Nogarola in which he commends her for delighting not in gold or embroidered robes but in Cicero and Virgil, through whom she pursues virtue and the highest good.[97] And Angelo Poliziano begins a letter to Cassandra Fedele with a

---

[92] *Delle eccellenze et dignità delle donne* (Venice, 1526), discussed in Jordan, *Renaissance Feminism*, 72–5.

[93] Jordan, *Renaissance Feminism*, 147 n. 16.

[94] *Discorso* (1572), discussed in Jordan, *Renaissance Feminism*, 146–9; see also 34.

[95] King, *Women*, 188–93.

[96] Discussed in Jordan, *Renaissance Feminism*, 138–43.

[97] Isota Nogarola Veronensis, *Opera quae supersunt omnia, accedunt Angelae et Zeneverae Nogarolae epistolae et carmina*, ed. E. Abel, 2 vols. (Vienna, 1886), ii. 50. A trans. of this letter may be found in Margaret L. King and Albert Rabil, Jr. (eds.), *Her Immaculate Hand: Selected Works by and about the Women Humanists of Quattrocento Italy*, Medieval and Renaissance Texts and Studies, 20 (Binghamton, NY, 1983), 120; see also 57, 117.

Virgilian tag (*o decus Italiae virgo*, 'O virgin ornament of Italy', *Aen.* II. 508) and continues with a reference to *Aeneid* I. 493, through which Cassandra is likened to the Amazon queen Penthesilea: *Audesque viris concurrere virgo, sic scilicet in doctrinarum stadio pulcherrimo, ut non sexus animo, non animus pudori, non ingenio pudor officiat.* ('You, as a virgin, dare to compete with men in the admirable race-course of learning in such a way that your sex does not hinder your spirit, nor your spirit your modesty, nor your modesty your talent.')[98] Thus the heroic women of Virgil's world could function as symbols through which new roles could be imagined for women in Renaissance Venice.

An especially interesting example of this process may be found in the poetry of Gaspara Stampa, a well-connected Venetian poet whose circle of acquaintances included Domenico Venier and the other prominent supporters of the Accademia della Fama.[99] Like the student who entered a crude version of Petrarch's *Rime* no. 61 into the front of the copy of the *c.*1488 Liga Boaria edition of Virgil now in the Biblioteca Comunale, Treviso, Stampa read Book 4 of the *Aeneid* through the lens of Petrarchan lyric conventions.[100] But unlike this (presumably) male student, Stampa used

[98] King and Rabil (eds.), *Her Immaculate Hand*, 126–7, 152 n. 21; and *Clarissimae feminae Cassandrae Fidelis Venetae epistolae et orationes …*, ed. J. P. Tomasini (Padua: Franciscus Bolzeteas, 1636), 155, 157.

[99] There are many problems connected to the interpretation of Stampa and her poetry, ranging from clarifying biographical data to evaluating serious editorial intervention into her work. Since most of these problems do not have a significant effect on Stampa's role in this study, I refer the interested reader to the treatment of Stampa by Patricia Berrahou Phillippy in *Love's Remedies: Recantation and Renaissance Lyric Poetry* (Lewisburg, Penn., 1995), 92–135 with notes, 215–23. Although I am approaching Stampa's work with different interests, I am indebted to Professor Phillippy for drawing my attention to Stampa, and my discussion is heavily indebted to her analysis on 114–20. For Stampa's relationship to the Accademia della Fama, see Martha Feldman, 'The Academy of Domenico Venier, Music's Literary Muse in Mid-Cinquecento Venice', *Renaissance Quarterly*, 44 (1991), 500–3; and ead., *City Culture and the Madrigal at Venice* (Berkeley and Los Angeles, Calif., 1995), 104–8.

[100] The student's poem reads: *Sia benedetto il giorno che nascesti* | *E l'hora e 'l penso che fusti creata.* | *Sia benedetto il letto ove giacesti* | *E la fonte ove fusti bagnata.* | *Sia benedetto il late che bevesti* | *e la tua madre che te ha nutricata.* | *Sia benedetta tu sempre da dio* | *Quando farai contento lo cor mio.* ('Blessed be the day when you were born | And the hour and the task when you were created. | Blessed be the bed where you have lain | and the fountain where you bathed. | Blessed be the milk that you have drunk | and your mother who has nourished you. | Blessed be you, always, by God, | when you will have made my heart content.') The poem is found on fo. 1ʳ, with the present shelf mark of the book being Inc. 13716. The same set of attitudes also colours a prose notice in a 1587 Sebastianus a Donnis edn. of the *Eclogues* (Verona, Biblioteca Civica, C.V.59), where the annotator discusses the proper

both the Petrarchan conventions and the Virgilian text to create an explicitly female voice that challenged the dominant literary and social values that these texts were generally believed to support.

Stampa's poem no. 93, for example, begins with Virgil's description of Dido as a doe, inflamed and wounded by the arrows of love (*Aen.* 4. 68–74). Since these lines are presented through the third-person epic narrator, they belong strictly speaking neither to Dido nor to Aeneas. For Venetian Renaissance readers, however, the poem celebrates the values of Aeneas, so that ultimately the image is tinged with all the negative valences that love takes on as a feminine threat to God, country, and morality. Stampa, though, challenges this interpretive matrix:

> Qual fuggitiva cerva e miserella,
>   C' havendo la saetta nel costato,
>   Seguita da' duo veltri in selva e 'n prato,
>   Fugge la morte che và pur con ella,
> Tal'io, ferita da l'empie quadrelle,
>   Del fiero cacciator crudo & alato,
>   Gelosia e disio havendo à lato,
>   Fuggo, e schivar non posso la mia stella.
> La qual mi mena à miserabil morte,
>   Se non ritorna à noi da gente strana
>   Il Sol degli occhi miei, che la conforte:
> Egli è 'l Dittamo mio, egli risana
>   La piaga mia; e può far la mia sorte,
>   D'aspra e noiosa, dilettosa e piana.[101]

(As a fugitive and miserable doe, having an arrow in her rib, followed by two greyhounds in wood and in meadow, flees death that yet keeps up with her; so I, wounded by the harsh arrows of the cruel and winged hunter, having jealousy and desire on either side, flee, and I cannot avoid my fate. This leads me to this miserable death, unless my eyes' sun, which comforts my life, returns from foreign people: he is my dittany, he heals my wound and can make my harsh and troublesome destiny delightful and light.)

This poem participates in a tradition of poems about deer, but it is different in one important way: Stampa as the deer is also the

---

order of gift-giving between a lover and his lady (38). For the role of these attitudes in the education of women in the Renaissance, see Zannini, *Motivi storici*, 71–116; for a general treatment of Stampa's work in relationship to Petrarchan conventions, see Phillippy, *Love's Remedies*, 92–135.

[101] The sonnets of Stampa I discuss are printed in Phillippy, *Love's Remedies*, 116–18, as are the English translations, which I have modified slightly.

speaker. As such, she rewrites Virgil's text so that as a woman, she has a voice in defining what is of value in the world around her.[102]

Where this leads can be seen more clearly in the preceding sonnet. Poem no. 92 begins with the famous Virgilian simile in which Aeneas' resolve is compared to an oak tree buffeted by Alpine winds:

> Ac velut annoso validam cum robore quercum
> Alpini Boreae nunc hinc nunc flatibus illinc
> eruere inter se certant; it stridor, et altae
> consternunt terram concusso stipite frondes;
> ipsa haeret scopulis et quantum vertice ad auras
> aetherias, tantum radice in Tartara tendit:
> haud secus adsiduis hinc atque hinc vocibus heros
> tunditur, et magno persentit pectore curas;
> mens immota manet, lacrimae volvuntur inanes.

> (... As when, among the Alps, north winds
> will strain against each other to root out
> with blasts—now on this side, now that—a stout
> oak tree whose wood is full of years; the roar
> is shattering, the trunk is shaken, and
> high branches scatter on the ground; but it
> still grips the rocks; as steeply as it thrusts
> its crown into the upper air, so deep
> the roots it reaches down to Tartarus:
> no less than this, the hero; he is battered
> on this side and on that by assiduous words;
> he feels care in his mighty chest, and yet
> his mind cannot be moved; the tears fall, useless.)

> (*Aen.* 4. 441–9)

In the context of the poem as it was customarily interpreted, these lines praised steadfastness in adherence to duty, as that concept was understood within the male-dominated epic world appropriated by those with power in Renaissance Venice. Stampa's version, however, challenges this interpretive context:

> Quasi quercia di monte urtata e scossa
> Da ogni lato e da contrari venti,

---

[102] Although the tradition of deer poetry can be traced back to Ovid's *Metamorphoses*, it flowered in the Renaissance, ranging from Petrarch's Sonnet 190 to Wyatt's 'They flee from me' and 'Whoso list to hunt' and Spenser's *Amoretti* 67. Most of these poems were written by men, although interestingly Wyatt's 'They flee from me' goes even farther than Stampa in silencing the man. I am grateful to Patricia Phillippy for help on this point.

Che, sendo hor questi, hor quelli più possenti,
Per cader mille volte e mille è mossa,
La vita mia, questa mia frale possa,
Combattuta hor da speme, hor da tormenti,
Non sà, lontani i chiari lumi ardenti,
In qual parte piegar' homai si possa.
Hor m'affidan le carte del mio bene,
Hor mi disperan poi l'altrui parole;
Ei mi dice, io pur vengo, altri, non viene.
Sia morte meco almen, più che non suole,
Pietosa à trarmi fuor di tante pene,
Se non debbo veder tosto il mio sole.

(As a mountain oak, pushed and shaken on all sides by contrary winds, now these winds, now those being more powerful, is moved to fall a thousand times and a thousand more; my life, this my frail strength, beaten now by hopes, now by torments, does not know, with the clear lights burning far away, in which direction it may bend. Now the pages of my lover encourage me, then the words of others cause me to despair. He tells me, 'I am certainly coming'; others say, 'he is not coming'. At least death may be with me, more than is usual, to remove pitiful me from so many pains, unless I soon see my sun.)

The major change, of course, is that Stampa has transformed the image of heroic resolution from Aeneas to herself. Her Aeneas, Collaltino di Collalto, is fickle—perhaps he is coming to her, perhaps not—but she is steadfast. As Patricia Phillippy has pointed out, this sonnet challenges the Petrarchist conventions of the day, but it also challenges the Virgilian underpinnings of Venetian Renaissance culture:[103] steadfastness, in other words, is transferred from the realm of martial and civic values to the realm of private relationships. Through this transferral, the speaking feminine voice validates itself and its own values at the expense of the silenced male and the values of his male-dominated world.

As poetry like Stampa's presented the possibility that women might begin to challenge the traditional male system of values, Renaissance men responded by oscillating between admiration and opposition.[104] For instance, the female scholar whose control

---

[103] Phillippy's discussion also highlights the role of Ovid's *Heroides* in shaping Stampa's work; see *Love's Remedies*, 114–20. See also John Watkins, *The Specter of Dido: Spenser and Virgilian Epic* (New Haven, 1995), 30–61 for further discussion of how later writers including Ovid challenged Virgil's handling of the Dido story.

[104] King, *Women*, 188–93. Kelso, *Doctrine for the Lady*, 5–37, offers a good survey of opinion regarding women's place in Renaissance thought.

of Latin allowed her to function with men on their terms was admired as a prodigy, but she was also feared as a threat, so that many of the scholarly exchanges between men and women are tinged with ambiguity. An example of this may be found in the letter of the Venetian patrician, humanist, and theologian Gregorio Correr to Cecilia Gonzaga (1443), in support of her desire to enter a convent. Both of them had studied with the great humanist educator Vittorino da Feltre, and Correr clearly recognized the desire for study as one of Gonzaga's aims in entering the convent. However in his advice to Gonzaga, Correr does not advise accommodation between Christianity and pagan culture, a humanist stance with roots going all the way back to the Church Fathers; instead he insists first that she abandon the classical Latin culture she has worked so hard to attain:

I forbid utterly the reading of secular literature, particularly the works of the poets. For how can I believe that you have renounced the world if you love the things that are of the world? ... a bride of Christ may read only sacred books and ecclesiastical writers. So you must put aside your beloved Virgil, with Vittorino's pardon. Take up instead the Psalter [and] instead of Cicero, the Gospel.[105]

Then he acknowledges that it may not be possible to expunge completely from her mind all that she has learned. If this is the case, she should imitate Proba, so that if a verse of Virgil comes to mind, it should be altered and brought into conformity with Christian doctrine.[106] The ambiguities here are striking. On the one hand the letter is written in Latin and acknowledges that Gonzaga's mastery of Latin literature, especially Virgil, is probably an ineradicable part of her intellectual life. On the other hand, however, the accommodation between Christianity and the pagan world that was available to many men, including many religious, through the concept of the *poeta theologus* was not available to her. As we see here, a woman's toehold in the world of Latin scholarship was tenuous at best.

Virgilian interpretation also reinforced the traditional patriarchal system when male writers simply failed to acknowledge any complexities involving gender issues in Virgil's texts and the implications these complexities might have for the lives of Virgil's

---

[105] King and Rabil (eds.), *Her Immaculate Hand*, 102–3; see also 91–3.
[106] Ibid. 104.

women readers in the Renaissance. For example, Luciana Borsetto has prepared a careful analysis of the prefaces addressed by the male translators to their women readers in each book of the popular *I sei primi libri del Eneide di Virgilio*. The *pietà* of Dido toward the Trojans in Book 1 of the *Aeneid* is equated to the *pietà* that the dedicatee, Aurelia Tolomei, should show toward the valorous wits in her circle of admirers. The dangers of Aeneas' sea journey in *Aeneid* 3 correspond to the dangers of *amore volgare*, and the felicity of divine love corresponds to the felicity of Giulia Petrucci and of whoever models a life on hers. The bitter death of Dido in *amore volgare* in turn contrasts to the happy end of felicity associated with the heavenly love of Aurelia Petrucci, to whom the translation of Book 4 is dedicated. The *pietà* and *bontà* that Aeneas shows to Anchises in Book 5 parallel the *pietà* and *bontà* shown by Giorolama Carli Piccolomini to her dead husband. And finally, the goodness and love shown by Aeneas to Anchises correspond to those shown by Frasia Venturi to Alessandro Piccolomini, the translator of Book 6, while the virtue of Frasia provides a guide to the travails of this life just as the golden bough allowed Aeneas to confront the dangers of the underworld.[107] The general references to pity and virtue, to earthly and heavenly love, are obviously taken from the matrix of a Neoplatonically tinged courtly love environment,[108] but they are striking here in their very banality: that is, when the text is specifically associated with women readers, any potentially subversive lines of interpretation are banished. Dido becomes the only negative *exemplum* in the group, and the positive *exempla* are moved decisively into an ambience where the interaction between men and women bears only a tangential relationship to the complicated realities of economic and political life in Renaissance Venice.

One of the most interesting, and decisive, uses of Virgil to reinforce the traditional, patriarchal hierarchy in Renaissance Venice is a play based on *Aeneid* 4. Although it was published by the prestigious Aldine press, *Didone: Tragedia di M. Lodovico Dolce*[109] has not fared well at the hands of modern critics: Vladimiro Zabughin

---

[107] Borsetto, *'Eneide' tradotta*, 26–32.

[108] A similar impulse motivated the copying or composition of original poetry in Italian with a courtly love flavour, like the octet discussed above (n. 100) in the *c.*1488 Liga Boaria Latin edn. now in Treviso, Biblioteca Comunale, Inc. 13716.

[109] References to the 1547 edn. will be placed in the text.

describes its author as 'a man with a distinctly impoverished imagination',[110] and Barbaro Bono feels that the play itself reveals a 'groping, partial, unassimilated historical consciousness'.[111] Nevertheless its author was the same man whose translation of the *Aeneid* would be published some twenty years later, and any shortcomings Dolce might have as a dramatist need not diminish his value as an interpreter of Virgil.

The most insightful analysis I have seen of this play is that of Corinne Lucas, who has argued that *Didone* presents honour as the key value in human existence and explores how this value manifests itself within the theme of marriage.[112] I would agree with this, but I would add that for Dolce, honour is a gendered concept that means something different for a man and a woman, even when both function as political leaders. For Aeneas, the honourable is defined by Achates, who reminds him that when a man leaves this life, he takes with him only *'l chiaro et honorato nome, | Che dal splendor de le belle opre segue* ('a famous and honoured name, which results from the distinction of good works'; fo. 11ʳ). That is, for a man, honour is linked to his deeds, to the successful completion of the political mission assigned to him by the gods (fo. 11ᵛ). For Dido, however, honour is associated with chastity, and when she is forced to admit to Aeneas that she has lost the one, she has to admit that she has lost the other as well: *Per voi l'antico mio gradito honore | Di castità ho perduto* ('Because of you I have lost my longstanding, well-received honour of chastity'; fo. 24ᵛ).[113] Again to Venus, Dido acknowledges that she has lost everything worth

---

[110] *Vergilio*, ii. 381.

[111] *Literary Transvaluation: From Vergilian Epic to Shakespearean Tragicomedy* (Berkeley and Los Angeles, Calif., 1984), 89. For discussion of other Renaissance plays about Dido, see ibid. 83–139; and Don Cameron Allen, 'Marlowe's *Dido* and the Tradition', in Richard Hosley (ed.), *Essays on Shakespeare and Elizabethan Drama in Honor of Hardin Craig* (Columbia, Mo., 1962), 55–68. I am grateful to Patricia Phillippy for this last reference.

[112] 'Didon: Trois réécritures tragiques du livre de l'*Eneide* dans le théâtre italien du XVIᵉ siècle', in Mazzacurati and Plaisance (eds.), *Scritture di scritture*, 593–604.

[113] As Ruth Kelso has observed (*Doctrine for the Lady*, 71), Dolce presents chastity as the virtue important beyond all others in women when he discusses their upbringing; see *Dialogo di M. Lodovico Dolce della institution delle donne: Secondo il tre stati, che cadono nella vita humana* (Venice: Gabriel Giolito, 1547), fo. 23ʳ. For a fascinating account of how gendered conceptions of honour can be recovered from archival documents of this period, see Guido Ruggiero, ' "Più che la vita caro": Onore, matrimonio e reputazione femminile nel tardo Rinascimento', *Quaderni storici*, 66 (1987), 753–75.

living for—*Dico la castità, dico l'honore* ('I mean chastity, I mean honour'; fo. 35ʳ).

A number of twentieth-century scholars have pointed out that in Renaissance culture, chastity was in essence a prerequisite for women who wanted opportunities for achievement in male-dominated arenas. The most famous woman ruler of the Renaissance, Elizabeth I, maintained her political power only by acting differently from Dido and remaining unmarried.[114] What is more, those who chose to compete with men in the arena of scholarship were faced with a similar choice. Those women who achieved some recognition for their accomplishments as humanists, for example, were eventually forced either to marry and virtually abandon their studies or to withdraw from the world as the price for continuing to read and write—although as we have seen with Cecilia Gonzaga, even entering a convent was no guarantee that the freedom to continue studying necessarily extended to humanist authors.[115] That is, the emphasis on female chastity in this play highlights a very real gender distinction in Renaissance life—that men could 'have it all', but women could not.

Aeneas was free to marry, but not to marry Dido, and what drama we find in this play results from his efforts to re-establish the

---

[114] The larger role of chastity in the suppression of women in the Renaissance was highlighted by Joan Kelly-Gadol, 'Did Women have a Renaissance?' in R. Bridenthal and C. Koonz (eds.), *Becoming Visible: Women in European History* (Boston, 1977), 152–61; and Margaret Ferguson, 'A Room not their Own: Renaissance Women as Readers and Writers', in Clayton Koelb and Susan Noakes (eds.), *The Comparative Perspective on Literature: Approaches to Theory and Practice* (Ithaca, NY, 1988), 93–116. Relevant material from the period is available in two treatises (discussed by Jordan, *Renaissance Feminism*, 41–7 and 68–70): Francesco Barbaro, *De re uxoria* (1416), and Lodovico Dolce, *Della institution delle donne* (Venice: Giolito, 1545). As regards Dido specifically, Jordan points out that as early as Boccaccio, humanist critics had noted that a woman ruling was a political impossibility, since if a wife is subordinate to a husband, at the moment of marriage she becomes politically impotent, leaving her citizens subject to the alien authority of a male consort (*Renaissance Feminism*, 37–9).

[115] King, 'Thwarted Ambitions', 280–301; ead., 'Book-Lined Cells', 68–9; and Lisa Jardine, 'Isotta Nogarola: Women Humanists—Education for What?' *History of Education*, 12 (1983), 231–44. For an interesting but somewhat eccentric effort to link chastity to the fundamental intellectual activities of humanism, see Stephanie H. Jed, *Chaste Thinking: The Rape of Lucretia and the Birth of Humanism*, Theories of Representation and Difference (Bloomington, Ind., 1989), with the review by Ronald Witt, *Renaissance Quarterly*, 43 (1990), 604–6. It is worth noting, however, that social historians have demonstrated that in practice women engaged in activities not approved of in theory, such that lower-class women often lived with men to whom they were not married and upper-class women in convents were not always chaste; see Guido Ruggiero, *The Boundaries of Eros: Sex Crime and Sexuality in Renaissance Venice* (New York, 1985), 77, 83, 100.

proper priorities in his life. Achates, who ends up articulating the traditional hierarchy underlying the vernacular versions of the *Aeneid*, reminds Aeneas of what he should already know, that he has erred in subordinating his will to that of Dido: *Peccaste à consentir à le sue voglie* (fo. 13ʳ). The solution is to take his proper place in the universal order by restoring order within himself: *Preponeste l'honesto à quel che piace*; | *Pur io dirò, che non comanda Giove* | *Cosa, che non sia giusta* ... ('Put the honourable before that which pleases, for I shall tell you that Jove orders only what is just'; fo. 12ᵛ; see also fo. 23ʳ). The gods have commanded and people must obey, since *Nessun' offende che obedisce à Giove* ('No one offends who obeys Jove'; fo. 27ʳ), for through obedience people accept their place in the social hierarchy and the just order willed by God can come to be.

As this just order is re-established in Dolce's play, there is no longer any place for Dido; she repents repeatedly in the final scenes, but her honour, unlike Aeneas', is lost for ever. The only choice is for her to be written out of the play, which is of course what happens, in the same way as the patriarchal hierarchy of Renaissance Venice so often wrote women out of its history.[116] Indeed it is striking that of the 251 Renaissance texts of Virgil that I have examined in the Veneto, not one can be securely linked to a woman owner. Thus most of the voices we hear today are male voices—male correspondents who urge educated women to abandon their studies, male translators who move to suppress potentially subversive interpretations, and male dramatists whose Virgilian plays celebrate a traditional hierarchy that closes off options for women.

Thus as we have also seen in the areas of morality and religion, subversive readings of Virgil emerged briefly, sometimes explicitly and sometimes only by implication, in the books of the period. Consistently, however, the social, economic, and political forces dominating Renaissance Venice functioned to contain these subversive readings. In part this happened because the various strands comprising the social fabric of Renaissance Venice turn out to have been inextricably interwoven: the Latin and Italian linguistic worlds were connected with one another, so that Latin

---

[116] For a review of 20th-cent. feminist efforts to deal with this aspect of the *Aeneid*, see Craig Kallendorf, 'Recent Trends in Vergilian Scholarship', *Helios*, 18 (1991), 76–8.

texts served everyone from patricians to the illiterate, and Italian translations made the moral and religious content of Virgil accessible to many people who did not work comfortably with Latin. Through these interconnections, the same basic interpretation of Virgil that originated among humanistically educated, upper-class men was disseminated through other groups as well and ultimately dominated their understanding of the poems. As Anthony Grafton has observed,

[M]en and women without formal education often had access to, and could express in their own way, the same sorts of concepts and images that put order into the universe, the past, and the diversities of the human race for scholars. ... [M]ercantile and learned cultures were not separated by an impermeable membrane. They met at many points.[117]

In this case, the result was that when women and the politically marginalized encountered the powerful in the pages of Virgil's poetry, the voices of the former were suppressed by the voices of the latter. Thus the study of Virgil's place in the history of printing provides a broader corroboration for the social and political unity that is at the foundation of the myth of Venice.

---

[117] *New Worlds, Ancient Texts: The Power of Tradition and the Shock of Discovery* (Cambridge, Mass., 1992), 74–5. From a somewhat different perspective, Jonathan Rose has also emphasized that working-class readers in 19th- and 20th-cent. England were just as capable as intellectuals of responding to canonical literature ('Rereading the English Common Reader: A Preface to a History of Audiences', *Journal of the History of Ideas*, 53 (1992), 54–5).

5

Afterword

One of the guiding premisses of this study has been that the meaning of a literary work is socially constructed, a protean, evolving negotiation between a text and its readers. What readers see in a text is in part determined by the basic paradigm through which they view the world around them, so that there is no privileged position from which literature can be interpreted objectively. From this premiss, it follows logically that if Venetian Renaissance readers viewed Virgil through the filter of their values and beliefs, we must in turn be viewing their acts of reading through our own ideological filter(s). In other words, if the myth of Venice in part determined what Venetian readers could and could not see in Virgil's poetry, then the assumptions and principles underlying my interpretive community will partially shape my observations about Renaissance readers encountering a classical text.[1] It is therefore incumbent on me to make some of these assumptions and principles explicit, for as Jean Howard has noted, 'what one discovers about the historical place and function of literary texts is in large measure a function of the angle from which one looks and the assumptions that enable the investigation'.[2]

The interpretive community from which this study has

[1] This point is developed further by Charles Martindale, *Redeeming the Text: Latin Poetry and the Hermeneutics of Reception*, Roman Literature and its Contexts (Cambridge, 1993), 1–34; and Stanley Fish, *Doing what comes naturally: Change, Rhetoric, and the Practice of Theory in Literary and Legal Studies* (Durham, NC, 1989), and *There's No Such Thing as Free Speech and it's a Good Thing too* (New York, 1994).

[2] 'The New Historicism in Renaissance Studies', in Arthur F. Kinney and Dan S. Collins (eds.), *Renaissance Historicism: Selections from English Literary Renaissance* (Amherst, Mass., 1987), 32–3. An excellent discussion of how the intellectual lives of individual scholars affect the way they view the past may be found in Norman F. Cantor, *Inventing the Middle Ages: The Lives, Works, and Ideas of the Great Medievalists of the Twentieth Century* (New York, 1991).

emerged is that of academic discourse generated in North America and Western Europe at the turn of the millennium. In a certain sense this is obvious, but it is worth dwelling on the point briefly because there are consequences that derive from it. If I were what used to be called a 'gentleman scholar', independently wealthy and not accountable to anyone for how I use my time, I suppose I could pursue any research I wish without regard to whether the results would interest anyone else or not. However, since I am a university professor with an institutional appointment, I am constrained at least in part to ask questions that interest other university professors, and to present my results in ways that are compatible with other scholarly activities of my day. For this reason, my study promotes the scholarly concerns of the twentieth century as much as those of the sixteenth.[3]

For one thing, the reader-response approach on which this book rests is very much a contemporary phenomenon. I suspect it is no longer terribly controversial among those who work in modern literature, but among classicists today the old philological model still exercises a powerful appeal. Originating with the humanists of the Italian Renaissance, refined by German scholars between 1750 and 1850, and applied in essentially the same way a hundred years later, philology rests on the belief that each text has one meaning, embedded within it at the moment of creation. The role of the interpreter is to recover this original signification, to see the text as it actually was—and is. According to this model, different interpretations are a sign of a methodological failure in which some or all of the interpreters have allowed their own values and beliefs to come between themselves and the text. The reader-response model, however, recognizes different interpretations as the inevitable result of interactions between a text and readers from different interpretive communities. There is no privileged position from which a text can be read objectively, so there is no way to reduce many readings to one and no reason to try. Studying the reception of a classical text is therefore transformed from the recording of a series of misreadings plotted against one philologically derived standard to the creation of many readings linking classical texts, later readers, and contemporary scholars.

---

[3] I am grateful to Charles Martindale for bringing up this point in his response to an earlier version of this book.

Contemporary theory has created a paradigm shift here, and this book depends very much on that shift.[4]

Another area in which present-day academic discourse has opened up new opportunities for discussion regards the material forms in which texts are encountered. Traditionally this has been the concern of analytical or descriptive bibliography, which 'deals with books and their relations solely as material objects' and 'in a strict sense has nothing to do with the historical or literary considerations of their subject matter or content',[5] and of textual criticism, which seeks to recover the text as it was originally created so that it can be presented (ideally) in a modern, critical edition.[6] These activities come first, as preludes to literary criticism.[6] Recently, however, a number of scholars have been applying pressure to this traditional model at several points. A printed text, one can argue, is not just the result of authorial intention, but also of the wishes of editors, typesetters, censors, and so forth. And when a text is presented in book form, physical elements of the presentation like typeface and book size can offer crucial cues for interpretation to various groups of potential readers. What is more, early printed books regularly contain dedicatory letters, illustrations, commentaries, and indexes, all of which were designed collectively to direct readers toward some interpretive possibilities within the text and away from others. Current work in this area stresses the importance of collaboration in the creation, production, and consumption of texts, and of the material form in which

[4] For a description of the philological model and relevant bibliography, see Anthony Grafton, *Defenders of the Text: The Traditions of Scholarship in an Age of Science, 1450–1800* (Cambridge, Mass., 1991), esp. ch. 1, 'Renaissance Readers and Ancient Texts', 23–46. The standard history of classical scholarship written from this perspective is still Rudolf Pfeiffer, *History of Classical Scholarship 1300–1850* (Oxford, 1976). Among works by classicists that explore the relationship between traditional philological practice and reception study, see William M. Calder III, 'Introduction', in Ward W. Briggs and William M. Calder III (eds.), *Classical Scholarship: A Bibliographical Dictionary* (New York, 1990), p. xv; Martindale, *Redeeming the Text*; and Craig Kallendorf, 'Philology, the Reader, and the *Nachleben* of Classical Texts', *Modern Philology*, 92 (1994), 137–56. The essays in Jan Ziolkowski (ed.), *On Philology* (University Park, Penn., 1990) also explore the relationship between traditional philology and various aspects of modern literary theory. The term 'paradigm shift', from Thomas Kuhn, *The Structure of Scientific Revolutions*, 2nd edn. (Chicago, 1970), has been overused almost to the point of becoming a cliché, but I believe the change in perspective I have described is significant enough to warrant its use here.

[5] Fredson Bowers, *Principles of Bibliographical Description* (Winchester, 1987; repr. of Princeton, 1949 edn.), 31.

[6] Ibid. 8.

a text appears as a crucial part of its meaning, not as a meaningless container to be examined and then discarded so that the real work of interpretation can get underway.[7] Thus the inclusion (and sometimes the exclusion) of particular commentaries in printed editions, book size and typeface as links to classes of readers, and the margins of early editions as places where various responses to the text can jostle against one another, have become key issues in the present project.

In the last couple of decades, the academic study of literature has taken a well-publicized turn from theory to history,[8] and this project has been informed as well by what is sometimes called 'cultural materialism' in the United Kingdom and 'new historicism' in the United States.[9] To be sure, it has become notoriously difficult to make a clean separation between 'old historicism' and the recent challenges to it, and that is as true for this book as for other projects of the day. On the one hand, some of my procedures and assumptions might well seem traditional enough. For one thing, while I confess to a healthy suspicion of period labels, I continue to find 'Renaissance' a useful term with which to begin research, at least in part because it says something about how some people of the period saw themselves. And I continue to be interested in the role of the classics in Renaissance culture, not because I hold to an essentialist view of the value of Greek and Roman literature but again because some people in the past chose to define themselves in relation to this literature. Finally, I still try to maintain some sort of distinction between writing the history of literature and writing other kinds of histories. I suspect, for example, that a good book could be written on how Virgilian values as understood in Renaissance Venice affected the writing of laws, the shaping of political policy, even the evolution of Christian

---

[7] One thinks primarily of Jerome J. McGann's work in this area: see, inter alia, A Critique of Modern Textual Criticism (Chicago, 1983), and The Beauty of Inflections: Literary Investigations in Historical Method and Theory (Oxford, 1988).

[8] The reference here is to J. Hillis Miller's 'Presidential Address 1986: The Triumph of Theory, the Resistance to Reading, and the Question of the Material Base', Publications of the Modern Language Association, 102 (1987), 281–91.

[9] By now the bibliography on this approach and the controversies it has generated is almost unmanageable, but a good orientation can be found in the essays (with notes) in the following collections: Kinney and Collins (eds.), Renaissance Historicism; H. Aram Veeser (ed.), The New Historicism (New York, 1989); and Jeffrey N. Cox and Larry J. Reynolds (eds.), New Historical Literary Study: Essays on Reproducing Texts, Representing History (Princeton, 1993).

doctrine, but such a book would require expertise I do not have in legal, institutional, and religious history. This book is restricted to the interaction between Virgil's texts and the basic cultural values of Renaissance Venice—a project I have found to be large enough in itself.

On the other hand, however, much of the earliest new historicist work developed in Renaissance studies, and this book could not have emerged in its present form without that work. For one thing, although I am reluctant to try to extend my own historical narrative into areas in which I have not been trained, it seems clear to me that the old reflective model relating literature to history is dangerously flawed. This model assumed that history recorded 'what actually happened' and literature in some way reflected historical reality. Literature, in other words, could hold a mirror up to the world around it, but it could not directly affect what happened in that world. Newer models for writing literary history help us see that literature, and the act of interpreting it, can affect how people live their lives outside the study and the school-room.[10] In this case, we have seen that the myth of Venice served as a dominant ideological paradigm for one group of people in the Renaissance, and that the myth shaped how Venetians approached the world around them at the same time as it was shaped by the ideas absorbed into it, including those derived from the reading of Virgil's poetry. That is, because literature affects the ideology of its readers, it ultimately affects their actions as well. This accords real power to poetry and literary criticism, for according to this model, literature and literary interpretation do not merely reflect what is happening in the world, but help to create the values and beliefs from which action results.[11]

To be sure, recent scholarship has taught us to be suspicious of totalizing claims and sweeping generalizations, and that suspicion has also affected what I have done. In writing this book, I have assumed that Venetian humanism might well have its own distinctive character that deserves to be encountered free of contamination from the Florentine model that still dominates present-day work in the history of classical scholarship in the Renaissance.

[10] Howard, 'New Historicism', 8.

[11] For an example of how readers of Virgil's *Eclogues* found themselves entangled in matters of ideology and power, see Annabel Patterson, *Pastoral and Ideology: Virgil to Valéry* (Berkeley and Los Angeles, Calif., 1987).

What is more, I have not assumed that every Venetian of this period saw Virgil's poetry in the same way—or more fundamentally, that everyone necessarily saw it at all. As I have tried to show, for example, those who were reading an Italian translation got a somewhat different picture from those who were reading in Latin. Furthermore, some Venetian readers resisted parts of the dominant Virgilian interpretive paradigm, annotating with loving care the obscenities of the *Priapea*, printing commentaries that contain challenges to orthodox faith, or imagining new roles for women in response to the Dido story. Such subversive readings, however, were ultimately contained within the prevalent interpretive grid, the Virgil who had been made to conform to the myth of Venice by the powerful patricians who dominated the city and its institutions. Dominance, subversion, containment—these are catchwords of the new historicism, connecting the modern period to its early modern roots.[12]

There are, of course, other points of connection, for the way I have divided my material reflects both my own interests as a member of my interpretive community and the interests of Virgil's early readers. In other words, I have concentrated on moral values in part because Virgil's Renaissance readers left frequent comments in this area, but in part because twentieth-century literary criticism in an academic setting often focuses on moral choice and its consequences as well. To be sure, an important change in the way this is done has developed over the centuries. Venetian Renaissance readers, for example, tended to work centripetally, using their study of Virgil as a way to reach a commonly accepted core of moral values that downplayed cultural difference. Modern work in this area, I believe, works centrifugally: the poem raises questions about moral choice and consequence, but few modern academics would try to abstract a transhistorical set of values from the poem, and a good number of scholars in this later interpretive

---

[12] This model of power relations owes a good deal to Stephen Greenblatt; see e.g. 'Invisible Bullets', in *Shakespearean Negotiations: The Circulation of Social Energy in Renaissance England* (Berkeley and Los Angeles, Calif., 1988), 21–65, and the essays in *Learning to Curse: Essays in Early Modern Culture* (New York, 1990), along with the critique by Mark Edmundson, *Literature against Philosophy, Plato to Derrida: A Defence of Poetry* (Cambridge, 1995), 185–98, which also discusses Greenblatt's debt to Foucault. I should probably note here that I do not wish to suggest that power always succeeds in containing subversion, only that the dominant ideological forces in Renaissance Venice used the myth of Venice successfully to contain subversive elements drawn from Virgil's poetry.

community have recently been stressing what they see as fundamental ambivalences in Virgil's moral world.[13]

A similar point can be made regarding the religious material
under consideration here. While the relationship between religion
and higher education has become increasingly tenuous through
the twentieth century,[14] students in North America at least often
see this issue differently from their instructors, and as a professor at
a publicly supported university in the American 'Bible belt', I am
constantly reminded of the need to continue thinking about this
part of our cultural life. Yet again, within an area of common
interest, we see difference where many Renaissance readers saw
similarity. To be sure, as we have seen, Renaissance readers in the
end knew that Virgil was not a Christian, but they consistently
went as far as they could in seeking points of contact, a procedure
that is impossible to legitimate in current academic discourse.

The relationship between the Venetian interpretive community
and that of today's university culture unfolds in a similar way in
regard to class and gender. This is, of course, a major area of concern
in contemporary academic life. Venetian society seems to have been
unusually static and hierarchical, and our own preoccupation with
issues of class and gender has certainly helped us see more clearly
some of the forces restricting social mobility in Renaissance Venice.
This preoccupation encouraged me to separate vernacular and Latin
material more sharply than I suspect I would have done if I were

---

[13] Modern scholarship of the so-called 'pessimistic' or 'Harvard school', developed
initially by Brooks, Parry, Clausen, and Putnam, is profoundly ambivalent, for it finds that
the *Aeneid* speaks in two voices, as Parry puts it, those of personal loss as well as public
achievement. That is, the poem's successes are accompanied by failure—of Aeneas, of the
Augustan order, and of human nature in general and its ability to attain its ideals. The
generally cited, seminal works are Robert A. Brooks, '*Discolor Aura*: Reflections on the
Golden Bough', *American Journal of Philology*, 74 (1953), 260–80; Adam Parry, 'The Two
Voices of Virgil's *Aeneid*', *Arion*, 2 (1963), 66–80, repr. in *The Language of Achilles and Other
Papers* (Oxford, 1989), 78–96; Wendell Clausen, 'An Interpretation of the *Aeneid*', *Harvard
Studies in Classical Philology*, 68 (1964), 139–47 (although written in 1949); and Michael C.
J. Putnam, *The Poetry of the Aeneid: Four Studies in Imaginative Unity and Design* (Ithaca, NY,
1988; repr. of Cambridge, Mass. 1965 edn.). This approach has been surveyed by F. Serpa,
Il punto su Virgilio (Bari, 1987), 76–88; a good overview of contemporary approaches to
Virgilian scholarship may be found in S. J. Harrison, 'Some Views of the *Aeneid* in the
Twentieth Century', in id. (ed.), *Oxford Readings in Vergil's Aeneid* (Oxford, 1990), 1–20.
Richard Thomas and I are currently exploring further ramifications of this approach in the
history of Virgilian reception.

[14] The role of religion in American university life has been thoughtfully surveyed in
George M. Marsden, *The Soul of the American University: From Protestant Establishment to*
Established Nonbelief (New York, 1994).

writing, say, forty years ago, and it has certainly helped me hear more clearly the voices of those who were responding to the socially marginalized figures in Virgil's poetry. Yet here, again, Renaissance readers sought unity where we glory in diversity. As we have seen, the myth of Venice promotes *unanimitas*, so that the officially sanctioned reading of Virgil ultimately confirmed the dominant ideology of Renaissance Venice. Today, in contrast, many academic readers prefer to listen to precisely those Virgilian voices that finally became inaudible in Renaissance Venice.[15]

In a way, this is perhaps just another way of saying that the history I have constructed both confirms and challenges the perspective from which I write. On the one hand, while many twentieth-century scholars may have given up their belief in transhistorical values and essential truths, it is reassuring (at least to me) that there are still several areas in which my interests and those of readers from five hundred years ago can converge. On the other hand, however, a project like this makes me acutely aware of the distance that separates me from those whose history I would write. The interpretive community of Renaissance Venice sought a centre, and it found that centre in an ideological construct that could accommodate itself to a poet from 1,500 years earlier as easily as, for example, to a religious reform movement like the Council of Trent. My interpretive community is a contentious one that not only lacks a centre but, on principle, would no longer try to create one. There are advantages to this, of course, as we are now beginning to hear the voices of those who have found it difficult to speak in the various totalizing systems of the past. But there are disadvantages as well, for it is much more difficult for literature and literary criticism to have real power in the world when there is so much disagreement about common aims and values.[16] But this, I suppose, is the fate of literary studies in our postmodern age.

---

[15] Although they begin from different theoretical stances, several influential critics have recently been treating the *Aeneid* as polyvocal: Gian Biagio Conte, *The Rhetoric of Imitation: Genre and Poetic Memory in Vergil and Other Latin Poets*, ed. Charles Segal (Ithaca, NY, 1986); R. O. A. M. Lyne, *Further Voices in Vergil's Aeneid* (Oxford, 1987); and Sarah Spence, *Rhetorics of Reason and Desire: Vergil, Augustine, and the Troubadours* (Ithaca, NY, 1988), 11–51.

[16] Stanley Fish, *Professional Correctness: Literary Studies and Political Change* (Oxford, 1995), develops a thought-provoking analysis of why the study of literature today is no longer able to affect political life as it did in the Renaissance. Fish is somewhat more pessimistic than I am, but his basic point seems reasonable to me.

APPENDIX 1

Chronology of Latin Editions

Date	Bibliography No.	Publisher

Editions published in Venice

Date	Bibliography No.	Publisher
1470	1	Vindelinus de Spira
1471	2	Adam de Ambergau
	3	Vindelinus de Spira
	4	Christophorus Valdarfer de Ratisbona
	5	Christophorus Valdarfer de Ratisbona
	6	Christophorus Valdarfer de Ratisbona
1472	7	Leonardus Achates de Basilea
	8	Bartholomaeus de Cremona
	9	'The Printer of Ausonius'
c.1472	10	Florentius de Argentina or Adam de Ambergau
1473	11	Leonardus Achates de Basilea
1475	12	Jacobus de Rubeis natione Gallicus
	13	Nicolaus Jenson Gallicus
1476	14	Nicolaus Jenson Gallicus
	15	Antonius Bartholomaei
1480	16	Petrus de Piasis Cremonensis, Bartholomaeus de Blaviis Alexandrinus, and Andreas de Torresanis de Asula
1482	17	Raynaldus de Novimagio Theutonicus
c.1482	18	Baptista de Tortis
1483	19	Baptista de Tortis
	20	Andreas Jacobi de Paltasichis Catharensis
1484	21	Thomas de Blaviis Alexandrinus
1486	22	Bernardinus de Celeris de Luere
1487	23	Baptista de Tortis
	24	Bernardinus de Benaliis Bergomensis
1488	25	Andreas Jacobi de Paltasichis Catharensis

Date	Bibliography No.	Publisher
c.1488	26	Liga Boaria
1489	27	Georgius Arrivabenus Mantuanus
1491	28	Lazarus de Soardis de Saviliano
	29	Baptista de Sessa
	30	Bartholomaeus de Zanis de Portesio
1491–2	31	Philippus Pintius de Caneto Mantuanus
1493	32	Bartholomaeus de Zanis de Portesio
1494	33	Damianus de Mediolano
	34	[printer unknown]
	35	Bartholomaeus de Zanis de Portesio
1495	36	Bartholomaeus de Zanis de Portesio
1497	37	Simon de Gabis dictus Bevilaqua Papiensis
1499	38	Philippus Pintius de Caneto Mantuanus
1500	39	Lucas Antonius Junta Florentinus
1501	40	Aldus Manutius Romanus
	41	[printer unknown]
1504	42	Bartholomaeus de Zanis de Portesio
	43	Philippus Pintius de Caneto Mantuanus
1505	44	Philippus Pintius de Caneto Mantuanus
	45	Aldus Manutius Romanus
1507	46	Bernardinus Stagninus de Tridino ex Monteferrato
1508	47	Bartholomaeus de Zanis de Portesio
1510	48	Bartholomaeus de Zanis de Portesio
1512	49	Georgius Arrivabenus Mantuanus
1514	50	Bartholomaeus de Zanis de Portesio
	51	Aldus Manutius Romanus and Andreas de Torresanis de Asula
	52	Aldus Manutius Romanus and Andreas de Torresanis de Asula
1515	53	Alexander de Paganinis Brixianus
1517	54	Aldus Manutius Romanus and Andreas de Torresanis de Asula
1519	55	Lucas Antonius Junta Florentinus and Augustinus de Zanis de Portesio

Date	Bibliography No.	Publisher
1520	56	Georgius de Rusconibus Mediolanensis
1522	57	Guglielmus de Fontaneto Montisferrati
	58	Lucas Antonius Junta Florentinus and Gregorius de Gregoriis
1525	59	Maphaeus Pasinus
	60	Melchior Sessa and Petrus de Ravanis
1527	61	Aldus Manutius Romanus and Andreas de Torresanis de Asula
1531	62	Aurelius Pintius
1532–3	63	Lucas Antonius Junta Florentinus
1534	64	Aurelius Pintius
	65	Heirs of Aldus Manutius Romanus and Andreas de Torresanis de Asula
	66	Petrus de Nicolinis de Sabio
1536	67	Aurelius Pintius
1536–7	68	Lucas Antonius Junta Florentinus
1538–9	69	Johannes Antonius de Nicolinis de Sabio
1539	70	Johannes Antonius de Nicolinis de Sabio and Federicus de Torresanis de Asula
1541	71	Sons of Aldus Manutius Romanus
	72	Aloisius de Tortis
1542	73	Heirs of Lucas Antonius Junta Florentinus
1543–4	74	Heirs of Lucas Antonius Junta Florentinus
1544	75	Hieronymus Scotus
1545	76	Sons of Aldus Manutius Romanus
1546	77	Cominus de Tridino Montisferrati
1547	78	Joannes Gryphius
1548	79	Vincentius Valgrisius
1549	80	Hieronymus Scotus
1551	81	Bartholomaeus Cesanus
1551–2	82	Bartholomaeus Cesanus
1552	83	Heirs of Lucas Antonius Junta Florentinus
1553	84	Hieronymus Scotus
	85	Paulus Manutius

Date	Bibliography No.	Publisher
1555	86	Paulus Manutius
	87	Hieronymus Scotus
1555–6	88	Franciscus Rampazetus and Melchior Sessa
1558	89	Paulus Manutius
	90	Joannes Maria Bonellus
1560	91	Paulus Manutius
1562	92	Joannes Maria Bonellus
1563	93	Paulus Manutius
1565	94	Paulus Manutius
	95	Franciscus Rampazetus and Melchior Sessa
1566	96	Joannes Maria Bonellus
	97	Franciscus Laurentinus
1567	98	Joannes Gryphius
1570	99	Paulus Manutius
1572	100	Heirs of Joannes Maria Bonellus
1573	101	Altobellus Salicatius
	102	Paulus Manutius
1574–5	103	Heirs of Joannes Maria Bonellus
1575–6	104	Joannes Baptista Sessa and Brothers
1576	105	Joannes Baptista Sessa and Brothers
	106	Aldus Manutius Minor
1578	107	Petrus Dusinellus
1580	108	Aldus Manutius Minor
	109	Petrus Dusinellus
1581	110	Joannes Baptista Sessa and Brothers, and Heirs of Franciscus Rampazetus
1582	111	Dominicus and Joannes Baptista Guerraeus
1582–3	112	Heirs of Franciscus Rampazetus and Melchior Sessa
1583–4	113	Joannes Gryphius Minor
1585	114	Joannes Gryphius Minor
	115	Aldus Manutius Minor, and Dominicus and Joannes Baptista Guerraeus
1585–6	116	Petrus Dusinellus

Date	Bibliography No.	Publisher
1586	117	Dominicus Nicolinus
	118	Heirs of Melchior Sessa
1587	119	Damianus Zenarus
	120	Aldus Manutius Minor
1588	121	Heirs of Melchior Sessa
	122	Joannes Gryphius Minor
1597	123	Joannes Baptista and Joannes Bernardus Sessa
	124	Joannes Baptista and Joannes Bernardus Sessa

Editions published in Treviso, Verona, and Vicenza

Date	Bibliography No.	Publisher
1475	124 bis[1]	Gerardus de Lisa de Flandria (Treviso)
1476	125	Johannes de Vienna (Vicenza)
1479	126	Leonardus Achates de Basilea (Vicenza)
c.1481	127	Paulus de Ferraria, Dionysius Bertochus Bononiensis, and Peregrinus de Pasqualibus Bononiensis (Treviso)
1482	128	Petrus Maufer Normannus Rothomagensis and Bartolomeus Confalonierus (Treviso)
1580	129	Sebastianus and Johannes a Donnis (Verona)
1587	130	Sebastianus a Donnis (Verona)
1598	131	Angelus Tamus (Verona)

[1] I am grateful to Martin Davies for bringing this edition to my attention.

APPENDIX 2

Chronology of Italian Editions

Editions published in Venice or the surrounding area, representing slightly over a 60 per cent market share, are signalled with an asterisk. Further information about these editions is available in my *A Bibliography of Renaissance Italian Translations of Virgil*, Biblioteca di bibliografia italiana, 136 (Florence: Leo S. Olschki, 1994).

Date	Bibliography No.	Publisher	Contents
1476	1*	Hermanno Levilapide da Colonia	*Aen.*
1481	2	Antonio Miscomini	*Buc.*
c.1490	3	Antonio Miscomini	*Georg.*
1491	4	Ugo Ruggieri	*Aen.*
1494	5	Antonio Miscomini	*Buc.*
	6*	Cristoforo Pensi and Giovanni Antonio Da Legnano	*Buc.*
1525	7*	Gregorio De Gregori	*Buc.* 5
1528	8*	Niccolò Zoppino	*Aen.*
c.1530	9	Niccolò Zoppino (?)	*Aen.* 7 & 8
1532	10*	Bernardino De Vitali	*Aen.*
1534	11*	Giovanni Antonio Nicolini Da Sabbio	*Aen.* 4
1538	12	Antonio Blado	*Aen.* 2
	13*	Bernardino De Vitali	*Aen.*
1538–9	14*	Bernardino De Vitali	*Aen.*
1539	15	Antonio Mazzocchi and Nicola Gucci	*Aen.* 2
1539–40	16*	Niccolò Zoppino, Giovanni Antonio and Domenico Volpini, and Comin da Trino	*Aen.* 1–6

Date	Bibliography No.	Publisher	Contents
1540	17★	Comin da Trino and Niccolò Zoppino	*Aen.* 1–6
	18★	Comin da Trino, Niccolò Zoppino, and Andrea Arrivabene	*Aen.* 1–6
1540–1	19★	Andrea Arrivabene	*Aen.* 1–6
1542	20★	Giovanni Antonio and Pietro Nicolini Da Sabbio, and Giovanni Francesco Torresano	*Aen.* 8
1543	21★	Melchiorre Sessa (sen.)	*Georg.*
after 1543	22	[printer unknown]	*Moreto*
1544	23	Girolamo Bianchini Del Leone	*Buc.*
	24	Antonio Blado	*Aen.* 7
	25★	Giovanni Padovano, Niccolò Zoppino, and Federico Torresano	*Aen.* 1–6
1545	26★	Giovanni Farri and Brothers	*Aen.* 11
	27★	Giovanni Farri and Brothers	*Georg.*
1546	28★	Comin da Trino	*Aen.* 7
1548	29★	Gabriele Giolito De' Ferrari	*Moreto*
	30	Bernardo Giunta (sen.)	*Aen.* 4
1549	31★	Giovanni Grifi (sen.)	*Georg.*
1551	32★	Paulo Gherardo	*Aen.* 1
c.1551	33★	Alberto di Gratia detto il Toscano	*Aen.* 1
1552	34★	Nicolò Bascarini	*Georg.*
	35	Achille Barbiroli	*Aen.* 1
	36	Valerio Dorico	*Aen.* 1
	37★	Gabriele Giolito De' Ferrari	*Buc.*
1555	38	Mattia Cancer	*Aen.* 7
	39	Mattia Cancer	*Aen.* 8
1556	40	Filippo Giunta (jun.)	*Opere*
1558	41	Alessandro Benacci	*Aen.* 1–4

Date	Bibliography No.	Publisher	Contents
	42	[printer unknown]	*Aen.* 6
1559	43★	Onofrio Farri and Brothers	*Opere*
1559–62	44★	Domenico Farri	*Opere*
1560	45★	Francesco Rampazzetto (sen.)	*Aen.* 2
	46	Lorenzo Torrentino (sen.)	*Aen.*
1560–67	47	Andrea Bresciano	*Aen.* 1–6
1560–70	48	Andrea Bresciano	*Aen.* 1–6
1562	49	Antonio Bellone	*Aen.* 4
	50★	Domenico Farri	*Opere*
1564	51★	Grazioso Percaccino	*Aen.* 1
1565	52★	Domenico Farri	*Aen.* 1
1566	53	Giulio Accolti	*Aen.* 2
	54	Giulio Accolti	*Aen.* 2
	55	Giulio Accolti	*Aen.* 6
	56★	Giorgio Cavalli	*Aen.* 1
	57	Astolfo De Grandis	*Buc.*
1567	58★	Domenico Farri	*Opere*
1567–8	59★	Giovanni Varisco	*Aen.*
1568	60	Heirs of Antonio Blado	*Aen.* 4
	61★	Giorgio Cavalli	*Opere*
	62★	Domenico Farri	*Opere*
1569	63	Agostino Colaldi	*Aen.* 4
	64★	Christoforo Cieco da Forlì and Domenico De Franceschi	*Aen.* 1
1570	65★	Christoforo Cieco da Forlì and Domenico De Franceschi	*Aen.* 1
	66★	Gabriele Giolito De' Ferrari	*Aen.*
1571	67★	Christoforo Cieco da Forlì and Domenico De Franceschi	*Aen.* 1
1571–72	68★	Gabriele Giolito De' Ferrari	*Aen.*
1572	69★	Christoforo Cieco da Forlì and Domenico De Franceschi	*Aen.* 1
	70★	Gabriele Giolito De' Ferrari	*Aen.*
1573	71★	Domenico Farri	*Opere*

Date	Bibliography No.	Publisher	Contents
	72	[printer unknown]	*Aen.* 1
	73★	Christoforo Cieco da Forlì	*Aen.* 2
1574	74	[printer unknown]	*Aen.* 2
1575–6	75★	Giovanni Battista Sessa (jun.)	*Aen.*
1576	76★	Giovanni Battista Sessa (jun.)	*Aen.*
	77	Paolo Gottardo Da Ponte	*Aen.* 6
1578	78	Christoforo Cieco da Forlì	*Aen.* 2
1579	79★	Christoforo Cieco da Forlì	*Aen.* 2
1581	80★	Bernardo Giunta (jun.) and Brothers	*Aen.*
	81★	Giovanni Battista Sessa (jun.)	*Aen.*
1582	82★	Domenico De Franceschi	*Aen.* 2
1585	83	Fausto Bonardi	*Aen.* 2
1586	84★	Giacomo Cornetti	*Opere*
	85	Francesco Osanna	*Opere*
	86	Francesco Osanna	*Aen.* 4
1588	87★	Heirs of Melchiorre Sessa (sen.)	*Opere*
1592	88★	Bernardo Giunta (jun.)	*Aen.*
1593	89★	Paulo Ugolini	*Opere*
1597	90★	Giovanni Battista Ciotti	*Aen.*
	91★	Giovanni Battista (jun.) and Giovanni Bernardo Sessa	*Opere*

Edition printed outside Italy

1568	92	Christophoro Plantino	*Aen.* 4

APPENDIX 3

The Indices to Moralized Virgilian Passages in Biblioteca Nazionale Marciana, Aldine 628

Aldine 628, a Marciana copy of the Aldine Virgil dated 1514 without the errata sheets in the back, has four additional folios bound in at the end of the book. These folios, containing two indices and keyed to the pages of the printed text, are transcribed below. Capitalization and punctuation have been regularized, abbreviations have been expanded, and line references have been added and placed within square brackets.

[fo. 1ʳ]
Loca lectorem pium commoventia
In prima Aegloga, ubi Melibeus loquitur, ubi de miseria exilii.
In secunda, ubi loquitur Corydon, ubi de miseria amoris.
In quinta, ubi Mopsus ibi *extinctum* [*Ecl.* 5. 20], ubi de morte Caesaris.
Libro primo Georgicorum, folio 24, ibi *ille etiam extincto* [*Georg.* 1. 466], ubi de obitu ... de Caesaris dictatoris.
Libro 2, folio 34, ibi *illum non populi* [*Georg.* 2. 495], ubi de urbis miseriis.
Libro 4, folio 52, ibi *ipse cava* [*Georg.* 4. 464], ibi ubi de Orpheo Eurydicen uxorem mortuam plorante.
Libro 1, folio 55 tergo, ibi *extemplo Aeneae* [*Aen.* 1. 92], ubi de Aenea naufragium timente et lamentante.
Libro 1, folio 57, ibi *o socii* [*Aen.* 1. 198], ubi Aeneas consolatur suos maestos.
Libro 1, folio 57 tergo, ibi *alloquitur Venus* [*Aen.* 1. 229], ubi queritur de Troianorum miseriis et nati ...
Libro 1, folio 59 tergo, ibi *hunc coniux Sicheus erat* [*Aen.* 1. 343], ubi de marito Didonis occiso a Pygmalione fratre Didonis propter avariciam clam ...

[fo. 1ᵛ]
Libro 2 Aeneidos, folio 70, ubi de Laocoo ...
Libro 2, folio 71, ibi *in somnis* [*Aen.* 2. 270], scilicet ubi de Hectore apparente in somnis Aeneae.
Libro 2, folio 72, ibi *venit summa* [*Aen.* 2. 324], ubi de Panthu Troiano dolente.

Libro 2, ibi *ecce trahebatur* [*Aen.* 2. 403], ubi de Cassandra capta a praeside.

Libro 2, carta 74 tergo, ibi *at domus interior* [*Aen.* 2. 486] et carta 75 et ibi *forsitan et Priami* [*Aen.* 2. 506].

Et carta 76, ibi *cui Pirrhus* [*Aen.* 2. 547] per totam paginam [ends *Aen.* 2. 576].

Iterum per totam cartam 77 [*Aen.* 2. 607–36].

Carta 78, in primo [*Aen.* 2. 667] usque *talia vociferans* [ends *Aen.* 2. 679].

Carta 78, ibi *dixerat ille* [*Aen.* 2. 705] per totam [*Aen.* 2. 726].

Carta 79, in primo et per totam [*Aen.* 2. 735–56].

Carta 80, in primo [*Aen.* 2. 790].

Libro 3°, carta 81, ibi *quid miserum* [*Aen.* 3. 41] usque *auri sacra fames* [*Aen.* 3. 57].

Libro 3, carta 82, ibi *iura domosque dabam* [*Aen.* 3. 137].

Libro 3, 83, ibi *postquam altum* [*Aen.* 3. 192].

[fo. 2^r]

Libro 3, 85 tergo, *O foelix una* [*Aen.* 3. 321].

Carta 88 tergo, ibi *accipe et haec* [*Aen.* 3. 486] et ibi *vivite faelices* [*Aen.* 3. 493].

Carta 90 fronte, ibi *cum subito e sylvis* [*Aen.* 3. 590].

92, ibi *hinc Drepani me portus* [*Aen.* 3. 707].

Libro 4, 97 tergo, ibi *dissimulare etiam* [*Aen.* 4. 305] usque *dixerat* [*Aen.* 4. 331].

98 tergo, ibi *nec tibi diva parens* [*Aen.* 4. 365] usque *at pius Aeneas* [*Aen.* 4. 393].

99 fronte, ibi *quis tibi tunc Dido* [*Aen.* 4. 408] usque *talibus orabat* [*Aen.* 4. 437].

101, *at non infoelix animi* [*Aen.* 4. 529] usque *tantos illa suo* [*Aen.* 4. 553].

102, *regina e speculis* [*Aen.* 4. 586] usque *haec ait et partes* [*Aen.* 4. 630].

103 fronte, ibi *at trepida* [*Aen.* 4. 642] usque *dixerat* [*Aen.* 4. 663].

[fo. 2^v]

103 tergo, *dixerat* [*Aen.* 4. 663] usque *tum Juno* [*Aen.* 4. 693].

Libro 5, nihil in hac materia.

Libro 6, 125 fronte, ibi *tres Notus hybernas* [*Aen.* 6. 355] usque *talia factus erat* [*Aen.* 6. 372], ibi de Palinuro se humari petente.

126 tergo, ibi *infelix Dido* [*Aen.* 6. 456] usque *talibus* [*Aen.* 6. 467].

127 fronte, ibi *atque hic Priameden* [*Aen.* 6. 494] [usque] *atque hic Priamedes* [*Aen.* 6. 509].

127 tergo, ibi *tum me confectum curis* [*Aen.* 6. 520] usque *qui te vivum* [*Aen.* 6. 531].

129 fronte, ibi *quid memorem Lapithas* [*Aen.* 6. 601] usque *non mihi si centum* [*Aen.* 6. 625].

[fo. 3^r]

130 tergo, ibi *venisti tandem* [*Aen.* 6. 687] usque *interea* [*Aen.* 6. 703].

Libro 7, nihil in hac materia.

Libro octavo, 154 tergo, ibi *inde ubi prima quies* [*Aen.* 8. 407] usque *insula* [*Aen.* 8. 416], de vidua casta.

156 fronte, ibi *quid memorem* [*Aen.* 8. 483] usque *his ego te* [*Aen.* 8. 496], de crudelitate tiranni.

157 tergo, ibi *at vos o superi* [*Aen.* 8. 572] usque *haec genitor* [*Aen.* 8. 583].

Libro IX, carta 165, ibi *unum oro* [*Aen.* 9. 284].

Carta 168, ibi *hunc ego te Euryale aspicio* [*Aen.* 9. 481].

[fo. 3^v]

Libro X, carta 188, ibi *tantane me tenuit* [*Aen.* 10. 846], usque *simul haec dicens* [*Aen.* 10. 856].

Libro XI, carta 190, ibi *tene inquit miserande puer* [*Aen.* 11. 42] usque *haec ubi deflevit* [*Aen.* 11. 59].

Carta 191 tergo, ibi *non haec o Palla* [*Aen.* 11. 152] usque *Aurora interea* [*Aen.* 11. 182].

Libro 12, 219 quid *nunc te tua Turne potest* [*Aen.* 12. 872] usque *tantum effata* [*Aen.* 12. 885].

[fo. 4^r]

Filius succurrit patri, scilicet Lausus libro X et Eneas Anchise libro 2.

Pater filio, scilicet Mezentius libro X, Priamus libro 2, et Laocoon libro 2.

Frater fratri, scilicet Pandarus libro 9 et Bitias ibidem et Timbrus libro X.

Maritus uxori, Eneas Creusae, Orpheus Eurydice libro 4 Georgicorum.

Soror sorori, Anna Didoni 4.

Amicus amico, Nisus Euryalo IX, Titirus Melibeo Aegloga 1.

Soror fratri, scilicet Iuturna Turno 12.

Mater filio, Venus Aeneae libro I.

SELECT BIBLIOGRAPHY

The bibliography that follows contains only a selection among the works consulted in preparing this book. It contains mostly works of modern scholarship and concentrates on two types of material: studies of basic methodological importance, and books and articles of sufficient breadth to provide guidance to the reader who wants to pursue further some of the issues raised here. The Renaissance editions of Virgil used in this study are listed in Appendices 1 and 2, and references to more specialized studies may be found in the notes.

ARMSTRONG, LILIAN, *Renaissance Miniature Painters and Classical Imagery: The Master of the Putti and his Venetian Workshop* (London: H. Miller, 1981).

ASCARELLI, FERNANDA, and MENATO, MARCO, *La tipografia del '500 in Italia*, Biblioteca di bibliografia italiana, 116 (Florence: Leo S. Olschki, 1989).

BALDASSARRI, GUIDO (ed.), *Quasi un picciolo mondo: Tentativi di codificazione del genere epico nel Cinquecento*, Università degli Studi di Padova, Quaderni dell'Istituto di Filologia e Letteratura Italiana, 1 (Milan: Edizioni Unicopli, 1982).

BARBARO, ERMOLAO (il Vecchio), *Orationes contra poetas, epistolae*, ed. Giorgio Ronconi, Facoltà di Magistero dell'Università di Padova, 14 (Florence: Sansoni, 1972).

BARKER, NICOLAS *et al.*, *A Catalogue of the Ahmanson-Murphy Aldine Collection at UCLA*, 5 fascicles (Los Angeles, Calif.: Department of Special Collections, University Research Library, University of California at Los Angeles, 1989).

BARNEY, STEPHEN A. (ed.), *Annotation and Its Texts* (New York: Oxford University Press, 1991).

BARON, HANS (ed.), *Leonardo Bruni Aretino: Humanistisch-philosophische Schriften* (Wiesbaden: M. Sändig, 1969; repr. of Leipzig, 1928 edn.).

BEC, CHRISTIAN, *Les Livres des Florentins (1413–1600)*, Biblioteca di 'Lettere Italiane', Studi e testi, 29 (Florence: Leo S. Olschki, 1984).

BEKKER-NIELSEN, HANS, BORCH, MARIANNE, and SORENSON, BENGT ALGOT (eds.), *From Script to Book: A Symposium*, Proceedings of the Seventh International Symposium organized by the Centre for the Study of Vernacular Literature in the Middle Ages, held at Odense

University on 15–16 Nov. 1982 (Odense: Odense University Press, 1986).

BENCI, ANTONIO, 'Volgarizzamenti antichi dell'*Eneide* di Virgilio', *Antologia*, 2 (1821), 161–200.

BENKO, S., 'Virgil's Fourth *Eclogue* in Christian Interpretation', *Aufstieg und Niedergang der römischen Welt*, 2. 31. 1 (1980), 646–69.

BLACK, ROBERT, 'Italian Renaissance Education: Changing Perspectives and Continuing Controversies', *Journal of the History of Ideas*, 52 (1991), 315–34.

BONO, BARBARA, *Literary Transvaluation: From Vergilian Epic to Shakespearean Tragicomedy* (Berkeley and Los Angeles, Calif.: University of California Press, 1984).

BORNSTEIN, DANIEL, 'Giovanni Dominici, the Bianchi, and Venice: Symbolic Action and Interpretive Grids', *Journal of Medieval and Renaissance Studies*, 23 (1993), 143–71.

BORSETTO, LUCIANA, *L''Eneida' tradotta: Riscritture poetiche del testo di Virgilio nel XVI secolo* (Milan: Unicopli, 1989).

BOUWSMA, WILLIAM, *Venice and the Defense of Republican Liberty: Renaissance Values in the Age of the Counter Reformation* (Berkeley and Los Angeles, Calif.: University of California Press, 1968).

BROWN, HORATIO F., *The Venetian Printing Press, 1469–1800: An Historical Study based upon Documents for the Most Part Hitherto Unpublished* (Amsterdam: Gérard Th. van Heusden, 1969; repr. of London, 1891 edn.).

—— *Studies in the History of Venice*, 2 vols. (London: J. Murray, 1907).

BROWN, PATRICIA FORTINI, *Venice and Antiquity: The Venetian Sense of the Past* (New Haven: Yale University Press, 1996).

BUCK, AUGUST, *Italienische Dichtungslehre vom Mittelalter bis zum Ausgang der Renaissance,* Beihefte zur Zeitschrift für romanische Philologie, Heft 94 (Tübingen: Max Niemeyer, 1952).

—— and HERDING, OTTO (eds.), *Der Kommentar in der Renaissance,* Deutsche Forschungsgemeinschaft, Kommission für Humanismusforschung, 1 (Boppard: Boldt, 1975).

BURCKHARDT, JACOB, *The Civilization of the Renaissance in Italy,* 2 vols. (New York: Harper and Row, 1958; repr. of New York, 1929 edn.).

BURKE, PETER, *The Fortunes of the Courtier: The European Reception of Castiglione's Cortegiano,* Penn State Series in the History of the Book, 1 (University Park, Penn.: The Pennsylvania State University Press, 1995).

CANOVA, GIORDANA MARIANI, *La miniatura veneta del Rinascimento* (Venice: Alfieri, 1969).

CASTELLANI, CARLO, *La stampa in Venezia: Dalla sua origine alla morte di Aldo Manuzio Seniore* (Trieste: Edizioni LINT, 1973; repr. of Venice, 1899 edn.).

CHAMBERS, D. S., *The Imperial Age of Venice 1380–1580* (New York: Harcourt Brace Jovanovich, 1970).

CHARTIER, ROGER, *The Cultural Uses of Print in Early Modern France*, trans. Lydia G. Cochrane (Princeton: Princeton University Press, 1987).

—— 'Texts, Printings, Readings', in Lynn Hunt (ed.), *The New Cultural History* (Berkeley and Los Angeles, Calif.: University of California Press, 1989), 154–75.

—— *The Order of Books: Readers, Authors, and Libraries in Europe between the Fourteenth and Eighteenth Centuries*, trans. Lydia G. Cochrane (Stanford, Calif.: Stanford University Press, 1994).

—— *Forms and Meanings: Texts, Performances, and Audiences from Codex to Computer*, New Cultural Studies (Philadelphia, Penn.: University of Pennsylvania Press, 1995).

CHRISMAN, MIRIAM USHER, *Lay Culture, Learned Culture: Books and Social Change in Strasbourg, 1480–1599* (New Haven, Conn.: Yale University Press, 1982).

CICCHITELLI, VINCENZO, *Sulle opere poetiche di Marco Girolamo Vida* (Naples: L. Pierro and Sons, 1904).

COCHRANE, ERICH, *Italy, 1530–1630*, ed. Julius Kirschner, Longman History of Italy (London: Longman, 1988).

COMPARETTI, DOMENICO, *Virgilio nel Medioevo*, ed. Giorgio Pasquali, 2 vols. (Florence: La Nuova Italia, 1981; repr. of Florence, 1943 edn.).

CONNELL, SUSAN, 'Books and their Owners in Venice, 1345–1480', *Journal of the Warburg and Courtauld Institutes*, 35 (1972), 163–86.

COPELAND, RITA, *Rhetoric, Hermeneutics, and Translation: Academic Traditions and Vernacular Texts*, Cambridge Studies in Medieval Literature (Cambridge: Cambridge University Press, 1991).

COX, JEFFREY N., and REYNOLDS, LARRY J. (eds.), *New Historical Literary Study: Essays on Reproducing Texts, Representing History* (Princeton: Princeton University Press, 1993).

DA PRATI, PINO, *Giovanni Dominici e l'Umanesimo* (Naples: Istituto Editoriale del Mezzogiorno, 1965).

DARNTON, ROBERT, 'What is the History of Books?' *Daedalus*, 111/3 (1982), 65–83, repr. in Davidson (ed.), *Reading in America*, 27–52.

—— *The Kiss of Lamourette: Reflections in Cultural History* (New York: Norton, 1990).

DAVIDSON, CATHY N. (ed.), *Reading in America: Literary and Social History* (Baltimore: Johns Hopkins University Press, 1989).

DEL COL, ANDREA, 'Il controllo della stampa a Venezia e i processi di Antonio Brucioli (1548–1559)', *Critica storica*, 17 (1980), 457–510.

DELLA CORTE, FRANCESCO (ed.), *Enciclopedia virgiliana*, 6 vols. (Rome: Istituto della Enciclopedia Italiana, 1984–91).

DE MARINIS, TAMMARO, *La legatura artistica in Italia nei secoli XV e XVI*, 3 vols. (Florence: Fratelli Alinari, 1960).

DI CESARE, MARIO, *Vida's Christiad and Vergilian Epic* (New York: Columbia University Press, 1964).

DI FILIPPO BAREGGI, CLAUDIA, *Il mestiere di scrivere: Lavoro intellettuale e mercato librario a Venezia nel Cinquecento*, 'Europa delle Corti', Centro Studi sulle Società di Antico Regime, Biblioteca del Cinquecento, 43 (Rome: Bulzoni, 1988).

DIONISOTTI, CARLO, *Gli umanisti e il volgare fra Quattro e Cinquecento* (Florence: Felice Le Monnier, 1968).

DOLCE, LODOVICO, *Didone: Tragedia di M. Lodovico Dolce* (Venice: Aldus Manutius, 1547).

DONATUS, TIBERIUS CLAUDIUS, *Interpretationes Vergilianae*, ed. Henricus Georgii (Leipzig: Teubner, 1905–6).

DRAKE, GERTRUDE C., and FORBES, CLARENCE A., *Marco Girolamo Vida's The Christiad* (Carbondale, Ill.: Southern Illinois University Press, 1978).

EISENSTEIN, ELIZABETH, *The Printing Press as an Agent of Change: Communications and Cultural Transformations in Early Modern Europe*, 2 vols. (Cambridge: Cambridge University Press, 1979).

ESCARPIT, ROBERT, *Sociology of Literature*, trans. Ernest Pick, Lake Erie College Studies, 4 (Painesville, Oh.: Lake Erie College, 1965).

ESSLING, V. M. PRINCE D', *Études sur l'art de la gravure sur bois à Venise: Les Livres à figures vénitiens de la fin du XVe siècle et du commencement du XVIe...* , 3 pts. in 4 vols. (Florence: Leo S. Olschki, 1907–14).

FAGIOLO, MARCELLO (ed.), *Virgilio nell'arte e nella cultura europea*, Catalogue of an exhibition held at the Biblioteca Nazionale Centrale, Rome, 24 Sept. to 24 Nov. 1981 (Rome: De Luca Editore, 1981).

FAHY, CONOR, 'The *Index Librorum Prohibitorum* and the Venetian Printing Industry in the Sixteenth Century', *Italian Studies*, 35 (1980), 52–61.

FASOLI, GINA, 'Nascita di un mito', in *Studi storici in onore di Gioacchino Volpe*, 2 vols. (Florence: Sansoni, 1958), ii. 445–79.

FEATHER, JOHN P., and MCKITTERICK, DAVID, *The History of Books and Libraries: Two Views* (Washington: Library of Congress, 1986).

FEBVRE, LUCIEN, and MARTIN, HENRI-JEAN, *The Coming of the Book: The Impact of Printing 1450–1800*, trans. David Gerard (London: Verso, 1990).

FELDMAN, MARTHA, *City Culture and the Madrigal at Venice* (Berkeley and Los Angeles, Calif.: University of California Press, 1995).

FIELD, ARTHUR, *The Origins of the Platonic Academy of Florence* (Princeton: Princeton University Press, 1988).

FISH, STANLEY, *Surprised by Sin: The Reader in Paradise Lost* (London: St Martin's Press, 1967).

—— *Is there a Text in this Class? The Authority of Interpretive Communities* (Cambridge, Mass.: Harvard University Press, 1980).

—— *Professional Correctness: Literary Studies and Political Change* (Oxford: Clarendon Press, 1995).

FLETCHER, H. GEORGE, III, *New Aldine Studies: Documentary Essays on the Life and Work of Aldus Manutius* (San Francisco, Calif.: Bernard M. Rosenthal, 1988).

FÜGEN, HANS NORBERT, *Die Hauptrichtungen der Literatursoziologie und ihre Methoden,* 6th edn., Abhandlungen zur Kunst-, Musik- und Literaturwissenschaft, 21 (Bonn: Bouvier Verlag Herbert Grundmann, 1974).

GAETA, FRANCO, 'Alcuni considerazioni sul mito di Venezia', *Bibliothèque d'humanisme et Renaissance,* 23 (1961), 58–75.

GARIN, EUGENIO, *Il pensiero pedagogico dello Umanesimo,* I classici della pedagogia italiana (Florence: Giuntine-Sansoni, 1958).

—— *Italian Humanism: Philosophy and Civic Life in the Renaissance,* trans. Peter Munz (New York: Harper and Row, 1965).

GARRISON, JAMES, *Pietas from Vergil to Dryden* (University Park, Penn.: Pennsylvania State University Press, 1992).

GEHL, PAUL F., *A Moral Art: Grammar, Society, and Culture in Trecento Florence* (Ithaca, NY: Cornell University Press, 1993).

GENETTE, GÉRARD, 'Introduction to the Paratext', *New Literary History,* 22 (1991), 261–72.

GERULAITIS, LEONARDO, *Printing and Publishing in Fifteenth-Century Venice* (Chicago: American Library Association, 1976).

GOLDSCHMIDT, E. P., *The Printed Book of the Renaissance: Three Lectures on Type, Illustration, Ornament* (Cambridge: Cambridge University Press, 1950).

GRAFTON, ANTHONY, *Defenders of the Text: The Traditions of Scholarship in an Age of Science, 1450–1800* (Cambridge, Mass.: Harvard University Press, 1991).

—— 'Is the History of Reading a Marginal Enterprise? Guillaume Budé and his Books', *Papers of the Bibliographical Society of America,* 91 (1997), 139–57.

—— *Commerce with the Classics: Ancient Books and Renaissance Readers,* Thomas Spencer Jerome Lectures, 20 (Ann Arbor: The University of Michigan Press, 1997).

—— and JARDINE, LISA, *From Humanism to the Humanities: Education and the Liberal Arts in Fifteenth- and Sixteenth-Century Europe* (Cambridge, Mass.: Harvard University Press, 1986).

GREENBLATT, STEPHEN, 'Invisible Bullets', in *Shakespearean Negotiations: The Circulation of Social Energy in Renaissance England* (Berkeley and Los Angeles, Calif.: University of California Press, 1988).

—— *Learning to Curse: Essays in Early Modern Culture* (New York: Routledge, 1990).

GREETHAM, D. C., 'Textual and Literary Theory: Redrawing the Matrix', *Studies in Bibliography*, 42 (1989), 1–24.

GRENDLER, PAUL, *The Roman Inquisition and the Venetian Press, 1540–1605* (Princeton: Princeton University Press, 1977).

—— *Schooling in Renaissance Italy: Literacy and Learning, 1300–1600* (Baltimore: The Johns Hopkins University Press, 1989).

GRUBB, JAMES, 'When Myths lose Their Power: Four Decades of Venetian Historiography', *Journal of Modern History*, 58 (1986), 43–94.

GUTHMÜLLER, BODO, *Ovidio Metamorphoseos Vulgare: Formen und Funktionen der volksprachlichen Wiedergabe klassischer Dichtung in der italienischen Renaissance*, Veröffentlichungen zur Humanismusforschung, 3 (Boppard: Boldt, 1981).

HALE, J. R. (ed.), *Renaissance Venice* (Totowa, NJ: Rowman and Littlefield, 1973).

HARDISON, O. B., Jr., *The Enduring Monument: A Study of the Idea of Praise in Renaissance Literary Theory and Practice* (Westport, Conn.: Greenwood Press, 1973; repr. of Chapel Hill, NC, 1962 edn.).

HARRISON, S. J., 'Some Views of the *Aeneid* in the Twentieth Century', in id. (ed.), *Oxford Readings in Vergil's Aeneid* (Oxford: Clarendon Press, 1990), 1–20.

HAUSMANN, FRANK-RUTHER, 'Carmina Priapea', in F. Edward Cranz and Paul O. Kristeller (eds.), *Catalogus translationum et commentariorum: Medieval and Renaissance Latin Translations and Commentaries, Annotated Lists and Guides*, 7 vols. to date (Washington: Catholic University Press, 1980–), iv. 423–50.

HELLINGA, LOTTE, and HÄRTEL, HELMAN (eds.), *Buch und Text im 15. Jahrhundert / Book and Text in the Fifteenth Century*, Proceedings of a Conference held in the Herzog August Bibliothek, Wolfenbüttel, 1–3 Mar. 1978, Wolfenbütteler Abhandlungen zur Renaissanceforschungen, 2 (Hamburg: Dr. Ernst Hauswedell and Company, 1981).

HENKEL, ARTHUR, and SCHÖNE, ALBRECHT (eds.), *Emblemata, Handbuch zur Sinnbildkunst des XVI. und XVII. Jahrhunderts* (Stuttgart: J. B. Metzlersche Verlagsbuchhandlung, 1967).

HENNINGSEN, GUSTAV, TEDESCHI, JOHN, and AMIEL, CHARLES (eds.), *The Inquisition in Early Modern Europe: Studies on Sources and Methods* (De Kalb, Ill.: Northern Illinois University Press, 1986).

HINDMAN, SANDRA (ed.), *Printing the Written Word: The Social History of Books, circa 1450–1520* (Ithaca, NY: Cornell University Press, 1991).

HIRSCH, RUDOLF, *Printing, Selling and Reading, 1450–1550* (Wiesbaden: Otto Harrassowitz, 1967).

HOBSON, ANTHONY, *Humanists and Bookbinders: The Origins and Diffusion of Humanist Bookbinding 1459–1559* (Cambridge: Cambridge University Press, 1989).

HOLUB, ROBERT C., *Reception Theory: A Critical Introduction* (London: Methuen, 1984).

ISER, WOLFGANG, *The Act of Reading: A Theory of Aesthetic Response* (Baltimore: Johns Hopkins University Press, 1978).

JAUSS, HANS ROBERT, *Toward an Aesthetic of Reception,* trans. Timothy Bahti, Theory and History of Literature, 2 (Minneapolis: University of Minnesota Press, 1982).

JAVITCH, DANIEL, *Proclaiming a Classic: The Canonization of Orlando Furioso* (Princeton: Princeton University Press, 1991).

JED, STEPHANIE, H., *Chaste Thinking: The Rape of Lucretia and the Birth of Humanism*, Theories of Representation and Difference (Bloomington, Ind.: Indiana University Press, 1989).

JENSEN, KRISTIAN, *Rhetorical Philosophy and Philosophical Grammar: Julius Caesar Scaliger's Theory of Language,* Humanistische Bibliothek, Texte und Abhandlungen, Reihe 1, Abhandlungen, 46 (Munich: Wilhelm Fink, 1990).

JORDAN, CONSTANCE, *Renaissance Feminism: Literary Texts and Political Models* (Ithaca, NY: Cornell University Press, 1990).

KALLENDORF, CRAIG, 'Virgil, Dante, and Empire in Italian Thought, 1300–1500', *Vergilius,* 34 (1988), 52–61.

—— *In Praise of Aeneas: Virgil and Epideictic Rhetoric in the Early Italian Renaissance* (Hanover, NH: University Press of New England, 1989).

—— *A Bibliography of Venetian Editions of Virgil, 1470–1599,* Biblioteca di bibliografia italiana, 123 (Florence: Leo S. Olschki, 1991).

—— *A Bibliography of Renaissance Italian Translations of Virgil,* Biblioteca di bibliografia italiana, 136 (Florence: Leo S. Olschki, 1994).

—— 'Philology, the Reader, and the *Nachleben* of Classical Texts', *Modern Philology,* 92 (1994), 137–56.

—— 'Historicizing the Harvard School: Pessimistic Readings of the *Aeneid* in Italian Renaissance Scholarship', *Harvard Studies in Classical Philology* (forthcoming).

KING, MARGARET L., *Venetian Humanism in an Age of Patrician Dominance* (Princeton, NJ: Princeton University Press, 1986).

—— *Women of the Renaissance,* Women in Culture and Society (Chicago: University of Chicago Press, 1991).

—— and RABIL, ALBERT, Jr. (eds.), *Her Immaculate Hand: Selected Works by and about the Women Humanists of Quattrocento Italy,* Medieval and Renaissance Texts and Studies, 20 (Binghamton, NY: MRTS, 1983).

KINNEY, ARTHUR F., and COLLINS, DAN S. (eds.), *Renaissance Historicism:*

Selections from English Literary Renaissance (Amherst, Mass.: University of Massachusetts Press, 1987).

KRAYE, JILL (ed.), *The Cambridge Companion to Renaissance Humanism* (Cambridge: Cambridge University Press, 1996).

KRISTELLER, PAUL OSKAR, *Renaissance Thought: The Classic, Scholastic, and Humanist Strains* (New York: Harper and Row, 1961; repr. of Cambridge, Mass., 1955 edn.).

—— *Renaissance Thought*, 2 vols. (New York: Harper and Row, 1965).

LABALME, PATRICIA H. (ed.), *Beyond Their Sex: Learned Women of the European Past* (New York: New York University Press, 1980).

LANDINO, CRISTOFORO, *Scritti critici e teorici,* ed. Roberto Cardini, 2 vols. (Rome: Bulzoni, 1974).

—— *Disputationes Camaldulenses,* ed. Peter Lohe (Florence: Sansoni, 1980).

LANE, FREDERIC C., *Venice: A Maritime Republic* (Baltimore: The Johns Hopkins University Press, 1973).

LOGAN, OLIVER, *Culture and Society in Venice 1470–1790: The Renaissance and its Heritage* (London: B. T. Batsford Ltd., 1972).

LOWRY, MARTIN, *The World of Aldus Manutius: Business and Scholarship in Renaissance Venice* (Ithaca, NY: Cornell University Press, 1979).

—— *Book Prices in Renaissance Venice: The Stockbook of Bernardo Giunti,* Occasional Papers, 5 (Los Angeles, Calif.: Department of Special Collections, University Research Library, University of California, Los Angeles, 1991).

—— *Nicholas Jenson and the Rise of Venetian Publishing in Renaissance Europe* (Oxford: Basil Blackwell, 1991).

MCGANN, JEROME J., *A Critique of Modern Textual Criticism* (Chicago: University of Chicago Press, 1983).

—— *The Beauty of Inflections: Literary Investigations in Historical Method and Theory* (Oxford: Clarendon Press, 1988).

MCKENZIE, D. F., 'Typography and Meaning: The Case of William Congreve', in Giles Barber and Bernhard Fabian (eds.), *Buch und Buchhandel in Europa im achtzehnten Jahrhundert—The Book and the Book Trade in 18th-Century Europe,* Wolfenbütteler Schriften zur Geschichte des Buchwesens, 4 (Hamburg: Dr. Ernst Hauswedell and Co., 1981), 81–125.

—— *Bibliography and the Sociology of Texts: The Panizzi Lectures, 1985* (London: The British Library, 1986).

MAMBELLI, GIULIANO, *Gli annali delle edizioni virgiliane*, Biblioteca di bibliografia italiana, 27 (Florence: Leo S. Olschki, 1954).

MARTIN, JOHN, *Venice's Hidden Enemies: Italian Heretics in a Renaissance City* (Berkeley and Los Angeles, Calif.: University of California Press, 1993).

MARTINDALE, CHARLES, *Redeeming the Text: Latin Poetry and the Hermeneutics of Reception,* Roman Literature and its Contexts (Cambridge: Cambridge University Press, 1993).

MARX, BARBARA, *Venezia—altera Roma? Ipotesi sull'umanesimo veneziano* (Venice: Centro Tedesco di Studi Veneziani, 1978).

MAZZACURATI, GIANCARLO, and PLAISANCE, MICHEL (eds.), *Scritture di scritture: Testi, generi, modelli nel Rinascimento,* 'Europa delle Corti', Centro Studi sulle Società di Antico Regime, Biblioteca del Cinquecento, 36 (Rome: Bulzoni, 1987).

MELTZOFF, STANLEY, *Botticelli, Signorelli and Savonarola: Theologia Poetica and Painting from Boccaccio to Poliziano,* Biblioteca di 'Lettere Italiane', Studi e testi, 32 (Florence: Leo S. Olschki, 1987).

MORSE, RUTH, *Truth and Convention in the Middle Ages: Rhetoric, Representation, and Reality* (Cambridge: Cambridge University Press, 1991).

MOSS, ANN, *Printed Commonplace-Books and the Structuring of Renaissance Thought* (Oxford: Clarendon Press, 1996).

MUIR, EDWARD, *Civic Ritual in Renaissance Venice* (Princeton: Princeton University Press, 1981).

MUSATTI, EUGENIO, *La donna in Venezia,* 2nd edn. (Padua: Angelo Draghi, 1892).

NARDI, BRUNO, *Saggi sulla cultura veneta del Quattro e Cinquecento,* ed. Paolo Mazzantini (Padua: Antenore, 1971).

ODORISIO, GINEVRA CONTI, *Donna e società nel Seicento: Lucrezia Marinelli e Arcangela Tarabotti,* Biblioteca di cultura, 167 (Rome: Bulzoni, 1979).

PARKER, DEBORAH, *Commentary and Ideology: Dante in the Renaissance* (Durham, NC: Duke University Press, 1993).

PARKER, W. H. (trans. and ed.), *Priapea: Poems for a Phallic God,* Croom Helm Classical Studies (London: Croom Helm, 1988).

PARODI, E. G., 'I rifacimenti e le traduzioni italiane dell'*Eneide* di Virgilio prima del Rinascimento', *Studi di filologia romanza,* 2 (1887), 97–368.

PATTERSON, ANNABEL, *Pastoral and Ideology: Virgil to Valéry* (Berkeley and Los Angeles, Calif.: University of California Press, 1987).

PETRUCCI, ARMANDO, 'Alle origini del libro moderno: Libro da banco, libri da bisaccia, libretti da mano', *Italia medioevale e umanistica,* 12 (1969), 295–313.

—— (ed.), *Libri, editori e pubblico nell'Europa moderna: Guida storica e critica,* Biblioteca Universale Laterza, 291 (Bari: Laterza, 1989).

PFEIFFER, RUDOLF, *History of Classical Scholarship 1300–1850* (Oxford: Clarendon Press, 1976).

PHILLIPPY, PATRICIA BERRAHOU, *Love's Remedies: Recantation and Renaissance Lyric Poetry* (Lewisburg, Penn.: Bucknell University Press, 1995).

PRAZ, MARIO, *Studies in Seventeenth-Century Imagery*, 2nd edn., Sussidi eruditi, 16 (Rome: Edizioni di Storia e Letteratura, 1964), with *Addenda et corrigenda* (Rome: Edizioni di Storia e Letteratura, 1974).

QUELLER, DONALD, *The Venetian Patriciate: Reality versus Myth* (Urbana, Ill.: University of Illinois Press, 1986).

QUONDAM, AMEDEO, ' "Mercanzia d'onore" / "Mercanzia d'utile": produzione libraria e lavoro intellettuale a Venezia nel Cinquecento', in Petrucci (ed.), *Libri, editori e pubblico*, 51–104.

RABIL, ALBERT, Jr. (ed.), *Renaissance Humanism: Foundations, Forms, and Legacy*, 3 vols. (Philadelphia: University of Pennsylvania Press, 1988).

RENOUARD, A.-A., *Annales de l'imprimerie des Alde, ou histoire des trois Manuce et de leurs éditions* (New Castle, Del.: Oak Knoll Books, 1991; repr. of Paris, 1834 edn.).

RENOUARD, P., *Bibliographie des impressions et des œuvres de Josse Badius Ascensius, imprimeur et humaniste, 1462–1535*, 3 vols. (New York: Burt Franklin, 1967; repr. of Paris, 1908 edn.).

REUSCH, Fr. HEINRICH, *Die Indices Librorum prohibitorum des sechzehnten Jahrhunderts* (Nieuwkoop: B. de Graaf, 1961; repr. of Tübingen, 1886 edn.).

RICHARDSON, BRIAN, *Print Culture in Renaissance Italy: The Editor and the Vernacular Text, 1470–1600* (Cambridge: Cambridge University Press, 1994).

RIDDELL, JAMES A., and STEWART, STANLEY, *Jonson's Spenser: Evidence and Historical Criticism*, Duquesne Studies, Language and Literature Series, 18 (Pittsburgh: Duquesne University Press, 1995).

ROMANO, DENNIS, *Patricians and Popolani: The Social Foundations of the Venetian State* (Baltimore: Johns Hopkins University Press, 1987).

RONCONI, GIORGIO, *Le origini delle dispute umanistiche sulla poesia (Mussato e Petrarca)*, Strumenti di ricerca, 11 (Rome: Bulzoni, 1976).

ROSE, JONATHAN, 'Rereading the English Common Reader: A Preface to a History of Audiences', *Journal of the History of Ideas*, 53 (1992), 47–70.

ROSENTHAL, BERNARD M., *The Rosenthal Collection of Printed Books with Manuscript Annotations: A Catalog of 242 Editions mostly before 1600 annotated by Contemporary or Near-Contemporary Readers* (New Haven: The Beinecke Rare Book and Manuscript Library, Yale University, 1997).

ROSENTHAL, MARGARET F., *The Honest Courtesan: Veronica Franco, Citizen and Writer in Sixteenth-Century Venice*, Women in Culture and Society (Chicago: University of Chicago Press, 1992).

ROSS, J. BRUCE, 'Venetian Schools and Teachers Fourteenth to Early Sixteenth Centuries: A Survey and Study of Giovanni Battista Egnazio', *Renaissance Quarterly*, 39 (1976), 521–36.

ROYDS, THOMAS FLETCHER, *Virgil and Isaiah: A Study of the Pollio* (Oxford: Basil Blackwell, 1918).

RÜEGG, WALTER, and WUTTKE, DIETER (eds.), *Ethik im Humanismus,* Beiträge zur Humanismusforschung, 5 (Boppard: Boldt, 1979).

RUGGIERO, GUIDO, *Violence in Early Renaissance Venice* (New Brunswick, NJ: Rutgers University Press, 1980).

—— *The Boundaries of Eros: Sex Crime and Sexuality in Renaissance Venice* (New York: Oxford University Press, 1985).

SABBADINI, REMIGIO, *Le scoperte dei codici latini e greci ne' secoli XIV e XV* (Florence: Sansoni, 1967; repr. of Florence, 1905–14 edn.).

SANDER, MAX, *Le Livre à figures italien depuis 1467 jusqu'à 1530: Essai de sa bibliographie et son histoire,* 4 vols. (Milan: U. Hoepli, 1942).

SHERMAN, WILLIAM H., *John Dee: The Politics of Reading and Writing in the English Renaissance,* Massachusetts Studies in Early Modern Culture (Amherst, Mass.: University of Massachusetts Press, 1995).

SŁAWÍNSKI, JANUSZ, 'Reading and Reader in the Literary Historical Process', *New Literary History,* 19 (1988), 521–40.

STIERLE, KARLHEINZ, '*Studium*: Perspectives on Institutionalized Modes of Reading', *New Literary History,* 22 (1991), 115–28.

STILLERS, RAINER, *Humanistische Deutung: Studien zu Kommentar und Literaturtheorie in der italienische Renaissance,* Studia humaniora, 11 (Düsseldorf: Droste Verlag, 1988).

Storia della cultura veneta, ii. Girolamo Arnaldi (ed.), *Il Trecento,* and iii. Girolamo Arnaldi and Manlio Pastore Stocchi (eds.), *Dal primo Quattrocento al Concilio di Trento* (Vicenza: Neri Pozza Editore, 1976–1981).

SULEIMAN, SUSAN R., and CROSMAN, INGE (eds.), *The Reader in the Text: Essays on Audience and Interpretation* (Princeton: Princeton University Press, 1980).

TANSELLE, G. THOMAS, *The History of Books as a Field of Study,* The Second Hanes Lecture (Chapel Hill, NC: University of North Carolina Library, 1981).

—— 'Textual Criticism and Literary Sociology', *Studies in Bibliography,* 44 (1991), 83–143.

TOFFANIN, GIUSEPPE, *History of Humanism,* trans. Elio Gianturco (New York: Las Americas Publishing Co., 1954).

TOMPKINS, JANE P. (ed.), *Reader-Response Criticism: From Formalism to Post-Structuralism* (Baltimore: The Johns Hopkins University Press, 1980).

TRAPP, J. B. (ed.), *Manuscripts in the Fifty Years after the Invention of Printing,* Some Papers read at a Colloquium at the Warburg Institute on 12–13 March 1982 (London: The Warburg Institute, University of London, 1983).

TRIBBLE, EVELYN B., *Margins and Marginality: The Printed Page in Early Modern England* (Charlottesville, Va.: The University Press of Virginia, 1993).

TRINKAUS, CHARLES, *In Our Image and Likeness: Humanity and Divinity in Italian Humanist Thought,* 2 vols. (Notre Dame, Ind.: University of Notre Dame Press, 1995; repr. of Chicago, 1970 edn.).

TROVATO, PAOLO, *Con ogni diligenza corretto: La stampa e le revisioni editoriali dei testi litterari italiani (1470–1570)* (Bologna: Il Mulino, 1991).

ULVIONI, PAOLO, 'Stampa e censura a Venezia nel Seicento', *Archivio veneto,* 106 (1975), 45–93.

VEESER, H. ARAM (ed.), *The New Historicism* (New York: Routledge, 1989).

VERDON, TIMOTHY, and HENDERSON, JOHN (eds.), *Christianity and the Renaissance: Image and Religious Imagination in the Quattrocento* (Syracuse, NY: Syracuse University Press, 1991).

VICKERS, BRIAN, 'Epideictic and Epic in the Renaissance', *New Literary History,* 14 (1982–3), 497–537.

WASWO, RICHARD, 'The History that Literature makes', *New Literary History,* 19 (1988), 541–64.

WILLISON, I. R., 'Remarks on the History of the Book in Britain as a Field of Study within the Humanities, with a Synopsis and Select List of Current Literature', *Library Chronicle,* 21/3–4 (1991), 95–145.

WITT, RONALD, 'Coluccio Salutati and the Conception of the *Poeta Theologus* in the Fourteenth Century', *Renaissance Quarterly,* 30 (1977), 538–63.

WLOSOK, ANTONIE, '*Gemina pictura*: Allegorisierende Aeneis-illustrationen in Handschriften des 15. Jahrhunderts', in Robert M. Wilhelm and Howard Jones (eds.), *The Two Worlds of the Poet: New Perspectives on Vergil* (Detroit: Wayne State University Press, 1992), 408–32.

WOODWARD, WILLIAM HARRISON, *Vittorino da Feltre and Other Humanist Educators,* Renaissance Society of America Reprint Texts, 5 (Toronto: University of Toronto Press, 1996; repr. of New York, 1963 edn.).

ZABUGHIN, VLADIMIRO, *Vergilio nel Rinascimento italiano da Dante a Torquato Tasso,* 2 vols. (Bologna: Zanichelli, 1921–3).

ZANNINI, GIAN LUDOVICO MASETTI, *Motivi storici della educazione femminile: Scienza, lavoro, giuochi* (Naples: M. D'Auria Editore, 1982).

ZORZI, MARINO, 'Le biblioteche a Venezia nel secondo Settecento', *Miscellanea Marciana,* 1 (1986), 253–324.

—— *La libreria di San Marco: Libri, lettori, società nella Venezia dei Dogi,* Ateneo Veneto, Collana di studi, 1 (Milan: Arnoldo Mondadori, 1987).

—— 'La circolazione del libro a Venezia nel Cinquecento: Biblioteche private e pubbliche', *Ateneo Veneto,* NS 28 (1990), 117–89.

INDEX LOCORUM

GENERAL INDEX

INDEX OF PRINTERS

Printers' names are in Latin for Latin editions, and in Italian for translations of Virgil's works.

INDEX OF ANNOTATED COPIES